OKANAGAN COLLEGE LIBRARY

MW01274049

African Philosophy and the Hermeneutics of Culture

Studies in African Philosophy

Series Editors

J. Obi Oguejiofor
(B. M. S., Enugu/Nigeria)

Mogobe B. Ramose
(UNISA, Pretoria/South Africa)

Godfrey I. Onah
(Urbaniana/Rome)

volume 2

LIT

OKANAGAN COLLEGE
LIBRARY
BRITISH COLUMBIA

African Philosophy and the Hermeneutics of Culture

Essays in Honour of Theophilus Okere

Edited by

J. Obi Oguejiofor
and
Godfrey Igwebuike Onah

LIT

Published with financial assistance from Bigard Memorial Seminary, Enugu;
St. Joseph's Seminary, Ikot Ekpene; and Seat of Wisdom Seminary, Owerri.

Bibliographic information published by Die Deutsche Bibliothek
Die Deutsche Bibliothek lists this publication in the Deutsche
Nationalbibliografie; detailed bibliographic data are available in the
Internet at http://dnb.ddb.de.

ISBN 3-8258-8217-9

© LIT VERLAG Münster   2005
Grevener Str./Fresnostr. 2   48159 Münster
Tel. 0251-620320   Fax 0251-23 1972
e-Mail: lit@lit-verlag.de   http://www.lit-verlag.de

Distributed in North America by:

Transaction Publishers
New Brunswick (U.S.A.) and London (U.K.)

Transaction Publishers   Tel.: (732) 445 - 2280
Rutgers University   Fax: (732) 445 - 3138
35 Berrue Circle   for orders (U. S. only):
Piscataway, NJ 08854   toll free (888) 999 - 6778

Contents

Acknowledgements

Msgr. Theophilus Okere has been, for more than three decades a golden voice in the task of critical reflections on the contexts of life in Nigeria/Africa in particular and in the world in general. As a philosophy teacher for more than twenty years, his thoughts and his inspirations left indelible traces on the minds of many of his students, and through them have been exerting profound influence on the evolution of philosophy in Nigeria. As Mgrs Okere turns 70 in 2005, it is with a deep sense of appreciation that we gather together this collection of essays in his honour. We are also grateful to all whose contributions have made this collection to see the light of the day.

We thank the contributors who spared valuable time to reflect on various aspects of Okere's thoughts. We are also grateful to Bigard Memorial Seminary, Enugu; St. Joseph's Major Seminary, Ikot Ekpene, and Seat of Wisdom Seminary, Owerri who together accepted without reservations to sponsor this publication, we are grateful for the generosity of their Rectors: Frs. John Okoye, Donatus Udoette, John Iwe and the rest of the members of their academic staff. The same dept of gratitude goes to our assistants Mssr. Christian Nwbuikwu, Anselm Ngana and Donatus Ekwe, and to the typesetter Mr. Victor Odigbo.

Finally we are most grateful to Msgr. T. Okere without whose cooperation the idea of this *Festschrift* would have been stillborn. We thank him for striving, despite many difficulties, to devote these long and fruitful years to deep and enriching philosophical researches and teaching. But to God, to whom all praise and glory is due, in whom we live and have our being, be all honour and glory forever.

J. Obi Oguejiofor and Godfrey Igwebuike Onah
Editors

Introduction

J. Obi Oguejiofor
Godfrey Igwebuike Onah

It already seems so long ago when the debate was raging, first in Europe, then in Africa and America, over the existence or non-existence of African philosophy. Whatever one may say of Placide Tempels, one has to admit that it was his work *Bantu Philosophy* that initiated that debate. Along with the question of its existence or non-existence, philosophers also argued about the nature, the method and the content of African philosophy as well as about the nature and the identity of the African. Not surprisingly, the debate was carried on with passion, also because of the historical circumstances of the time. It is only a little more than a decade since the heat of the debate was doused by the establishment of courses in African philosophy in many universities and colleges in Africa, Europe and America, yet it already seems very long ago and there seems to be some nostalgia among some African philosophers for that period. This is because, like what happened among the Early Fathers of the Church in Africa in the first centuries of Christianity, the philosophical discussions of the 70s and 80s gave rise to a very fruitful exchange between African philosophers of different persuasions, the renewal of philosophical rigour within the continent and, more importantly, the production of the first significant body of philosophical literature on African philosophy.

Fortunately, though, the debate is not yet over. It has only changed form. Philosophers in Africa certainly know that philosophy has not yet finished the job of its self-definition anywhere in the world. With every new insight that a philosopher brings into the arena, every new formulation of old problems and every fresh application of philosophical reasoning to human problems (old and new), philosophy adds something new to its self-definition. African philosophers today who ask philosophical questions about the African condition as well as those who search the cultural heritage of Africa for a philosophical understanding of the human being and the world are, in effect, carrying on the debate. So are those who are now returning to the assertions of the pioneers of African philosophical revival in order to think some of their thoughts through to their ultimate conclusions, to question some of their assumptions or to reveal some of their limitations.

Significantly, some of the pioneers themselves have had the opportunity of modifying their earlier positions, adding flesh to some of their skeletal thoughts and answering some of their critics. Since many of them were and still are academic philosophers, they have also had the opportunity, as teachers of philosophy, of stimulating further reflection in others through their lectures. As a result, their intellectual influence has gone beyond what is usually read in their publications.

Theophilus Okere first added his voice to the debate on Africa philosophy in 1971 with a doctoral dissertation he defended at the Catholic University of Louvain (an extract was published in 1983). He immediately caught the attention of others because he pointed a new direction in the discussion. In addition to tackling the question of the foundations of method in African philosophy, he also brought to the fore, for the first time, the relevance of hermeneutics "to the founding of the tradition of rational philosophy in Africa."[1] Okere is thus recognized as the initiator of the hermeneutical orientation in African philosophy.[2]

But besides being just the initiator of an orientation in African philosophical scholarship, Okere was and still is addressing the issue of particularism and universalism in philosophy. When philosophies are classified as African or Western, Christian or Islamic, are these classifications merely convenient or are they based on any essential characteristics of the philosophies thus classified? Is there any need at all to attach such regional, cultural or religious labels to philosophy? These and other similar questions obviously go beyond the limited area of African philosophy since they concern the nature of philosophy as such. Taking inspiration from some European hermeneutic philosophers, Okere argues that philosophy, every philosophy, is essentially a hermeneutic of culture (in the fullest meaning of the term culture). Therefore, while philosophy possesses some qualities that distinguish it from other forms of knowledge, qualities which account for its universal character, every philosophy is, nonetheless, closely bound to the culture in which it was produced, in other words, the culture whose hermeneutic it is. This would imply that whereas it would be improper to classify philosophies *aprioristically* according to cultures,[3] it would be safe to assume that every philosophy has a cultural label, even when that label is not easily legible.

A serious difficulty follows on the heels of the above affirmation: How can one avoid the risk of cultural relativism and eventually of absolute relativism if even philosophical knowledge cannot claim universality? In fact, relativism seems to be the natural conclusion to the hermeneutic argument and the Postmodernists, with their most radical statement in Vattimo's so-called weak thought (*pensiero debole*), may claim to be the rightful heirs of a tradition that began with Nietzsche. But this is only *apparently* so. First, it ought to be born in mind that every philosophical knowledge, insofar as it contains some truth has a universal claim to *that* truth, though not to *the* truth as such. To that extent it is universal. What is contested, at least by Okere and those who hold a similar view, is the claim of absolute universality by any philosophy or philosophical tradition, the type found, for instance, in some system-builders. In philosophy, absolute relativism is as absurd as absolute universalism. The former would negate the possibility of the human mind to know any truth at all and the latter feigns ignorance of the limitedness of the human mode of knowing.

Both one and the other extreme position can be avoided through a commitment to dialogue in philosophical inquiry interpersonal and intercultural dialogue. It is part of his nature as a social and socializing being that man does not and cannot search for knowledge alone and in isolation. This is true both of the single individual and of cultural groups. The search for absolute truth, which is natural to the human being, can be satisfied only piece meal and in communion, not once and for all by any single person or culture. Not only do individuals and cultures need to listen to one another, different forms of human knowledge also need to listen to one another. And philosophy has shown through the ages the obvious advantages of interpersonal, intercultural and interdisciplinary dialogue. The apparent refusal by some philosophers or philosophical traditions to dialogue with other cultures and disciplines is a novel development in philosophy. There is ample documentation of the positive results of the exchange and borrowing between Egyptian philosophy and Greek philosophy, between Greek philosophy and Roman philosophy, between the "pagan" Greeks and Romans and the

Christian theologians of Africa (despite the protestations of Tertulian) and also between theology and philosophy in Medieval Europe. Medieval European philosophy would have been very different, perhaps a lot poorer, without the input of some Arab Moslems. Anglicanism, Pietism and Prussian Lutheranism influenced Locke, Kant and Hegel more than is usually openly acknowledged, to say nothing of the French Revolution. Many modern and contemporary philosophers in Europe were scientists and mathematicians who also had deep interest in philosophy, with or without formal training in the discipline. The examples could be multiplied. To stop this dialogue now, in an age of monumental increase in intercultural contact, or to transform it into cultural confrontation or a clash of cultures, would only impoverish not just philosophy but humanity in general. The Akan of Ghana have a proverb, which says that no single individual, however long his arms may be, can ever encircle the baobab in an embrace. And there is an Igbo proverb, which says that the guinea fowls choose to go in groups so that what the pair of eyes of one of them misses, another pair of eyes may see, to the benefit of the group.

Theophilus Okere has not published much since after the extract from his doctoral dissertation. A couple of booklets on social questions, a few articles in philosophical journals and some chapters in the collection he edited in the Nigerian philosophical studies series[4] are the only other published works to his credit *as at now*. But he has continued to research, to teach, to stimulate and to inspire. Although his *African Philosophy* has already made remarkable impact on African philosophical scholarship,[5] those whose knowledge of his thoughts stopped with this work, may not be aware of the way he has tried to apply his preferred method to other specific areas of the philosophical investigation in Africa and how he has tried to overcome the risk of relativism through the promotion of intercultural dialogue in philosophy. The essays published in this volume bear eloquent testimony to the multivalent character of Okere's contribution to African philosophy and to the philosophical discourse in Africa and beyond. As would be expected, most of the essays are about Okere's hermeneutics of culture, both as a method and as a type of philosophy. Some of the authors examine the method in itself, while others focus their attention on its application to specific philosophical themes. In either case, there are serious attempts to move Okere's thoughts beyond Okere and sometimes even beyond the confines of African philosophy. A few essays, though not referred directly to Okere and his thoughts, nevertheless maintain the spirit of his method. In an interview part of which serves as a fitting conclusion to this volume, he shows how committed he still is to his philosophical project within a cultural context that is never permanently fixed, but is constantly presenting new challenges as well as insights.

In a work like this, repetitions are very likely and the fewness of Okere's publications just referred to above makes repetitions inevitable. But that in itself may add force to Okere's argument. Culture is dynamic and the individual's relation to it is personal. Hence, each philosophical work is personal to the philosopher. This would imply that the essays in this collection represent not the philosophy of Theophilus Okere, but of their individual authors, who may have been inspiried by Okere. In bringing these essays together, we hope to provide a forum for the enriching dialogue that Okere advocates in philosophy. Seeing how different persons interpret the same author may draw attention to the prespectivity of human knowledge (including philosophical knowledge) and underline the need the philosopher has of being aware of his or her particular context and of making *conscious* use of it, while at the same time trying to overcome its limitations by listening to others. This, we believe, would be a fitting way of *marking the seventieth birthday of a man who has had such a profound influence on so many of us.*

Notes

[1] Theophilus Okere, *African Philosophy: A Historico-Hermeneutical Investigation of the Conditions of its Possibility*, University Press of America, Lanham, 1983, p. v.

[2] See V. Y. Mudimbe, *The Invention of Africa: Gnosis, Philosophy and the Order of Knowledge*, Indiana University Press, Bloomington and Indianapolis, 1988, pp. 173f; Bruce Janz, "Alterity, Dialogue and African Philosophy," in Emmanuel Chukwudi Eze (ed.), *Postcolonial African Philosophy: A Critical Reader*, Blackwell, Cambridge, Mass., 1997, p. 223; J. Obi Oguejiofor, *Philosophy and the African Predicament*, Hope Publications, Ibadan, 2001, pp. 118ff.

[3] Cf. Godfrey Igwebuike Onah, "The Universal and the Particular in Wiredu's Philosophy of Human Nature," in Olsegun Oladipo (ed.), *The Third Way in African Philosophy: Essays in Honour of Kwasi Wiredu*, Hope Publications, Ibadan, 2002, pp. 64ff.

[4] Theophilus Okere (ed.), *Identity and Change: Nigerian Philosophical Studies*, I, Washington, D.C., Paideia, 1996.

[5] Tsenay Serequeberhan's *The Hermeneutics of African Philosophy: Horizons and Discourse*, Routledge, New York 1994, is one of the most systematic expressions of this impact.

1

The Philosopher and The Society: A Portrait of Msgr T Okere

B. E. Nwigwe

1. Introduction

Msgr. Okere is well known as being a highly gifted person in many fields of human endeavour. For this reason it would only be looking at him from one perspective alone, if his intellectual virtues alone were stressed. It is obvious that he is an exceptionally intelligent man; but to give credit to his intellect alone would mean giving him only partial merit. The phrase "intellectual virtue" is an academic expression, especially in discussions involving Aristotle's *Ethics.*[1] To commend a man's intellect is just like commending some enviable gift of fortune like beauty or health or high-birth. But a man cannot be counted as meritorious for a gift of nature; he should rather be counted as meritorious for the real virtues like moral virtues that are truly his own achievements. One cannot single out intellectual virtue alone in Msgr. Okere because in him, head and heart form a perfect blend. His head, heart and all the endowments form a piece with his whole life.

One very evident and most enviable quality is his simplicity. Simplicity in this sense is a harmonious blend of virtues and of opposites. He can be a high-flying intellectual and at the same time has the capacity to mix up, joke, eat and drink, and enjoy the company of simple people. Intelligent people and philosophers in particular are often disposed to censor or quarrel or condemn the work and lives of others. In Msgr. Okere, passionate concern for truth does not go with a desire to run others down. On the contrary, he has a remarkable listening ear, especially towards students whom he sees as materials for molding in his hands. This is evident in the patient and caring manner with which he engages and encounters his students and even colleagues, giving listening ear and looking at every detail to ensure satisfaction to all. But one thing he does not tolerate is laziness (mental or physical), for whatever one becomes in life often depends on personal effort and commitment to duty.

Another quality that characterizes Msgr. Okere's life and dealings with his fellows and could not but come in his work and person is a great directness and honesty. He says just what he thinks and why he thinks it in plain words. He has a fine judgment of what measure of exactness at what place and time a quality which Aristotle counts as a mark of a well educated man.

As a Catholic priest, his is a life of selfless service, a fact which he has exhibited in the numerous functions which he has held in the service of the Church. He does not know or regard artificial boundaries of religion, rich or poor, educated or uncouth, etc. He thinks that everyone deserves respect, recognition and fair play.

In his austerity of life, moral and intellectual virtues, simplicity, commitment to duty, sense of justice and equity towards everyone, desire for individual and societal advancement, etc., Okere shows a strong affinity of mind and disposition with certain well known traditional philosophers - Socrates, Immanuel Kant, Arthur Schopenhauer, etc., for whom commitment to duty overrides everything else. Though a philosopher, his overall attitude to life shows that philosophy even though often regarded as a high-flying speculative intellectual engagement, can be made part of our practical day-to-day life. We will see in what follows how Okere's work shows how this can be achieved.

2. The Philosopher And Society

Let this be an overall impression of my conception of a philosopher in society. I see the philosopher as one who has the courage to question those issues on which a great deal of our normal beliefs rest. Belief systems are often looked upon as sacrosanct: People do not look kindly at anyone who tries to raise questions on their assumptions. People very easily get upset and uncomfortable when they are asked to justify the basis of their beliefs. But in fact a lot of the presuppositions of the ordinary day-to-day common beliefs serve as matters for philosophical considerations.

When our day-to-day presumptions and beliefs are critically examined they often turn out to be a great deal less secure, and their meanings and implications become a good deal less clear than they seemed at first sight. In critically examining our day-to-day presumptions and beliefs, man's self-knowledge is thereby increased and enhanced. Critical examination of beliefs and presuppositions also implies examination of self and the society as a whole. The importance of such self-examination is evident when Plato makes Socrates say that "an unexamined life is not worth living." If beliefs and presuppositions are unexamined but simply uncritically accepted, society becomes ossified, beliefs harden into dogma, the imagination is warped and the intellect becomes sterile. If the imagination is to be kept awake, if the intellect is to work and if mental life is to be kept dynamic and the pursuit of truth, justice or self-fulfilment is not to cease, assumptions must be questioned and presuppositions must be challenged. This simply shows that philosophy is a practical discipline, which is at the basis of every search for knowledge. And any one who reads Plato's or Augustine's or Locke's or Descartes' or Kant's conception of the world can see that they are down to earth, they deal with basic day-to-day issues which laymen do not perceive.

In other words, philosophy seeks to elucidate any concept or analyse any activity whatsoever. This is what Ludwig Wittgenstein meant when he insists that philosophy is an activity and not a body of doctrines. It follows from that, of course, that the activity of philosophy is therefore subject to investigation; and it is, indeed, the case that an enormous amount of such investigation goes on perpetually among philosophers (of different schools and persuasions).

The engagement of philosophers regarding society is aimed at exposing the presumptions and the beliefs of society, dragging them to light. If one doesn't drag out to light the very presumptions of one's thinking, one remains simply the prisoner of whatever the reigning orthodoxy in the matter at issue happens to be. Plato tells us in an allegory that that is the way human society often is:

Human beings are held prisoners in a cave and they see

only shadows of objects on the wall. Some of them are
liberated and they see real things and lastly the sun itself.
They go back to the cave in order to take the other
prisoners to flight[2]

This summarizes the basic job of philosophy or of knowledge in
general, for man and for the human society. With this we see that the
dialogues of Plato and the writings of philosophers generally, constitute
fertile sources of discussion of ultimate values which are indispensable
for the survival and sustenance of every human society. They also serve
as opportunity to question conventional wisdom, and through such
questioning the human society grows and prospers. Every good
philosopher has to do this. Good novelists and social critics also do it.
And this is what Msgr. Okere has done and continues to do for the
human society. In order not to make any empty generalizations about
this, let us examine some of his contributions to philosophy.

3. Contributions To Philosophy

My judgment of Msgr. Okere is that he is not only knowledgeable but is
as well a wise man. To be knowledgeable is to be competent in some
specific area of human endeavour, but to be wise is to have the ability or
insight to be engaged in almost every aspect of human endeavour. This
is evident in the scope and variety of literary works which go to show
that he has the ability to philosophize on any topic whatsoever with
much success. Plato, Aristotle, Michelle de Montaigne and the Roman
Emperor and philosopher, Marcus Aurelius, achieved this same feat. It
is a rare phenomenon.

     Even from ordinary day-to-day conversation, it is observable
how much he knows, ranging from the most typical native ideas (village
expressions) to the loftiest and professionalized ideas. Indeed, Okere is
very versatile in the sense of being a leader, diplomat, writer, musician,
teacher, economist, and so on.

     As part of his contribution to philosophy, Okere addressed a
seminar on "Culture" in 1975 at the College of Science and Technology,
Port Harcourt. There he used his profound and lucid philosophical mind
to analyse the notion of culture, lifting it, as it were, from the common-

place or naïve understanding as "way of life" or mode of dancing to a more intricate and comprehensive apprehension of the phenomenon. Culture, for him, is something created by man as contrasted with that which is natural to man. For instance, to eat in order to survive is something natural, but, then, the type of food one eats becomes a matter of culture. He stresses that culture touches a number of issues ranging from language, marriage, art, music, commerce, religion, belief systems, symbols, law, politics, social structures and institutions, to customs in general.

Moreover, he was able to prove the thesis that culture change was a principle of cultural development. Henceforth, to contemplate culture in terms of development is "to think of culture with a richer meaning, beyond the merely descriptive and qualitatively neutral way of life of a people."[3] He, accordingly, retraced the term *culture* to its etymology (*colo colere colui - cultum*: meaning "to till" or "to tend") and insists that culture is that which is originally oriented "towards more refinement"; that which "involves a conscious effort, a common pursuit, a forward march towards higher values."[4] Therefore, the idea of a static culture is a contradiction in terms, since culture as a great monument of human genius is a perpetual project, a becoming.

Bringing Africa into focus, Okere neatly observes that one major factor that brought about cultural inferiority in the African is the story of material success of the imperialist West. Another crucial factor is that Africans got themselves locked up for centuries as "cultural islands" without experiencing the benefits of culture-contact (which would have injected "the new blood necessary for productivity in any culture"). Today the African is put in the dilemma of either dumping or reviving his past cultural heritage; and in the quagmire of "to borrow or not to borrow and if to borrow, what to borrow." Looking at this predicament, then, Okere counselled that African cultures should try to retain their identities by borrowing only judiciously and selectively i.e., by discriminatory borrowing. Cross-cultural borrowing does not negate the identity of any given culture, so long as the new element is infused in such a way that it becomes properly integrated or assimilated, evolving "as it were from the old". African cultures must always aim at borrowing that which is positive and functional.

This becomes a critical lesson in socio-cultural reformation for the African continent. And Okere ultimately called for a war to be waged on the ideological front, so as to restore our cultural dignity, pride and independence.

In a very recent paper (2003) he presented on "Crisis of Governance in Africa: the Root of the Problem",⁵ Okere paints one of the most brilliant and graphic pictures of the socio-political scenario of our continent. He points to the phenomenon of war as "the quintessence of the failure of governance." Apart from the reign of combat war and overthrow of the rule of law, there are spates of other "forms of reign of terror", leading to insecurity of life and property; these include armed robbery, riots or civil disturbances (politically or religiously motivated), hired assassinations, and much more besides.

Furthermore, Africa is overburdened with all forms of malaise ranging from refugees, massive unemployment, poverty, debt burdens, secessionist bids, hopelessness, roguery, to virulent diseases, etc. And to worsen the matter, most African leaders never work in the interest of the masses. Since *exploitation* is their political ideal, they have even "gone beyond maximum corruption to looting the national treasuries."⁶ But, then, Okere quickly makes the following deduction: the people themselves are so bad; the leaders are taken from among the people; they, then, "get the leaders they deserve."⁷ In order words, the people share a greater responsibility in the crisis of governance.

Besides, Okere attributes the total failure of governance in Africa to "a lack of understanding or a misunderstanding of the main purpose of government itself." He notes that colonial rule was the early microbial substance that started the decay of African politics. Okere even avers that the imperialist menace is still being felt in the Bakassi Saga.

For Okere, Africa is at the cross-roads and leads the world in "virtually every form of crime against good government." He then suggests that philosophy must now come to the aid of African politics, since nobody digs deeper than the philosopher in getting to the roots of problems. As such, Okere endorses the view that politics is "far too serious a thing to be left to politicians and rulers." Incidentally, philosophy has this radical way of looking at issues such that all these peripheral anomalies in the political history of Africa might simply be "symptoms of a more deep-seated, spiritual malaise." It is then left for the philosopher to construct the theoretical run-way through which Africa can escape from incessant crises and unjust social structures.

As a guest speaker to NTV (channel 8) discussion programme of May 9, 1976, Okere talked on "The Secret Societies and Us."[8] There he defined *secret society* and gave a panorama of nefarious activities carried out by such organizations. For Okere, the cultist is an antisocial and a perverter of justice, so long as *his* notion of justice is mutilated, partial and selective. "But justice mutilated is not only justice destroyed, it is injustice."[9] Apart from the cultists diabolic and destructive influences on our society, they also aid and abate the enthronement of mediocrity through "favoritism".

The most interesting part of the discussion is that he holds substantive logic and proof for any case made against the so delineated cult groups. And I believe he sampled the principle of justice largely because the plenitude of justice guarantees social cohesion and political stability. Remove justice from the state, as St. Augustine said, it eventually turns into bandwaggon of criminals and robbers.[10] Okere, however, ended the discussion in this organ tone:

> If any society, secret or otherwise, is known to exist just to neutralize justice, is it not a mortal enemy of the state and of the people? Has such an organization any right to exist? I think our rulers must have the courage to face their responsibility in this matter and the sooner, the better.[11]

All these are mere representative examples to whet one's appetite on the immense philosophical contributions of Okere. And I add that to run commentary on any of Okere's piece is simply to deface its structural and linguistic beauty. For example, through his mastery of language, Okere was able to analyse the concept of New Year Resolution in a paper he delivered on "New Year, New Man, New Society", and brought it to bear on how the entire society can be moved forward through this same act of resolution. But since we cannot go on and on, we then turn to his philosophical system.

4. Philosophical System

Having talked generally about Msgr. Okere's overall engagement to the

well-being of man and society, let us now say a few things about his
system of philosophy.

He is generally well schooled in the Western philosophical
tradition; and with such background knowledge he has been able to
assert his influence as an important figure and one of the early founders
of what is today referred to as *African Philosophy*. He is convinced that
the African must not ape the European to be able to establish some
identity of his own. Though humiliated, degraded, unjustly treated by
the combined onslaught of imperialism and colonialism; though at
cross-roads in the various influences and intervening cultures that
impinge on him; though rendered almost sterile and barren by the
economic plunder of the West, the African, in Okere's estimation, still
has a culture very rich in values that could serve as an identity if well
harnessed and revived. But this quest or project is not every man's
business, it is something that involves deep thought, articulate methodological approach and critical orientation.

As no culture is totally sealed off from others without any
intervening influence, as no philosophy can exist without a methodology, the African quest for self identity and intellectual contribution to
the overall well-being of humanity must have a methodological
approach. Okere, then, borrows such an approach which could serve as a
way leading to the birth of African philosophy in *Hermeneutics*. But
before we look at this all-important terminology let us explain in a
nutshell the meaning, origin and applicability of this word.

5. Hermeneutics: A Philosophical Approach

Hermeneutics as a philosophical approach is a reaction against phenomenology. It is a reaction against Husserl's philosophy which claimed to
be able to achieve a level of human experience that would be common to
all people and to all historical periods. That level of experience is
identified by Husserl as "Ideas." In other words, for Husserl, *ideas* are
the most basic or fundamental level of experience. As a result of this,
every other human creation (be it national or ethnological cultures,
empirical sciences, religion and so forth) are simply, in Husserl's
estimation, structures erected to distort the very fundamental ideas. Of
course, what Hurssel is saying here is a form of intolerable idealism

which Hermeneutics as a philosophical approach was out to counter.
True enough, *universality* and *necessity*, as Kant tells us, are vital elements to any claim to authentic knowledge that transcends cultural, empirical or religious prejudices. Yet it is the same Kant that reminds us that any claim to knowledge must be tied to *historicity* which implies segmentation across the board of universality. For Gadamer, the various frameworks that have been created by human beings over the course of history (including the arts and sciences) should constitute the objects of obvious and important hermeneutical exercise. Gadamer's reason for this is that we all are products of specific historical cultural, and intellectual backgrounds. To say this of Gadamer would not mean that he was the first to envisage this position. What Gadamer worked out and expressed in his book, *Wahrheit und Methode* was already in its early beginnings present in the writings of Schleiermacher, Dilthey, Herder, Friedrich Wolf, etc. Whatever the early beginnings of this understanding of Hermeneutics, the main thrust of hermeneutical thinking began with the publication of *Gadamer's Wahrheit und Methode.* For him, understanding as is involved in interpreting the actions of men and their works in the past is not a subjective matter but rather an entering into another tradition such that *past* and *present* constantly mediate and encounter each other.[12]

Gadamer sees understanding and interpretation as involving a creative process in which the observer through penetrating an alien mode of existence enriches his own self-knowledge through acquiring knowledge of others. We can see in this that Gadamer and Wittgenstein have a lot in common, because what Gadamer regards as penetrating to get the meaning of a culture is what Wittgenstein refers to as a form of life. And for both, this level of understanding and interpreting a people's form of life can only be achieved through a commensurate understanding of the language that people speak. Both Gadamer and Wittgenstein are thus agreed on the indispensable role of language in knowledge. In fact, both stress the view that the limits of language are the limits of the world. For both, language is not first and foremost a system of signs or representations which in some way stand for objects, they are rather our expression of human mode of being in the world.[13] This inseparable link between language and meaning is of vital importance in hermeneutics.

Having acquired some knowledge of what hermeneutics means,

let us now examine Msgr Okere's application of it in the study of African philosophy.

6. Hermeneutics And African Philosophy

Several writers in this subject have employed all forms of methods ranging from analytic, phenomenological to hermeneutical approaches. And as we earlier mentioned, Msgr. Okere adopts the hermeneutical method. His application of hermeneutics in the study of African philosophy is not in the Diltheyan sense of interpretation, but in the Heideggerian- Gadaman sense of interpretation as an ontological event. This sense of interpretation has one aim in view, namely the production of objective knowledge of man and his society which are not obtainable in the empirical sciences.

Hermeneutical approach in the HeideggerianGadaman sense points to the finite and context-bound nature of human knowledge. In this sense *universalism* as characteristic feature or essence of knowledge is highly suppressed. Knowledge is rather situated, time-bound and historical. In a sense, there is relativity in what could be referred to as knowledge or truth.

In his thesis "Can there be an African Philosophy" submitted in 1971 to the University of Louvain part of which eventually got published in 1983 as *African Philosophy: A Historico-Hermeneutical Investigation of the Conditions of its Possibility*, Msgr. Okere enunciates in a very succinct manner how the hermeneutical approach could be applied in the on-going strive for African philosophical identity. For him, the encounter with western culture and or civilization, and the influences this has brought about on the African psyche, worldviews, ways of life and cultural heritage notwithstanding, the possibility still looms large that the authentic African cultural values could be wrest from such unfortunate circumstances. He singled out some such values as extended family system, polygamy, respect for elders, deep religious instincts, ability for social organisations as veritable elements on which the cultural identity could be pegged and from where we could launch our own mode of life. But, then, he was against anybody who took a pedestrian understanding of African philosophy as involving ethnography alone. In other words, African philosophy could not exist on mere past beliefs, poems, mythologies, proverbs, and so on. Even though these on their own could not constitute the philosophy of a people, vital elements could be sieved out of them which could then be used in forging a coherent and articulate mode of existence (i.e. way of life) of a people. What he suggests here is of course obvious to any one who has read the systematic works of Plato, Aristotle, etc. Even though Alfred Whitehead believes that every European philosophy is a footnote to Plato[14] and Bertrand Russell thinks it is rather Pythagoras that forms the bedrock of European philosophy, no one doubts the all-encompassing role of poets like Homer, Hesiod, Sophocles, etc., in the construction of the philosophies of Plato, Aristotle or anyone else. In a similar vein, and in line with Okere's suggestion, our traditional world views, myths, proverbs, and so on, could constitute veritable ingredients for an African philosophy.

The question, which of course is inevitable is whether truth is relative, as the hermeneutical approach seems to suggest. In asking this question, one calls to mind Kant's doubt about the *correspondence theory* of truth. Before him truth was always understood as correspondence between mind and object in which case truth was understood as something indubitably objective. But Kant and his critical philosophy on which all subsequent critical philosophies seem to revolve, including the philosophy of Gadamer, the neopositivists, Wittgenstein, analytic philosophers of all strands never understood truth in that absolute objective sense. The relativity of truth as he understands it, and in the sense in which we conceive it in this hermeneutical approach is that in which truth involves historicity and time. And it is to my mind that Msgr. Okere understands truth as relative. In a way it is truth as we can and do attend it. It is on this particular understanding of relativity of truth that the hermeneutical approach has its method logical stress. This approach as suggested by Okere has yielded very rich fruits, as we can see in the maze and volumes of literature produced ever since then on African philosophy. But has hermeneutics as a philosophical approach the last word in African philosophy?

7. Critical Reflection

From our analysis so far we can see that a Euro-centric philosophy or a

one-dimensional cultural understanding of philosophy is totally misguided. This makes nonsense of all theories of society which try to
produce or establish a natural science of society which would possess
the same sort of logical structure and pursue the same achievement as the
science of nature. Unfortunately there are quite a number of English-
speaking social scientists who believe in this sort of asseration. Unlike
social sciences which are guided by natural laws, human society is
human production not by any single person but by the participant in
every social encounter. For this reason society is always in the process
of creation or recreation, and the parameters that apply in the creation of
a particular social milieu may not apply in other social circumstances.
The phenomenon of language bears this out. And hermeneutical
approach as we have seen involves an appreciation of the nature of
language and its significance in social life. As Gadamer puts it:
Verstehen ist sprachgebunden[15] (that means, "philosophy is tied to
language")
      These views, however, have been criticized by Habermas and
K.O. Apel on the ground that the study of human activity cannot be
purely hermeneutic.[16] According to them, the thesis of the universality
of hermeneutics could only be sustained if man were wholly transparent
to himself in the world of perfect Hegelian rationality. It is necessary in
fact to resist the claim to universality with regard to the explanation of
human conduct, of the two main competing traditions in philosophy-
hermeneutics and positivism. Each aspires to cover the whole range of
human behaviour to accommodate it to its particular logical scheme.
According to hermeneutical philosophers, all human actions have to be
understood and are refractory to normological type of explanation
which characterizes the natural sciences. In the eyes of positivistically
minded philosophers, on the other hand, the logical form of natural
sciences applies, broadly speaking, in social sciences also. For Apel and
Habermas, however, both hermeneutics and positivism are two sorts of
endeavours or philosophical approaches that cannot stand on their own
alone, they need a third moderating factor, namely, critical theory.
Applied to hermeneutics (which is our major area of interest), what
Habermas and Apel are saying is that there should be a critical analysis
of the data obtained from our cultural background which should then be
subjected to the normal rule of logic, which is itself, of course, a univer-

sal phenomenon.
This is a great insight for would-be African philosophers and writers in African philosophy.

8. Conclusion

Msgr. Okere is in every sense a social critic, a philosopher and a prophet. He has said whatever needs to be said to touch the minds and hearts of all who have had the opportunity to listen to or read him. He is for the liberation, mental and material, of the African continent. Prophets are usually great gifts to every society, especially if their messages are understood and applied.

It is a free, proud people which keep a nation or a continent alife. A nation or continent becomes a huge flabby power when the people cease to feel themselves free and responsible. But there is vibrant progress when the leadership is aim-oriented and when sincerity and hard work are the bedrock of the people's outlook in life. This is Msgr. Okere's clarion call.

Msgr. Okere deserves our praise for having the courage to say and to do all he has been able to say and do.

Notes

[1] Aristole, *Nichomachian Ethics*, 1094a 27b11.

[2]. Plato, *Republic*, Bk. 7, 514-516.

[3]. T. Okere, "Culture", an unpublished Paper delivered at the College of Science and Technology, Port Harcourt, Nov. 15, 1975 p.3.

[4]. Loc. Cit.

[5]. T Okere, "Crisis of Governance in Africa": The Root of the Problem", in: J. O. Oguejiofor (ed.), *Philosophy, Democracy and Responsible Governance in Africa*, Munster: Lit Verlag, 2003, pp.3-11.

[6]. Ibid., pp 6ff.

[7]. Ibid., Pp.8f.

[8]. T. Okere, "The Secret Societies and Us", An NTV (Channel 18) Talk: Guest, Speaker, 9th May 1976.

[9]. Ibid., p. 5.

[10] St. Augustine, *The City of God*. Ch. 4, Bk 4.

[11] T. Okere, "The Secret Societies and Us", P. 5f.

[12]. H.G. Gadamer, *Wahrheit und Methode*, Tubingen: 1960, p.275.

[13]. K. O. Apel has tried to show in some detail that these affinities are already present in Heidegger. But he indicates, together with Habermas, that Gadamer's philosophy also provides a source of a critical approach to Wittgenstein's work

[14] A. N. Whitehead: The safest general characterization of the European Philosophical tradition is that it consists of a series of footnotes to Plato R. R. Rust, et al, *Doctrines of the Great Educators*, Hongkong: The Macmillan Press Ltd, 1979, p. 33.

[15] H. G. Gadamer, *Kleine Schriften*, Vol. 1, Tubingen: 1967, p. 109.

[16] See Habermas, „Der Universalitats anspruch der Hermeneutik," in: *Apel, Hermeneutik und Ideologiekritik,* Frankfurt: 1971.

2

In Search Of Reason's Traces

Emmanuel Chukwudi Eze

1. Introduction

In postcolonial African philosophy, Theophilus Okere belongs to the "continental" side. In fact, in Africa, Okere is to the continental style of philosophizing what Kwasi Wiredu is to the "analytical" side. Both are accomplished, widely read, and still professionally active.

We have had to put the designators "continental" and "analytical" in scare quotes because, as methodological orientation, each tells us little about the philosophical ideas that the philosopher has pursued.[1] It is also self-evident that, when these ideas are considered in their African context, the continental/analytical designators may appear inappropriate. Arguably, beyond the international classification of contemporary thinkers as either continental (European) or analytical (Anglo-American), in Okere as in Wiredu's works, there may be other more appropriately African characterizations that best capture both the substance or style of their philosophical works. For the purposes of this essay, I have chosen to employ the qualifier "postcolonial" to refer to these African writings.[2] There are, however, other forms of recognizable division of philosophical labor in postcolonial Africa. While some philosophers work in ethnophilosophy (dogmatic or critical restatement of so-called pre-modern or pre-colonial indigenous African systems of thought), others are interested in analyzing in what should then be modern or post-modern, and colonial postcolonial conditions of the continent in the immediate present, with particular references to the global circulations of culture, commerce, and political power. Okere is among the few African thinkers whose works have managed to straddle this historical division of labor.

The substance of Okere's work is marked by its claim to ontological and hermeneutical depth. It is only among francophone African
thinkers (e.g., Ebousi Boulaga in Cameroun or Paulin Hountondji in
Benin) that one may encounter similar, implicit, claim to philosophical
profundity. But it is also possible that what, ultimately, sets Okere apart
from his African peers may be found neither in the distinctions between
the analytical and continental nor in the ethnographic and the
postcolonial; the relevant difference may lie in Okere's highly unique
conception of a relation between philosophy and theology. On the
surface, the theological interests seem quite obvious. In a lecture he
gave on 6 April 2000 at the Centre for Liberation Theologies, a Center
based in the theological faculty of his alma mater, K. U. Leuven, Okere,
spoke on the topic, "The Saving Grace of Reason: Philosophy and
Theology in the Service of Religion and Society."[3] The necessary items -
- philosophy, theology, religion, culture, and society: these are the
structuring issues that have ontologically marked Okere's intellectual
preoccupations. In this regard, his work might be as close to the traditions of liberation theologies in Latin America and Brazil as it is deeply
rooted in late 20th century Africa's peripheral capitalist post-colonialism.
        But the commentary and critique I offer from here onwards are
entirely about the philosophical aspects of Okere's work. My references
are primarily to *African Philosophy: The Historico-Hermeneutical
Conditions of Its Possibility*; the four essays in *Identity and Change*;[4]
and the papers "The Saving Grace of Reason" and "Philosophy and
Intercultural Dialogue." Okere's contributions in philosophy, I will
argue, are located in the specific ideas he proposes about the nature of
philosophical reason, culture, and *history*, and in the relationships he
thinks must exist across these terms. But before I get into the substance
of my remarks, let me say something, even if indirectly, about my
procedure.
        On 4 November 2000 at Bard College on Annandale-On-
Hudson, New York, major African and African American intellectuals
gathered in one hall with one purpose: to celebrate Chinua Achebe's
seventieth birthday. In the audience were Toni Morrison, Wole Soyinka,
Ali Mazrui, Ngugi wa Th'iongo, John Edgar Wideman, and many
others. The president of Nigeria, Olesegun Obasanjo, sent a cabinet
minister to deliver a birthday salute. President Jimmy Carter sent a

letter, and President Nelson Mandela sent birthday greetings. In a representative homage, Mandela, for example, referring to his prison experiences, wrote: "There was a writer named Chinua Achebe ... in whose company the prison walls fell down." Wideman credited *Things Fall Apart*, Mr. Achebe's groundbreaking 1958 book about an Igbo village before colonialism, with teaching him about the literary uses of "primal language," the power of gesture. Wa Th'iongo came with his grandchildren, who at one point climbed onstage to give Mr. Achebe a birthday card. Morrison spoke about how Mr. Achebe's writing had not only induced her love affair with African literature more than 30 years ago, but also helped her think about her own tussle with English, a language, she said, at once rich and deeply racist. What she gleaned from Mr. Achebe's work, she said, was not simply to write against the "white gaze," but outside it, so as to "postulate its irrelevance." She described her debt to Mr. Achebe as one that was "very large, had no repayment schedule, and was interest-free." And so forth.

For two days, Achebe, wearing the traditional Igbo red cap reserved for important men, sat in the front row with his wife Christie, and listened to the pegans rolling down from the stage. When it came time for him to speak, however, he confided to Somini Sengupta, the *New York Times* reporter, who described the exchange as follows:

> To be sure, he was grateful for the praise, he said privately, but he found it all a little odd, too. "It's a funny feeling," said the author, who has written five novels, five books of nonfiction and numerous short stories, children's books and poems. "I am pleased. But it's not intended to be that way -- to be sitting in the front row and everyone's singing your praises -- unless you're a third world dictator."[5]

Or the Holy Father.

2. The Postcolonial African Condition

As some of the participants noted, it was significant that Achebe's seventieth birthday was celebrated on the banks of the Hudson rather than the Niger. Or that so many of Africa's prominent intellectuals just happened to be there assembled: Soyinka from his teaching post at Emory University in Atlanta; Wa Thiong'o from New York University; Mazrui from the University of Binghamton; and so forth. These are writers who, obviously, have experienced what Achebe himself eloquently captured in the title of his most recent book, *Home and Exile.*[6] It seems that the African intellectuals are part of what the Romanian writer Norman Manea called "displaced dreamers and messengers." Okere's social and political philosophical reflections, I wish to suggest, guide us a long way to understanding the forces of the postcolonial conditions that make the displacement appear so routine a phenomenon.

For Okere is a philosopher of the socially or historically oppressed. Along with Boff and Gutierrez, Friere, and Dussel, Okere represents a Third-World stream in theologically-inflected philosophical traditions where the power of reason is brought to bear on historical conditions of the poor or the culturally marginalized -- in view of illuminating the root causes of those conditions. Even as a "man of the cloth," Okere is ready to praise the official Church where the Church's social and historical missions in the Third World have been in conformity with the Beatitudes; but he is also ready to criticize the Church when its missions fail to live up to the rhetorical commitments to the marginal members of the human family. It is in this context, for example, that Okere praises this Pope for accepting responsibility for some of Christianity's problematic relations with Judaism and the Jewish people, even as he criticizes the Pontiff for not yet accepting equivalent moral responsibility for the Church's official implications in the institutions of the African slave trade, nor for the Church's complicities in the activities of the purveyors of predatory capitalist colonialism.[7]

Speaking as he does from the complexities of the standpoint of a Third World thinker, with expertise in the philosophical traditions of the West, Okere observes: "The contradictions of the West between, on the one hand, the philosophy of universal love and peace and the eschatological emphasis of Christianity, and, on the other hand, its perceived xenophobic and predatory self-centeredness and the hedonistic materialism of its secular arm contribute to create monumental ambiguities."[8] What is the role of the philosopher of Africa, faced with these Western cultures? We notice that whether the object of his philosophical critique is religion in specific, or culture in general, Okere's aim remains the

same. His aim is to enhance in all cultures the power of rational reflection; to encourage intellectual traditions to cultivate greater self-
understanding and intellectual humility; and to lead thus chastened and
philosophically sober historical actors and institutions to recognize and
respect difference through acts of dialogues.

Although Okere's method of critique may strike some as
iconoclastic, the iconoclasm and radicalism derive from his expectations about the cultural and social role of philosophy. The goal of
philosophical critique, according to Okere, must always be animated by
an unwavering commitment to the dignity of persons and of cultures.
Writing about his awareness of the disconcertment a people might feel
when confronted by iconoclastic philosophical interrogation, or by
broader human experiences that signal transformations in philosophical
points of view within a culture, Okere remarks: "However it came about,
like the triumph of Elias against the priests of Baal, the undermining of
belief in the traditional gods [by rational reflection is] a devastating rout
that [shakes] more than confidence. It [leads] to the collapse of a whole
philosophico-theological, moral and social, system. It reduces to
meaninglessness and absurdity the panoply of beings, agents and factors
that gave sense and purpose to life."[9] Yet, instead of lamenting such
"catastrophe" to a religion or a culture's self-image, Okere, because of
his Socratic commitments, must see the social and historical opportunities opened up by such otherwise disruptive events. The emergence of
the sobriety of reason, Okere seems to suggest, has no historical substitute. It is such rational sobriety, alone, that marks the attainment of
maturity by both the individual and society, and signals their readiness
in fact constitutes the only condition for a democratic culture. A rational
and democratic culture is one that accepts creativity and pluralism as the
rule rather than as exception, while shunning fundamentalism and
zealotry, whether of religion or politics.

3. The Philosophical Autonomy of the African Subject

What most strongly marks *The Hermeneutics of African Philosophy* is
its ambivalent relationship to Heidegger. I will devote this section to
discussion of the ambivalence because it holds the key to understanding
both Okere's conception of hermeneutics and his application of this

method to an African culture.

In general, Okere seems to be in agreement with Heidegger on the subject of "reason qua being."[10] In an argument he called the "The Uses Of Ontology," for example, Okere repeats some of the main arguments of *The Hermeneutics*. He says:

> One of the better-known characteristics of philosophy as a knowledge form is what one might call its ontological bias. Philosophy ultimately is not poetry or narrative history, or descriptive phenomenology, but rather a discourse on the being of things. It is a statement with an ontological bias, a statement of how things are in themselves - an ontology.[11]

However, unlike Heidegger, Okere is aware of the misleading nature of this statement. He accordingly cautions the reader: "granting ontology such a status was capable of opening it up to abuse." This is because "an ontological determination is a statement on the deepest meaning and level of being of a thing. As such it was definitive and ultimate and has unfortunately been often used in a negative way, in a way that compromised both its claims to real, accurate knowledge and its claims to universality and objectivity."[12]

But, following what I had characterized as an ambivalence, one wonders if the problem we should express in regard to this idea of the ontological, and of a philosophy that depends upon it, is located elsewhere than Okere has conceded. On the one hand, the problem is *not* the abuses that ontology might lend itself to. The problem lies, rather, in the prior claim that ontology is a philosophical "statement of how things are *in themselves*." This, simply, may not be true. For example, if, today, one wants to know how an existing object really is in itself, one must subject it to batteries of tests: chemical, biological, physical, etc., not merely, or even primarily, to ontological philosophical reflection. But it is even more erroneous, and entirely misleading, to believe that, in order for philosophy to be adequate to its tasks, it must be the ontological kind of philosophy in the sense that ontology has been defined. Likewise, to claim that any meaningful philosophical statement must be "an ontological determination," or "a statement on the deepest meaning and level of being of a thing," could not be more debatable. One falls into this and similar errors precisely because one started with what we must regard as a problematic conception of both ontology and philosophy.

On the other hand, if we agree with the hermeneutical Okere that both being and reason are historical, one avenue to find our way out of the problems I have raised is to return to certain aspects of Heidegger. Okere, as Heidegger does of German and European history, wishes to establish the historical grounds for an Igbo and African philosophical consciousness. "In regard to the affiliation of ratio with being," for example, Heidegger says, "we fumble around in the dark because it all too easily slips our mind that the word 'being' also always only speaks historically." Therefore, "the question of the extent to which being and ratio belong together can only be asked in terms of the *Geschick* of being and answered by thinking back into the *Geschick* of being." Then, he added: "But we only experience the *Geschick* of being in traversing the history of western thinking," a history which, for Heidegger, "starts with the Greeks."[13]

Heidegger maneuvers his interpretation of the history of philosophy in the West in this way: "we went from *Grund* back to *ratio*. But ratio speaks in a Latin-Roman way and not Greek way, which means, not such that in the hearing of this word we would already be in a position to ask our question in an inaugural-historical way." When he asks: "might the Roman word ratio also simultaneously speak in a Greek manner," he answers in the affirmative, thus paving the way to the claim of at least an interpretive continuity between the Greek *ousia*, Latin-Roman *ratio*, and his German *Grund*.[14]

In *The Hermeneutics*, Okere, like Heidegger, requires his own Igbo and African "grund" (*omimi*) of being, and therefore of both reason and history.[15] Philosophical dialogue becomes a meeting of such diverse grounds of the world leading to a fuller, if not full, Account of Reason, or History of Being. This under-current of Heideggerianism is also in line with Okere's own Igbo roots. For example, when Heidegger asked himself, "What caused the incubation and end of incubation of reason in the West," he answered: the destiny of Being. He accordingly laments the West's modernity as a period when "the incubation period of the principle of reason ... came to an end." The question of reason or rather the historical crisis of reason henceforth, would be elevated or elevates itself in philosophy to philosophy's "supreme fundamental principle."[16]

The difference between the African Okere and the European

Heidegger lies in the facts that whereas Heiddeger's anti-rationalistic streaks lead him to lament the advent of reason in modernity as a recess of Being, or a liquidation of Being into the principle of calculation, Okere celebrates the African emergence of African reason in an anti-colonial, dialogical, modernity. Reason, for Okere, is the advent of increasing rationalization or interpretative understanding of the onto-logical backgrounds of cultures and life-worlds, leading to increasing rationalization of world-processes and cross-cultural understanding.

If challenged that the rationalization of the social and cultural spheres might lead to consequences such as epistemic imperialism and cultural colonialism, or the predatory practices of modernity such as have just been observed by Okere (or others: Weber, Senghor, etc.), Okere could simply deny that his conception of modern Igbo or African reason shares the historical weakness he attributes, as above, to classical European, Enlightenment, ideal of capitalist rationality. But this defense, on one level, merely begs the question: how is the culturally African reason different from the classically European? If one would not could not -- return to a Senghorian Afro-animism, or to a High Art Negritudist cult of the mystical emotion, what are the common grounds that must sustain *any* reason's claim to either ontological universality or trans-cultural significance?

Okere, it seems, paints in big brushes. Whereas he and Heidegger might share commitments to the transcendental element in hermeneutics, they part ways in their actual theories of reason. In Heidegger, for example, "The surpassing [*Übersteig*] of objects to objectness is the passage into Reason which thereby first comes to light in its ground-positing essence. This surpassing of objects that is expressly the passage into subjectivity is, said in Latin, a *transcendere*. Therefore Kant names his critical procedure that investigates the a priori conditions for the possibility of objects, the method that surpasse, the transcendental method."[17] With dismay, however, one cannot but watch how, in Heidegger, "method" becomes merely evocative, poetic mourning/affirmation of the absence of being. The method, in the end, seems to yield nothing other than exposure of misappropriation by Dasein of the essence of being as false i.e., inauthentic consciousness. Okere's African cultural historico-transcendental critique of reason, it seems to me, is precisely an antidote to Heidegger hyper transcendentalism. But this is also what makes it puzzling to hear Okere, in the 2000s, suggesting, without detailed and stronger qualifications, that philosophy might be, after all, a form of a Heideggerian "ontology."

Consider that elsewhere, in Heidegger, we read that what is "distinctive about the transcendental method is the fact that as the determination of the objectness of objects, this method belongs [not to objects] but to objectness" -- in other words, to the being of beings. Thus, "cognition" is nothing other than the rendering of "sufficient reasons for objects when ... it brings forward and securely establishes the objectness of objects and thereby itself belong to objectness."[18] The transcendental method is said to allow one to, as it were, isolate and hold in view the objectness of object, an objectness that constitutes the principle of sufficient condition for the cognitive reason.

But in other to avert the inevitable accusation of subjectivism, one must make the radical proposition that "subjectivity," after all, is *not* subjective. As Heidegger puts it and it is this assertion that ultimately justifies Okere's qualified embrace of the ontology the subjective "is not something subjective in the sense of being confined to a single person, to the fortuitousness of their particularity and discretion." Instead, "subjectivity is the essential lawfulness of reasons which *pro*vide the possibility of an object." Or, it is also argued, "subjectivity does not mean a subjectivism; rather it refers to that lodging of the claim of the principle of reason which today has as its consequence the atomic age in which the particularity, separation, and validity of the individual disappears at breakneck speed in favor of total uniformity."[19] What is obscured in this apocalyptic disdain for the mundane characterized as "uniformity" -- is, however, a lack of strong deontological consideration and restraints. The Age of Europe may be atomic, but Okere, obviously, is very aware that Africa, in all its present human suffering, may not lay claim to such a grandiose, otherworldly, vision of either philosophy or the forces in its history. While Europe and the West may fear nuclear or atomic catastrophe, atomic nuclear science also has other, peaceful and constructive, uses: it has propelled Europe and the West to a level of unparallel technological, economic, and political achievements. A critique of rationality, especially of the culture and rationality of science in Africa, must require something short of the Heideggerian ontological apocalyptics.

For this reason, it seems, Okere could be only ambivalently Heideggerian. In Okere, it is not clear, for example, that Africa is suffering, as Heidegger thinks of Europe, from the idea of truth as "information technology." It is also not clear that African cultures suffer from reason as "something obvious." Okere is aware of all these when he argues, in his 2000 Luven Liberation Theology Center lecture, for a "saving grace of reason," in both religion and society, not just in Nigeria but also in other parts of Africa.

4. The Dream of Being and the Reality of History

As we have seen, in *The Hermeneutics* Okere follows Heidegger in the awareness of the social and historical forms that any rationality must take. In *The Principle of Reason*, for example, Heidegger had wondered, in the case of the history of reason in the West: "How odd that such an obvious principle, which always directs all human cognition and conduct without being stated, needed so many centuries to be expressly stated as a principle." But then, he says, "It is even odder that we never wonder about the slowness with which the principle of reason came to light. One would like to call the long time it needed its 'incubation period': two thousand three hundred years for the positing of this simple principle. Where and how did the principle of reason sleep for so long and presciently dream what is unthought in it?"[20] In *Identity and Change*, Okere's meditations on the African condition is no less puzzled. On the one hand, speaking about the contradiction in the subject of philosophical reason in postcolonial Africa, he observes:

> Though trained in systems dominated by European culture, the African's concern is not with an inner voyage of discovery of a self. The African's problem is his public role, not his private self. Where the European intellectual, though comfortable inside his culture and tradition, has an image of himself as an outsider, the African intellectual is an uncomfortable outsider, seeking to develop his culture in the directions that will give him a role.[21]

On the other hand, Okere must question the universal applicability of even this claim. Is the dichotomy between the "private" and the "public" spheres of reason so extreme in Africa? Or so comfortable in Europe?

How is one to theorize not just the subjectivity of the reflective subject in Africa but also the extra-rational dimensions of life against which the philosophical subject must compete for civic space?

In the four essays that constitute Okere's intervention in *Identity and Change*, one can detect a common perspective. In fact, it could be argued that the thematic unity of the wide-ranging book is held together by Okere's points of view, which range from the most general to the highly specific: "African Culture: the Past and the Present as an Indivisible Whole"; "The Poverty of Christian Individualist Morality and an African Alternative"; "Names as Building Blocks of an African Philosophy"; and "The Structure of the Self in Igbo Thought." In each of the essays, Okere's writing demonstrates the dilemma articulated earlier: a philosophy (or philosopher) in search of a social role beyond the Faculty Club. Beyond what the essays tell us about contemporary Nigeria or Igbo culture, the interventions suggest a way out of a professional contradiction. If it is the case that philosophers everywhere must *invent* their own cultural and social relevance, and maintain or fail to maintain the relevance according to the ingenuities of the philosophers' social and political class; or if it is the case that philosophers, like members of most professions, work with other social actors to create and maintain spaces for their own self- and collective flourishing, then, one cannot expect, by some ontological design, to find what it means to philosophize in some pre-existing rational order of "Being." In contemporary Nigeria, and as the essays enumerated make clear, there are many reasons why the principle of reason "slept," or sleeps, so long. It seems that the philosophical principle of reason must not just be invented: it needs to be institutionally sustained.

The difficulties of inventing and sustaining such institutions of reason anywhere are well known and not all of the difficulties are deontological. On the matter, Heidegger remarked: "Everywhere we use the principle of reason and adhere to it as a prop for support. But it also immediately propels us into groundlessness."[22] This assertion was, of course, in regard to Kant's insights into the antinomy of reason, in the "Transcendental Deductions" sections of the *Critique of Pure Reason*. Perplexed by this particular dimension of reason, Novalis, for example, eloquently asked: "Should the highest principle contain the highest paradox? Being a principle that allows absolutely no peace, that always attracts and repels, that always anew would become unintelligible as soon as one had understood it? That ceaselessly stirs up our activity without ever exhausting it, without ever becoming familiar?"[23] This extraordinary, romantic, view of reason, it seems, is what Okere must work through if his highly ontological conception of hermeneutics were to succeed. The fact that Okere distances himself from Heidegger's crypto- or overt Nazism does not sufficiently free Okere up as I think he should be freed up from a commitment to the idea of groundless "grounding" of rationality in culture, language, or tradition.

Because of his intellectual struggles to bring to reason the postcolonial conditions of Igbo and Nigerian culture, Okere must radicalize ordinary ideas of culture and history. In this historical radicalism he found more accessible and more acceptable objective grounds for the social roles of the African modern philosophical subject. But these objective grounds could no longer be clearly deeply metaphysical in the "groundless," deep-ontological, sense. Deep-historicality rather of deep-ontology leads one to emphasize not the old gods, nor tradition and "prejudice"; instead, what opens to thought is radical contingency and open-ended revisability of tradition, language, and culture.

The difference between the ontologism of *The Hermeneutics* and the essays in *Identity and Change* could not be any clearer. Implied in the later, more radical conception of history and tradition is a more robust notion of freedom: freedom of thought, but also freedom for action. Both freedoms are grounded not in "Being" but merely on entirely new sets of historical responsibilities. These non-metaphysical grounds of subjectivity, or reason and agency, it seems, are no less "deeper" than the imaginary and practical institutions of societies. Contrary to *The Hermeneutics*, there is little attempt in *Identity and Change* to justify either the imaginary or the institutions by metaphysical intuitions into a "History of Being"; rather, the newer conceptions represent a displacement of commitments to reason from onto-metaphysical to historico-pragmatic considerations. These considerations include, of course, religious thought; but they also include this thought in a wider social and political economy.[24]

The implicit in the earlier and later Okere, however, requires further contextual elaboration. Similar to Okigbo's poetry[25] or Soyinka's[26] drama, the later Okere understands that we are not able to speak, in a postcolonial context, about rationality other than as historical *products* of a transnational, trans-cultural, global environment. The production activity is both subjective and objectively historical, bound up as it is with pre-existing and culturally inherited institutions. These institutions are not purely formed by culturally philosophical or artistic rationality but also the social, economic, and political. But even where Okere would prefer to insist on these conditions as the "prejudicial" disposition implied in subjective and historical embeddedness of intellectual institutions and our procedures of thought, he equally emphasizes the power of reflection on the conditions, the coming to self-awareness of thought, and thus the forcing of traditional and everyday practices to become more nearly rational. This newer Okere perspective presupposes, of course, the earlier, more transformational, claims about history and the contingency, so that philosophical creativity goes all the way up, and the functions of critique could have no bounds ontological or otherwise other than what the historical structures that provide the space for reflection and critique could be made to bear.

In summary, the perspectives of Okere's essays in *Identity and Change* project the task of the Nigerian or African philosopher as consisting of both creation and conservation; building and preservation; and reconstruction because one must deconstruct as much as one constructs. This is a radical affirmation of creativity and the democratic reason as a principle of social change. In comparison to the standpoints of *The Hermeneutics*, this is a philosophical posture derived more from later than earlier Heidegger both shun of the fascist tendencies. Perhaps Okere is more accessible in this regard if read through a Derridean lens; or, if one prefers this in a religious mode, through the idea of radical self-transcendence made popular by Kierkegaard. But, as I have indicated, it seems to me that Okere's work in *Identity and Change* is most in context with Okigbo and Soyinka. A Heidegger that would be compatible with these Nigerian thinkers would have an eye not only "for grounds in all that surrounds, concerns, and meets us," but also for a greater specification of the reasons that form the foundation of the existential attitude.

5. Philosophy as Universal Histories of Reason

In "Philosophy and Intercultural Dialogue," Okere argues: "a philosophy that will enable intercultural dialogue will be not an over-reaching but an over-arching philosophy. It will be a mega-philosophy incorporating and integrating all that is best in the philosophies of the world's cultures."[27] This is an important claim but also a difficult one. Some of the difficulties are obvious, and Okere himself points them out when he remarks that "ignorance, indeed mutual ignorance has often characterized the relations between cultures, and ignorance and error have vitiated relations rather than built bridges." He points out that the problem is compounded when such ignorance comes, as sometimes the case, "in the name of philosophy." It is also noted that "even if it had the knowledge of other cultures, philosophy encounters other obstacles in fulfilling the role of a bridge over cultures." For example, the proverbial "gap" between theory and practice, which Okere claims is inherent in all philosophies, gap could cripple philosophy in its role cultural mediator, by portraying this role as unrealistic or hypocritical.[28]

Yet, Okere hopes that philosophy an overarching one is within reach *because* the fact of dialogue is within philosophy's reach. Hope for enlightened, good, philosophy thus rests on the universal power of dialogue. As Okere imagines this hope:

> Up till now, cultures seem to have interacted with each other at the level of praxis, action and often brutal force; in mutual ignorance or at the level of anecdotes, suspicions, guess work and raw generalization passed on through interpreters, ambassadors, journalists and travelers. It would surely be different if they could learn and reflect on each other's reflexions, self articulations and self assessments. Such a process and discipline of learning would promote a much needed and fruitful exchange. The result should be a creative, cross-pollination of ideas that would lead to intercultural understanding. This would, in turn, contribute immensely to peace among peoples. Philosophy would, for once, be at the service of peace.[28]

This is a hope any philosopher would share; a hope for philosophical enterprises that could see themselves not just *using* dialogue but also see philosophy as such as essentially and intrinsically dialogical. It is through such traditional yet radical conception of philosophical practice that philosophers might hope to better contribute to universal growth of enlightenment and cultures' self-awareness in various nations. Such universal development, Okere understood, would enhance global development of freedom in the forms of civil societies, constitutional democratic institutions, and general commerce and understanding among peoples.

This universal role, in fact, is *traditional* to philosophy because, as Okere points out from a reading of the history of philosophy in the West:

> Two philosophers par excellence, Plato and Aquinas point the way through their quintessentially philosophical methods. Plato's dialogues show the dialectic or Socratic method. Questions draw forth answers and further questions to sharpen and modify the answers in order finally to arrive at some agreement or at least clarify matters. Often the result is inconclusive, indicating that real philosophical questions cannot have a final, definitive answer, but are meant to continue to encourage the human mind to keep wondering about being and nature and man. Thomas Aquinas in his method of philosophizing, though he knows his answer to the question, takes a serious view of all relevant questions, doubts and objections. His answer is also a reasoned choice among many plausible answers.[30]

But this is also a *radical* idea of philosophy because perhaps for the second time in recorded history, and on account of what is known as "globalization" of civil societies humans are capable to come into intensive contacts, and are therefore able to place themselves in positions from which they can offer meaningful critiques of both self and other.

It is also understood that the inter-cultural critiques must include the objects that constitute both the substance and the media of the intense cultural commerce and the social contacts. Okere is, for example, is explicit in the claim that dialogue cannot be understood as an imposition from one partner in dialogue upon others. He says: "[T]he honest search, the openness, the reaching out to other ideas and opinions with respect, defines the truly philosophical process and temperament." Again using Plato and Aquinas as models, he says:

> These two show off philosophy's potentials ... They show that

> philosophy is a search and is a truth seeker; ready to see it,
> recognize and embrace it wherever it can be found. This
> dialogic/dialectical method stands also for the role of philoso-
> phy in mediating between views, worldviews, and cultures.
> Every viewpoint is taken seriously and when taken together,
> several viewpoints rub off on each other by interaction and
> gentle, respectful persuasion. [31]

Persuasion on the basis of the stronger argument: this is the ideal of
philosophical dialogues. [32]

The advantages attributed by Okere to these conceptions of
philosophical practice are unmistakable in their nobility. Speaking
about "the promise of philosophy for intercultural dialogue," he says:

> [Philosophy] can be seen ... clearly in its well known function
> as a clarifier of ideas, words and concepts. This work of
> clarification is carried on by a sustained, critical teasing out of
> hidden layers of meaning in words, the analysis of concepts and
> demanding rigour in logical reasoning. In the real world
> environment of a pluralism of customs, a Babel of languages
> and opaque symbols, anything that brings clarity can only bring
> greater understanding among peoples and cultures. By the
> nature of philosophy, it poses questions of ultimacy which seem
> to be, in the last analysis, the questions all men [sic] ask. In its
> being the concern of all men, [philosophy] becomes accessible
> to all cultures. [33]

Most philosophers would agree with these noble descriptions. But some
of us might argue that in order for philosophy to accomplish the admirable goals or at least to better pursue them -- it must give up on some of
its most profound dreams about Being, some of which, incidentally,
Okere himself appears committed to. Notice, for example, that philosophy, even as Okere described it in relation to the enumerated advantages, may or may not require the heavy Ontology that Okere had
ascribed to philosophy's historical conditions of possibility. Philosophy,
when effective, Okere says, is merely a "critical teasing out of hidden
layers of meaning in words, the analysis of concepts and demanding
rigour in logical reasoning." Unless one were to read more than is
necessary into the word "hidden" (an over-determination that we should

characterize as mystification), or revert to pre-modern -- mythical or religious -- concept of "reason" (e.g., a conception of reasoning as deriving from a theologically sanctioned act of Divination or Revelation), it appears that philosophy, to be successful, requires no more sufficiency than what one would prefer to call the ordinary vocation of an empirical and historical reason. This ordinary form of reason needs neither be anti-tradition nor anti-religious: it merely reserves for itself the radical category of the ordinary. Why *risk* what Okere himself has called the "abuse" of deep-ontology if, as it is implied, philosophy could be reasonably expected to get on with its work without it?

6. The Force of Reason and the Reasons of Force

In "The Saving Grace of Reason," Okere thinks that "contrary to Nietzsche's assertion that Christianity's embrace of rationality led to its own death," the truth of the matter is that rational reflection has played a redeeming role to both religion and society.[304] Among these benefits of reason in religion are the results of a culture characterized in the Europe of the eighteenth and nineteenth centuries by "toleration." Because of the growth of reason in the form of science, and the demand of the scientific mind-set for regulation of conduct and governance of society on the bases of evidence (rather than purely theological beliefs), official Christianity, Okere argues, lost its cultural and social capacity for fundamentalism. Rationalism at least created a framework (e.g., the separation of Church and State) within which religious fundamentalism could be held in check, and religious institutions forced to become more self-reflective. Okere, it seems, expects that other religions, notably 21st century Islam, in Nigeria as elsewhere, will follow this historical example of Christianity.

Okere's reading of the fate of cultural chauvinism is equally critical. The problem of difference (e.g., of language, race, religion, gender, class or sexual orientation) within cultures or across them, he implies, are best managed by recognizing the ontological fact of identity-in-difference. This, as he defines it, is a rational attitude that allows one to give a hearing even to a point of view that one may not personally hold. Citing what are by now his favorite examples, Plato's dialectics and Aquinas's method of questioning, he remarks: "[T]he questions in the *Summas* start with "Whether" a gesture of receptivity formulated as an open-ended query."[35]

It is quite appropriate to raise in relation to this third and the last of the units of Okere's writing currently available to us the question of the relationships of reason (philosophical reason in particular) to force. This is because, if we followed Okere's train of thought, one would think that the orders governing global social and cultural relations are, or could become, as transparent as a philosophical conversation. But we know that, even laying aside the potential gap between theory and practice in philosophy, or the blatant facts of ignorance, the truth about politics and modern economic relations, for example, must include the knowledge that these relations are often intentionally founded on partial truths or outright untruths and on relations of force.

What is the role of violence in the history of human civilizations? Is it possible, for example, that the State's right to a ready use of violence, or credible threat of it, in domestic as in international relations, is as much instruments of "understanding" and order and of national and world peace as any non-coercive universal ideas philosophers could jointly think up at a Seminar? This is not to suggest that there are no enlightenment states or diplomacy. Or that there are no enlightenment principles of governance that philosophical traditions, as Okere understands them, have contributed to good governance. More circumspectively, what we would be interested in is more purely philosophical: to clarify for ourselves the conceptual relations or lack of relations, if this is the case between reason and power. Such distinction, no matter how philosophical intra-mural it might, provides the philosopher the conditions for the possibility of distinguishing between, say, irrational claims to "authority" or "tradition" as sources of arbitrary exercises of power on the one hand, and rational justifications of sources and traditions of non-arbitrary, enlightened, political authority on the other.

If there were two paradigms of human interactions persuasion by reason (e.g., appeal to democratic "freedom") and brute threat of violence or actual of it (e.g., justification of repression of freedoms on grounds of provision of "security"), the philosopher needs to at least try to understand how the two paradigms have played out, in antagonistic or mutual relations, within and across civilization. Are both paradigms incompatible for the philosophical development of culture? Or are they compatible? What are the implications of the possible answers for philosophical critiques of cultures and traditions? These questions may be considered useful for at least one reason: we know that the concept of "Reason," "Democracy," "Revolution," etc. has often been claimed in the cause of violent and morally questionable ends. Are there, for example; as Michel Foucault has argued, forms of epistemic violence, Violence of Reason?

Although no one could doubt his sincerity, Okere's ontological, hermeneutical, and universal "mega-philosophy" raises such question. Is it not precisely on account of metaphysical and epistemic abstemiousness that postmodern critiques of philosophy, such as Lyotard's or Feyerbrand's, have had to counsel resistance to mega- and meta-narratives? Okere rightly suspects the potential for abuse in mega-ontology, but not in his own meta-narrative of a mega-dialogue. (We do not point this out as a criticism, because it is easy to see how Okere is correct: he explicitly expressed a conceptual *hope* much as Kant did in the essay "On Perpetual Peace" for universal civil society or encounters of cultures dialogically mediated and sustained by international systems of rules of law, not force.) Okere also rightly attributes to philosophers a level of humility and open-mindedness that could serve such transnational and transcultural developments. But further accountability on the part of philosophy would, it seems to me, require that philosophical dialogue take into account the historical and even class positions of the philosophers themselves. What makes philosophers better agents of reason than, say, economists, sociologists, or novelists? It is not enough to say that philosophy, because of its relation to ontology, encompasses the interests of the sciences of economics, sociology, literature, etc. We know that novelists and sociologists and economists also study ontological philosophy, and could not be presumed to be incapable of thinking dialogically in search of the universal. If, therefore, the implicit claim is that all cultures and traditions are potentially dialogic and implicitly universal, we would require that further efforts be made to show that the philosopher (apart from, or together with, the novelist, the sociologist, the economist, etc.) is defending a universal that transcends the separate or collective, national or trans-national, class interests of the intellectual.

In a related manner, it seems that philosophy could play the expected role of harbinger of reason, or the role of a secularized social "savior" for religion, either from a position of superiority or inferiority to the object of the salvation. Any of these statuses is possible but it could not be *presumed*: it calls for some kind of *justification*. Even if philosophy neither subordinates nor superordinates itself to the object it is called upon to rationally rescue, if we assumed a relationship of peers and equality between say, philosophy's claims to the authority of reason and religion's doctrinal claims to Revelation, the basis of the peer relationships needs to be made explicit. For example, which authority defers to the other, on what subjects, and under what circumstances? This and similar question are part of the dialogue, as Okere seems well aware; but the questions bring back to the conversation table the issue of sources of philosophical and religious claims to authority or to tradition.

7. The Extraordinary as Enemy of the Ordinary

Another way to make sense of the last issue might be to ask: How would Okere take more seriously an idea of the universal that bears the radical mark of actual historical institutions of "reason"? I am convinced that Okere could do this - but, as I have indicated, on condition of a revision of his hermeneutical ontologism. The strong onotologization - some might say, his hermeneutical "purification" of the rational, I fear, gets in the way of a more truly scientific and historical task of thinking. This later form of thinking requires that the problem of the ontological crises of the historical autonomy of the modern African subject not be ontologically papered over but instead intellectually radicalized. By refusing to confront so radically the crises of post-missionary and postcolonial subjectivity among the Igbo in particular, or in Africa and the postcolonial Third World generally; or by refusing to engage in the confrontation as openly even with a theological sensitivity as, for example, Ebousi Boulaga in *La Crise du Muntu* or *Christianisme sans fetiche*, Okere, it seems to me, remains stuck within the orbit of at least three obstacles to historical thought.

First, in the traditional narration of History in the West (e.g., Weber's, Comte's, or Habermas's), reason is not only historical in its emergence (from the mythical or religious worldviews to the philosophical and scientific), the philosophical self-interrogation of reason must also be seen, as Heidegger's works demonstrate, as a recent development requiring a different set of conditions. Okere as well as Heidegger must concede that, culturally in the western world, while "philosophy has been reigning and transforming itself ever since the sixteenth century BC," it took as long as "two thousand three hundred years" before "Western European thinking" discovered, and formulated, questions about the simple "principle" of reason. Heidegger, for example, believed that it was only in Leibniz's work that, for the first time, the question "What is reason?" became a problem in western thought.[36]

African philosophy, by contrast, and in Okere hands, appears to have been forced to discover and articulate, at once, a history of philosophy *and* the question of the principle of reason. I am not convinced that Okere's onto-hermeneutical claims vis-à-vis the historical conditions of postcolony in Africa sufficiently justify this conflation. To evaluate the sources of the factors contributing to the success or failure of Okere's project in this regard, one must ask whether or not his "accelerated" hermeneutics of both tradition and modernity in African philosophy equally conflates a passive finding of (grounds of) reason in tradition with reason's more active, pioneering, historical spirit. The question here, of course, is not about installing a historical division between the cultures of "tradition" and "modernity" (Okere's dynamic conception of language does not allow this); instead, our question is regarding the degree of freedom, freedom of thought as well as the thought of freedom.

Second, taking the idea of freedom seriously requires that Okere confront the question of peripheral postcolony in reason's own history. We could easily rephrase this question in a favored language of ontology. When we say, for example, that a tradition of reason governs the law of non-contradiction, or that the law of non-contradiction governs the law of reason, what do we mean by "tradition"? Heidegger's choicewhich becomes Okere's, but also in the footsteps of Nietzsche, Kierkegaard, and several poets, e.g., Novalis was to question not only the scope but also the legitimacy of what we have just recognized as the law. "How valid," Heidegger strangely asks, "is the fundamental principle of contradiction?" Without denying the necessity or influence of this principle for the practices of the sciences, or in everyday life, the poet in Heidegger nevertheless resorts to questioning whether science (strictly conceived and in its modern form), or the everyday he derogates as the condition of *das Man*, ought to have the last word on what is or is not rational. In what amounts to putting into question not just the rationality of European modernity but also of science as such, Heidegger claims that "the constant appeal to the principle of contradiction may be the most illuminating thing in the world of the sciences; but whoever knows the (western) history of the principle of contradiction must concede that the interpretation of its content really remain questionable."[37] What is Okere's "Igbo" or "African" (or Christian theological) relations to this debate? What claims could he make, from his existential positions, for or against the arguments and the consequences?

Finally, Okere must address the main problem in Africa's experience of philosophy's own recent history. Again, under Heidegger's influence, he could exploit Africa's history to argue that certain versions of historical reason may be simply a form of irrationality. For example, speaking about the contents of philosophical histories, Okere stipulates: "Any philosophy that denies the full humanity of other humans or the value of certain cultures is obviously in error and was based in the first place on ignorance, no matter how wittily or brilliantly the philosophy was conceived."[38] But if one must do deep ontology why not go all the way, as Heidegger did, to stake a claim for lack of "rational" bottom to reason any reason? Whereas Heidegger used his story about the rise of science and technology in the West to justify his claim that the grounds of reason may indeed be in its self groundless, Okere seems ready to consign only the predatory Enlightenment model of capitalist rationality (e.g., the reason of Las Casas when he recommends to the Spanish Crown to spare Indians from forced labor by importation of African slaves to the plantations) to the domain of the "ontologically" irrational. But what stops one from taking the more radical stand, as Heidegger did? For Heidegger, "for the last one hundred and fifty years there has been Hegel's *Science of Logic*. It shows that contradiction and conflict are not reasons against something being real. Rather, contradiction is the inner life of the reality of the real."[39]

This insight on the surface, an interpretation of the essence of contradiction in Hegel is very revealing when read along with Foucault's works on the ontological nature of power. Heidegger, too, is adamant on the matters: "Ever since Hegel's *Logic* it is no longer immediately certain that where a contradiction is present what contradicts itself cannot be real." He therefore claims that "within the context of our considerations of the fundamental principle of reason in many respects it remains an overhasty procedure if, without hesitation and without reflection, we appeal to the fundamental principle of contradiction and say that the principle of reason is without reason, that this contradicts itself and therefore is impossible." I cite Heidegger at length because it is not clear to me how Okere could have it both ways: just as it was not easy for Heidegger to exorcise the "demon" from the history of reason in the West, we are not sure that Okere could simply wish away the predictable consequences not just of Heidegger's ambivalence but also the ambivalence at the heart of *his own* philosophical or hermeneutical ontology. It seems to me that Okere has merely looked into the abyss and pulled back. We do not, of course, disagree with this decision; the question is: why?

If Okere were to remedy any of the above three problems, he would at least attempt to stabilize the dialectical oscillation between the extremities of "reason" and its "ground." Hegel, as we have seen, chose to entirely reinterpret the meaning of the word, "dialectic," finding in it not the abstract, dogmatic, confrontations between reason and unreason in the form of the logical and the illogical, the abstract and the concrete, or the formal and the existential. For Hegel, this duality is located both at the heart of existence, in Being itself, so that any logic faithful to itself and to the world must take account of and encompass in itself this opposition. It is only after this acknowledgement or recognition of non-identity of the real that one can then construct a dialectical logic that would do justice to both the idea of logic in itself, and to that existence which logic is supposed to be a logic of. In the case of Okere's hermeneutical conception, it is not clear to me how he might go about reconciling the discrepancies he duly notes not just in the affinity between philosophy and culture, but also across the cultural reasons of philosophic traditions, which he hopes to put in dialogue with one another.

Perhaps Okere's ontology might respond to this challenge by proposing a theory of evil -- a theodicy. Or he may abandon ontology altogether. If it did the first, he would re-tread Heidegger, for this was implicit in Heidegger's denigrations of science and technology as a "Fall." Heidegger tried "methodically to eliminate" the contradictions he believed "now and again surface in theories and the conflicts that crop up in observed facts." But then Heidegger also devalued this form of remediational thinking: "This style of cognition," he declaimed, "defines the passion of modern science."?[40] If Okere were Heideggerian enough, would he resort to this anti-science poetics, a poetics that, in phrases like "only the god can save us now," relinquishes to the power of myth (or to nihilism) the historical crises of reason that would have been already so astutely articulated?

But we could also say that Okere has simply carefully chosen his Heidegger, the Heidegger, who says: "Let us take good note of it: the principle of reason indeed speaks of reason and yet it is not a statement about reason qua reason."[401] For *this* Heidegger, reason qua reason, ultimately, is without reason *because* it belongs, as he says, to the "being" of beings. In other words, reason *is*, and there is nothing humans can do about it. Whether or not reason could permeates all human conducts or only parts of it; whether reason is universal and constant or culturally determined and contingent; whether or not reason *ought* to regulate all human affairs; and if yes what *kind* of rationality this regulative reason must exhibit; etc.: these, for Okere, might become primary rather than secondary questions.

But the vocation of "philosophy" which, I believe, Okere sketched above provides enough clues as to what he may or may not do. He might say that while distinct from ontology, yet presupposing it, hermeneutics "rescued philosophy from itself and enabled it to take the first step to act as a bridge among cultures and peoples." He could think that hermeneutics does this "by reminding philosophy of its own cultural origins and clearing the ground about its prejudgments, originating biases, initial and abiding interests and unconscious presuppositions." Etc. The potential problem here, of course, is not in the hermeneutical conception of philosophy; it is rather the indistinct, confused and confusing, "background" of this philosophy. What is Being? What is this dream of a cultural philosophy of Being? A philosophy that would be capable of "full" awareness of its own background as well as its limits? The truth is that because there is no fully conscious philosophy, there is no totality called Being that inexorably forms the object or background of this philosophy. If philosophy is to achieve greater self-awareness -- in culturally artistic, political, economic, and social terms it must, as I see it, orient itself with greater awareness towards its ordinary *historical institutions*, not its putative "deep" or mystical *ontological structures*. Philosophy will grow in Africa only if it focused its attention not on the History of Being but rather on the ordinary stories that account for its humble origins in ancient, traditional, and rudimentary religious sentiments as well as in its increasingly independent, professional, developments in the differentiated (religious, secular, etc.) cultures of a peripheral, postcolonial, and transnational social and political economy.

Whereas Okere might believe that his idea of a philosophy, purified of imperial intentions, "will be in a position to appreciate statements, ideas and philosophies from other cultures and ultimately generate a dialogue among ontologies and philosophies," I am inclined to argue that such cross-cultural dialogue is inhibited, not enhanced, by equating philosophy to ontological reflections, or at least by reducing hermeneutics to a set of ontological reflections. There is a critical edge to philosophy present in Okere's thought, but this critical edge easily gets blunted when he tries to prove that philosophical consciousness must be rooted in a prior, indistinct or vaguely distinguishable, Background of Being. My concern is not that this claim may be untrue, but rather the burden it imposes not only on philosophy but on the spiritual vocation of the philosopher. For example, if philosophy is to allow us as Okere wishes to create fora for cross-cultural understanding, and for seeing the rich pluralism as well as basic compatibilities of cultures, we must ask to what extent they are pre- or extra-philosophical "background" with a small *b* -- that enable philosophy to play this role. No one would belittle the power of ideas or philosophical theories; but it is wise on our parts to ask: are we burdening philosophy with more than its mortal vocation when we ask it to play for our minds the roles traditionally reserved for, say, religion or politics? To put non-philosophical burden on philosophy beyond what philosophy's material institutions can bear would, it seems to me, run the risk of minimally nursing the pre-modern Platonic dream of the Philosopher as King. Or a postcolonial dream of the Philosopher as High Priest.

If one does not wish to make philosophy the servant or hand-maid of Power, secular or religious then, it is imperative that philosophy declines the invitation to usurp any claims to a power of Being, a claim usually reserved in religion to the priest or in politics to the sovereign. The modest dream of philosophy could consist in the ordinary demand for a right to civil, public, space in which to speak the truth (even if, as the case may arise, such truth needs be spoken to power).

Since Socrates, Immanuel Kant, it seems to me, was one of the firsts to grasp this insight into the public nature of philosophy. Although he knew that the faculty of philosophy in Prussia was officially called the *inferior* faculty, just as the faculties of Theology, Law, and Medicine were accordingly called the *superior* faculty, Kant nevertheless insisted that philosophy's power, in relations to the other disciplines, consisted in its powerlessness. There could be only one source of philosopher's power: reason's lack of claim to a heteronomous authority.

In "What is Enlightenment" as well in *The Conflict of Faculties*, Kant argued for the independence of reason and of philosophy in these and similar words: "Enlightenment is man's emergence from his self-incurred immaturity.... For enlightenment of this kind, all that is needed is freedom. And the freedom in question is the most innocuous form of all: freedom to make public use of one's reason."[42] Likewise, yet explicitly in *The Conflict*, Kant points out that while only the members of the lower faculty can provide the principles underlying this faculty's functions, it is enough for the members of the higher faculties to "retain empirical knowledge of the statutes relevant to their offices (hence what has to do with practice)." On account of this epistemological and juridical division of labor, unlike the philosophers who belong to the inferior faculty, the superior members of the faculties of theology, law, and medicine "can be called the businessmen or technicians of learning." This is because they seek "legal influence on the public," and thus "form a special class of the intelligentsia who are not free to make public use of their learning."[43]

The philosopher, however, is accorded none of this or similar status, power, nor protection. Part of the reasons for this irregularity of the discipline of philosophy is that philosophy would loose its intrinsic

character, as free inquiry, if it were legally empowered and, recipro-
cally, regulated by the sovereign or a censoring authority. It seems to me
that whether in Prussia or in Igbo country, the freedom to think and the
cultures of science and enlightenment government will grow not in the
blurring of these boundaries between the philosopher, the scientist, the
theologian, and the sovereign, but in institutionalizing and cultivating
the professional and juridical differences. For philosophy, obviously,
this means a readiness to accept the humblest though radical, because
indispensable role of reason in the ordinary.[44]

8. Concluding Remarks

D.C. Ugwu, a citizen of Nsukka who lived through British colonial
conquest of the Igbo parts of Nigeria had this to say about the experience:

> When the Britishers came to the East, they struck terror into
> people's hearts by shooting people. When villages surrendered
> to the British force, there arose the problem of how to meet the
> British soldiers to negotiate peace. Any brave man who risked
> his head and met the Britishers first was made the 'Chief' of the
> village by the Britishers… None could rebel since such ['Chief']
> had the backing of the soldiers who went about shooting even
> though unprovoked.[45]

In many ways this observation "on the ground" provides further evidence for what Mahmood Mamdani, in his magisterial study, *Citizen
and Subject*, described as the colonial politics of "decentralized despotism."[46] What Ugwu's first-hand report also provides, however, are
largely the forgotten (except when we encounter its truth in novels such
as Achebe's *Things Fall Apart*) grounds of anti-colonial nationalism.
For the citizens of Nsukka, as Ugwu duly noted, the threat of colonial
subjection struck at the deepest institutions through which an African
social and political life was transmitted. In a tone familiar to those who
have read another Igbo memoir, Olaudah Equiano's *The Interesting
Narrative of the Life of Olaudah Equiano, or Gustavus Vassa the
African*,[47] Ugwu reflected:

> We have our customs which from time immemorial had worked
> in the best interest of the greatest number of people in the
> community. It offered the best democratic government in West
> Africa at least, and gave to men and women in our region the
> opportunity which helped to develop their personalities more
> than you could have any where in West Africa. Why should we
> hate it only to copy anachronistic feudalism just for the joy of
> pageantry which feeds on the masses?[48]

Far from defending "anachronism" or a purely emotional attachment to
any "tradition," Ugwu's concerns were about the fates of the explicitly
democratic institutions that he new sustained the material and cultural
reproductions of a society. These institutional provisions, he claimed,
had been particularly effectively made ("men and women in our region
… develop their personalities"); so he warned that the upset of the
democratic political and social order by arbitrary colonialist despotism
could only leave the people "to grope in the dark"; and that unless the
situation is overcome ("If things are left like this"), the customs and the
institutions "which led us proudly through the dark ages" into the light,
will soon die forgotten.[49]

Ugwu's ideas about the prospects of a, at one point, colonially
changing Nsukka resonates, I believe, in Okere's philosophical understandings of Africa and the continent current global marginalization in
economic and political terms. Just as Ugwu concluded his warnings by
proposing: "We must retain them [the democratic institutions] and if
possible progressively renovate them," Okere's work poignantly asks:
In which directions must African societies *progress* after the colonial
experience? Okere's key answer seems to be that one cannot make
progress by merely forgetting the past or misunderstanding the conditions of the present. Likewise, for those who ask what *means* are available for achieving such progress, the answer seems equally clear:
intellectual and cultural democratic citizenship, because it is only this
form of participation in the works of culture and society that guarantees,
for African "men and women," the developments of their talents and
personalities.

Okere's philosophical work makes clear that the "saving grace
of reason" is an indispensable element in the work of culture in a demo-

cratic society. After the traumas of colonialism and a genocidal civil war aimed at them, one hopes that the example of the minority experiences of the Igbo in Nigeria, as that of Africa in the rest of the current orders of the world, continues to provide shining examples of progress in culture and politics through exercises of the democratic reason. It is in the contexts of this universal project that one must send best wishes to Okere and the Whelan Research Academy in Owerri, Nigeria. African intellectuals, the Center's existence seems to announce, must find ways to stage in Africa a debate between those who think that Africa in general, or Igbo modernity in particular, is declining and those who believe that it is rising. In other words, the debate must be between the pessimist and the optimist about the prospects of the human conditions in Africa and about the prospects of the disciplines of natural, social, and humanistic sciences that reproduce global and universal humanity in postcolonial Africa.

Okere, clearly, is in the camp of the optimist. This is the camp of those who believe that recovery of order in the soul and order in society is a first necessity for postcolonial Africans. Therefore, for optimists like Ugwu and Okere, the question is not, as some might erroneously think, *Faut-il ethniciser de nouveau les esprits?* This is not the right question because the globally peripheral postcolonial conditions of Africa are not primarily a conflict between the universal and the particular. The challenge is to see that the "particular" is also universal and to build for all through intercultural dialogue the vocabularies that would allow such universality to become also a more universally shared cultural facts. Just as there could be no universal mind that does not arise from spheres of what is already, specifically, culturally located, Okere's work shows us that the true enemy of the universal is not the particular but the ignorant, the greedy, and the bigoted.

Notes

[1] For the most up-to-date discussion of the continental-analytical divide, see: C. G. Prado (ed.), *A House Divided: Comparing Analytic and Continental Philosophy*, New York: Humanity Books, 2003.

[2] In *Postcolonial African Philosophy: A Critical Reader* (Oxford: Blackwell, 1998)

I tried to explain what "postcolonial" could mean in the philosophical contexts. See also Kwame A. Appiah, "The Postcolonial and the Postmodern," in *In My Father's House: Africa in the Philosophy of Culture* (New York: Oxford University Press, 1992).

[3] Forum for Liberation Theologies, Annual Report 1999-2000, Leuven, 2 October 2000.

[4] University Press of America, 1983.

[5] Somini Sengupta, "Chinua Achebe: A Literary Diaspora Toasts One of Its Own," *The New York Times*, 4 November 2000. My description of this event liberally depends on Sengupta's report. (Achebe's exact birthday is 16 November.)

[6] Achebe, *Home and Exile*, Oxford University Press, 2000.

[7] Okere, "The Saving Grace of Reason." V. Y. Mudimbe's *The Invention of Africa* and *The Idea of Africa* also chronicle Papal justifications   often explicit authorization of African colonialism.

[8] Okere, "Philosophy and Intercultural Dialogue"; hereafter, *PID*.

[9] Okere, *Identity and Change: Nigerian Philosophical Studies, I*; Washington, D.C., 1995; hereafter, *IC*.

[10] Heidegger, *The Principle of Reason*, Bloomington, Indiana: Indiana University Press, p. 105; hereafter, *PR*.

[11] Okere, *PID*.

[12] Ibid.

[12] Heidegger, *PR*, p. 105. Martin Bernal has shown the problems of facts associated with this German reconstructions of European history. See Bernal, *The Black Athena*, 2 vols., Rutgers: Rutgers University Press, 1996 and 1998.

[13] Heidegger, *PR*, p. 105.

[14] This diversity in being is entirely conceivable because Okere's ontological conceptions of Being, like Heidegger's, is not only historical (as destined, *geschick*, or *akara-aka*); it is also linguistic and polysemic. Okere's conception of tradition, *ome-n'ala*, is therefore in agreement with the linguistically Heideggerian. "In terms of the essence of language," argues Heidegger, "this means that language speaks, not humans. Humans only speak inasmuch as they respond to language on the basis of the *Geschick*. But this responding is the genuine manner in which humans belong in the lighting and clearing of being." The polysemy is not of "the word" but rather of the history of the word, and "springs from the fact that in the speaking of language we ourselves are at times, according to the *Geschick* of being, struck, that means addressed, differently by the being of beings." See Heidegger, *PR*, p. 96.

[15] Heidegger *PR*, p. 55.

[16] Heidegger, *PR*, p. 77.

[17] Heidegger, *PR*, p. 80.

[18] Ibid.

[19] Heidegger, *PR*, p. 4.

[20] Okere, *IC*, p.

[21] Heidegger, *PR*, p. 13. In this work, for Heidegger the question was not how to logically ground this or that fact; he is not even interested in investigating the processes of coherence of rational demonstrations such as we find in a standard syllogism; his interest is far more reaching and, as he calls it, "fundamental." He wants to lead the reader to the "ground" of reason. Predictably, he runs into the two easily recognized problems: either infinite regress (what grounds the ground of ground ... etc. of reason?) or the circular: how can, under what condition might it be possible to say that reason is its own ground?

[22] Novalis, *Minor III*, p. 171; "Logische Fragmente," No. 9, in *Schriften: Die Werke Friedich von Hardenbergs*, Berlin: Verlag W. Kolhammer, 1981; 2: 523-524.

[23] The remaining essays in *Identity and Change* include: Joseph I. Asike, "Cultural Identity and Modernity in Africa: A Case for a New Philosophy"; C.B. Okolo, "Urbanization and African Traditional Values"; C. Nze, "The Influence of Christian Values on Culture"; etc.

[24] See, for example, Okigbo,"Heaven's Gate," in *The Labyrinths* New York: African Publishing Corporation, 1971.

[25] See, in particular, *Death and the King's Horsemen*. In the Preface to this play, which is often referred to as Soyinka's first "post-Biafra" play (1975; my reference is to the 2002 Norton and Company edition), the author states: "The Colonial Factor [in the play's question about equality of cultures, e.g., what rights does the British colonialist has to disrupt everyone else's order of the world] is an incident, a catalytic incident merely. The confrontation in the play is largely metaphysical, contained in the human vehicle which is Elesin and the universe of the Yoruba mind - the world of the living, the dead, and the unborn, and the numinous passage which links all: transition."

[26] Okere, *PID*.

[27] Ibid.

[28] Ibid.

[29] Ibid.

[30] Ibid.

[31] As a friendly amendment, one needs to also recognize the historically contextual conditions under which such philosophical dialogue take place: the inequities of power relations, both explicit and implicit; the dynamics of identities and difference on grounds of experiences of factors such as race, culture, gender, class, etc. These are factors of social existence that, if ignored, even with the best of honest expressions, could distort the conditions of productions of truth. In *Identity and Change*, George F. McLean describes his own perspective on Okere's hermeneutics in the following way: "It is not incidental that this philosophical work in hermeneutics has emerged as central in philosophy at the same time that culture has taken its place as a locus philosophicus, or source for philosophical insight, just as scripture is a locus theologicus. As with other fields under intensive

development, this is not an area of philosophical concord, but that very fact is a richness. An appendix to this volume surveys the hermeneutics of H.G. Gadamer for its development of the nature of a cultural tradition and its application to changing circumstances. It reviews also the *critical hermeneutics* of Jurgen Habermas for its effort to provide a way of reading tradition that will protect against its becoming a means of perpetuating structures of injustice. Finally it considers their interrelation in searching out the meaning of a tradition and relating it to the task of building the future." (McClean, "Preface," *Nigerian Philosophical Studies, I*; italics added.)

[32] *PID*.

[33] Okere, "The Saving Grace of Reason," hereafter, *SGR*.

[34] Okere, *SGR*.

[35] Heidegger, *PR*, p. 4.

[36] Heidegger, *PR*, p. 18.

[37] Okere, *PID*.

[38] Heidegger, *PR*, p. 17

[39] Ibid.

[40] Heidegger, *PR*, p. 39.

[41] Immanuel Kant, "An Answer to the Question: "What is Enlightenment?" (1784). Compare these insights to the manifesto in the Preface to the First Edition of the *Critique of Pure Reason*: "Our age is, in especial degree, the age of criticism, and to criticism everything must submit. Religion through its sanctity, and law-giving through its majesty, may seek to exempt themselves from it. But they then awaken just suspicion, and cannot claim the sincere respect which reason accords only to that which has been able to sustain the test of free and open examination."

[42] Kant, *The Conflict of the Faculties* [Der Strit Der Fakultaten, 1798]. My reference is to Mary J. Gregor's translation, University of Nebraska Press, 1992 edition.

[43] In a passage that comes closest to what I have called the "ordinary," Heidegger describes the process of philosophical reasoning as follows: "We content ourselves with the most immediate reasons. But after a while we investigate the more remote reasons; finally we try to get at the first reasons and ask about the ultimate reason." Yet "in all founding and getting to the bottom we are already on the path to reason," so that we "find that what the principle of reason states is commonplace, and because it is commonplace, it is immediately illuminating." The path of the ordinary -- the way of the entirely human, even if daringly Promethean or Agwushike: this remains, I think, for us as mere philosophical mortals, the sum and the model of truth.

[44] D. C. Ugwu, *This is Nsukka!*, Apapa, Lagos: Nigerian National Press [1958], 2nd ed., 1964; p. 21; hereafter, *TIN*.

[45] Mamdani, *Citizen and Subject: Contemporary Africa and the Legacy of Late Colonialism*, Princeton, NJ: Princeton University Press, 1996.

[46] Originally published in London, 1789; my reference is to the

[47] Ugwu, *TIN,* p. 23.

[48] Ugwu, *TIN*, p. 24.

[49] An example of a philosophy textbook that might hold a particular interest to Okere could be Robert Solomon's and Kathleen Higgins's anthology, *World Philosophy: A Text with Readings* (Oxford University Press, 1994). It includes selections by culture: "Japanese Philosophy," "Chinese Philosophy," "South Asian Philosophy," "Arabic Philosophy," "Persian Philosophy," "American Indian Philosophy," "Latin American Philosophy," "African Philosophy," "Western Philosophy," etc.

3

Philosophy Of Non-philosophy: Okere's Trilogy On African Philosophy

I. Maduakolam Osuagwu

Preamble

Fathom a mere mortal attempting to talk about a more-than-a-spirit *Okere wu agbara*. If I accept to dare, it is for a student's enthusiasm to pay homage to his teacher, for a harbinger's humility to witness to the master.[1] My apologetic discretion to our intellectual giant towering high not so much by his imposing stature as by his magisterial finesse. Okere is a repository, a phenomenal compendium of knowledge, an *oba ako* to say it in Igbo, and to put it another way in French, *doyen* of the disciplines. We can justifiably call him an oracle thundering clear and distinct ideas, with melodious and admirable voice of authority that commands profound respect and assent, any where, any time.

Since early in the 1970s, Okere initiated many of us into the intricacies of philosophy. It was a very impressive initiation, with long-lasting impact which made many of us walk his footsteps along the same pathway, home and abroad, during our postgraduate studies and later on during our professional engagements. For those of us who followed him, since the 1980s and 1990s, to the famous Catholic University of Louvain (Belgium) our scholarly interests and areas of specialization tallied very much with his.

Topic of our Essay

Okere's major work, the 1983 published version of his 1971 dissertation, is our major source and focus: *African Philosophy: A Historico-*

Hermeneutical Investigation of the Conditions of its Possibility (1983)[2] He demonstrates in this work the inescapable intimacy and invaluable mutuality which, thanks to hermeneutics, he establishes between philosophy and culture. This submission of his is valid for philosophy everywhere. Africa will be no exception to the rule. Okere's philosophical career can rightly be summed up as *a trilogy on philosophy, culture and hermeneutics*. This trilogy echoes and reechoes all through his works, forming a recurrent decimal that has endured since his dissertation, and still endures in his lectures, articles and books. Okere has doggedly remained consistent in dedicating his intellectual life to this principal preoccupation. The same crucial matters of the trilogy inform this essay of homage we are paying our revered master and mentor. It is a trilogy on and for African philosophy whose fundamental objective is to establish a philosophy of non-philosophy.

A philosophy of non-philosophy gives privilege to culture and builds on it. Okere lays down the general philosophic rule using it to argue its applicability to the African case. Like hermeneutics, culture is also a condition for the possibility of African philosophy. For Africans to do and have their African philosophy, they need to turn to their cultures using hermeneutics to work with and on them. This is not just a hypothetical statement, it is more a categorical one. We can see how philosophy, hermeneutics and culture provide Okere the context, problem and preoccupation to build up his thesis.

Stating the Problematic and the Thesis

For Okere, the major task is "to inquire into the triple problem: Is there, can there be, and in what sense can there be such a thing as African Philosophy?" He considers these three questions the basic problems of African philosophy at the crucial inception of its historical development. To answer these questions raised about African philosophy, he symbiotically links up culture to philosophy and hermeneutics: "...somehow black Africa's own philosophy must have something to do with its culture. Philosophy must be related to culture." It "is a unique cultural form." But "What aspect of culture is philosophy?" And, "what is the nature of this relationship?"[7] But "what is Philosophy in the first place, and what is not philosophy?" That is, "What is culture, and what is

philosophy?" To "what is philosophy?" there is the coordinate question
of "What is culture,....?" or synonymously "what is not philosophy, or
what is non-philosophy?"

Okere takes the question further: "What can happen to culture so
that it brings forth philosophy?" How is philosophy created out of
culture? "How does non philosophy become philosophy?"
Hermeneutics! Okere answers. Hermeneutics is that which can happen
to culture in order to bear or become philosophy. It is in, with and
through hermeneutics that philosophy symbiotically relates to and
methodologically mediates culture. Thus, hermeneutics becomes, for
Okere, the conditions of possibility, we can add, the categorical imperative for the existence, of African philosophy. Hermeneutics is one major
triad of his enterprise. It is therefore necessary to also know what
hermeneutics is, and what is its relational status or function to philosophy and culture. In essence, the hermeneutical relationship of philosophy and culture constitutes a core issue of his investigation. His main
research impetus attempts to found a tradition of rational philosophy in
Africa. In this trilogy lies his basic problematic and preoccupation. He
will strive to symbiotically identify the hermeneutic method with
philosophy and culture, and in this way, to midwife African philosophy.
Okere declares his thesis intention as a matter of procedure or method.
And so his book "does not purport to present an African philosophy."
Instead, it principally

> explores in depth the nature of the relationship between
> philosophy and hermeneutics, exposing mainly by implication,
> how and under what conditions an African philosophical
> tradition could emerge. .....
> In other words, it is essentially a study of hermeneutics and of its
> relevance to the founding of the tradition of rational philosophy
> in Africa.

Philosophy Formally Defined in the Strict and Narrow Sense:
The formal and strict or narrow meaning of scientific philosophy constitutes, for Okere, part of the problem and therefore part of the
trilogy. He insists on this formal scientificity for African philosophy to
worth its salt and respect. Seeking this level of relationship between

philosophy and culture clearly demands identifying, establishing and specifying philosophy, and doing it formally and scientifically *in stricto sensu*. The claim here is that "designating what is African Philosophy needs some criteria." Everything about philosophy might be culture, but not everything about culture is philosophy pure. Moreover, despite culture's involvement, it is philosophy that is the rule in the matter. Therefore, Okere underscores the demands of the scientific frontiers and disciplinary requirements of philosophy. While expecting philosophy to do the same, he demands other sciences and their scholars to respect philosophy's territorial integrity. "Philosophy is a unique cultural form", it must not, "despite affinities" "be confused with other forms" or elements of culture like myth, proverb, worldview, poetry, ideology, nor with study areas like sociology, anthropology, literature, politics, psychology, theology or religion, etc.

I deeply share with Okere this counsel. It is important to honour philosophy in its strict sense in order lest one falls into disciplinary reductionism and professional confusion whose pitfall leads to scientific inertia and decay, if not to scientific suicide. Thus, to guarantee philosophy's formal integrity, its scientific identity and specific difference, Okere brackets out its non-formal, non-scientific and nonprofessional conceptions and practices. As we shall further explain, he challenges defective conceptions of philosophy, the confusion of culture for philosophy, as well as the defective relationship hitherto established between them. The problem of African philosophy is not unconnected with this defective African conception and practice of philosophy. This defect must be addressed and corrected and Okere goes on to do so in his book which we shall consider presently.

Context of the Problematic: Controversy over African Philosophy

The context of the many heated-up controversies is home-based and foreign-influenced. This controversial context also heated up the problematic. Okere raises many more questions in this regard. The questions are raised with reference to the problem of philosophy in general but inescapably also with special reference to the problem of

African philosophy. In the final analysis, it has to do with the conditions of possibility of African philosophy. More specifically, the concern is all about defining African philosophy in its particular and universal characters, its identity and difference, its principles, methods and aims, its actuality, practicability and productivity.

Opinions were divided and positions were taken, in opposition or in proposition. There is also a third position of indisposition, identifiable with indifference, antipathy, disrespect and agnosticism toward African philosophy. It is within the controversial context of opposition and proposition by both indigenous and expatriate philosophers, that Okere develops his philosophy of non-philosophy seen as a prolegomenon to defining and doing African philosophy. Before demonstrating his own position, he critically confronts views jeopardizing the genuine conception of and quest for a true African philosophy of our time. He classifies the opposition as easy but false road of some thinkers to African philosophy. This *false route* called ethnophilosophy has attracted, not only much patronage and popularity, but also much criticism.

Okere's Critique of Ethnophilosophy:[3] an *Apologia Pro Vita Sua*

Okere specifies that his work

> takes a critical look at those works published so far under such or similar titles, or with such intentions. Dissatisfied with their naivety and simplistic assumptions, it suggests that their main fault is a fault of method, a misunderstanding of the nature of philosophy and a failure to see that the nature of the problem is essentially hermeneutical.

In order to constitute an authentic conception, and *a fortiori*, a genuine institution of African philosophy, by claiming for it, its strict scientific concept, its *philosophemenal* expectations from culture, and the methodological (hermeneutical) relationships between them, Okere needs to first and foremost challenge the opposition party. Two grades of opposition are discernible. The camp of skeptics unscientifically denying, dismissing and negating the possibility and reality of African philosophy. And for the other camp of ethnophilosophers, while affirming the possibility and even actuality of African philosophy, it falls victim of its own overzealousness by which it identifies and practices philosophy in a highly questionable, indeed defective, way. It is to this other opposition camp that Okere particularly addresses his criticism, and to it, we shall now turn.

Chapter one of his work identifies, for his criticism, three chief protagonists of ethnophilosophy notably, Placide Tempels (*La philosophie bantoue*, 1948), Aléxis Kagame (*La philosophie bantou-rewandaise de l'être*, 1956) and John Mbiti, *African Religions and Philosophy*, 1969).[4] Okere took his place among avant-garde critics of ethnophilosophy after F. Eboussi Boulaga, P. F. Hountondji and Aimé Césaire.[5] Like them, he was not swayed by the popular euphoria generated by the epoch-making efforts of Tempels and co. To detect its defects, and defects he did detect, our critic dispassionately blazed his searchlight, to, respectively, sharing the racist, theoretical and political objections of the other critics.

Okere also identifies for his critique a form of European ethnophilosophy which is racially pretentious in its prescription for African philosophy, and whose ideological categorization idolizes itself as philosophy *par excellence* and exclusively, posing as the ideal on which African philosophy must model itself for it not to be an abortive enterprise.

Although he acknowledges the significant cultural turn of ethnophilosophers, Okere rejects, on two count charges, their pretentious and exaggerated *ethnologic*. Philosophy is not just an ethnic enterprise, neither in the subject (content) nor in the manner (method) of the enterprise. With a similar premise, we can add that philosophy's instrument and intention are far from being exclusively ethnic affairs. Ethnologic or ethnophilosophy confuses philosophy with culture, and confuses culture for philosophy. "Suffice it to emphasize that there is no art whereby one can automatically deduce a philosophical system from a culture." Thus, it cannot be a "mere 'bricolage,' no mere collecting together of heterogeneous and prefabricated elements which belong to a culture."

According to Okere, ethnologic, ethnophilosophy, or collective philosophy is a "vain search," call it a philosophical fallacy or heresy.

Philosophy is a formal science, a disciplined enterprise with its rules and regulations, principles and methods to be obeyed. Okere insists on a meticulous respect for the rules and regulations of philosophy. In this his delimitation, he issues his caveat and dissuasive recommendation to proponents and practitioners of African philosophy: "The black African philosopher is not to become a cultural historian, a laudator temporis acti, or a curator of the ethnic museum, jealously guarding the purity of ancestral heritage and protecting it from the adulterating encroachment of time and evolution."

What Okere proffers as the way out of this aporetic misconception is for ethnophilosophy to retrace its step in the right direction, first by dropping its defective ethnologic and next to go on to make the absolutely needed methodological hermeneutical turn in order to balance the equation. In this his critique of ethnophilosophy lies his own proactively corrective and creative contribution for a genuine African philosophy. Let us here rest Okere's apologetic trajectory in order to pursue the important pathway of his own investigation and proposition on the crucial and core issue of what we recognize and designate as his philosophy of non-philosophy.

Okere's Philosophy of Non-Philosophy. The Dialectical Dynamics of His Cultural and Hermeneutical Turns

With time, culture became progressively less prominent to philosophers, if not almost outrightly ignored by them as the premier environment and major focus of their profession. But they went only as far as a shadow from its object. Inevitably culture, like nature, remains and will ever remain at the core of the philosophic enterprise, the background, basis, preoccupation, presupposition and inspiration of the philosopher's mission. History contains copious evidences in this regard. In our times and across the continents, the number is on the increase of philosophers who,[6] like Okere, are reclaiming and reinstating for culture its old-age pride of place and irreplaceable role in philosophy, its primacy, constancy and perenniality for philosophy.

Okere takes his reader down the memory lane on a historical

excursus. He demonstrates that, with culture's enduring presence, philosophy cannot be baseless and presuppositionless. He reminds us of the practice of the earliest philosophers and the tradition followed by their successors in Greece, Europe and Asia, where philosophers made their peoples' cultures the focus and thrust of their task. Philosophy is a *scientia cum fundamentum in re*, with culture, like nature   as this foundational thing.

For Okere, the term non-philosophy is the technical jargon for culture. He prefers this *modus loquendi* to underscore the not-to-be-forgotten fact that, while culture, pure and simple, is not the same as philosophy *qua tale*, it has something essential to do with philosophy. Culture is synonymously called non-philosophy in order to demonstrate its intimate and inevitable connection with philosophy. It is non-philosophy without being anti-philosophy or enemy of philosophy. It is rather pro-philosophy as a friend providing philosophy with the enabling sources and resources, locus and environment to thrive. Qualifying it as essentially philosophical, Okere describes culture with the special term "*philosopheme*": the necessary background, ingredient, raw material, vessel, source, nourishment of philosophy. From the other perspective, Okere equally recognizes the necessary and essential cultural character of philosophy. Philosophy anchors its roots and tentacles on culture because it is necessarily culture-bound (limited). It is inevitably culture-contextualized, culture-suffused, culture-inspired, culture-sustained as well as culture-sustaining.

Okere's is a critical theory of philosophy and culture, turning them to dialectically face each other. Philosophy is meant to inevitably turn to culture as its origin and source, its provision and sustenance. To borrow from an equally culture-concerned contemporary European philosopher, the point is that along with many others, "Philosophy is one of the cultural activities of humanity". "It is not the least of these, nor is it the best; it is merely unique and indispensable." [7] Although culture is the core issue, it is so only insofar as it is an expression, articulation, exten-sion and objectivization of nature or life that is at the core of philoso-phy's perennial quest for meaning and understanding. Culture is part of reality, the abstract and material product of man's mental and manual efforts, unlike nature, that part of reality not made by man but is rather the product of the Supreme also denominated God.

Okere dedicates the greater part of his five-chapter work to major historical cases for the demonstration of his thesis concerning the methodological dynamic of hermeneutics that reigns between philosophy with culture. This has ever been the case since philosophy's inception with the Pre-Socratics of Ionia and with Socrates and Plato of Greece. In European history of philosophy, the story is the same. Okere seeks out principal European figures including, among many others, Paul Ricoeur, Martin Heidegger, Hans-Georg Gadamer, G. W. F. Hegel and Alphonse de Waelhens. Philosophy in Asia reflects a similar tendency. Okere argues and draws the conclusion and lesson. Africa is not and cannot be an exception to the rule. What is being pursued is to arrive at establishing the fact that and how philosophy emerges from culture, and how this is also very valid for Africa:

> philosophy is so related and dependent on its cultural universe that each genuine philosophy would have to grow and evolve from its particular culture. If the latter is the case, then philosophy in black Africa would have to emerge from the cultural context of black Africa, nay, in Africa philosophy would have to be homegrown if it is to be philosophy

Okere adds to this his thesis declaration:

> if this is the type of dialectical relationship there is between philosophy and culture, our thesis is this: that Black Africans, having their own cultures, can have their own proper philosophies by deriving and elaborating them from their own cultures. But it is not enough to have a culture in order to have also a philosophy. A mediation, a passage from culture to philosophy is necessary.

He also finds African justification and authority to support his thesis proposition. He draws from the recognitions, provision and recommendation of the sub-commission on philosophy during the second congress of Black Writers and Artists (Rome, March 26 - April 18, 1959) regarding the vital role which, on the one hand, philosophy plays in the elaboration and development of African culture, and on the other hand, the vital sources and resources which African culture provides for the African philosophical enterprise (*op. cit.*, p. 129f.).

Contemporary European philosophers impressively catch Okere's fancy. They provide him with the best historical examples of the cultural and hermeneutical turns. He learns from Europe how hermeneutics is the quantum leap of culture to philosophy. Philosophy is never ready made, neither in culture nor in nature. Culture like nature is not synonymous to philosophy. Philosophy is a disciplined enterprise and product of the human reason[8] working hermeneutically on the raw materials of culture and nature in order to emerge. Culture, like nature, provides philosophy, as has been severally noted, with the background, context and raw material, while hermeneutics intervenes, as philosophy's required method and mediator, to transform it into philosophy. With this understanding, Okere declares:

> Hence, any question of the relationship between culture and philosophy is a hermeneutical problem and calls for appropriate methods of procedure before one can jump from one to the other. We have put hermeneutics in perspective, that is, in relation to culture and philosophy. Hermeneutics, that is, interpretation is the mediating factor between the two poles.

This has ever been the orthodoxy and orthopraxis, the tradition of philosophers through the ages. The philosopher employs hermeneutics to rationally work on culture, as on nature, in order to produce philosophy. As this concerns African philosophers, Okere, to reiterate, stipulates:

> that Black Africans, having their own cultures, can have their own proper philosophies by deriving and elaborating them from their own cultures. But it is not enough to have a culture in order to have a philosophy. A mediation, a passage from culture to philosophy to culture is necessary.

Because, "it is only within the context of hermeneutics that African culture can give birth to African philosophy." Because "It is by interpreting the symbols of a culture that one can arrive at reflexion, philosophy." In this way, Okere understands and defines philosophy as an interpretation of culture - as of nature. Equipped with the philosophy of hermeneutics, he concludes that "African philosophy is a philosophy which gets its initial impulse and its nourishment from the African source, from

African culture." Ultimately, it is not only hermeneutics, but culture also, that constitute the categorical conditions imperative for the possibility, and we add for the reality, of African philosophy.

Critical Considerations - In Critique of Okere

In this part of our essay, we undertake a critical insight into some aporetic stands of Okere. Our critiques agree with his submissions to the extent that they are agreeable, but also differ from them as the problematic cases may be. The following three crucial points of contention make up our critical considerations on Okere: an ethnophilosophical boomerang on Okere, the *aporia* of Okere's *egologization* of philosophy and the impossibility of a genuine ethnophilosophy, the *aporia* of Afrocentrism vis-a-vis philosophy's scientific liberty and universality.

The Ethnophilosophical Boomerang on Okere: First, Sharing Okere's Egological Critique of Ethnophilosophy

We have, earlier on above, looked into Okere's criticism against ethnophilosophy. The drive of his contention anchors on a strict and narrow sense of philosophy which distances philosophy from being a collective enterprise, an ethnology or ethnologic. We agree with Okere that philosophy is essentially and primarily *egologic (cogito), not ethnologic*. What he wants to see established, and henceforth practiced by Africans, is an *ego-philosophy, not an ethnophilosophy*, the type patronized and popularized by P. Tempels, A. Kagame, J. Mbiti and their disciples and admirers. Okere strongly and justifiably argues that philosophy, everywhere, remains an effort necessarily undertaken and realized by an "I." This means that philosophy is not a collective project. It is only when a collective culture is labored on by an "I" that the philosophical signification appears. That a culture is understood and interpreted means that this culture is re-assumed, re-appropriated, retrieved, and made to live again by a new and creative act done in the first person. This is why philosophy can neither be a collective effort, not yet an impersonal enterprise. The authentic philosophical project is undertaken by an "I" from within his culture, involved in it and part of it, and not like a scientist reporting impersonally and objectively from outside.

> It is rather a project of appropriation, of assumption and identification with one's total culture in a process of intellectual alchemy from which results a new creation, the meaning of this culture as interpreted by this unique experience which is the philosopher's insertion in it.

Okere makes philosophy to strongly contrast with a people's worldview (*Weltanschauung*). Philosophy which is essentially an individual enterprise differs from collective philosophy. Collective philosophy here means total consensus, total adherence and total unity and uniformity. But philosophy as an individual enterprise "is often a mise-en-cause, and a radical questioning of the collective image. By reflecting and the questioning of this image, one makes an individual effort to find, that is, to give meaning to one's world." The recommendation of Okere is for Africans to make philosophy their individual personal efforts at self understanding, "a giving of meaning to one's own world and existence. It is always "my" philosophy - in other words, a first-person effort." This is philosophy's tradition as Okere exemplifies in Socrates and Plato, in contemporary European hermeneuticists like Ricoeur, Heidegger, de Waelhens. This is philosophy's rule of thumb that he highly recommends for African philosophers to make philosophy "always the creative work of an individual intellect."

Critique of Okere's Aporiae

But some of Okere's claims turn around to raise crucial issues that question his very views, positions and recommendations. He criticized ethnophilosophy and its ethnologic, but did he not, in spite of himself, fall into the same pitfall? Besides, Okere does agree with ethnophilosophers' concentration on African cultures! But his call on philosophers to busy themselves only with their people's particular cultures creates a serious problem. With the task to be executed and objective to be achieved, his individualization or personalization of philosophy creates the problematic impression of the *egologization* or of philosophy.

One might very well doubt that Okere succeeded, in the long run, in escaping the ethnological or ethnophilosophical pitfall that he, with good reasons, criticized so vehemently. To what extent are his claims on Igbo philosophy[9] not ethnophilosophical, differing really from Tempels', Kagame's and Mbiti's? In philosophizing, does he make it an ethno-Igbo undertaking and an ethno-Igbo product? Or is not all about his personal enterprise and the fruit of his personal labour? The signature of philosophy may be personal (*my-own*) on the level of engagement, but certainly not with respect to the task to be done, the objective to be achieved and the use to be made of it which are all *our-own*. The project, purpose and employment of philosophy are matters of *our-own*. In other words, with this collective dimension, philosophy cannot be so personalized, made matters of "in my opinion", "in my view", "in my understanding", and many of such ego-base clichés. Ultimately, philosophy is, at the same time, inescapably egocentric and ethnocentric, egologic and ethnologic, *egophorus* and *ethnophorus*. We only need to establish the necessary levels and aspects of the identifications and differentiations of the personal and the communal.

To play the *defensor vinculi*, the personal touch to philosophizing is surely far from being an absolute matter of the individualization of philosophy - as just submitted, philosophy is not a matter of opinionatedness, of one's opinion (*doxa*) and taste (*gustus*). A clear and strong distinction must be made between a perverse individualist and a scientific individualist. Further distinction needs to be established between a psychological individualist concerned with relative matters or subject areas and a philosophical individualist - a more-than-psychological individual - concerned with matters of objective or universal principles. Although the philosopher does his work of thinking, reasoning, individually, scientifically speaking, his philosophical individuality (ego) essentially means his community individuality, with community capacity and authority to work on a common project for a common use and common purpose. To reiterate, the philosopher should not, and cannot be an individualist (egoist) in the pejorative sense of the term. The work he does is community work. His vocational and missionary personality is meant to represent the community.

Okere quarrels with ethnophilosophy on the two count charges of their philosophic deficiency and of their exaggerated ethnicity and ethnologic. But is ethnophilosophy diametrically opposed to and exclusive of formal scientific philosophy? Considering its strong impacts that have generated a thriving current of African philosophy, can ethnophilosophy not be legitimized by making it become proper?

By respecting the requirements of scientific, personalized and hermeneutical philosophy, can there not be a legitimate passage from crude and defective ethnophilosophy of the Tempelsian brand to a critical genuine ethnophilosophy,[10] into which, with deference Okere might well fit.

Furthermore, the recommendations of Okere's well-intentioned autochthony proposition creates its *aporiae* for African philosophy. This Afrocentricism[11] might well be a strategic puritanism to call the African scholar back to his roots, to motivate him to be interested in his heritage, with the necessary attention, allegiance and coverage. African philosophers must be about their own people's cultural business, and stop the distractions, deviations and derailments occasioned by Eurocentrism[12] - and progressively in recent times Asiacentrism.

Okere criticizes Eurocentrism but professes Afrocentrism.[13] Since African culture differs from European or Asian culture, this gives African philosophy its identity differentiating it from European philosophy. It is all a matter of authenticity and independence.[14] African philosophy must chart its own specific course. Okere and others like him represent the premier attempts of Africans to overcome the European pull. But how far have we gone since then? Today, Tshibangu-wa-Mulumba might still be relevantly right for "Until otherwise proved, we are all European philosophers of black African origin. Thus, - as long as we continue to reason and reflect in the European manner - we have no right to qualify this intellectual 'extension' 'African philosophy'."[15] H. Maurier (1977) might also be still right that we do not yet have African philosophers or African philosophy, since the necessary conditions are yet to be met.[16]

Of course, Okere rightly demands an authentic African philosophy. Just as Kinyongo says:

> it is not just by mere desire to be á la mode to postulate that just as there are western, Chinese, Indian, etc., philosophies, so too an African philosophy - which however would still be its right. It is rather a way by which the philosophical project, having become a regional project and a regional science, engages itself in the Black continent, and identifies with its history, geography and social customs.[17]

Legitimate as this expectation and demand may be, we hope, however, that Okere's Afrocentrism is not at the expense of attempts by scientific philosophers and philosophizing to attain universals and objectives common to humanity and cosmology, and common to epistemology, religiosity and technicity of a common scientific interest, concern, quest, endeavour and conclusion? Noble as it may sound, Okere's Africanity risks succumbing to problematic relativism, isolationism and incompatibility in the face of the cultures and philosophies of the peoples of the world. Despite his cursory caveat against introversion, does his privilege for African originality, focus, relativism, disconnection and departure, not pose a grave obstacle to legitimate architectonic inter-cultural or cross-cultural contact, dialogue, communication, community, commerce and exchange with other peoples of the world?[18] If stretched to the extreme, Okere's Afrocentric advocacy will attract a Hountondjian criticism:

> To require thinkers to be content with reaffirming the beliefs of their people or social group is exactly the same as prohibiting them from thinking freely and condemning them in the long term to intellectual asphyxia. Deep down such a demand lies radical skepticism and stubborn relativism, and perhaps worse still, behind the apparently anti-racial and anti-Eurocentric stance lurks a secret contempt for non-western thinkers, who are thus subtly excluded from any claim to universality - that is to say to *truth* - and denied the right to any authentic research, simply being expected to display the peculiarities of their culture in philosophical form. .... Africans today should be capable of ... freely seizing the whole existing philosophical and scientific heritage, assimilating and mastering it in order to be able to transcend it.[19]

In his bid to boycott the boycottables, Okere, like the vast majority of contemporary African philosophers, hardly succeeded in totally avoiding borrowing the borrowables of other peoples, cultures and philosophies. Many of our African philosophers are still heavily dosed and dazed with the European philosophic spirit. Like many others, Okere still parades European philosophers who serve him as model authorities and sources to be relied on and imitated. He still uses their

European languages,[20] concepts and methods. European philosophy has taken its proper historical place in our African tradition. Despite its regrettable defects and rejectable excesses, Africans have been inescapably marked by it. I share Kinyongo's realistic counsel:

> *volens nolens* and by necessity of a historical order, our philosophy wears and will always wear in a profound way the Greek image of its designation, even in its very rejection of Greekness. It is therefore, not only by the necessity of the tactics of struggle advocated by M. Towa and Nkombe Oleko that we must adopt Western philosophy..., it is also and above all by the necessity of a historico-ontological order, and because, theoretically and in principle, we are constrained to do so.[21]

Whatever the constraint, it is not without a light at the other end of the tunnel, the light of the liberty to be, at the same time, truly (authentically) African and truly human. Our quest for our African relativity/particularity must not be opposed to our human objectivity/universality. Our Africanity must transcend and indeed has transcended its ethnic culturality and continental spatiality. Scientifically and historically, our Africanity means more a tribal and a geographical mark; it is more than biology, physics and psychology. It is now defined, no longer only by its blood and cultural ancestry. It has acquired a scientific and spiritual meaning to transcend its hitherto myopic intentionality. With its historical encounters and experiences, it has acquired new expanded conceptualizations and contextualizations. Even without these historical factors, it is capable of an unlimited extentionality.[22]

Africans can no longer pretend or continue to be blind to these novelties and overtures that are not necessarily, all and always, obstacles to their African autochthony. If so, we cannot be doing African philosophy only when we are focused on and using our pure indigenous African cultural and natural matters. An African can, legitimately, use philosophically interesting cultural and natural issues of other peoples to do his African philosophy. Just as much as it is legitimate for an African to philosophize on the cultural and natural issue of other peoples and places, so too is it equally legitimate for European or Asian philosopher to make African culture and nature issue of his philosophical endeavour.

Conclusion: Okere's Significance, Fame and Influence

The foregoing critical reservations must not be allowed to diminish or dismiss Okere's significance and influence for African philosophy. In the preamble, we declared Okere an intellectual giant, towering high by his admirable magisterial finesse and by his compelling oracular authority. We acknowledge him as master and mentor.

By his trilogy, Okere significantly reinstates for African philosophy in its basic formal meaning, depositing and demanding for it the principal criteria for its definition. These criteria constitute the categorical conditions of the possibility as of the existentiality of African philosophy. In this way, Okere makes a case for scientific African philosophy, elevating African philosophy rungs higher than was the situation hitherto. His trilogy is a scientific apologia and a booster project for the African philosophical tradition.

In addition, his trilogy founds African philosophy on the scientific *cogito*, on the scientific or professional individual engaged on the personal reflective (*egology*) effort of interpretation or explicitation of culture and nature, of life and reality. Scientific *cogito* accords genuine philosophic primacy to the human reason (mind, spirit) as the principal subject and canon - not to dream, myth, narrative, and even to faith.

Okere stands African philosophy on its proper and authentic footing, African cultures. Once, African cultures were neglected, denigrated, denied or forgotten. If at all they were spoken of, it was not for anything serious, creative and acknowledged. With great apologists like Okere, African cultures receive their true scientific status and function in the various life endeavours of Africans. Thanks to his promotions, Africans, more than ever, have come to a higher appreciation of their cultures and its scientific value. Okere has given a great impetus to the African *fons et origo* or *redeuntes ad fontem*: more than ever, many more Africans are embarking on a return to their cultural roots and origins. Okere contributes immensely to African cultural revival, restoration and revolution in our time. Heeding the warning against scientific suicide, the way to be at and bring out their best, is for African philosophers to accord priority and preeminence to their cultures, and to invest all energies and resources on it.

Furthermore, in connecting the cultural revolution to philosophy, Okere ignited the unstoppable high philosophic waves rippling across Africa of our time. His trilogy produces a psychological or psychedelic effect on Africans, elevating them out of their passion of inferiority to the dignifying status of self pride. This scientific psychedelism carries with it other elating consequences that concern the African's existential authenticity, morality and productivity. Accordingly, Okere recommends:

> that one should go back to one's own roots and sources. The sources, the headwater region of creative and original thought, are one's own culture. No familiarity with the foreign and borrowed element can suffice for the articulation of something so deep-felt as one's understanding of one's own world. It is not a question of fruitlessness when one undertakes to think foreign to oneself. It is also a moral question of being honest and true to one's self.

The challenge is also for a creative, never a mechanical, philosophy. It is a new project, an African mission and mandate. Talking of Okere's significance already introduces his fame and influence in the world of African philosophy. We can justifiably proclaim him the grand patron of the African school of hermeneutics. The truth of the matter is that, in both Anglophone and Francophone Africa, He enjoys the historical-scientific credit of being the pioneer of hermeneutics in African philosophy. Acknowledged East and West, and North and South, it is Okere's merit, to have, with his 1971 dissertation, given the premier impetus to the hermeneutical current in contemporary continental African philosophy. Others, in this African hermeneutical tradition, came after him.

Okere is not a prophet without honour in his own country. Back home, he has considerably inspired many scholars as well made a remarkable number of disciples, immediately and proximately. He is an inspiration behind many of us who went to the famous Catholic University of Louvain, Belgium, as he is behind many others who went elsewhere like Rome, Germany, Austria, U.S.A. The present essayist is part of the litany that includes S. Nnoruka, R. O. Madu, J. Uwalaka, P. Iroegbu, J. Oguejiofor, G. Onah. The list continues... of the many ever eager to listen to the oracle with rapture and deference, following closely in his footsteps as disciples and/or entrepreneurs.

Notes

[1] Since 1993, Okere has continued to received prominence in my works, both in my postgraduate works: *Towards a Phenomenology of Social Existence* (1989) and *The Ontological Destiny of Man (1993)*, and later on in my published three-volume lecture series on African Philosophy: Volume 1: *African Historical Reconstruction.* "A Methodological Option for African Studies. The North African Case of the Ancient History of Philosophy". (Enugu, SNAPP, 1999), Volume II: *Early Medieval History of African Philosophy.* "The Africanity of the Early Medieval History of Philosophy or of the Christian Phase of North African Catholic Thinkers". (Enugu, SNAAP, 2001); Volume IV: *A Contemporary History of African Philosophy,* (Enugu, SNAAP, 1999).

[2] See principally his doctoral dissertation *Can there be an African Philosophy?* "A Hermeneutical Study with Special Reference to Igbo Culture". (Louvain, University Catholique de Louvain, 1971); "The Relation Between Culture and Philosophy" in *Uche,* Journal of the Department of Philosophy and Classics, (University of Nigeria, Nsukka, Vol. 2; *African Philosophy: A History-Hermeneutical investigation of the Conditions of its possibility,* (Lanham: Univeristy Press of America, 1983), and his many talks and articles. For more details, see general bibliographical compilation on Okere.

[3] See Chapter 5 of my critique of ethnophilosophy in *A Contemporary History of African Philosophy, op cit.*

[4] We hope that Okere will oblige us to do like P.E. Bodunrin and include, in this popular current, Leopold Sadat Senghor's *Negritude* written earlier on. Ethnophilosophy made its glorious appearance in the forties and fifties. With its big-bang impact in the sixties and seventies, and even in the eighties till date, it grew like the African wild fire gaining, by leaps and nounds, popularity, patronage and discipleship. See my *A Contemporary History of African Philosophy, op. cit.* Chapter Five.

[5]. Paulin F. Hountondji who coined the term ethnophilosophy, see his "Remarques sur la philosophie africaine" in *Diogene,* no. 71 (1970), his *Sur la "philosophie africaine", Critique de l'ethnophilosophie,* (Paris, Maspero, 1977) and *African Philosophy,* "Myth and Reality", (London: Hutchinson, 1983 of 1973) French); see F. Ebousi Boulaga, "La bantou problematique" in *Presence Africana,* no. 66 (1958).

[6] Okere is not alone in the cultural turn in African Philosophy. the 1970s and

thereafter were decades of this critical African cultural turn or revolution. See P.F. Hountondji, *African Philosophy:* "Myth and Reality" *(op. cit)*; Kwasi Wiredu, *Philosophy and African Culture,* (Cambridge: Cambridge University Press, 1980); O. O. W'oleko, *Pour une philosophie de la culture et du development, recherche d'hermeneutique et de paxis africains,* 1986; A Diemer & P. J. Hountondji, (eds), *Africa and the Problem of its Identity, International Philosphical Symposium on Culture and Identity of Africa, 1982,* (1985). Okere shares with European philosophers like Ernst Cassirer, Paul Ricoeur, M. Heideger, H.G. Gadamer, A de Waelhens, etc.

[7] L. E. Cahoone, *The Dilemma of Modernity, Philosophy, Culture and Anti-Culture,* (Albany, State University of New York, 1988), p. 263, see p. 196, 246.

[8]. Although all men are rational by culture, it does not necessarily follow that all are also by nature philosophical. philosophy or philosophic reason is not natural, it is cultural and needs to be developed.

[9] Compare with Okere indications on Igbo symbols and institutions such as *Chi, Ikenga, Mbari, Uwa,* etc. (Okere, 1983, p. 115, 124), and on Igbo conception of history as cyclic rather than linear, or as reincarnational rather than eschatological (*op. cit.*, p. 122), or again, as particular or relative rather than universal and objective (*op. cit.*, p. 123).

[10] See my *A Contemporary History of African Philosophy, op. cit.* p. 153f.

[11]. See I.C. Onyewuenyi's definition of Philosophical Afrocentrism in his *The African Origin of Greek Philosophy"*, "An Exercise in Afrocentrism". (Nsukka: University of Nigeria Press, 1993).

[12] Many Contemporary African Philosopher share, *grosso modo,* in this position of Okere. It is all about the great controversy over the African uses of Western Philosophical - Linguistic, conceptual and methodological models. See my *African Historical Reconstruction.* "A Methodological Option for African Studies...", *op cit.,* Chapter One: See P.F. Hountondji, *African Philosophy,* "Myth and Reality", *op cit.*

[13] Okere is not alone in calling for the critique of Eurocentrism in African Philosophy. About three decades after hsiu first say, Tsenay Serequeberhan issues his "The Critique of Eurocentrism and the Practice of African Philosophy" in Emmanuel Chukwudi Eze, (ed.), *Postcolonial African Philosophy.* "A Critical Reader", (Oxford: Blackwell, 1997), p. 141-160, p. 130, Onyewuenyi's Afrocentrism also presents a critique of Eurocentrism, see his *The African Origin of Greek Philosophy:* "An Exercise in Afrocentrism", *op cit.*

[14] Some African authors talk of intellectual or literary decolonization. Chinweizu, O. Jamike & I. Madubuike, *Toward the Decolonization of African Literature,* Volume 1: "African Fiction and Poetry and their Critics", (Enugu: Fourth Dimension Publishers, 1980); Wa Thiongo Ngugi, *Decolonizing the Mind: The Politics of Language Literature,* (Nairobi: East Africa Publishers, 1992).

[15] A. Tsshibangu-wa-Mulumba, "Metaphysique, cette philosophie qui nos vient

d'ailleus", in *Cahiers philosophiques africains,* 3-4 (1973); my translation.
[16] Henri Maurier, "Do we have an African Philosophy?" in Richard Wright (ed.)
African Philosophy "An Introduction", (Lanham: Univeristy of America Press,
1984, 1977).
[17] Jekki Kinyongo, *Ephiphanies de la philosophie africaine et afro-americaine.*
"Esquisse historique du debat sur leur existence et leur essence", (Munich-
Kinshasa-Lubumbashi: Publications universatires africanes, 1989), p. 79; my
translation.
[18] We agree with to J. Kinyongo that "real and certified development of philosophy
in western Europe does not exclude the possibility of appropriation or re-
appropriation of the western philosophical mode of thinking by other
civilizations..."*Epiphanies de la philosophie africane et afro-americaine.*
"Esquisse historique de debat sur leur existence et leur essence", *op. cit.,* 16. My
translation.
[19] See P. Hountondji, *African Philosophy,* "Myth and Reality", *op. cit., p.* 128-129.
[20] The use of African Languages to define and do African Philosophy has become
bone of contention for contemporary African scholars. See my *A Contemporary
History of African Philosophy,* (1999), *op. cit,* p. 72-80. Language must not be so
absolutized a criterion for defining and doing African Philosophy. Importance as
African indigenous language undeniably are, it is also possible to define and do
African philosophy by or in non-African languages. This is currently the situation
of African philosophers who, willy nilly or out of scientific liberty or legitimacy,
are using non-African, notably European, language to do their African
philosophy. let us share with Tran van Toan his most judicious and balanced
reflection and counsel on this matter.

> One can say that these two languages (English and French) actually
> play, in the majority of African countries, the role which Latin played
> for Europe in the middle ages. i know that the problem is complex. i do
> not mind what his happening in African countries in which the official
> langauge os administration and education is in an African language.
> In these countries, it seems to me, the birth or birth of an original
> African thought constitutes no problem.
> If the philosophers of Europe gradually detached themselves from
> Latin in order to write in their national language, it is not theoretically
> excluded that one day African philosophers, having been nourished
> with foreign philosophical traditions, will began to philosophize in
> their own national languages, in this way initiate a fruitful and original
> philosophical life in Africa. Nobody would be able to say if it is
> necessary to regret the loss of false universality, because, on the one
> hand, it is in order to see clearer ourselves, in our situation, that we
> philosophize, and on the other hand, no foreign language permits us
> more point of view on the universal. "A propse de la question des

langues dan la philosophie africaine" in *Cahiers philosophiques africains,*(1972), p. 173; my translation.

It is more due to lack of the political will on the part of African public leaders coupled with lack of scientific courage on the part of African scholars that African languages are still being dominated by foreign languages and so not in use in African scholarship. In the absence of official and institutional interventions in favour of African languages, individual philosophers must carry on the crusade.
[21] J. Kinyongo, *Epiphanies de lar philosphie africaine et afro-americaine.* "Esquisse historique d debat sur leur existence at leur esence", *op. cit.*, p. 16 my translation.
22 In a very formal or professional consideration, Africanity requires the science or author being determined to bear the following characters. No one character suffices. All four must be considered in their proper combinations and requirements: (a) *Ethno-African character* acquired by birth, that is, by partial or total sanguinity, ancestry and cultural–*cum*-natural tradition. (b) *Spatio-temporal African character* acquires by virtue of space and time where the author is functioning or the event is happening; the spatio-termporal factor is both physical and spiritual or symbolic. It circumscribes the African, not only within the immediate boundaries of the African continent, but also spiritually or symbolically beyond it, wherever, the world over, an ethnic or legitimate African finds himself functioning as such. (c) *Lego-African character* acquired through the law, be it naturalized, civil, academic or ecclesiastical which authorizes especially a foreigner to assume African scholarly citizenship. he is not African by ethnicity, but he certainly has a legitimate claim to the African citizenship that enables him to function within the African spatio-temporal order and to do so as a legally agent of the African enterprise. (d) *Techno African character* acquired by virtues of the works by an indigenous African or a foreign African, who is operating be it within the immediate physical boundaries of Africa or symbolically outside it. See my *A Contemporary History of African Philosophy, op. cit,* p. 29f. We are making a case for non-indigenes from Europe and other parts of the world, who, by process of depth insertion or inculturation, properly assume our Africaness, sharing in those typical characters that identify and differentiate us.. We must not all be born Africans by full or partial parentage. besides natural Africanity, there is also cultural Africanity, being African by cultivating African characters. the same logic holds for thet African classified as European or Asian philosopher or scholar.

4

Ethnophilosophy and Hermeneutics
Reviewing Okere's Critique of Traditional African Philosophy

J. Obi Oguejiofor

1. Introduction

A very standard practice appears to have developed in contemporary African philosophy. This procedure is seen in the ease with which thinkers are classified into different identifiable philosophical trends. The classification is done in such a manner that it is almost iron-cast with rigid boundaries. Thus in the works of authors like H. O. Oruka, P. Hountondji, M. Towa, O. Oladipo and A. Mosley African philosophic thinkers are somehow easily categorized as ethnophilosophers, professional philosophers, members of the national ideological school, etc. Philosophical categorization has its convenience.[1] It introduces order into an otherwise fluid discipline, making predictability easier, and facilitating more clear cut discussions. But such an example as A. J. Ayer's *Language, Truth and Logic* is a caveat that the job of categorizing philosophic thinkers and their thought may not be as easy as it is often seen in practice. Ayer in an overarching attempt to give philosophical analysis a historical backing claimed that the history of Western philosophy is in the main history of philosophical analysis, and that such philosophers as Plato, Aristotle, etc were in fact doing philosophical analysis and not metaphysics.[2]

The facility afforded by philosophic classification has not been lost to contemporary African philosophers, and this has given rise to its different currents. But the attendant problems have also not eluded the discipline. One typical instance is H. O. Oruka's critique of ethnophilosophy which in his view is philosophy only in the debased sense, since it is not critical.[3] However, the counter-current he championed in order to get around the problems that gave rise to ethnophilosophy is accused of being a throwback to the same current it is escaping from. In view of this problem, this essay is a brief overview of Theophilus Okere's critique of ethnophilophy. The aim is to examine the major points of the critique, and to argue that the issue may not all be too clear cut. It argues that while Okere's main thrust that African philosophy should emerge through the process of hermeneutics has a lot to commend it, many of the so-called ethnophilosophers have, perhaps without knowing it been engaging in the process of hermeneutics.

2. The Meaning of Ethnophilosophy

The word ethnophilosophy is a coinage from ethnology and philosophy. It was first used by Paulin Hountondji in the context of contemporary African philosophical discussions. It refers to the trend in contemporary African philosophy, which originated from Placide Tempels' *Bantu Philosophy* published in 1948. The advent of colonialism in Africa was followed by attempt to understand the African people through expert studies provided by official colonial anthropologists and ethnologists, as well as by other independent colonial administrators, missionaries and academics. In the English colonies, these efforts gave rise to works of such writers as Northcote Thomas, A. G. Leonard, G. T. Basden, S. Leith-Ross, M. M. Green, C. J. Meek, Daryl Ford, etc. Placide Tempels' work follows the line traced by such studies on African societies, but he brought a completely new dimension to the result of his field study of Bantu people by seeing a philosophical system in their thought pattern. For Placide Tempels, the Bantu have a philosophy proper to them, a philosophy that guides their lives, their comprehension of realities and their activities.[4] It is this attempt to find philosophy in what would generally be regarded as ethnological work that was designated ethnophilosophy. Hountondji traces the origin of the word much earlier in American writings, as far back as the nineteen forties where it was already associated with the flourishing ethnosciences of the time. According to Hountondji, this origin makes the word ethnophilosophy to be associated with inventories of knowledge dubbed "primitive" in American university circles. For him therefore, Ethnophilosophy is a specialized branch of ethnology "tasked with studying the "philosophy" of so-called primitive, archaic, or traditional people in any case, peoples who are the object of ethnology."[5] In the view of Hountondji, African philosophy is not to be exhumed from the debris of the past and tradition, but belongs to the future just as African science. Other thinkers critical of ethonophilosophy have slightly different view but converge on the point that it is not properly philosophical. Marcien Towa for example does not believe that philosophy is a given of all cultures. In his view Judaic and Islamic cultures are not only not philosophical, but are anti-philosophical. But that reality is far from traditional African culture. Africans of yore permit critical view of their society in different genres.[6] But that does not however settle the case for ethnophilosophy. Ethnophilosophy is guilty of what he called a methodological confusion.[7] It begins by asserting the existence of traditional African philosophy, but then goes on from there to engage in defending an African philosophy that it has succeeded in exhuming, a turn that Towa considers to be philosophically unorthodox.

For Towa, to bring to light an authentic African philosophy would establish with certainty that our ancestors were philosophers, without dispensing us in turn from philosophizing. That we have a philosophy does not mean that we are philosophers. The West can pride itself with possessing a brilliant philosophical heritage. But the West which recognizes the existence of this tradition and which acquires its content has not as yet started to philosophize.[8]

Towa's problem with ethnophilosophy is thus that it fails to follow a proper philosophical method. Philosophy for him begins with the decision to submit all cultural and philosophical heritage to implacable criticism. Such philosophical critique does not receive any idea, no matter how venerable it might be without subjecting it to the process of critical appraisal. Like Towa, Peter Bodunrin's idea about ethnophilosophy appears through his outline of what genuine philosophy must be. For Bodunrin, to be philosophical a thesis must be clearly stated, and clearly and consciously argued, and must not be dogmatic. Ethnophilosophy fails on all three counts and that is largely due to its origin: it is "the works of those anthropologists, sociologists, ethnologists and philosophers who present the collective worldviews of African peoples, their myths and folk-lores and folk-wisdom as philosophy."[9]

The above paragraph would make it appear that ethnophilosophy is being defined from the lenses of its opponents. But Joseph Omoregbe's view is distinctive. Philosophy for him evolves in three stages. The stage of wonder that is attendant on man's contact with his world, the stage of questioning that follows the initial wonder, and the stage of reflection in answer to questions. Omoregbe's view of philosophy is therefore very akin to hermeneutics as we shall see shortly, but then he did not reserve this process to any specialized group of people. The basic questions[10] about life are universal, and "there is no part of the world where men never reflect on such basic questions about the human person and about the physical universe."[11] Every human society has its thinking class constituted by those who devote more time and attention to the art of reflection than others. The preservation of the results of philosophic reflection introduces a huge difference in the nature of extant philosophy. Where there is the art of writing, the facility for safeguarding and transmitting the outcome of philosophic reflection is abundant. But where writing does not exists, such reflections, for Omoregbe, usually filters into the proverbs, mythologies, wise-sayings, stories and religious beliefs.

For Omoregbe, the philosophy that can be sieved out of these genres is what constitutes traditional philosophy. It does not in his view need to be in the form of western philosophy or to be couched in what he calls western style arguments. What is significant in this view is that in it, traditional or ethnophilosophy does not constitute African philosophy of today. It is rather, as in Towa, the philosophy of yesteryears. It really belongs to the history of African philosophy, and contemporary African philosophy should be seen in the output of numerous philosophic workers of this epoch who have been blessed with the facility of writing.[12] This view differs significantly from Theophilus Okere's view which does not concede the genres that Omoregbe and Towa see as mirrors of philosophy any philosophical import.

3. The Meaning of Hermeneutics

Broadly speaking, the term hermeneutics means interpretation. Though many thinkers add different slants to the meaning of the term, in general, hermeneutics involves the bringing out the inner meaning to the open. It entails making explicit what is implicit. It is thus a quest for meaning, one's own meaning in one's life, society, milieu, in short the totality of one's universe which could be said to be constituted by one's cultural symbols. Modern hermeneutics first started in connection with the scriptures given the need to rise beyond mere text to the question of its meaning for the present epoch. Philosophical hermeneutics as a discipline is comparatively more recent. W. Dilthey saw it as the core discipline that should be the foundation of all the arts or humanities (Geisteswissenschaften).[13] While before him Schleiermacher emphasized two elements of the grammatical and the psychological, Dilthey emphasized the historicity of all interpretations. But it was the older thinker who first defined hermeneutics as the "doctrine of the act of understanding." For Dilthey, man is basically made in history. There is first and foremost self-understanding which is akin to the psychological, but there is understanding of things through history. Edmund Hurserl's transcendental phenomenology aimed at arriving at presuppositionless understanding by bracketing all the factors that could constitute a wedge between the object and its comprehension as it is. Martin Heidegger turns against Hurserl's claim to presuppositionless understanding with his analysis of the different modes of the object. To arrive at the real nature of understanding for him would require an appreciation of that being whose nature it is to understand, the only being that is capable of understanding. In Heidegger hermeneutics thus turns to fundamental ontology, which in itself is understood as understanding and interpretation of man's being. This attempt to explain the ontological condition of understanding is what he calls hermeneutics. It involves historicity and commitment to the existential horizon of one's time, which is the constituent element of being in the world. Understanding is the basis and the presupposition of interpretation and it is deeply related to one's situation, but not closed in on it. In any case, it is not presuppositionless with its elements of *Vorhabe, Vorsicht, Vorgriff*, representing respectively something we have, see and grasp in advance.[14]

On his own part H.-G. Gadamer begins with analysis of *Vorurteil* (prejudice). He goes counter to Dilthey and Husserl with his presuppositionless understanding. He follows the lead provided by Heidegger, but his theory is a throwback to the enlightenment with its support for the claims of reason against authority, tradition and prejudice. Gadamer discountenanced the bad connotation given to the word 'prejudice' by the Enlightenment. Etymologically, the word prejudice originates from *pre-judicium*, pre-judgement, and represents all the paraphernalia that usually accompanies our act of understanding. He follows the lead traced by Heidegger, underlining what he names the *Vorstructur des Verstehens* which indicates the predetermined structure of our current act of understanding. For Gadamer, understanding should be seen in the context of tradition, and thus, it becomes an activity in which the past and the present are fused.[14] One major element in this tradition is the language, which serves as the vehicle of our understanding. Language imposes a limit as well as marks the promise of creative possibility. Because thinking is tied to the boundaries of language, our "understanding is language bound." One's own language world in which one lives is not a barrier preventing objective knowledge, but rather includes everything, which our insight can reach or extend to. Of course, those who are brought up in a certain linguistic and cultural tradition see the world differently from those coming form other traditions. Of course, the "historical worlds" succeeding each other in the course of history differ from each other and from the world of today. However, it is always a world, which is linguistically constituted which expressed itself in some tradition or other.[16]

Standing on the gains of these thinkers, Paul Ricoeur dwells a great deal on the question of method, and views philosophy as a process, which starts from a phenomenological level to the hermeneutical to the reflexive states. It is "a reflection upon existence and upon all those means by which that existence can be understood."[17] It is a recovery of the self, a separation between the self and one's true being. Despite its inclination it is inherently impossible to achieve universality due to the impossibility of presuppositionless starting point in reflection. It is the actual existential situation that provides the starting point for reflection, and thus there arises a tension between philosophy's aim at universality and its anchor on particular contexts from which it must operate, but which it must strive to transcend. Philosophy "begins with non-philosophical presuppositions which in the end cannot themselves be confidently justified with finality."[18]

From this very brief excursus on the thought of a few hermeneutic thinkers, it is clear that despite the different slants that have been observed, certain element are identifiable as basic in the process of hermeneutics. We can say the central elements in the operative under-standing of hermeneutics include the roles of psychology, of history, context, nature of being, nature of understanding, prejudice, tradition, and language. Philosophical hermeneutics operates within the bounds of the tension created by the desire for universality and the inevitable particularity of philosophical reflection.

4. Okere's Crique of Three Ethnophilosophers

At the beginning of his famous book: *African Philosophy: A Historico-Hermeneutical Investigation into the Conditions of Its Possibility*, Theophilus Okere clearly stated his understanding of the nature of philosophy. His is like a via media between two views of philosophy. The first is philosophy seen as the work of untainted or pure reason abhors qualifications that would confine it to any region, people or nation. Philosophy in this conception would then not be African, European or Indian, and must remain philosophy as such. At the opposed end is the understanding of philosophy as necessarily present in every culture, in line with J. Omoregbe's view stated above. If philoso-phy is present in every culture and in every society of men, the task of the researcher would be to discover and articulate what it is in order to outline the philosophy of the people under consideration.[19] The work is however, mainly an indictment of ethnophilosophy as well as an attempt to show the way that African philosophy, properly so-called must follow the path of hermeneutics of African culture. It is because the writers he criticizes do not take proper account of the nature of philosophy that they erred in presenting as African philosophy what for Okere is not philo-sophical at all. Philosophy may not have any definition that enjoys unanimity of agreement, nevertheless, for Okere it has a hard-core of content which should not be neglected. It carves out its own niche from such cultural phenomena as myth, *Weltanschauung*, religion, ideology, proverb, poetry, etc.[20]

The critique of Okere is first directed against Placide Tempels' *Bantu Philosophy* and its theory of vital force. For Tempels, vital force and its operations are enough to explain everything in the Bantu meta-physics. Vital force is synonymous with being, and its operation is overwhelmingly determinant in all the activities of beings, spiritual, rational and material. Any positive activity is due to the increase in vital causality while any diminution of vitality is due to the reduction of the appropriate vital force. Vital force also determines the relationship of being with beings, especially rational beings, as one rational being can increase or reduce the being of another through the manipulation of vital force. A rational being can also manipulate other lower beings to increase or decrease the vital force of a fellow rational being. That is what Tempels names the laws of vital causality.[21] He applies the same principles derived from the idea of vital force to outline Bantu Theodicy, Epistemology, Ethics, etc.

The efforts of Tempels is, for Okere, not more than the ontologization of primitive magic. His use of vital force as a concept that explains everything is, in his view, akin to the concept of mana among anthropologists. But the greater weight of Okere's critique lies on the point that Tempels was trying to outline a collective philosophy while philosophy is essentially an individual enterprise. In addition, philosophy more often than not is a mise-en-cause of collective image, thinking, prejudice or presumptions. That this is amply exemplified in early Greek philosophy is abundantly signified by the death of Socrates. Philosophical traditions exhibit the essential individuality of their engagement by the perennial divergence and disagreement between individual philosophers. It means that rightly speaking, philosophy cannot really be qualified as Greek, African or American if by that is meant a philosophy that is shared by each of the members of these communities. Greek philosophy refers to the corpus of Greek philosophical writing. These writings are thus Greek only in the sense that they are inspired by the Greek culture and world-view, and not that they are shared by all the Greeks of their time.[22]

Alexis Kagame's philosophy is based on the assumption that philosophy of a people is deductible from the analysis of their language structure and grammar and deducting from these the philosophical implications and teachings about life and reality. Again Okere described this project as an effort to ontologize Ruandese grammar, through a systematic application of Aristotle's philosophy to this grammar. It is for him also an effort to establish a bi-univocal correspondence between Aristotle and the Ruandese language structure. Though there is an important and close relationship between language and thought, language cannot thereby be erected as a photocopy of any philosophy, nor can the structure of language be assumed to correspond to the structure of philosophy. Again, Okere brings in as his witness the history of philosophy that amply contradicts the aims of Kagame. Were there to be any semblance of truth in this project, then philosophy would be predetermined by language in such a way that there would not be any difference between one philosophical system and another when the two are derived from the same language. This is far from the experience of divergence among philosophers who share and work in the same languages in the history of philosophy.[23]

Finally J. S. Mbiti's concept of African time is also used as an example of the errors of ethnophilosophy.[24] By doing field research among the Kikuyu of East Africa, Mbiti came to the conclusion that Africans have a special concept of time. This concept is the usual three dimensional time with its past, present and future. African time includes a long past and an ample idea of the present, but the future is so limited and does not go beyond the projection of a few years. As a consequence the Africans of Mbiti have no lineal understanding of time, and as a result have no lineal conception of history, no idea of the end of the world, and also no strictly eschatological concepts. For Okere, the errors of Mbiti arise from the failure to make relevant distinctions between time as social, scientific, mythological and philosophical. Again it is doubtful whether it is really true that African time is two dimensional. Still, the most important factor here is the confusion that one can derive a people's philosophy from their conception of time, just as Kagame attempted from the analysis of grammar, a philosophy that would be attributable to a people as a whole.

5. Elements of Hermeneutics in Ethnophilosophy

The above summary may perhaps achieve the unintended effect of mellowing the incisiveness of Okere's critique of ethnophilosophy. Nevertheless it goes without saying that one must give due recognition to the correctness of most of the points he raised against the efforts of a certain generation of African thinkers to furnish, almost at any cost, some samples that one could take as African philosophy. Still, it must be said that the measurement of the value of these critiques depends on certain conditions. In the first place, if western experience of philosophy is taken as paradigmatic in any way, then there is no disagreeing with practically any of the points raised against Tempels and his cohorts. Secondly, the critiques would also be unassailable if the actual outcome of the reflection of the ethnophilosophers is brought into focus. This means that Okere's critique would be mainly correct were we to subject to criticism the content of what the three traditional philosophers presented as samples of African philosophy. It appears, however, that these may not be that important in determining whether the ethnophilosophers are engaged in the hermeneutical process in their works.

Concerning the position of western philosophy, there seems to be no doubt that this tradition of philosophy subtly pops up its head to assume the position of a model in Okere's critique. The aim of the critique is, of course, to strike a balance between the exponents of monolithic philosophy valid for everyone, everywhere, and those who insist that philosophy in the words of Okere is "a cultural universal." But perhaps unwittingly, the justification of Okere's characterization of philosophy as a discipline with some hard-core of content takes almost all its features from western philosophy. Among these features are the following: the special, and unique addition to wisdom that the Greek made that makes the discipline of philosophy specific;[25] the mise-en-cause of philosophers of the image of their society, exemplified in the life of Socrates;[26] and finally, the divergence and often contradictions that is the hallmark of any comparison between one philosopher and the other.[27] True to the point as these characterizations may appear, it is an important question whether these features must be essential features in any correct understanding of the nature of the discipline. This issue, of course, touches on the self understanding of philosophy itself. The question which arises from the basic point of Okere's critique is whether this understanding is clear-cut enough to exclude the possibility of a collective philosophy without further ado.

It appears that philosophers are not so agreed on the nature of their engagement as to exclude the possibility of collective philosophy.[28] The characterization of the nature of philosophy is itself a project that most philosophic workers often prefer to side track. The reason for this is that there is practically no such effort that is objective. It means that due to the special nature of the discipline, any effort to explain the nature of philosophy implies taking one philosophical position among others. In western philosophy, for instance, Plato would understand the philosopher as the person in touch with the world of Ideas, a world the presupposition of which makes possible our claim to knowledge. For Aristotle, that would hardly have any meaning, since in his view, the problem of justifying our knowledge is so difficult that Plato's theory becomes *obscurus per obscurius* (trying to explain the obscure by recourse to the more obscure!). This divergence underscores the individuality of the giants of Greek philosophy, but the point is that the nature of philosophy even among individuals as near historically as Plato is to Aristotle is far removed from being settled with any measure of unanimity.

Further down in the history of Western philosophy, one encounters thinkers like Russell and other British analysts for whom metaphysical and ethical questions are not at all part of the concerns of philosophy. For Russell, philosophy is analysis, and analysis is an effort to clarify the meaning of linguistic symbols in use. In his theory of description, the effort was to find out how a non-entity can be the subject of a proposition through careful analysis of what the normal user of the English language understands by such statements as 'the king of France is bald.' Or again the attempt to find the real meaning of such descriptive statements as Walter Scott is the author of Waverly, which may appear to be a tautology. For Russell, the major duty of philosophy is to try to clarify such statements, basing squarely on the collective understanding of the statement in the language concerned.[29]   From this it seems clear that Russell, and the men of his ilk were not very far from what some ethnophilosophers were doing. Of course one who rejects the project of ethnophilosophers could as well reject that of the British analysts for the sake of consistency. But it appears that it would raise more eyebrows in the philosophic community to reject the works of philosophical analysts because their project is aimed at expounding collective thought and understanding.

Furthermore, the collective nature of ethnophilosophy is not uncontested. Joseph Omoregbe's view is a case in point. For him, what we have as proverbs, wise sayings, myths, religious beliefs, etc, are all thoughts that emanate from individuals who because of the absence of efficient means of recording can no longer be identified. It seems obvious that the collectivity as such does not think, and in so far as these genres are, no doubt, the inventions of thinking beings, they must have emanated from individuals not groups of individuals. Omoregbe goes further to assert that such individuals are the philosophers of their societies, and thus he would not accept the view that what ethnophilophers are expounding is collective thought. In his view, the philosophy of a people without the art of writing or other more efficient means of recording should be sought in such genres, since they are sediments of more elaborate philosophical thoughts. Nevertheless, contemporary African philosophy should be sought in the works of present day philosophic workers everywhere in Africa who are now endowed with the art of writing and who have been producing works of philosophy aided by this art.[30]   It implies that for Joseph Omoregbe, ethnophilosophy belongs really to the history of philosophy, and this goes against T. Okere's idea of a philosophy that must not only be the work of an individual, but must be attributable to such an individual.

Another point that calls for consideration is the actual result of the work of ethnophilosophers. Concerning this, there seems to be no doubt that if one takes the intention of the individual thinkers as a guide, then there seems to be no doubt one would assume they are outlining a collective philosophy for Africa. In reality, however, there is more than meets the eyes in this assumption. Okere, for example, criticizes Tempels for ontologizing magic. True as this may be, the vital question is who is carrying out the process of ontologization, the Bantu or Tempels himself? There appears to be no doubt here that the work of Tempels is not just a pure presentation of what any and every Bantu is thinking. There is therefore much more individual reflection that goes on in the work of ethnophilosophers. This passage from Tempels serves as an example:

> Man is the dominant force among all created visible forces. His force, his life, his fullness of being consists in his participation to a greater or lesser extent in the force of God. God, the Bantu would say, possesses (or, more exactly, He is) THE supreme, complete, perfect force. He is the Strong One, in and by Himself; . . . He has his existential cause within himself. In relation to the beings whom he has created, God is regarded by the Bantu as the causative agent, the

> sustainer of these resultant forces, as being the creation cause. Man is one of these resultant living forces, created, maintained and developed by the vital, creative influence of God.[31]

Tempels puts this reflection in the mouth of the Bantu. But even if they hold the theory of vital force, and accept the broad outline of its operations as adumbrated by Tempels, it can hardly be said that collectively the Bantu rise to the level of reflection that Tempels is foisting on them. He is clearly influenced by the scholastic philosophy in which he was schooled before his quest for an African philosophy, and his statement can conceivably fit into any manual of thomistic theodicy. It means that while ethnophilosophers are busy doing, in some cases, very serious personal philosophical reflection, they do not wink in attributing the result of their efforts to the Bantu or the Africans as the case may be. This puts into question the extent that ethnophilosophy as a whole is collective philosophy.

Much the same critique is applicable to Kagame's attempt to see the philosophic import of the analysis of Bantu-Ruandese language. Kagame believes that through the analysis of linguistic structure and its implications, one can arrive at Bantu-Ruandaise philosophy of being. The raw material of this analysis is what he calls the institutionalized languages like proverbs, myths, poems, etc. But here again, the question is to what extent is Kagame outlining a philosophy which can be called the common patrimony of the Ruandese. Okere inveighs against this project on the ground that if it were to be assumed as the way to true philosophy, then there would be no divergence between the philosophy of one individual and another. But even the analysis of the grammar of languages presents many intricacies for disagreement and divergence among grammarians. Once we leave this shore however, and sail into the areas of meaning and implication, when this grammar becomes 'ontologized' one wonders how much the result can be uniform. Thus Okere's view that Kagame was ontologizing Ruandese grammar while making a systematic application of Aristotle's philosophy to this grammar may not be as devastating as it would appear. There is *a priori* no reason why a hermeneutical process would not ontologize any grammar, and the application of Aristotle's philosophy may be a pointer to the cultural (educational) background of the thinker over which, in the best tradition of hermeneutical thinkers he may not step. What is there-fore important is the extent of individual reflection that goes on in the claim made by the thinkers of presenting a collective philosophy for the Africans.

Similarly, J. S. Mbiti's presentation of the concept of time in East Africa comes under the same purview. It is surprising that he talks of two-dimensional time. Granted that his field of research is limited to the Kikuyu, still it goes without saying that the idea of time is part of the paraphernalia of the human mind. The mind is structurally endowed with the conception of the past, the present and the future, based on the faculties of memory, consciousness of the present and expectation of the future, as Augustine rightly points out.[32] Thus a traditional Kikuyu who plants a tree has a projection into the future when he or his children would enjoy the fruits of his tree. Again when a new child is born in the family, it would be inconceivable that mature Kikuyu minds would not immediately imagine a distant future, forty or fifty year to come when the toddler would be a mature adult, a warrior, or even an elder in his clan. The implication of all this is that Mbiti's idea of African time is indeed his own idea and not that of the African on whom he hangs the idea.

Thus far from being simply a collective philosophy, a gathering of proverbs, folk tales, myths, etc, as Bodunrin would call it, ethnophilosophy is much more complicated than it is often presented. In pretending to speak for Africans in general, ethnophilosophers indeed speak for themselves. It is clear instance of presenting one's own interpretation of one's cultural symbols as a collective interpretation. The vital question is why would a thinker want to substitute the result of his efforts for those of his people, why would he substitute his individual endeavor for the collectivity? The fact of this practice is relevant in understanding the hermeneutical import of the efforts of ethnophilosophers.

The history of the people of Africa leaves in its wake, both a psychological burden of inferiority complex and the physical burden of underdevelopment on the Africans. This burden, reinforced and exacer-bated by colonialism and missionary evangelism of all sorts, was accompanied by a real doubt of the humanity of the Africans. This doubt, or even outright denial is seen in numerous western philosophic thinkers: Hume, Hegel, Locke, Jaspers, Montesquieu, Toynbee, etc. The special position of philosophy in this dehumanization is evident since man is taken to be a rational animal, and for many, the ultimate exercise of his rationality is his ability to philosophize. It is not surprising that Tempels aims first and foremost to establish the humanity of the African by establishing that he has a philosophy, any philosophy. It is a quest for the White man's acknowledgement.

> What they want more than anything else is not improvement of their economic or material circumstances, but recognition of and respect of their full value as men by the Whites. Their greatest and deepest sorrow is that they are treated perpetually as half-wits, as "monkeys."[33]

Given this quest, together with the honorific conception of philosophy as a measure of the humanity of the human, and the most lofty expression of the engagement of man in the humanistic sciences,[34] the project of Tempels and men of his ilk becomes more understandable. It is also this quest that has nudged the emphasis of the so-called ethnophilosophy from the assertion of personal reflection to that of the reflection of the community, of the collectivity. Thus the quest for African philosophy is written in the history of the thinkers, and in the context of their lives. The major concern was to prove that Africans are humans, and since philosophy was taken as a measure of human, that they have a philosophy. It appears obvious that since this revisionist quest is not aimed at the individual, but at the whole of the African community, it would also be projected to the past. That means it was necessary to prove, not just that Africans can philosophize now that they are endowed with western education but that they have, as it were, always philosophized. This underlying aim may not be explicit, except in Placide Tempels, but it is abundantly evident from the paradigmatic position of western tradition of philosophy, as well as the uncritical assumption of the link between the philosophy and the measure of humanity.

This underlying quest extrapolated into philosophy is what many critics of ethnophilosophy often fail[35] to take adequate account of. This failure is seen in Towa's aspersion on having a philosophy and being philosophers. Even though Hountondji gives a grudging recognition of its origin,[36] he again fails to give it its due importance in asserting that "the facile apology of our system, belief and other collective representation only leads to an impasse." To start with, only a superficial reading of ethnophilosophy would lead to this description. Again, there is no doubt that in his words, "what we need is a renewed creativity on every level, in every sphere." But if the discipline of hermeneutics has any contribution to make to the process of understanding, it is to warn us that such creativity that Hountondji advocates does not come from no where. In any case, it cannot bury underground the origin, the history and the context of its agents.

What this means is that the so-called ethnophilosophers do indeed reflect on their culture, environment, their history, in short on their world. The outcome of such reflections are usually unpredictable. It may not be able to withstand the searchlight of critical appraisal; nor be acceptable to a host of other philosophic thinkers. But a bad philosophy is no less a philosophy than a good one,[35] as prominently proven by the history of western philosophy. It must also not be a bashing of one's society because in this case, that society has already received enough battering from history. It may not be overwhelmingly necessary to place the individual's tag on such reflections since the aim of philosophy in this case is the hominization of the African, which purpose is served better, in the understanding of ethnophilosophers, when the trade mark of a single individual takes the back seat. On these grounds, we can say that there are many elements of hermeneutics that are traceable in ethnophilosophy, while not disparaging many of the points of Okere's critique.

6. Senghor's Negritude as Hermeneutics

Let us end this essay by making a brief exploration of the philosophy of L. S. Senghor, to show that in their interpretation of Negritude, many African thinkers made an overly uncritical characterization of ethnophilosophy. Senghor is one of the best known modern African philosophic thinkers. The idea of Negritude which he popularized is perhaps one of the most widely known philosophic ideas in contemporary African philosophy. His literary prowess as well as his political career as the President of Senegal for two scores of years appears to have provided him a forum through which to disseminate his thought on Negritude. However, the understanding of that philosophy is, in our view, very often flawed. Senghor is more often than none presented as the apostle of ethnophilosophy. We mean ethnophilosophy understood in the terms we have explained briefly above as a reconstitution of the collective representation of the Africa of yore, presented as a philosophy. For Hountondji, such can never constitute a philosophy (as though the world has agreed on what should constitute it!). "Instead, one should admit that current system of thought, present in all personal thought is always, precisely, the obstacle to surmount, the anonymous unthinkable of which the critical interrogation should constitute, when possible the beginning of philosophy."[39]

Senghor's project, far from being a facile assemblage of a collective representation, arose from the cultural world made possible by the rampaging cultural obliteration of colonialism. Colonialism was rooted on the absence of any culture, language, history, civilization, value in the colonized. It was a comprehensive civilizing mission, ostensibly aimed at making the colonized share a little of the unassailable western life, history, culture, language, political organization, social ethos, etc. While almost all colonial powers were backed by basically the same philosophy, the French and the Portuguese, with their doctrine of assimilation appeared to have gone a step further in this direction. Education became a process of making the subject a French man or woman, and those adjudged sufficiently civilized, the evolué, were then given French citizenship. That was the history that Senghor, despite his African origin, lived to the full. The result was intellectual and cultural alienation. As a young man in Paris, in spite of his privileges, Senghor, together with his companions, Leon Dumas, and Aime Cesaire, felt his alienation very deeply. A verse of his many poems clearly points to his alienation:

Let my mind turn to my dead!
Yesterday was all saints, the solemn anniversary of all the sun
In all the cemeteries, there was no one to remember.
O dead who have always refused to die, who have resisted dead
From the Sine to the Seine, and in my fragile veins you my unyielding blood.[40]

It is this experience of inner resistance towards the planned assimilation of the French colonial project that jotted out in the philosophy of Negritude. The reaction of Negritude is not only to emphasize the African difference, but also to glorify this difference. It was an avenue that led to cultural survival. As a politician, Senghor believe that political liberation is important, but he takes cultural liberation to be more fundamental: "Our renaissance will be more the work of African writers and artists than of politicians. We have seen from experience that there can be no political liberation without cultural liberation."[41] Thus the main focus of his thinking is to underpin the authenticity of African culture, its civilization, its way of life. Already here we can perceive by a sort of Copernican revolution the critical interrogation which Hountondji was alluding to if we take the experience of colonialism into due consideration. In spite of his schooling in the French system, with all its assumptions of superiority, Senghor is reacting in the name of his original background. His concern is first and foremost what specificity the African experience can bring unto the world arena. To him, there must be some aspect of civilization in which a people excel, where they are different, and with regard to which they must be valued, without this specificity, such people do not deserve the respect of the world. They become a museum piece.[42]

No doubt in his quest for difference, Senghor is unwittingly strengthening the concept of the otherness of the Other on which the colonial project was built.[43] But it must be emphasized that while the Other of colonial philosophy was aimed at obliteration, at conquest and exploitation, Senghor's whole aim is to give equality and dignity to the humanity of the Other. It is in this sense that his oft cited and pilloried assertion that emotion is African and reason is Hellenic should be understood. Senghor sees emotion here in a very positive sense. In his view, there is a world of difference between the African and European apprehension of reality. Before an object, the European distinguishes the object from himself, keeps it at a distance. He dissects, and somehow kills the object. This is in order to make use of it; to make a means of the object, and this he calls "domesticating nature." The African on the other hand does not form distance, he does not analyze the object. Rather with his inner being, he discovers the Other. He is more faithful to the stimulus of the object. He is at one with its rhythm. Thus the African "abandons his I to sympathize and identify with the THOU."[44]

Senghor believes that the attitude towards the object is innate. For him it follows all aspects of the African life. Distinguishing the African attitude from that of the European does not make emotion to be an inferior level of knowledge. For Senghor, the emotive attitude towards the world which "explains the cultural value of the Africans" may look like a failure of consciousness, but it is in reality a higher state of consciousness. It is not anti-reason. It is only a different type of reason. Different from the "eye-reason" of the European, it is *reason-by-embrace*. It is akin to *logos* in its original pre-Aristotelian sense while the European reason is nearer to ratio. "Classical European reason is analytical and makes use of the object. African reason is intuitive and participates in the object." [45]

Translated into the human society, African participation in the object makes him create a society endowed with unity, a society that is a "seamless whole."[46] Man is the center of this universe, but this man is not the isolated man but man understood as meaningful within the family. The family is the actual constitutive element of the African society, and all its facets are but extensions of the same family, which enlarges as a web of concentric circles to eventually include the whole of humanity.

All these theories of the Senegalese are in turn based on another more fundamental foundation, the metaphysical. Senghor supports whole and entire Tempels' theory of vital force. In *The Foundations of 'Africanité',* he asserts that reality, be it vegetal, animal or mineral are varied in form. This notwithstanding, they all are manifestations of the one universe, which in turn is a network of different but complementary forces which are nothing but the emanation of the powers of God. God is the only true being and the force of all forces. The universe achieves its unity through the convergence of all these forces which find their origin in God. In his own word, Negro-African ontology "proceeds by polymorphic dialectic, by induction: by involution and extension. By integration in the etymological sense of the word."[47]

Comparing his idea of African ontology with Arab ontology, he says that Arab ontology 'is reduced to the rank of other creatures,' thus leaving God as sublimated in an analogical movement. While the Arab insists on one God, the African lays emphasis on the Ancestors. Thus for him, Arab thought is "transcendentalism by the concrete but transparent." This contrast in Senghor is like a dress rehearsal for drawing a convergence between the two ontologies:

> Negro dialectics, ontology and thought do not conclude, do not shut down, like the 'therefore' of Greek syllogism; they open on limitless time, on the transcendent, like Arab dialectics, ontology and thought.[48]

Senghor sees all these characteristics of the Negro-African as marks left by the circumstances of his evolution. According to him, the Negro-African homo sapiens primordial context was one in which reality was abundantly accessible and "friendly." It is because of this that a sort of good-neighbourliness, understanding and friendship grew between him and nature. This is the origin of the harmony that Senghor sees between the black man and nature, so much so that he has grown to be "integrated" in nature. The influence of this pre-history conditions his mode of knowing and perceiving, making it, so to say a sort of inner recollection instead of totally new encounter as would be the case were the object of knowledge to be estranged from the being of the subject. "So, when the Negro-African responds to the object and throws himself upon it, knows it, his knowledge stems more from analogical images of real experience that surge up within him, than from the novelty of his impression."[49]

The above indications of Senghor's thought are in all respects eminently hermeneutical. It goes without saying that the Senegalese is here engaged in deep reflection on his culture, his history, and the actual context of his life. He is not presenting the thought of all who share his culture, or what Okere would call 'non-philosophy.' Rather, basing on the given of this cultural and historical experience, he is attempting to come to an interpretation which is wholly directed by the most pressing need of his personal history and by extension that of his fellow blacks and Africans. It is therefore very incongruous to present Senghor's Negritude as an example of ethnophilosophy without fundamentally altering the usual definition of the term.

7. Conclusion

We have tried to show that the grouping of contemporary African philosophers into distinctive trends may not be as clear cut as it is very often presented. Through a brief presentation of the meaning of ethnophilosophy and hermeneutics, we have seen that Okere's critique of the former, without prejudice to its incisiveness, tends to occlude the fact that there are many elements of hermeneutics in the works of ethnophilosophers. It means that many African philosophic thinkers hitherto designated as ethnophilosophers are in fact engaging in individual reflections and interpretations based on their cultural heritage, which include their individual and collective experiences. Leopold Sedar Senghor comes out as a shining example of this process of hermeneutics. An appreciation of our arguments here, if it does not lead to a total review of much of the categorization that has been entrenched in the writings of African philosophers, would at least lead to a more attentive reading and interpretation of the output of contemporary African thinkers.

Notes

[1] See H. O. Oruka, Four Trends in Contemporary African Philosophy," in Alwin Diemer, *Philosophy in the Present Situation of Africa*, Wiesbaden: Franz Steiner, 1981; H. O. Oruka (ed.), *Sage Philosophy: Indiginous Thinkers and Modern Debate on African Philosophy*, Leiden: E. J. Brill, 1990, pp. 11 22; P. Hountodji, *African Philosophy: Myth and Reality*, London: Hutchinson Univ. Press, 1983, pp. 30 35; O. Oladipo, *The Idea of African Philosophy*, Ibadan: Hope, Publications, 1998. Peter O. Bodunrin, "The Question of African Philosophy," in Tsenay Serequeberhan, *African Philosophy, the Essential Readings*, New York: Paragon House, 1991, pp. 63 65.

[2] A. J. Ayer, *Language, Truth and Logic*, London: Victor Gollanz, 1955, pp. 52 58.

[3] H. Odera Oruka, "Four Trends in Current African Philosophy," in Alwin Diemer (ed.), *Philosophy in the Present Situation of Africa*, p. 3.

[4] Placide Tempels, *Bantu Philosophy*, Paris: Presence Africaine, 1959, p. 21. For Tempels, Bantu ontology may not be self evident, but this does not mean it does not

exist and exercise enormous influence on the people "This ontology exists; and it penetrates and informs all the thought of these primitives; it dominates and orientates all their behaviour."

[5] P. Hountodji, "The Particular and the Universal," in Albert Mosley, *African Philosophy: Selected Readings*, New Jersey: Prentice Hall, 1995, p. 175.

[6] Marcien Towa, *L'idee d'une philosophie Negro-africaine*, Yaounde: Edition Cle, 1971, p. 19ff.

[7] P. Hountodji, "The Particular and the Universal," p. 178.

[8] Marcien Towa, *Essai sur la problematique philosophique dans l' Afrique actuelle*, Yaounde: Editiion Cle, 1981, pp. 31 32.

[9] Peter O. Bodunrin, p. 63.

[10] Joseph I. Omeregbe, "African Philosophy: Yesterday and Today," in P. O. Bodunrin, *Philosophy in Africa: Trends and Perspectives*, Ile Ife, University of Ife Press, 1985, p. 1.

[11] Ibid., pp. 3-4.

[12] Ibid., p. 10.

[13] R. O. Madu, *African Symbols, Proverbs and Myth: The Hermeneutics of Destiny*, New York: Peter Lang, 1992, p. 11.

[14] Ibid,. p. 19.

[15] H. G. Gadamer, *Truth and Method*, London: Sheed and Ward, 1975, p. 258.

[16] H. G. Gadamer, *Weisheit und Methode*, quoted in T. Okere, *African Philosophy: A Hermeneutico-Historical Inquiry into the Conditions of its Possibility*, Lanham: University Press of America, 1983, p. 71 72.

[17] S. C. Hacketh, "Philosophical Objectivity and Existential Involvement in the Methology of Paul Ricoeur," quoted in R. O. Madu, *African Symbols, Proverbs and Myths: The Hermeneutics of Destiny*, p. 26.

[18] Ibid., p. 27 28.

[19] Theophilus Okere, *African Philosophy*, p. vii viii.

[20] Ibid., p. viii.

[21] Placide Tempels, pp. 66 - 69

[22] Theophilus Okere, pp. 4 6.

[23] Ibid., p. 5 6, 8 9.

[24] See his *African Religion and Philosophy*, London: Heinemann, 1969.

[25] Theophilus Okere, p. viii.

[26] Ibid., p. 7.

[27] Ibid., p. 9.

[28] See P. Bodunrin, p. 73, 75.

[29] B. Russell, 'On Denoting,' *Mind* (1905)

[30] J. Omeregbe, op. cit., pp. 4-9.

[31] Placide Tempels, pp. 98 99.

[32] See St. Augustine, *Confessions*, chapter 11.

[33] Placide Tempels, pp. 178

[34] Tsaney Serequeberhan, The Hermeneutics of African Philosophy: Horizen and Discourse, London, Routledge, 1984, p. 3; Kwame Anthony Appiah, *In My Father's House: African in the Philosophy of Culture*, New York: Oxford University Press, 1992, p.

[35] Paulin Hountondji, "The Particular and the Universal," p181

[36] Ibid., p.194.

[37] Cf. P. Bodunrin, "The Question of African Philosophy," p.

[38] The thought of such philosophers as Machiavelli, Hobbes, Hegel, Marx are up till today given prominence in the study of Western philosophy. This is so even when some of the consequences of their thoughts have been largely negative. Hegel's thought gave birth to the twins of Nazism and communism, but that does not deny him a pride of place in the annals of Western philosophy.

[39] Paulin Hountondji, "The Particular and the Universal," p. 191.

[40] Leopold Sedar Senghor, "In Memoriam," in *Senghor Prose and Poetry*, edited and translated by J. Reed and C. Wake, London: Heinemann, 1976, p. 103

[41] Leopold Sedar Senghor, 'L'Esprit de la Civilization ou les Lois de la Culture Negro-Africaine,' in *Senghor Prose and Poetry*, p. 76.

[42] Ibid., p. 98.

[43] Tsanay Serequeberhan, *The Heremeneutics of African Philosophy, Horizen and Discourse*, London: Routledge, 1994, p.

[44] Cf. De la Negritude. Psychologie du Negro-Africaine, in *Senghor Prose and Poetry*, pp. 29-34

[45] Ibid., p. 34.

[46] Leopold Sedar Senghor, Elements constructif d'une civilization d'inspiration negro-Africaine, in *Senghor Prose and Poetry*, p. 43.

[47] Leopold Sedar Senghor, *The Foundations of 'Africanié' or 'Négritude' and 'Arabité,'* Paris: Présence Africaine, 1971, p. 80.

[48] Ibid., pp. 81 82.

[49] Ibid., pp. 51-52.

5

The Originality of African Philosophy as a Hermeneutical Problem in Okere

Francis O. C. Njoku

1. Introduction

Scholars who start off on the idea of 'originality' or 'authenticity' of African philosophy without a methodological clarity and good intellectual map take off on false premise. This is a conviction Theophilus Okere presses on his readers. After all, "our view of realty is like a map with which to negotiate the terrain of life. If the map is true and accurate, we will generally know where we are, and if we have decided where we want to go, we will generally know how to get there. If the map is false and inaccurate, we generally will be lost."[1] In the desire to negotiate a good terrain with a good map for African philosophy, Okere claims that the question of the existence or the possibility of African philosophy precedes the question of its authenticity or originality. Like John Locke, who advised his contemporaries that before one claimed an unlimited horizon of knowledge for the mind, it was proper to examine the mind itself to see what it was capable of, Okere looks for the possibility, and conditions of searching for, African philosophy. Until that is done, the search risks being misguided. A methodological starting point will reassure hope of what are possible within the confines of the research. In taking the position of an under-labourer in the area of seeking or establishing the conditions of philosophy, then African philosophy, Okere shows that he has a better grasp of the issue of African philosophy. How does Okere wade the muddled waters of inquiry in the way of African philosophy? In a large part, this paper will attempt to demonstrate that Okere, in his book *African Philosophy: A Historico-Hermeneutical*

Investigation of the Conditions of its Possibility, addresses the issue of originality as a hermeneutical problem. Before we advance further on what Okere takes to be a false start in African philosophy, it is instructive to put into perspective the issue of search for an original or authentic African philosophy.

2. Does Africa Have Its own Philosophy?

The intellectual bias perpetrated especially by David Hume[2] and G. W. Hegel[3] denied reason to Africa. The denial of reason meant the denial of reflection and a philosophical tradition. Even, when history proved that the African had come of age in reasoning, some remained sceptical about the attribution of some kind of original philosophy to him. Many Africans responded in the affirmative, that is, there is such a philosophy the African can call his own - a philosophy that is original to him.

To say that something is 'original' is to say that it exists from the beginning; it is innate; serves as a pattern; and underived or not imitated. Something that is original is first, primary, indigenous, true and authentic. In this essay, I will be using 'originality' to mean primary/underived or authentic.

Europe has been accused of stealing African intellectual legacy. One understands why some African scholars are prepared to castigate Europe for not being humble enough to acknowledge the intellectual feeding it received in the bosom of Africa. The issue of originality of Africa's contribution to philosophy has troubled many before Theophilus Okere gave a hermeneutical twist to it.

The argument for the authenticity or originality of African philosophy has been presented from two major fronts.

There are those who argue that African philosophy has Greek roots. Their reason is that African philosophy cannot be put on the shelf as a philosophy characterised by conventional or primitive mentality. By tracing its roots to the Greeks origin, they claim that they are appealing to authenticity. Since the Greeks are known for being the forerunners of written philosophy, then by tracing African philosophy to Greek roots, scholars feel satisfied that African philosophy is also a genuine philosophy. Claude Sumner, in his article 'The Ethiopian Philosophy of Greek Origin,' argues that if Greece is taken to be the paradigm of all philosophy, and Ethiopian philosophy is traced to the Greeks, then Ethiopian or African philosophy is original.[4] Furthermore, the *Book of Philosophers,* written in Ethiopian language, later translated into Greek had Ethiopian philosophers. This argues favourably for the authenticity of African philosophy since Ethiopian philosophy can be traced to Greek philosophy, that is, "if the latter is philosophical in the strict sense, it follows logically that the former is also philosophical in the same sense."[5]

However, the location of African philosophy within Greek or European quarters only satisfies a psychological need, and a weak argument too. To define African philosophy in European gabs does not necessarily make it original or prove its authenticity. Originality is not something that Europe should be looked upon to confer and confirm. Such an honorary title is not very commendable, for it depends on the person who confers rather than the person who receives it. Originality, in this direction, Okere would disallow, as an uncritical assumption of Western philosophy or the importation of some kind of extra-African material into the African philosophic space.

The attempt to establish the African origin of European philosophy satisfies another need: to tell Europe how ungrateful it has been, having failed to acknowledge its sources. In this regard, African philosophers condemn Europe for willingly stealing a legacy that does not belong to it. Martin Bernal in his *Black Anthena* claims that African philosophy predates Greek philosophy. Bernal argues that "it was only after the collapse of the Egyptian religion in the second century AD that other Oriental cults, notably Christianity, began to replace it."[6] Bernal confirms his claim by quoting the Greek historian, Heroditus who said that "the names of nearly all the gods came to Greece from Egypt"[7] or "were borrowed by the Greeks from Egypt." Bernal believes that both Isocrates and Plato owe much to Egypt.[8]

G. R. Levy, in his *Plato in Sicily,* quotes Plato's acknowledgement of his debts to the Egyptians after serving in the new wars in Egypt, that he got some quiet and kindness from Egyptian priests who taught him something about the divine basis of the society and its relation to the heavenly circuits.[9]

Edward Blyden traces the history of Blacks to the sons of Ham recorded in the tenth Chapter of book of Genesis. Blyden claims that the city built by the descendants of Ham was Egypt. In other words, the original descendants of the Egypt were blacks.[10]

G. G. M. James has written that years of study brought home to him the fact of *Stolen Legacy*, which Europe does not want to acknowledge.[11]

However, the judgement as to the authenticity of African philosophy has acquired some theoretical aims; that is, the debate is not neutral. Europe maintains that the superiority of reason is the parameter for defining philosophy, and thus claims it as its pride; hence the reluctance to take Africa on board their philosophy or intellectual ship. Europe can point to its achievement in the areas of philosophy, science and technology as a reason for not taking Africans seriously. Africans on their own side have problems appealing to historical records in the present scheme of things to convince Europe. Thus those who claim that Africans have philosophy of their own, in the academic sense, simply propose arguments that are only of historical interest and belatedly defensive.

3. Ethno-philosophers' False Start, and the Hermeneutical Re-direction

Ethno-philosophy is the view that philosophy is retrievable from cultural symbols. Placid Tempels, Alexis Kagame, and John Mbiti already take it for granted that African philosophy exists. Tempels, studying Bantoue philosophy, locates it in the overriding concept of 'vital force';[12] Kagame believes that linguistic analysis of Bantoue-Rwnandaise world yields certain ontology   African ontology. Mbiti merges religion and philosophy.[13] By considering the African idea of time, Mbiti claims to have found an understanding of a basic religious and philosophical concept in Africa.[14] The starting point of these ethno-philosophers (Tempels, Kagame and Mbiti) is bold, but Okere claims that they are false and unsatisfactory. Their failure is essentially the inability to "pose and answer the basic, initial questions: What is philosophy in the first place, and what is not philosophy? How does non-philosophy become philosophy?"[15] If one establishes what philosophy is, then one will know how to move from philosophy to non-philosophy. In short, what ethno-philosophers have failed to do is to lay the conditions for sieving philosophy from cultural, collective or 'primitive' mentality. Until the conditions of philosophy are specified, one might be masquerading cultural sentiments as philosophy.

The issue of culture and philosophy must be addressed from the point of view of hermeneutics. Hermeneutics is a question of interpretation. Through hermeneutics, an intellectual highway could be constructed between philosophy and culture. In bringing to light this fact, Okere notes that hermeneutics has a long history: from the Greeks through the Jewish-Christian traditions to Edmund Husserl and beyond. Within a certain historical perspective, he seeks the help of the masters of hermeneutical philosophy.

Paul Ricoeur unites the whole field of hermeneutics under the umbrella of semantics - a question of meaning. Through interpretation, Ricoeur deciphers hidden meanings in symbols and their environment of occurrence, thereby arriving at reflection or philosophy. Husserl uses the concept of intentionality to show that there is an *a priori* correlation between subject and object.[17]

Okere treats with admiration Martin Heidegger's understanding of the task of philosophy and the essence of hermeneutics. Heidegger relates ontology and meaning as existential correlative signification:

> The aim of the study is to reveal the inter-connectedness of these concepts and prepare the way for showing that since philosophy is an attempt to interpret reality and since all interpretation of reality is historical, relative and limited, all philosophy is necessarily also historical, relative, and limited.[18]

Heidegger's method reveals that the meaning of being is embedded in the fundamental structure of every question. When we pose a question, it implies that the subject who asks has a partial or some kind of intuitive grasp of the answer already. Therefore, the meaning of being is accessible to experience; we posses an initial understanding of being, however vague it may be. In Heidegger's scheme, whereas the business of philosophy is ontology, the business of hermeneutics is interpretation whose starting point is *Dasein*.

Dasein opens and widens the horizon of interpretation and the condition of possibility of all ontological project. It is a fundamental way to being and basis of philosophy and scientific method.[19] Thus, philosophy is an interpretations and the interpretation of Dasein opens the gate for all interpretation of reality. But the fundamental characteristics of *Dasein* as 'finite,' 'limited,' 'historical,' 'relative,' and 'situated' affect philosophy itself. If this is the case, the inevitable conclusion is that all philosophy is finite, historical and time-bound in the interpretation of being.[20] In this regard, philosophy and its tools are limited, situated and contingent. The world of its context is the world of relative symbols of interpretation.[21] The anthropological fact that confronts everyone is that meaning is context-bound. From the study of Heidegger, Okere concludes that man is constitutively and inescapably time-bound, historical, contextual, cultural and relative to this environment of occurrence; hence "his environment will prescribe the terminology, provoke the questions and predetermine the answers."[22]

Our interpretation, as Hans G. Gadamar has revealed, is not always impartial; hence there is a certain presupposition in our experience, knowledge, interpretation or philosophy itself.[23] One then acknowledges that humans labour under some kind of prejudice in their interpretation of reality. This fact is inescapable, in the conceptual schemes of the hermeneutical school, because every question is a search for what is already preordained or predetermined by the object of inquiry. There are then no presuppositionless grounds for knowledge. Context determines meaning; hence to give meaning is to give a context, to define,[24] and this defining Is always contingent.

4. The Basic Lesson for All: Dealing With Non-Philosophy

Anthropological and cultural presuppositions show that there is always an extra-philosophical material in philosophy.

Philosophy is an exercise in interpretation or "an interpretative commentary on reality against the guiding, determining and suggestive background of a culture."[25] There is always a hand of non-philosophy, that is, elements of language, history, scientific, or other lores, religion, mythology, values and beliefs, social and individual experience" that serve as raw materials for philosophical reflection.[26] And in philosophers, such as Hegel and Heidegger, Okere could see the finger of non-philosophy at work. For example, besides building on the thoughts of his predecessors, Hegel's time, his country's history, and Christian theology aroused the philosophical disquietude in him. Christian scriptures have had their hand in Heidegger's thought. Okere could deep his hand further back to show that Greek mythology and religion gave background to Pre-Socratic and Socratic periods in Greek philosophy.[27] Therefore, philosophy and non-philosophy have always shared borders in the thoughts of individual philosophers, albeit philosophy is characterised by reflection and non philosophy is taken to be an "unreflective baggage of cultural background."

Non-philosophy is the pre-judgements or prejudices, individual and cultural presuppositions which the hermeneutical method wants to get beyond to reveal the real world structure. Ethnophilosophers' error, in Okere's conceptual schemes, is to assume non-philosophy as philosophy or to appropriate life-world without reflection. However, Okere is aware that reason cannot operate independent of us. The question of "truth of things" becomes as suspicious as it is unattainable, for we cannot know all about things and ourselves in advance.

5. What African Philosophy Will Amount To

Okere stakes his intellectual harvest by concluding that philosophy is context-bound; all philosophy involves a situated exercise and extra-philosophical materials too:

> Philosophical reflection is the process of explicitation, an uncovering, a disclosure, an unfolding of the meaning and sense implied in those objectivations of life which are symbols. Reflection means *implicita explicare* - making the implicit, explicit. African cultures have their own symbols pregnant with meaning. A reflection on these symbols with a view to making the implicit meanings explicit would constitute African philosophy.[28]

Does African philosophy then exist? Okere answers that he does not quarrel with the *fact* of its existence but he worries over what *its existence* is claimed to be, when he writes:

> Whether there is some black African philosophy or not, can be decided only after an exhaustive examination of every individual in the culture concerned. More practically, we have on examination of the current philosophy literature objected not so much to the fact that they claimed the existence of philosophy in Africa as to what they claimed to be philosophy.[29]

Given the hermeneutical intuition that the interpretation of cultural symbols provides an outlet for articulating both the individuals' and communities' philosophy, Okere leans on Heidegger's line of thought to assure that African philosophy takes off from its environment of occurrence: "From Heidegger's philosophy of hermeneutics, one can validly infer that an African philosophy is a philosophy which gets its initial impulse and its nourishment from the African source, from African culture."[30] Africans have a philosophy that is original to them. Whereas, however, the sources of African philosophy will include traditional institutions, colonial and post-colonial experience, these cannot be uncritically assumed without questions. Symbols are context-bound, thus "a philosophical interpretation of the symbols of African culture would be African philosophy."[31]

The materials for philosophy are already there in the African environment waiting to receive philosophical reflection. What seems to be noticeable now is that African symbols are presupposed without being given critical reflection. An individual is situated in their cultural context; "it is by relating the elements of culture to himself that one creates and constitutes meaning and becomes a philosopher. The relation of culture to philosophy is explained from the structural constitution of man."[32] African philosophy exists as Okere implies, and with this platform created by the individual's culture and the climate of opinion around him,[33] but is not what ethno-philosophers are presenting.

6. The Relativistic Implication of Okere's Standpoint

The facts with which to do philosophy are there in African culture. Philosophy comes out of them through individual, critical and reflective attitude; that is, philosophy is hewed out of man's cultural environment through interpretation. This is a great insight Okere presents in clearing the rubble in the way to constructing African philosophy.

There is the glaring implication that every culture is *a* culture; every meaning is culture-bound, therefore, in Okere one lands into the inevitable conclusion that, since philosophy is culturally situated, meaning and truth become relative. Ordinarily, factual statements about cultures do not presuppose statements about the truth of their philosophy. While Okere will accept the preceding claim, the relativism he lands into seems to stem from the fact that, when we have come to do a reflection on factual suppositions, it will be discovered that the outcome will be relative. His position and those of enthnophilosophers he sets out to criticise become a matter of scratching at the same place at different times. Ethnophilosophers uncritically assume facts of culture as philosophy; Okere says 'wait a moment! Say you are doing a reflection on those facts; then you will discover your philosophy, and that philosophy will be particular to you.' If there is no universal measure for determining which reflections are truly critical, does it matter to the on-looker whether I have reflected critically on my materials since statements about those materials will turn out to be particular and culture-bound? Philosophy seems to lose its enduring universal structure in Okere - the great master of the African hermeneutic school of philosophy in the following words:

> The possibility of an African philosophy raises the question of the validity and universality of truth and the communicability of cultures and their respective philosophies. Is truth relative? It seems this conclusion is inevitable. The historicity and relativity of truth - and this always means truth as we can and do attain it - is one of the main insights of the hermeneutical revolution in philosophy and it is in it that this thesis hangs.[34]

Okere is correct to insist that there is an element of the particular in whatever is generalised as philosophy. But the problem is that this particular or non-philosophy remains at the end of the tunnel without acquiring a philosophical universality in Okere, where philosophers can ply or negotiate each other's intellectual worlds.

We must accept Aristotle's observation in his *Metaphysics* that "all men by nature desire to know." In other words, humans have a natural inclination to know and take delight in knowledge. The senses furnish them with information about the world. The particularity in the human intellect that has a universal vocation is an indication that the history of humans starts within a certain occurrence in time; the tribe, the clan, the village and the small town represent kinds of small worlds within which all his living is done.[35] So, one wonders within a certain environment, at least, as a starting point. The sense of wonder is universal to humans; but its point of departure is situated in time and place. Adopting a philosophical position of wonder, one tries to understand one's life and place in the universe. It is against this background that some claim that philosophy also has a cultural root or bent to it, for every experience has an environment of occurrence; hence the temptation into relativism to which some of the hermeneutical school have landed. Does the fact that people are situated mean that they have a different mentality that will yield a different philosophy, other things being equal? This is unlikely.[36]

Certainly humans are situated beings; they do not speak from nowhere. They speak from within their environment or culture, with their particular expressions and language. Philosophy is thus embellished by a variety of experiences. We should accept that varieties in culture and experience are evidenced in the different bents of intellectual worlds. The variety of philosophy is due to variety of cultures, races, nationalities. However this is not to say that people have different characteristic mentalities:

> It is more accurate to point out that different characteristic mentalities in the categories of race, culture, and nationality ... do not determine but rather influence the attitudes and methods adopted and the choice of questions asked. A philosophy always springs, however indirectly, from the society in which the philosopher grows up, with its religious

proclivities or lack thereof, the social class from which the philosopher has been drawn, the events that have shaped the philosopher's education.[37]

One insists that the variety of philosophical experiences arises from the characteristic complexity of the universe, namely, human experience in its rich and varied forms. In other words, ordinary experience can lead to philosophical questions. For example, from the suffering, pain and death of friends and relatives, we may begin to wonder about the whole question of human toil, meaning and end of human life and hereafter. Therefore experiences of a particular lived-world can evoke questions and problems of universal concern. Such varied questions have been grouped over the years by philosophers into different branches of philosophy -- ethics, epistemology, metaphysics, logic and social and political philosophy. However, "what philosophers share is an open-mindedness which allows for the digging up of unacknowledged presuppositions, an openness that allows for the existence of competing and alternative explanations of possibilities, and a willingness to suspend judgement in the absence of evidence":[38] albeit there reflection will be coloured by their particularities.

7. Cannot A Particular Be Universalizable?

Okere gives the impression that a truth that is a product of hermeneutics is not universalizable. I do not think this is very correct. Science follows the inductive method: accumulates a body of particular truths, then generalises them as having universal appeals. A truth of culture may be relative, but is does not have to be.

Culture is idea expressed as a set of adaptive materials by humans to cope with their environment. Whether the mind records information about objects disinterestedly or gives its own laws, it is arguable that ideas have recurrent universal structures evidenced in the human intellect, regardless of particular mentalities. If the intellect sieves the partial truths in every particular culture; that it has something that is general that draws the particular to an identifiable universal status becomes undeniable. If this reasoning is correct, nothing then blocks a possible particular from being universalizable. Western philosophy presents itself as a philosophy with a universal appeal, why must African philosophy be relegated to cultural relativity as a birthright? If African philosophy is a philosophy by humans, it has an intelligible universality, unless we want to claim that humans have no common ground on which to converse as humans.

One recalls that Okere in an article titled 'The Assumption of African Values As Christian Values' affirms a "pan-African cultural base" for African values because there are values that are basic to all African cultures.[39] His basis for a claim about pan-African base of African values is that some "values are not only more permanent in time but seem destined for a more universal vocation, eventually being accepted beyond their time and place of birth."[40] On the same token, Okere will have to accept that certain philosophical truths transcend cultures or their initial places of origin; there are certain truths about humans and their environment that are destined for universal vocation. There must be then a hermeneutics that goes beyond the relativistic outlook of reality, which Okere's present school of hermeneutics advocates.

8. Meaning as Political

We must be grateful to Okere however for drawing our attention to the fact that meaning and interpretation are not only contextual, but also political. Meanings do not always possess untainted and abstract essences that are applied as determined axioms of a book of mathematics. Words such as 'African philosophy,' 'European philosophy,' 'colonialism,' 'black race,' 'democracy,' 'freedom' 'economics,' and many others are not neutral. They can be languages of power, control and domination. In other words, the meanings and languages of the philosophical sphere are contestable. The hand of non-philosophy in philosophy can wear some socio-political gab that affects the philosophical space. When the non-philosophy breaks into the space of philosophy, it does not go away without a fight, if it goes away at all. It politicises the whole intellectual atmosphere. Much as reasoning is a general attribute of humans, its exercise is not presuppositionless. If every philosophy is culture-bound, at least according to the hermeneutical reasoning, it is then political or ideological where a set of cultural truths amounts the so-called tribunal of pure reason to judge other sets of truths. Okere will be glad to call for some kind of psychoanalysis in our cross-cultural intercourse and intellectual highways for self-appointed judges of philosophies to back off.

Following the hermeneutical method, one reasonably agrees with the implication of Okere's study that every philosophy is local, but this implication should not be pushed to assume a position of a denial of a possible truth that local philosophies are not universalizable. If the meaning of philosophy of being is accessible to experience as Okere accepts, why cannot the experience be at once 'our' and 'my' experience? A scientist, first, stumbles on a particular truth while researching, then he brings it to the public arena where it becomes our truth.

9. Relativism-cum-Uniqueness as a Hermeneutical Problem

The fact of originality or non-originality of African philosophy is understandably contestable. However that a concept is contested does not mean that it may not have a core of meaning; it partly means that whatever it is, interlocutors in the debate are talking pass each other; and views are dangerously polemicised. This reminds one of John Stuart Mill's observations that "the principles which men profess on any controverted subject are usually a very imperfect exponent of the opinions they really hold."[41]

Both African philosophy and European philosophies are original in their own right as arising from their cultures and individual experiences. If we attempt to define philosophy in a less sophisticated manner, as a way of life, then *that* way of life is always original to the people involved, for philosophy arise out of people's life situations. Philosophy is the whole mode of being; adjusting and coping by a human group in its own environment of occurrence. It is not something they have to import from outside. In this regard, no group would claim superiority in the way it copes with life-riddles within its own port. One can ridicule the view of equality of environmental sustainability and vitality by reminding us that since fossils are traced to Africa, the first ape-like humans whose fossils are found in Africa argues then that African philosophy precedes Europe's. Fossils however do not tell us that the ape-like man was a human being in the way we know humans today.

The originality of a thing does not need to be defined in terms of others. The principle of identity states that every being is determined in itself, is one with itself and is consistent in itself. If a thing is identical in itself, it is genuine or original. Instead of defining the originality of African philosophy in terms of Europe or vice versa, let us explain African philosophy in its own right. Okere just wants intellectuals to do their homework.

Contemporary studies in African philosophy brand the problem of originality or relativism in African philosophy as the problem of uniqueness. Is African philosophy unique? To answer this question two schools of thought emerge.

There are those who answer in the affirmative. Placide Tempels argues that African philosophy is unique. He attempts to defend the native against the Western impatience and charge that the native has no philosophy; hence Tempels reminds them that he has a philosophy, albeit a different or unique one. Tempels sees himself as supplying the native with the instruments he requires to articulate his thought since he lacks them. He presents the uniqueness of African philosophy to his European brothers to assuage their curiosity. It is accepted that Tempels may not have used the word 'native' in pejorative terms, but could he raise African philosophy to the level of European philosophy? It is likely that Tempels would not. He is satisfied to point out that the natives have 'their philosophy,' which should not be denied them, albeit a kind of philosophy.

Leopald Sedar Senghor buys the idea that African philosophy is unique. He restricts Africa to emotions and gift of myth making, dance and rhythms, and traded off reason, implying that Europe can stick to its claim of superiority on the basis of reason.

Uniqueness plays a negative role in Tempels: Africans have their own philosophy; it is different from European philosophy. Senghor assumes the negative quality with which the African is defined and derogated and turns it as a positive attribute without arguments; that the African gift of emotions is also a valid mode of being in the world. Thus the value of African uniqueness is complimentary and not discriminatory.

If African philosophy is unique (following the line Tempels and Senghor, then Okere), then it is closed to others. It is an 'African thing.' Is philosophy then a thing the individual appropriates? Paulin Hountondji does not think that philosophy is an African thing. Philosophy, for him, is universal. What makes the difference is the geography from which authors make their contribution. Hountondji rejects the ethnophilosophy group to which Tempels and Senghor are classified. He blames them for masquerading African rites, rituals and music as African philosophy. Hountondji himself reduces philosophy to written work, and disregards the oral tradition from which ethno-philosophers carve out their philosophy. There is then in Hountondji's conceptual schemes nothing unique about African philosophy.

Hountondji has been criticised for thinking that European literacy sets the paradigm for philosophy. The thinking that written tradition is what counts as philosophy seems to place Africa behind Europe in terms of the issue of originality. However, African narrative philosophy is not prepared to be dismissed without a fight. Sage philosophers have argued that orality as expressed by sage counts as a text. Paul Ricoeur corroborates the view that text is not restricted to the written word, when he states that text implies texture (complexity of composition) and inscription in a durable monument of language.[42] Therefore the word 'text' is an inclusive term and cannot be confined to issues of orality and literacy.

If the uniqueness of Africa philosophy closes the doors to others from experiencing the African's own reality in a broader human context, it does not fare any better. The whole problem is not so much the originality or authenticity of African philosophy in face of European or Greek philosophy as *the difficulty of the African reality or any African reality has in universalising its particular experience, as Europe or the West do*. The attempt to do this through unearthing its historical past or records as evidence of its possibility or that it had been done is complicated by the present inaction of Africa in catching up with a fast moving world of science and technology. The present inaction or ineptitude places a great divide in recuperating the so-called ancient and stolen legacy in the present scheme of things. However, a relativistic interpretation of philosophy or politics shuts off Africa from the mainstream scholarship.

The arena of hermeneutics is arguably political; however, African philosophy should be there to negotiate its way by convincing other interlocutors that its intellectual and material products are marketable as human goods that appeal to persons and transcend cultures.

Too much insistence on a relativistic understanding of cultures and philosophies does not make African intellectual tradition fair any better. An unreflective parading of the uniqueness of African philosophy risks the conclusion that the intellectual baggage Africa is presenting is simply 'an African thing,' in a derogatory sense.

Okolo Okonda and Tsney Serequeberhan took to Okere's hermeneutical approach. Okonda follows Okere to indicate that using the hermeneutical approach provides the African an initial intellectual space; hence African tradition is to be viewed in progressive light.[43]

Like Okere, Serequeberhan applauds the hermeneutical method, but Serequeberhan calls our attention to the fact that hermeneutics itself as a method is of European origin.[44] Thus the hermeneutical method that is imported into the African space has to undergo certain psychoanalysis to fit the dual traditional and colonial experiences of the African: "Thus, in terms of contemporary concerns - political, economic, scientific, cultural, etc. - the hermeneutics of African philosophy must engage in situated reflections aimed at the pragmatic and practical aim of enhancing the lived actuality of post-colonial Africa. It is only in this way that African philosophy, as the reflexive hermeneutics of its own historicalness, can grow and cultivate itself as a concrete contemporary philosophic discourse."[45] It is not enough then to employ the hermeneutical method. One has to recognise that the hermeneutical method is part of the Western intellectual tradition and politics. So hermeneutics itself is in need of hermeneutics; hence one must be clear as to what kind of hermeneutics one is adopting or advocating. As Barry Hallen, in interpreting Serequeberhan says, "an African hermeneutics, if developed and applied in a sensitive manner, can make a positive contribution to Africa's social, cultural, and political restoration."[46] Since there are no presuppositionless grounds for hermeneutics, African hermeneutics has to be prioritised interpretation that liberates the continent and advocates the rediscovery and re-evaluation of authentic African values in all spheres.[47]

And a further step will be to insist before the West that one has come to recognise that the judgement as to the superiority of philosophies in term of rationality is a matter of politics of choice, which the West has hijacked till date. African scholars have come to realise that African and Western perceptions of reality yield equally valid epistemologies. My contention is, however, that whatever politics is adopted, the intellectual harvests at both sides of the divide are equally negotiable and trans-cultural in the final analysis. There is a rationality that transcends cultures that can subsume the West and Africa alike as species of rationalities in the gamut of human rationality.

Notes

[1] David L. Bender, ed., *Constructing A Life Philosophy: Opposing View Points*, San Diego: Greenhaven Press, Inc., 1993, p. 18..

[2] Cf. Hume's essay, 'On National Character' quoted from E. Chukwudi Eze, 'Modern Western Philosophy and African Colonialism,' in *African Philosophy: An Anthology*, ed. E. C. Eze, Oxford: Blackwell Publishers, 1998, p. 214.

[3] See G. W. F. Hegel, *The Philosophy of History*, New York: Dover Publications, 1956, p. 93.

[4] Claude Sumner, 'The Ethiopian Philosophy of Greek Origin,' Collectanea Aethiopica, Stuttgart: Franz Steeiner Verlag, 1988, 146.

[5] F. Ochieng-Odhiambo, *African Philosophy An Introduction* 2d. Nairobi: Consolata Institute of Philosophy Press, 1997, p. 36.

[6] Martin Bernal, *Black Athena: The Afroasiatic Roots of Classical Civilisation*, Vol. 1, The Fabrication of Ancient Greece 1785-1985, New Jersey: Rutgers University Press, 1987, p. 23.

[7] *Ibid.*, p. 99.

[8] See *Ibid.*, p. 108.

[9] G. R. Levy, *Plato in Sicily*, London: Faber and Faber, pp. 25-26.

[10] Edward Blyden, 'The Negro in Ancient History,' in *The People of Africa: a series of Papers on their Character, Condition and Future Prospects* ed. Henry M.

Schieffelin, 2d., Ibadan: Ibadan University Press, 1974, p. 8. (This article first appeared in Methodist Quarterly Review, January, 1869). Cf. also Luc Croegaert, *The African Continent: An Insight into its Earliest History,* Nairobi: Paulines Publications Africa especially Ch 2.

[11] F. Ochieng-Odhiambo, *African Philosophy An Introduction* 2d., 25

[12] Placide Tempels, 'Bantu Philosophy,' in *African Philosophy An Anthology* ed., E. C. Eze, 430-431. See also Placid Tempel, *Bantu Philosophy,* trans. Rev. Colin King , Paris: Présence Africaine, 1959.

[13] See John S. Mbiti, *African Religion and Philosophy* 2d., Oxford: Heinemann Educational Publishers, 1989, p. 1.

[14] See *Ibid.,* 14.

[15] Theophilus Okere, *African Philosophy: A Historico-Hermeneutical Investigation of the Conditions of Its Possibility,* London: University Press of America, 1983, p. 11.

[16] See *Ibid.,* pp. 16-18.

[17] *Ibid.,* p. 26.

[18] *Ibid.,* pp. 32-33.

[19] See *Ibid.,* p. 37.

[20] See *Ibid.,* p. 38.

[21] See *Ibid.,* pp. 38-40.

[22] *Ibid.,* p. 54.

[23] See *Ibid.,* p. 59.

[24] See *Ibid.,* pp. 76-77.

[25] *Ibid.,* p. 81.

[26] See *Ibid.,* p. 82.

[27] See *Ibid.,* pp. 107-108.

[28] *Ibid.,* pp. 114-115.

[29] *Ibid.,* p. 114.

[30] *Ibid.,* p. 118.

[31] *Ibid.,* p. 115.

[32] *Ibid.,* p. 116.

[33] See Innocent Onyewuenyi, 'Towards An African Philosophy,' in *Readings in African Humanities: African Cultural Development* ed.; Ogbu U. Kalu, Enugu: Fourth Dimension Publishers, 1982, p. 247.

[34] Theophilus Okere, *African Philosophy: A Historico-Hermeneutical Investigation of the Conditions of Its Possibility,* 124.

[35] Benita Luckmann, 'The Small Life-Worlds of Modern man,' in *Phenomenology and Sociology* ed. Thomas Luckmann, London: Penguin Books, 1978, p. 276.

[36] See Francis O. C. Njoku, *Essays in African Philosophy, Thought and Theology,*

Owerri: Claretian Institute of Philosophy, 2002, Ch., 1.

[37] Samuel Oluoch Imbo, *An Introduction to African Philosophy*, Maryland: Rowman & Littlefield Publishers, Inc., 1998, pp. 3-4.

[38] *Ibid.*, p. 6-7.

[39] See Theophilus Okere, 'The Assumption of African Values As Christian Values,' in *Lucerna* 1 (July-December 1978), 6.

[40] *Ibid.*, 11.

[41] John Stuart Mill, *Considerations on Representative Government,,* New York: Prometheus Books, 1991, p. 11.

[42] Paul Ricoeur, *Hermeneutics and the Social Sciences*, ed. and trans. John B. Thomson, Cambridge: Cambridge University Press, 1981, 37.

[43] See Okolo Okonda, 'Tradition and Destiny: Horizons of an African Philosophical Hermeneutics,' in *African Philosophy: The Essential Readings*, ed., T. Serequeberhan, New York: Paragon House, 1991, 204-205.

[44] See T. Serequeberhan, *The Hermeneutics of African Philosophy*, London: Routledge, 1994, 10-11.

[45] *Ibid.*, p. 114.

[46] Barry Hallen, *A Short History of African Philosophy* , Bloomington: Indiana University Press, 2002, pp. 65-66.

[47] See *Ibid.*, p. 66.

6

The Paradigmatic Status of Western Philosophy in Okere's Philosophical Hermeneutics

Sylvanus Ifeanyi Nnoruka

1. Introduction

In popular terms philosophy is understood as love of wisdom. The authenticity of one's philosophy depends on the adequate conception of the term 'love of wisdom'. The wisdom we are talking about here is more of practical experiential wisdom. The wisdom of a philosopher is not supernaturally infused. He also does not posses it by virtue of his superhuman illumination. He does not posses this wisdom through a natural instinct. It is the wisdom of man which he acquires through consistent intellectual hard work However it is done, philosophy aims at clarification of thoughts, concepts and meaning of language. To philosophize is to think clearly and accurately. Philosophy is always suggesting new ways of looking at questions, new ways of expressing ideas, and new views about the purpose and function of philosophy itself. A philosopher does not operate in a vacuum. He always tackles the problems that solicit the mind of his race. He undertakes an intellectual adventure and above all exercises a liberty of thought. He is there to show the light, to propose solutions to problems. Wittgenstein for instance understands his task as being to show the fly the way out of the bottle.

Monsignor Theophilus Okere possesses the qualities of a philosopher among other qualities. He is undoubtedly one of the eminent philosophical thinkers in Africa. His philosophical reflection finds its setting within the period of the great debate on the nature and character of philosophic activity in Africa. The basic questions were: Can there be African philosophy? If yes, what nature or character should it assume? Was it to be esoteric in character or should it just maintain its specific characteristics while at the same time forming part of the universal philosophical enterprise? Okere opted for the latter. He maintains that African philosophy is possible and that its methodology is hermeneutics. In fact, for him, philosophy is hermeneutics.

Our task here is to show that western philosophy, in fact that western hermeneutical thinkers played a model and indispensable role in the shaping of his hermeneutical thought.

2. Context of the Emergence of Okere's Hermeneutics

The context is the debate on whether or not there can be African philosophy. We shall consider the views of four principal contributors to the debate: Henri Maurier, Ramose, Paulin Hountondji, and Bodunrin.

In his answer to the question, do we have African philosophy? Maurier clearly answers: "No! Not Yet!" He then goes ahead to stipulate what he considers to be the conditions for genuine philosophy. As discipline, philosophy is reflective, rational and systematic.[1] Most thinkers meet up with the demands of the reflective character. But above all, philosophy ought to be a rational discipline. This means in effect that all "philosophy should be a thorough and rational critique of concepts in general use."[2] cultural practices: riddles, jokes, proverbs, folk tales etc. should not be accepted at their face value. They ought necessarily to be subjected to rational criticism. It is only through such efforts that the objective of African philosophy would be accomplished. Specifically to say that philosophy ought to be critical should be understood in the Kantian sense of the term. That is, "philosophy should question itself about the proper value of its rational procedure and on the epistemological or gnostic validity of its results." He thus identifies the basic difference between an African philosopher and a western philosopher. It concerns basically the situation in which each finds himself. While the western philosopher works "within a long vein of philosophical thinking", the African philosopher has a more arduous task. He has no philosophical tradition to draw from. He is "a ground breaker, he plunges straight into African life as seen in its myths, its beliefs, its rites, and in its everyday language." The studies of sociologists and ethnographers are of advantage to him. The procedures he employs remain, however, his greatest obstacle. The procedure he employs must be such that will make African philosophy truly African. This is possible only when African philosophy is thought through a conceptual framework properly African and adapted to African realities. "For were we to impose upon these realities a foreign framework, we would be placing on them an iron collar, we would torture them in a Procrustean bed, we would not be able to readily connect reality with the particular savor it has..., we would be posing all sorts of false problems and then pseudosolutions."[4]

How then do we get at the correct framework for African philosophy? Maurier opts for the process of elimination. Stoicism would not be suitable because the cosmos is indispensable in African thought. The same also applies to the objectivistic framework where subject is opposed to the object and which considers the object independent of the subject. A better framework here would be one that is relational or participative. Even though man is at the center of African philosophy it is not in the style of Descartes and his *Cogito*. That is, African philosophy would completely miss its target if it took up a solipsistic or individualistic option. A number of problems have polarized African philosophy. They include the problem of universals, the problem of immediate awareness, the problem of empiricism, the problem of philosophical critique and within the past century, the problem of phenomenology. These are not the sort of problems that should borge African thinking. For the African, the problem of living, of life is far more important than gnoseological. African subjectivism is real but we can speak of it in a different sense from western subjectivism. Western subjectivism "evolved in an individualistist and objectivist perspective, looks upon the subject as self-sufficient, autonomous, a consciousness, a free agent, a strong personality, competitive, who should assert himself in and by the independence he is assumed to have."[5] African subjectivism on the other hand will manifest itself in a different way. This is because it will be developed in a relational circle. The subject manifests self-affirmation not just through mere self-affirmation per se but through cultivating contacts with others and exchanging with them. This conceptual framework could be framed thus: 'I-with'. In a general way, African subjectivity is oriented to the exterior, to the group, the others. There is incessant renewal of the need for relations. It could be called the subjectivity of the group. (*Moi le groupe*) "L'Africain aime la compagnie, multiplie les contacts. Il quete les protections et avance..., il accepte le paternalisme. Piusque les relations sont réglées par la Tradition, ;a personne est peu inventive, elle s'en tien a une solidarité obligtoire."[6] An indispensable point to be made here is that even though African philosophy must begin from the African and the realities of his life, it must maintain the character of universality. It is in this way that African thought can indisputably contribute to universal culture; its polarization by the vital relationship that every one necessarily maintains with others and the world. This is in sharp contrast to the West that for many centuries has centered its thought on the isolated individual. It has thus for centuries used an individualistic and obectivist framework. The individual is powerful, liberty is extolled and the world is full of scientific and technological developments. In Africa, it is a different story since African civilization is characterized by solidarity, communitarianism, traditionalism, participation. In Africa, philosophy ought, therefore, to flow, to influence life and subsequently political development. The point of departure for African philosophy ought to be African life as it is actually lived. "Comme toute philosophie, la philosophie de l'Afrique doit partir d'une donné premier. La vie africaine concrètement vécue, pour remonter aux principes ou fondements ultimes qui la constituent."[7] The individual cannot be separated from what precedes it: mythical ancestors, historical ancestors, immediate ancestors, immediate parents, etc. In this way, it could be seen that contrary to the assertions and pretensions of some foreign anthropologists and ethnographers, the African continent has never been a closed one. At the same time, it should also be remarked that it was never as receptive of external influences as other cultures.[8]

Does African Philosophy exist? Ramose is of the opinion that this question was initiated outside of Africa. The indigenous African people could not have initiated it. He adduces three reasons for this position. In the first place, it is obvious that "if this is construed as an empirical, statistical question" even by the Africans, "then it is an otiose question." He regards the question as insignificant. The only possible merit of the question could be that it helps to identify and count "people of African origin who have either pursued philosophy as an academic discipline or have philosophized even before the recognition of philosophy as an academic discipline." On this merit alone, "it could be argued that only downright ignorance or perverse intellectual dishonesty would deny the fact that there are African philosophers." It is, however, completely another matter whether or not academically trained professional philosophers do African philosophy. The second reason is that such question can be the subject of philosophical debate only if we understand the questioner as seeking to determine that " were the people of African origin from time immemorial capable of and competent to do philosophy." That is, - do people of African origin from time immemorial possess the same qualities and capabilities as the others who perform philosophic activity. This is "an ontological question which in its directedness and immediacy calls into question the very humanity of the indigenous African people." Ramose puts the question in another way: "the people of African origin from time immemorial do not as living beings, possess and are by their very being incapable of acquiring or having that quality or qualities the possession of which and by virtue of which other living beings, apparently like them qualify to be called human beings who can do philosophy, as well."[9] Rationality has been singled out as the most outstanding and distinctive quality for membership of *homo sapiens.* This quality implies that the being in question speaks and acts. He is *homo loquens* and *homo agens.* Ontologically and biologically, Africans belong to this group. No research in any discipline has so far proved that they are exempt from this group. Ramose accordingly posits the thesis that "the indigenous African people have always been potential and actual participants in and are full members of homo sapiens."

There is yet the third reason. It is that "through their autopietic activity underlined by their faculty of perception, the people of African origin from time immemorial have conceivably cognised themselves as specific entities of a particular kind and quality, thereby being distinguished and differentiated from other entities in the overall environment of their existence."[10] So if they ever posed the question "what or who am I?, it does not in any way imply a denial of the fact that they already exist. They did obviously perceive themselves as distinct kind of beings in their environment. But this does not mean that the question is insignificant. The "significance of this question lies in the quest to determine the meaning of what it is to be the kind of beings they actually are." Since the indigenous African people have ever regarded themselves as full members of *homo sapiens* and real and complete human beings, the central question they were posing could be said to be "the fundamental one pertaining to what it means to be a human being." Ramose, therefore, suggests " neither in the remotest past of human history nor the contemporary history have the people of African origin from time immemorial espoused either a philosophy or a science aimed to disprove their humanness: their membership of or participation in *homo sapiens*. It is only non-African people in their encounter with indigenous Africans who have developed both a philosophy and a science aimed at disproving the humanity of African people. They have persistently defended this position even till this day. The thesis is, therefore, posited that "there is no ontological defect inherent in the indigenous African people by virtue of which they may be excluded from the membership of *homo sapiens*."[11] Finally Ramose makes bold to assert "that if Africa is indeed the cradle of *homo sapiens,* then it is the indigenous African people who are the first members of and the very root from which the tree of *homo sapiens* took shape and grew."[12]

Hountondji is the foremost and fiercest critique of ethno-philosophy. However, he concedes that Tempels had some positive motives. Most outstanding in this regard is Tempel's intention to correct certain false images of the black man as disseminated by early European anthropologists who did research in Africa. An example is Lévy-Bruhl and his school. They tagged African weltanschauung, 'primitive mentality.' Tempels dismissed this view and set out to prove that African weltanschauung is not insensitive to contradiction; that to some extent, it conforms to the elementary laws of logic, that it is a systematic conception of the universe. This conception may be different or in fact is different from western system of thought but it deserved the name philosophy. He accepts that the primary objective of Tempels was "to rehabilitate the black man and his culture and to redeem them from the contempt from which they had suffered until then."[13] In spite of Tempels' good intentions, Hountondji characterizes the enterprise as ambitious. In an outstanding way, he observes that the work is not addressed to

Africans but to Europeans precisely to colonials and missionaries. The implication is that

> contemporary African philosophy, inasmuch as it remains an ethnophilosophy, has been built up essentially *for a European public.* The African ethnophilosopher's discourse is not intended for Africans. It has not been produced for their benefit, and its authors understood that it would be challenged, if at all, not by Africans but by Europeans alone...In short, the African ethnophilosopher made himself the spokesman of All-Africa facing All-Europe at the imaginary rendezvous of give and take - from which we observe that 'Africanist' particularism goes hand in glove, *objectively,* with an abstract universalism, since the African intellectual who adopts it thereby expounds it, over the heads of his own people, in a mythical dialogue with his European colleagues...,[14]

Thus the Africans are excluded from the discussion. This is clear from the title of the last chapter of the work: 'Bantu philosophy and our mission to civilize.' The black man remains a topic for discussion; a voiceless individual subjected to private investigation. He can only be defined and cannot be a part of the discourse. In fact, he cannot genuinely be an interlocutor. With regard to Bantu philosophy, the Bantu have no part to play in the discussion. They appear only as an object or a pretext. Following this methodology, what would be left for African intellectuals would be to describe the main features of African civilization for the benefit of their European counterparts. Their target would be to secure the respect of Europeans on their own terms for African cultural originality. One can at this time contrast the views of Kagame with those of Tempels. The latter identifies the main difference between European philosophy and African philosophy (concretely Bantu philosophy) to lie in their respective conceptions of being. For the Europeans, being is static while for the Bantu, it is dynamic, that is, being is synonymous with power. Ontology then becomes a general theory of forces, of their natural hierarchy and interaction. Kagame disagrees with Tempels on the ground that it is artificial to contrast *being* at rest and *being* in motion. This is because in each case we are confronted with the same being. Hountondji regards Kagame's critic as unradical, weak and cloudy. He thereby makes himself a prisoner of the same myth. He strongly rebukes him in these terms:

Kagame should not have been content to confute Tempels, he should have asked himself what the reasons were for his error. Then he might have noticed that Tempels' insistence on emphasizing the differences was part and parcel of the whole scheme, the reconstruction of the Bantu *Weltanschauung,* inasmuch as the scheme was not inscribed in the *Weltanschauung* itself but was external to it. Kagamé should have seen that this theoretical undertaking took its meaning only from a desire, the desire to differentiate African from European civilization at any cost, and that in these conditions the author of *Bantu Philosophy* would inevitably regard all as grist to his mill and would massively project on to the Bantu soul his own metaphysical reveries, reinforced for the occasion by a few delusive fragments of ethnography.[15]

It is clear that Hountondji does not recommend Kagamé's mode of approach to African intellectuals especially if such intellectuals wish to talk to their fellow Africans. Without dismissing the ethno-philosophers with ignominy, we must grant that they have tried with the means at their disposal to defend their cultural identity against the designs of imperialism. This is what he identifies as their only merit. But their ethno-philosophical methodology is ambiguous and their greatest demerit is failure to perceive the ambiguity. If this methodology is accepted, it means that African philosophy is relevant only to the past. It has no significance for the future. Such a methodology is by its very nature absurd. To get away from the impasse, we must relearn how to think. According to Hountondji, this can be done only in one way, in form of a debate. The task of African philosophers is to reorganize and take part in such a debate. It is not just to talk about Africa but also to talk among Africans. The result should be a useful corpus for an African public. But it would be a mistake to think that the word 'philosophy' changes its meaning simply because 'Africa' is added to it. This debate must avoid the danger of unanimity. This was the greatest shortcoming of ethno-philosophy. This philosophy attempted to "account for an imaginary unanimity, to interpret a text which nowhere exists and has to be constantly re-invented." Hountondji refers to it in the most abject of terms: "a science without an object," " a discourse that has no referent."[16] Philosophy can neither be found in the collective unconscious of African people nor in the silent folds of their explicit discourse. Ethnophilosophy exists only in the anthropologist's imagination. Instead of presenting its own rational justification, it "shelters lazily behind the authority of tradition and projects its own theses and beliefs on to that tradition."[17] Such a debate should permit constant free discussions about all the problems confronting the possibility of scientific discourse in Africa.

On his own part, Bodunrin outlines the sources of ethnophilosophy as follows: folklore, tales, myths, proverbs, religious beliefs and practices and African cultures at large. This does not mean that he accepts every aspect of the sources mentioned. At the same time, he states explicitly what he is denying. He does not deny that in Africa, there exist respectable and in many ways complex, rational, logical conceptual analysis. A number of foremost European ethnologists also confirm this point. Some of them are: Jean-Paul Lebeuf, Professor Evans-Pritchard, Professor Robin Horton. Jean-Paul Lebeuf even admitted that there exist in Africa perfectly balanced metaphysical systems in which all the phenomena of the sensible world are bound together in harmony. But Bodunrin does not hesitate to warn that "not every rational coherent and complicated conceptual system is philosophy. Science and mathematics are eminently rational, logical and, to a large extent, consistent conceptual systems, but they are not philosophical systems. This for him is the mistake of many ethno-philosophers. They erroneously "believe that all rational logical and complicated conceptual systems are philosophical systems." He identifies the following as being the forms taken by the usual criticism of ethnophilosophy.

Some of the things they say about African culture are false and unfounded. Examples are Mbiti's claim that Africans have no conception of the future beyond the immediate future. There is also Senghor's claim that Negro African reasoning is intuitive by participation. To counter the latter, Anthropologists such as Robin Horton have clearly shown the unemotional rationality of some African thinking. Another characteristic form of ethno-philosophy is that it is collective philosophy. The collective thought of peoples upon which they concentrate is not genuine philosophy. Bodunrin is himself not convinced of this point for according to him, "it is not clear why the thought of groups, if there is such a thing, cannot be a proper subject for philosophical study." This is because in the history of philosophy, we find abundant discussions of different sorts of things and various approaches to the subject." One, therefore, needs a genuine and critical argument before he can dismiss the discussions of anything and the use of any method as unphilosophical. He then makes bold to assert that there "is no a priori reason why proverbs, myths of gods and angels, social practices, etc, could not be proper subjects for philosophical inquiry."[18] It is only a matter of philosophical stance. All who engage in cognitive endeavors including ethno-philosophers have a common object of inquiry. It is the burning desire to know more about our universe: its content, the events and activities, which take place within it. One can get about this task by asking several questions and thereby expect several and varied answers. Both the question and method of inquiry determine the answer. This explains why different disciplines approach the study of the work from different perspectives. They seek to understand reality at different levels and with different goals. From this optic, he lays down the criteria to be met by one putting forward a philosophical thesis for acceptance; "we expect him to state his case clearly, to state the issues at stake as clearly as possible so that we know what we are being invited to accept." He should clearly and distinctly show us why we must accept his case. A number of ethno-philosophers, indeed many of them, fall short of these and other expectations. It is precisely on this account that we find their work philosophically unacceptable.

> The pity is that ethno-philosophers usually fall in love so much with the thought system they seek to expound that they become dogmatic in the veneration of the culture to which the thought system belongs. They hardly see why others may refuse totally to share their esteem for the system they describe. They do not raise philosophical issues about the system (because for them no problems arise once we 'understand' the system); therefore they do not attempt to give a philosophical justification of the belief system or of issues that arise in it.[19]

He and others who share the same point of view do not therefore; reject the project of ethno-philosophers because they consider the outcome of their research unworthy of a philosopher's attention, or their work unscholarly. It would be unbecoming of an African philosopher to *deliberately* ignore the study of the traditional belief systems of his people. His role should rather be that of objective criticism. His critical study of traditional societies may be an answer to the problems of today. If the problem he is treating is philosophical, then it must be universally relevant to all men.

So for Bodunrin, philosophy is basically a conscious creation. For him, one's philosophy is always his conscious reflection on his beliefs. It is not just enough to have men capable of philosophical dialogue in Africa. Philosophers in Africa must be able to engage "in organized systematic reflections on the thoughts, beliefs and practices of their people."[20] He thus sees a philosopher's role as that of objective criticism. A philosopher's objective criticism of traditional societies may be an answer to the problems of today. However, a philosophical problem must have universal relevance.[21] Even if for him, writing is not a prerequisite for philosophy, it is an indispensable aspect of it. With regard to the definition of philosophy, he points out that "... the philosophy of a country or of the world is not definable in terms of the thought-content of the tradition nor in terms of the national origins of the thinkers."[22] He supports his position by noting that the very influential British philosophers such as Wittgenstein and Popper were not English by birth. Without explicitly saying so, he is obviously against Hountondji's definition of philosophy.

2. Western Root of Okere's Hermeneutics

Okere's philosophical thoughts have a number of similarities with those we considered in the preceding section. He on his part rejected the attempts made so far at the time to write African philosophy. His rejection is based mainly on two grounds: "the failure of these authors to realize that philosophy and culture (a) are heterogeneous and (b) must be mediated by preliminary hermeneutical work which comprises various levels."[23] He thus asserts unequivocally that African culture can give birth to an African philosophy only within the context of hermeneutics. Okere's hermeneutics has its basis and roots in western philosophy. The time is now ripe for us to explore this thesis in considerable detail. Firstly, we shall endeavor very briefly to answer the question: what is western philosophy?

Western Philosophy was born in a definite culture, in a world that already had its characteristic conception of reality. This conception of reality is generally regarded as naive view of the world. It is uncritical. The works of Homer and Hesiod give us valuable insights into this world. It was a world of mythology. They explained reality through poetry and mythology We do not mean here that poetry and myth are "irrational" in the sense that they are related to truth. Instead, they are non-rational in the sense that they attempted to explain things from a more abstract, unrestricted, or do we say "emotional" perspective. For instance, according to this mythological world-view, round the earth-disc, flowed the vast river Okeanos. This concept was of considerable importance in pre-scientific Greek thought. Okeanos is the river surrounding the earth, the source of all waters whether fresh or salt, which are enclosed within its orbit, on or under the earth. The earth-encircling river differs from other elements of the popular world-picture in that it is not so obviously based on experience.

However, at its inception in Ionia in the 6th century B.C., it was reflection that characterized philosophy. The birth of philosophy basically refers to the passage from myth to rationality, from the principle of explication of the world through the medium of beings that symbolically represent nature-zeus, the earth, the ocean et cetera to method of rational explication. Instead of studying the Athenian gods and their effects on nature, philosophy now pays attention to the study of the natural causes. It is the supremacy of reason over myth. The immediate result of this supremacy of reason over myth was the attempt by the pre-Socratic philosophers to respond to the decisive and basic question: of what material is this world made of? What characterized the various responses to this question was the personal reflection of each philosopher on the constitution of the world; the use of reason to identify the principles of all things. So, it is clear to us that philosophy at its birth tackled the questions concerning nature, the city and being. The response to the questions concerning nature led to the initial formulations of the basic notions of physics. The response to the questions concerning the city of men laid the foundation for aesthetics, ethics and political philosophy while the early discussions on being marked the birth of metaphysics.

Medieval thinkers differed according to their philosophical tradition, according to whether they were Platonists or, after the

Aristotelian revival in the 13th century, Aristotelians. The main dispute, however, was over the theories of universals. Since the dispute had theological implication, it was heated. The argument had its source in certain questions put by Porphyry, a disciple of Plotinus, about the exact status of species and universals, these questions, the answers to which Porphyry thought were obscure, were discussed by Boethius in a commentary. The main schools of thought on the subject were the realists, conceptualists, and nominalists. Realists thought the universals had an objective existence, although their view on this existence depended on whether they were Platonists or Aristotelians. Conceptualists held that universals existed only as concepts in the mind; nominalists held that the only universal things were words. A more pertinent stage to our work is the Renaissance period. Generally, the Renaissance is regarded as the period of literary, artistic and scientific renovation, which occurred in Europe from the second half of the 15th century to the 16th century. It is a period of rebirth and revival. It has many aspects. We are here principally concerned with the philosophical aspect. In philosophy, it is a period difficult to classify. Some regard it as a period when the medieval Christian faith is replaced by secularism. But it does not seem that Renaissance philosophers saw their role as such. They regarded themselves as devout and orthodox Christians in line with Bonaventure and Aquinas. They, therefore, differ from medieval philosophers in their ability to give philosophy a greater degree of independence over theology. They equally boldly gave unadulterated interpretation to Greek pagan philosophy. New themes were developed from this source. It was no longer the Greeks as interpreted by the medieval philosophers.

Above all, humanism is an important theme of the Renaissance. Generally, humanism designates notion that man is the supreme value and the foundation of all moral values. But Renaissance philosophy is humanist in a larger sense: in its concrete and total approach to man. The renaissance philosophy concerns itself with the fact about man's activity. It talks of what man does. Where Plato would talk of the ideal city, Machiaveli would simply consider the success and failure in the activity of government. The philosophy of this period also gave birth to a new science in the sense that the scientists of the renaissance brought about unique alterations in the mode of knowledge. The medieval thinkers read mainly the traditional texts. The scientists of this time laid emphasis on observation. They made use of controlled experiments and equally relied on mathematics to test their hypotheses. This made them supersede their predecessors: Aristotelian and medieval scientists. Experimental observation and mathematics thus characterized renaissance science.

The importance of this period to our subject is that it ushered in a climate of re-awakening. Before this time, the problem of hermeneutics was mainly a biblical problem. This time, the problem is focused to a different region. This was principally owing to the discovery of the ancient literature of Rome and Greece. This gave a new impetus to the science of hermeneutics. Okere observes that the "humanists set themselves the task of mastering the classical languages with a view to appropriating the enormous classical tradition deposited in literature and philosophy." This in deed marked the beginning of philological hermeneutics. It brought the problem again to the forefront. Okere once again remarks that in both cases, "the classics and the Bible, hermeneutics aimed at re-discovering the original meaning of the texts by an appropriate technique." The question in both cases was on the one hand, the foreign languages and on the other hand, "the rediscovering of something that was not altogether new and unknown but whose meaning had been blurred."[25]

Another stage that inevitably merits our attention is the Enlightenment. It was an intellectual movement, which began in England in the seventeenth century and developed in France in the eighteenth century. Virtually every European country, and every sphere of life and thought, was affected by it. Reason is man's central capacity, and it enables him not only to think, but also to act, correctly. Man is by nature rational and good. It follows that both the individual and humanity as a whole can progress to perfection. In a certain sense, the Enlightenment could be said to be 'unhistorical'. This is because it holds that all men are at all times and in all places fundamentally the same in nature and that the difference between them that has arisen over history is superficial and dispensable. The Enlightenment, therefore, devalues local prejudices and customs, which owe their development to historical peculiarities rather than to the exercise of reason. We can interpret this to mean that what matters to the Enlightenment is not whether one is

European or African, but that one is an individual man, united in brother-hood with all other men by the rationality one shares with them. Okere holds the view that this period is of unique importance in the develop-ment of hermeneutics. It prescribed the constitution of the generality and unity of the hermeneutical problem that became recognizable at the time. There was "the tendency to treat all texts, religious or profane, biblical or philological from the same standpoint, the hermeneutical standpoint." It was the beginning of the historico-critical method. "This method provides for fidelity to the text, a fidelity guaranteed by a continuous and critical verification of the text itself." [26]

The philosophy of Hegel could by all standards be said to be the most profound manifestation of reason. He is credited with the notion that thought governs reality, instead of the other way round. His philoso-phy emerged from the unique ordering of a set of distinctive themes. The first of these was his affirmation not only that reason is the guide to reality but, finally, that the rational is the real, and conversely. The rational and the real are identified. The second theme concerns the constancy of change in the universe. In the manner of Heraclitus, Hegel gives emphasis to the role of opposites, and of opposition, in the analysis of change. We should also add to these a belief in progress and a belief in God. One can easily discern the outline of a system of thought in which these could be affirmed jointly. The view would stress process over product; the process would embody progress; but the progress could come only through opposition. It would be a troubled process leading to the unfolding of new qualities through the tension of the opposites involved in the process itself. The emergent quality might preserve the relevant values of the opposed points of view within a higher synthesis. The pattern of opposition in physical processes and in reason would need to be identical in structure. Also every achieved standpoint would be partial and one-sided, neither utterly false nor utterly true. The process would continue indefinitely. The consequence is that if the world is under the control of God then the entire process might be appropriately interpreted as the divine Reason realizing itself in history.

It should be emphasized here that Hegel is credited with increas-ing the attention paid to history. That is, in a sense Hegel has historicized the world. Thus in *The Phenomenology of the Spirit*, Hegel develops the successive steps by which spirit rises from individual sensation to universal reason. While the abstract universals of the understanding are inert and lifeless, the ideas of reason have something like carriers and lives of their own. The ideas of Reason are Notions, which are at once implicitly universal, particular, and singular. They relate to other universal ideas, to further ideational specification, and to particular instances of themselves. Notions are self-specifying and self-particularizing. Hegel calls them "concrete universals." Their unusual nature is what makes the Dialectic possible and necessary. According to Okere, Hegel represents the apotheosis of the "unlimited belief in Reason." With regard to Christian religion, he understood the contents "as moments in the self-development and self-revelation of the absolute spirit in the world and in history." There is thus an integration of revelation in the Hegelian system. It now becomes a system where reality and thought; that is reason becomes identified. A significant point to make is that it is generally agreed that the collapse of the Hegelian system "in a way marked the end of the entire tradition of the logos philosophy starting from the Greeks and spanning the whole history of western thought." The implication of Hegel's principle of reason for hermeneutics is that "it becomes hardly distinguishable from the history of theology and philosophy."[27] Okere further identifies two key concepts that contributed to the final and general rejection of Hegel's idealism and rationalism. They are, "the ideas of life and existence." So existential philosophy and philosophy of life became subsequently the successors of idealism. This collapse marked a turning point in the history of hermeneutics. It is to this that we now turn our attention.

3. What is Hermeneutics?

We are now so to say at the core of our work. But first of all, let us give a brief explication of the term, hermeneutics. We shall now examine the main hermeneutical currents to see the indispensable role they play in the shaping of Okere's hermeneutics.

Etymologically, hermeneutics is from the Greek, *hermeneuein*: to express, to explain, to interpret, to say. The adjectival form is *hermeneutikos,* the art of interpretation (called by Schleiermacher, "the art of understanding" and by Gadamer, "the art of technique of understanding and interpretation") Historically, the noun, *hermeneia* refers to the Greek wing-footed messenger-god Hermes, whose function is associated with announcing, promulgating and interpreting the mind of the gods. In ancient mythology, Hermes is used to translate what is originally beyond human understanding into a form that is humanly understandable. Hence in its various nuances, hermeneutics suggests the process of bringing a thing or situation or text from unintelligibility to intelligibility. The problem of hermeneutics concerns the nature of the act of understanding in relation to the interpretation of texts. Deriving from the need for interpretation in the studies of rhetoric and of scripture, the art came to be applied to any text. Even scientists, to make the scope of hermeneutics universal, may be said to be studying the text of nature.

The word itself is not modern. It is already known since Greek antiquity. It appeared in classical Greek in the works of Plato. In the Alexandrian period, it designated various things: translation of foreign texts or combination of ancient texts. The central idea, however, remain: to render language understandable be it foreign or obscure or difficult language by means of reformulations, of transpositions. We should note that translation is only a part of this activity of transposition. In this context, cultural difference can mean the same thing as different language. Interpretation can then mean the same thing as translating a foreign language.

The Greek *hermeneutike (techne)* is the "art of interpretation". It came to be rendered in Latin as *ars interpretandi* as it is used in Latin Christian exegesis. It became important after the Reformation, when Protestants needed to interpret the Bible accurately. Medieval hermeneutics ascribed to the Bible four levels of meaning: literal, allegorical, tropological (moral), and analogical (eschatological). But the Reformation insisted on literal or 'grammatical' exegesis and on the study of Hebrew and Greek.

In the 18th century, the term, *Hermeneutik* reappeared in Germany. This reappearance took place in a certain cultural situation, which was determined by three problems:
- The relationship between biblical exegesis and the philology of profane classical texts
- The development of historical sciences. Within this context, the question was: what is history? What is the place of history in the human

sciences?
- The debate at the end of the 19th century on the concept of *verstehen* (understanding) in relation to explanation in the natural sciences.

It is, therefore, the accumulation of the three problems that is at the base of the rebirth of the problem of hermeneutics. In interpreting history and thought, hermeneutics denies both that there is a single objective true interpretation transcending all viewpoints and that we are forever confined within our own viewpoint. Interpretation is rather something to be arrived at by a gradual display between the subject-matter and the interpreter's initial position.

4. The Main Actors in Modern Hermeneutics

We shall now examine the main hermeneutical currents to see the indispensable role they play in the shaping of Okere's hermeneutics. It basically consists in a considerable analysis of the following figures: Schleiermacher, Dilthey, Heidegger, and Gadamer.

Schleiermacher was a professor of New Testament in Halle at the time he got the hermeneutical inspiration. A text has two points of view: 'grammatical', in relation to the language in which it is written, and 'psychological', in relation to the mentality and development of the author. We cannot gain complete understanding of either of these aspects, since we cannot have complete knowledge of a language or a person. He identifies two faults in the philology of his age:
- Philology presents only particular rules. This is the source of the problem of understanding how to elevate exegesis to the status of *Kunstlehre*, that is technology which is not just a collection of simple operation without connection.
- Hermeneutic is found here and there in various disciplines especially in classical philology and biblical exegesis. He proposes a *general hermenutics* which goes beyond particular applications and the characteristics of which should be found in the two major areas of hermeneutics. Defining hermeneutics as "the art of avoiding misunderstandings", he stressed both grammatical, and technical or psychological interpretation. His main application of hermeneutics is to Scripture. Beyond scripture, however, his techniques could be applied to any individual work cast in language and, beyond lan-

guage, to all human manifestation, including conversations and works of art. So the presupposition that there is exegesis or philology only with regard to ancient texts, in particular foreign languages should be dismissed. It is true that historically the problem of exegesis came out of the difficulty posed by Hebrew, Greek, et cetera; but historical distance is only one case of the real distance that gave rise to the problem of understanding. This difficulty is connected to the *central act, "Die Rede" - Speech-act.* For Schleiermacher speech-act is every thought which is expressed in signs. These signs could be forms of speech or written texts. There is further the tension between the intention to speak and the verbal vehicle. This is what raises the problem of hermeneutics. One now understands in what measure the problem of understanding goes beyond the living languages. It is not the language as ancient but the speech as foreign/strange/unknown which poses the problem of hermeneutics. Foreign languages or ancient authors constitute only particular or extreme cases.

We can now precisely state that there is problem of hermeneutics each time that there is cultural distance, each time we are separated geographically, by time or by culture. In all, it concerns *bringing nearer what is farther away.* What is fundamental is the relationship between the other and myself. Technically, therefore, it is the view of Schleiermacher that there is hermeneutics principally because there is misunderstanding. The critical problem of hermeneutics is always to correct the misunderstanding.

Okere ranks Schleiermacher with Ranke and Droysen. So like these two, Schleiermacher maintains that the correct understanding of a text cannot be separated from the perfect understanding of history. "The business of history is the construction of this hidden text. Just as the part can only be understood in relation to the whole, so can a historical event be understood only in relation to the sense of world history, a sense whose existence is presupposed."[29] In this sense, history is grasped in aesthetic-hermeneutical categories.

Wilhelm Dilthey, a German philosopher and Schleiermacher's biographer is regarded as a neo-Kantian philosopher; extending the Kantian analysis to history. He extended Kant's method to the cultural sciences (*Geisteswissenschften*). The sciences rest on lived experiences

(*Erlebnis*)-expression and understanding (Verstehen). It involves the lived experiences of our culture. He thus extended hermeneutics to the understanding of all human behavior and products. Our understanding of an author, artist, or historical agent is not direct, but by way of analogies to our own experience. We relive past decisions, et cetera in imaginative sympathy. The problem, he argued, was to develop a method for *understanding* human differences. But he believed that all of these were ultimately superficial and thus not incommensurable at all. Thus for him, interpretation or *verstehen* is a method for the historical and human sciences. There should be rules or criteria for understanding what an author or native "really" meant.

It is, therefore, with Dilthey that the general problem of understanding considerably goes beyond the interpretation of texts and gets to a more general level: that of the *knowledge of the other* and *historical understanding.* Let us note that history, art, religion, law express the spirit of their authors. We understand them by grasping this spirit. How is understanding of the other possible? It is in his first work: *Introduction to Human Sciences* (1883) that Dilthey gives his first contribution to the critic of historical reason. In his second work: *Ideas for a Descriptive and Analytic Psychology* (1894), he treats the important subject: How can a being who is in a historical time understand another being who is also in a historical time and how can this understanding attain the statute of science and not simply fugitive intuition. He answers the question by developing the notion *Zusammenhang* structures of togetherness, linking, connection. Life in its growth produces the forms. Life is the continuity and unity of all cultures (*Leben*). It enables us to relive (*nacherleben*) and thus understand the past. The historian employs categories such as 'meaning, value, purpose, development, ideal', which are not a priori but lie in the nature of life itself. Life has no single meaning. Our idea of its meaning is always changing and the purpose we set forth for the future conditions our account of the meaning of the past. Every expression of life stabilizes itself in a stable configuration. The possibility to understand the other depends on the capacity of the psychical life to lay down the acquired structure around which is organized man's evaluations: sentiments, will, representations, et cetera. Life is a process that produces norms. Life is norm itself. This is what Dilthey calls theological structure. It is this theological structure that makes the classification of historical attitudes in a general manner possible, that permits the introduction of conceptuality in the following orders: contingent, individual and singular. It is this production of an acquired structure that makes it possible for the social sciences to reconstruct proper types. This problem is also found in Max Weber and his ideal types.

Setting himself, therefore, the task of completing the Kantian set of critiques with a critique of the historical reason, Dilthey separated the natural sciences from the sciences of the spirit whose content is known somehow with one's whole life, and not in the abstract, partial manner in which we gain knowledge of the natural sciences. He considers our lives as part of the life of society and of history, a result of evolutionary processes. Historical relations replace substantive human natures. The sciences of the spirit are, therefore, primarily historical. And the information they seek cannot be gained apart from the method of understanding called *Verstehen*. This is experienced in situations. Such subtle and elusive meaningfulness qualifies the conclusions of the cultural and spiritual sciences.

Within this context, the basic questions are: How does Hermeneutics add a supplementary stage to the understanding of the other? What in effect does interpretation add to understanding? Dilthey answers these and similar questions in the essay: "Descriptive Psychology and Analytic Psychology." The internal perception of psychic states uses the understanding of the other to compliment itself. We complete the internal perception by the understanding of people foreign and external to us.

Also in "Contributions to the study of the individuality", the word hermeneutic is richer in meaning. It concerns the transfer of my proper self to a strange domain. It is also correlatively of transformation of this my proper self. It is the hermeneutic or critical method, which is not only utilized by the philologist and the historian but without which any social science is possible. There is, therefore, a hermeneutical moment in every science that has to do with the other. The fundamental act here is to reproduce the link, the entire structure by holding to the objective signs of life. To reproduce, to reconstruct by interpreting the objective signs this is the hermeneutical act. This means that every singularity moves to another singularity in favor of the domain that they have in common the domain of signs where each goes to lay down its proper intentions. So it is the research of the individual, which is at the base of the historical experience, which led to the addition of hermeneutics to psychology.

What should be emphasized is the notion of reproduction and reconstruction (*Nachbilden*). It is a recreation in favor of which the link with the other is placed at a distance, transmuted, clarified, done in a lighter and transparent atmosphere. The characteristic of hermeneutics becomes to add to the clarification of the *logos* the profound process and mystery of creation. It is a victory over the romantic obscurity. The point is that historical judgments and systems of philosophy, once defined, become inert; and history, since it is relative, has no final authority. Dilthey holds in fact, that historians are bound by the judgments of the ages in which they live -the doctrine is called Historicism and one can transcend his age only by entering imaginatively and uncritically into other ages. Thus, neither the historical judgment nor the philosophical system has the final word. Introducing the term *Weltanschauung* (world-view) to philosophy, Dilthey defined it as a comprehensive view of the universe and of man's place in it. World-views are projections of dominant personality traits: intellect dominant/naturalism; will dominant/libertarian idealism; feeling dominant/ objective idealism. He believed individuals could combine two of the three types, and that Descartes and Kant, for example, combined intellect and will.

The indispensable role that Dilthey plays in Okere's philosophical hermeneurics cannot but be glaring. It does not, therefore, surprise us when he observes that the "ideas of Erlebnis (experience), Leben (life) and Struktur (structure) are the operative concepts of Dilthey. Leben, life - delimits the specific area of human sciences as distinct from the lifeless and abstract forms, which form the object of the natural sciences. To understand the human, one has to understand it as lived - erlebt." Dilthey thus conceives objects of knowledge as "objectivations of life." It should be recalled that Dilthey borrowed his idea of structure from the romantics. It is often illustrated by the unifying and centralizing role, which a musical motif plays in a movement. This in turn "designates for the human sciences, the matrix of ideas and forces which constitutes the unit of meaning."[30] When this notion is applied to history, an epoch would constitute such a meaning-matrix. It is *Bedeutungszusammenhang.*

With Heidegger, we are brought face-to-face with the revolution brought about by *Sein und Zeit* with regard to the fundamental problem. Hermeneutics is no longer the extension of the problem of methodology raised by the exegesis of the sacred or profane texts, by philology, by psychology, by the theory of culture. The hermeneutical problem now concerns a new question how do we know? We now ask, "what is the mode of being of this being which exists only by understanding. The focus of Heidegger's phenomenological analysis is human existence, although the object of the quest is a rediscovery of being (sein). In the ontological perspective, one looks at the world from the standpoint of being. This is also the existential standpoint. His term for human existence is Dasein, meaning simply "being there." The term signals at once both the mystery and arbitrariness in one's being where and as one is. Okere in this respect opines that Heidegger in a unique way "widens the concept of hermeneutics to embrace all quest of meaning starting from the interpretation of Dasein."[31]   So the problem of hermeneutics now concerns the ontological constitution of understanding. It "is originally hermeneutics of Dasein which becomes the basis of all philosophy and of scientific methodology."[32] But even if one is hurled (from *werfen*) into the world, still one possesses freedom. Heidegger's philosophy centers in the uses of this freedom. One decides for example to live authentically, or allows oneself to be inauthentic. To live authentically is to discover oneself in direct relation to the things-that-are; it is to be capable of genuine understanding and originative thinking; and it is to be capable of genuine discourse. To be inauthentic is to be characterized by a kind of ambiguity in which one's relation is to the crowd and the requirements of daily life rather than to oneself; one substitutes curiosity and calculative thinking for genuine understanding (and one substitutes "prattle" for discourse). To live authentically, grasping the structure of time, being there among the things that is, while appreciating the possible, is living with *Verstehen*. *Verstehen* relates one in devotion to *seiendes*, the things that are. To experience the world from this standpoint is to take the ontic perspective. It is also the *existenziell* standpoint. *Verstehen* leads to *Ek-sistenz.* This stands in contrast to the life in which one relates to the things that are by concern for the *Zuhandenen,* the instruments which provide control of things and take up one's time. So the problem of hermeneutics now concerns the ontological constitution of understanding.[33]

From the introduction of *Sein und Zeit*, the forgotten question of being is announced as *Auslegung;* that is, an exegesis, and an interpretation. There is a reversal of the theory of knowledge by the interrogation that precedes it and which concerns the way a being is a being before it becomes an object before a subject. The philosophy of Heidegger begins by a challenge against the pretension of putting the question of method before the investigation of the thing in itself. It aims at subordinating the method to the object. Heidegger borrowed this approach from the Husserlian phenomenology, the famous slogan: to the things themselves. This is a challenge to every pretension to subordinate the things to the methodology that precedes examination. This explains why section seven of the introduction develops in a manner non-Husserlian (non-transcendental and non-idealist) the two parts of the word phenomenology. 'Phenomen' signifies that which shows itself in itself, the manifest. Accordingly, phenomena are the totality of what lies in the light of day or can be brought to the light; what the Greeks sometimes identified simply with entities. *Logos* signifies to show, to make manifest. This is the Heideggerian return to the Greek meaning of the term instead of the German usage as found in Kant, the post-Kantian and Husserl. It puts aside the transcendental phenomenology. Heidegger thus reforms the idea of truth. Truth no longer signifies coherence nor verification. It is a *manifestation*. This implies a warning: never prescribe procedures before the study itself; it is the mode of being of the object that dictates the method. This is the meaning of: leave the things to be seen.

But why is this task that of hermeneutics? After saying that philosophy is possible only as phenomenology and having insisted that behind the phenomen, there is nothing, Heidegger now characterizes this phenomenological ontology as hermeneutics. Between the thing which has left itself to be seen and manifestation, Heidegger sees a narrow relationship between it and authentic understanding. It is because the question of being is forgotten that phenomenology is hermeneutics. The trilogy - situation, understanding, and interpretation - is of unique significance here. When one is treating the trilogy, one is already depending heavily on the theory of sign and signification that belong to the structure of worldness as such. It is in this preliminary analysis and in the movement of pole-world and pole-there that the trilogy, situation, understanding and interpretation manifest itself. What is common to the trilogy is the existential constitution of there.

The first term is *Befindlichkeit*: to be found (well or bad, to be in a mood), to be found (there), to feel. This precedence of the sentiment of situation has a considerable hermeneutical signification. It is this relation of taking root or having a *locus standi* that assures in a way the firmness of every linguistic system and, therefore, of the books and texts in something that is not primordially a phenomenon of articulation or speech-act. Okere identifies three fundamental characteristics of *Befindlichkeit*. The first is the existential of *Geworfenheit*. It denotes the reality of being thrown into existence. What is abundantly clear to *Dasein* is the fact that he is - *Dass es ist.* The second concerns the fact that the disposition is both original and entirely embraces all possible experience. The result is that the structure of *Dasein* is thus revealed -*In-der-Welt-sein.* The third is *Betroffenheit, Dasein* has the capability to be affected. Generally, this is related to the various elements of *In-der-Welt-sein*. It is this characteristic receptivity that constitutes existentially the openness of *Dasein* to the world. Okere further points out two ways in which the doctrine of *Befindlichkeit* is of unique importance. Firstly, "as *Geworfenheit* (Being thrown into it), it underlies the pure facticity of man's historical existence. One finds himself as it were there, without being consulted. One does not choose one's history, one's culture, one's language. One is born into them." Secondly, this doctrine "makes it possible for *Dasein* to be appealed to, to be receptive, to be concerned. But *Dasein* can discover and open up the world because it is predisposed to it by *Betroffenheit*. It contributes to a more penetrating understanding of the constitution of the world." The sentiment of situation makes use of certain sentiments like fear and anguish not for existentialist reasons but in order to attain contact with reality more fundamental than the relationship of subject-object. By the act of knowing, we have always the object in front of us. The sentiment of situation is more firmly rooted than knowing.

Next is the consideration of *Dasein* as *verstehen*. This like *Befindlichkeit* charaterizes *Dasein* as Being-in-the-world. In ordinary language, verstehen means understanding something and how to handle it. It implies the aptitude to do something. Basically, verstehen has a project character (*Entwurfscharakter*) *Entwurf* means plan, project. The term stresses that all our behaviour towards the world is projected as a possibility. It follows that the first function of understanding is to orient us. Just as we are first and foremost beings that are situated, we are also beings, which have possibilities of being oriented. The function of understanding is to outline the projects orientation. What are important is not the taking cognizance of a fact but essentially the apprehension of a possibility of being. Understanding a text is not to find the passive meaning that it contains. It is to open up the possibility of being indicated by text. Understanding in Heidegger is essentially a *throwness.* More exactly, it is the meeting point of being-situated and being-projected that constitutes the act of understanding. Heidegger uses the beautiful expression, *thrown possibility.* We are, therefore, abandoning the classical image of judge and tribunal. Understanding projects the being there in an original way towards the worldness of the world. As a being there, it is always already projected and remains a project as long as it is. The project is not at the level of existential choice but at the level of ontological conditions of the constitutions of a being, which is to be.

In interpretation, it is not the methodology of exegesis that is our primary concern.   Interpretation is above all to make explicit (*Auslegung*). It is a development of understanding, a development that does not transform it into something else but makes it become itself.[34]

Heidegger introduces the important words: *Vorhabe, Vorsicht,* and *Vorgriff.*
Vorhabe: 'what we have in advance' or 'what we have before us.' It is something we have in advance, 'fore-having.'
Vorsicht: 'that we see in advance', fore-sight, caution, prudence.
Vorgriff: 'what we grasp in advance', 'foreconception'.

Each time something is interpreted as something, the interpretation will be founded essentially upon fore-having, fore-sight, fore-conception. In an interpretative approach, there lies such an assumption as that which has been taken for granted with the interpretation as such, that is to say, as that which has been presented in our fore-having, our fore-sight and our fore-conception.[35]

Okere acknowledges that Heidegger's hermeneutics is unmistakably significant in the shaping of his own hermeneutics. Thus, he is of the opinion that philosophy "is also an interpretation, a making explicit of one's understanding of one's self and one's world." The very concept of interpretation implies that it works only with presuppositions; that is, "within the framework of a certain culture."[36] Okere's conclusion is that Heidegger in his "magisteral exposition....has identified philosophy as the activation of man's natural inclination and privilege to give meaning to reality. In practice it boils down to a thematic explicitation of an implicit understanding of the meaning of being." It is this explicit meaning that is an interpretation or do we better say hermeneutics. While giving meaning to reality, man's effort is inevitably colored with his own perspective, which is determined by his own very constitution. Okere does not fail to point out that constitutionally "man is inescapably time-bound, historical, contextual and relative, relative that is, to his immediate environment." His perspective cannot, therefore, but be marked by these same characteristics. An obvious question now is: what does meaning-giving consist in? Okere answers by saying that it "consists in building up, out of the elements of one's environment, a complex of references and relationships". He further asserts unequivocally that "man's ultimate interpretation, his philosophy will be necessarily historical and culture-bound, articulated relatively to his environment and world, His environment will prescribe the terminology, provoke the questions and predetermine the answers." What advantage does this have for philosophy? The first is that it is "the most revolutionary result of the hermeneutical movement." Philosophy no longer teaches us just how to read and understand ancient authors nor is it any longer an x-ray of the art of philosophizing; above all and pre-eminently "it becomes the Magna Charta of all those of other cultures who aim to build up a philosophical tradition which will be more than a mere footnote on the pages of Greek and Western Philosophy."[37]

Another western philosopher that played a key role in the development of Okere's philosophical hermeneutics is Gadamer. In *Truth and Method (Wahrheit und Methode, Grundzüge einer philosophischen Hermeneutik)* Gadamer treats disciplines like philosophy, theology, legal theories and literary criticisms in the light of understanding, interpretation and application in concrete life situations. The various parts of the work underscore the fact that the problem of hermeneutics, that is, the problem of understanding and interpretation, is not the problem of method. Thus truth and method are not models of under-standing and interpretation. Hermeneutics is not concerned primarily with the verification of knowledge (truth) and the methodology of doing so (method).

The central question in Gadamer's investigation is the nature of understanding, particularly as it is revealed in hermeneutic study. Understanding for Gadamer is a dialogue. In a true dialogue, no one party determines the truth. Rather each is open to the contributions of the other. Understanding as dialogue is a three-way process. First there is the person who comes to understand. Secondly, there is the interlocutor - the person or text he comes to an understanding with. Then there is the subject of their understanding. The subject or something to be under-stood is not just an individual opinion. When we understand, we under-stand not just the person's view or opinion, but we also consider the validity of such a view in our own concrete existential situation. Understanding has language as its medium. Language is the interactive or communicative medium, which provides the common ground for understanding. It is, therefore, indispensable to the relativity and historicity of understanding. Toeing the line of Heidegger, Gadamer emphasizes that language is a possibility. All our thinking and indeed all our experience find their setting within language. The approach to language here is different from that of linguistics or philosophers of language. These think of language in terms of the imposition of limits to our world. Language should rather be "conceived more as an orientation than a limitation." The character of language as universal is also inevita-ble. Okere identifies Gadamer's unique insight here. "It is the develop-ment of the idea of openness of language and of its creativity that Gadamer arrives at insights which prove very fruitful because in show-ing the relation between language and philosophy it exemplarily illustrates the purpose and process of philosophising."[38]

From the foregoing, Gadamer subdivided hermeneutics as follows: understanding (*subtitatis intelligendi*), interpretation (*subtitatis explicandi*) and application (*subtitatis applicandi*). These are the elements of the process of understanding. The three are interwoven. Interpretation does not come after understanding, rather understanding is always interpretation and interpretation is the explicit form of under-standing. These two lead to the third element - application. So understanding implies applying the text in the concrete life situation of the interpreter. Understanding is always application. Interpretation is of four kinds: cognitive, normative, reproductive and performative. All these constitute one unitary phenomenon. To separate them is to separate what originally belong to a whole.

It must be clear by now that Gadamer gave hermeneutics a wider look. Okere sees the main contribution of Gadamer to the hermeneutical discuss as being "to spell out the implications of Heidegger's pregnant but often cryptic statements about man's destiny as a meaning giver and as interpreter of Being."[39] Thus hermeneutics for Gadamer is no longer the act of interpretation or of historical understanding only; rather it acquired the dimension of application in practical life situation. It is no longer limited to the theoretical interpretation of sacred scripture or legal code but it embraces their application to existential circumstances. Hermeneutic thus becomes a performative system of understanding and interpretation. So it follows that an absolute truth would be a truth without context. This would naturally be meaningless to mortals who can only live and understand within a limited horizon. The implication this has for us according to Okere "is that all philosophical discourse is first and foremost an answer to problems and questions raised within a questioning horizon which means always, a culture."[40] He thereby rehabilitates the notion of prejudice. Thus, "to know we must already have known; to know explicitly we must first know implicitly,.... We get out of a thing only what we have put into it. There is no open discourse without hidden presuppositions; no explicit statement without an implicit, subterranean, subconscious background. There is no reflection except against a background of the unreflected."[41]

The undeniable result of the illumination, which Okere received from Gadamer's hermeneutics, is his assertion that there is a relationship "between any philosophy and its culture." Philosophy is always the interpretation of reality within a certain culture. It follows then that the relationship between philosophy and culture is "governed by the dialectics of background to foreground, of presupposition to explicit statement, of prejudgment to judgment..." In this relationship, both play definite roles. While culture "plays the role of background, presupposition and prejudgment" philosophy on its own side "plays the role of foreground, thematic statement and explicit judgment."[42]

5. Conclusion

It should by now have become clear that western philosophy played an indispensable role in the shaping of Okere's philosophical hermeneutics. We should at this time recall Okere's original objective: a critical inquiry into the possibility of African philosophy. If African philosophy is possible, the next question is, how? As a method of inquiry, Okere opted for a historical phenomenological approach. It is here that the context of his hermeneutics differs from those of the key players we saw earlier. While Schleiermacher situates hermeneutics within a systematic theory of interpretation of texts and speech, Dilthey his biographer extended hermeneutics to the understanding of all human behaviour and products. In his *Being and Time,* Heidegger gives hermeneutics a deeper and wider meaning. It is concerned with the interpretation of the being who interprets texts and other artifacts, who may become, but is not essentially, either a natural or a cultural scientist: the human being or *Dasein.* Heidegger's student, Hans Georg Gadamer is generally regarded as the most important proponent of hermeneutics. He was so wary of the fact that method - and not only the scientific method - may distort our understanding that he insists that hermeneutics must resist the temptation to become another method. His, is an attempt to overcome methods, to dispense with the overemphasis on proofs and arguments and the quest for certainty and emphasize instead the shared understandings that we already have with one another. The substance of philosophy then becomes dialogue rather than individual phenomenology or abstract proofs. Interpretation thus becomes not an abstract function of the intellect but a process that permeates our every activity. Paul Ricoeur finds himself within the setting of the relationship between culture and philosophy. Ricoeur chooses the method of philosophical hermeneutics for this relationship. This consists essentially in a reflection of the symbols of a given culture and the objectivations of life as found in the said culture. For Ricoeur, therefore, philosophy is a reflection on symbols; but it is a distinctive type of reflection, concrete reflection. More than any other western philosopher, Ricoeur's context seem to be the nearest to that of Okere. However, Okere ingeniously develops both Ricoeur's hermeneutics and those of his predecessors within the context

of a definite culture, African culture. Thus he makes two explicit
statements concerning the possibility of African philosophy. First is that
a reflection on symbols "with a view to making the implicit meanings
explicit would constitute African philosophy." From the assertion that
symbols give food for thought (*le symbole donne a penser*), he makes
the second assertion that a "philosophical interpretation of the symbols
of African cultures would be African philosophy."[43] He concretizes
these assertions with a hermeneutical analysis of a definite African
culture, the culture of the Igbo people of Nigeria. We should also add
that Husserl's intentionality equally played a unique role in the development of Okere's hermeneutics. However, point that should not in any
way be forgotten is that Okere's context is the heated debate on the
possibility of African philosophy. At the initial stage of our work, we
saw the contributions of Maurier, Ramose, Hountondji, and Bodunrin to
this debate.

It must be pointed out that Okere's presentation of his hermeneutics presents a unique difficulty. It is that of distinguishing precisely the
basic contents of his hermeneutics from the key players of European
philosophy. More precisely, one can hardly distinguish Okere's hermeneutics from the hermeneutics of Ricoeur. However, viewed from
another perspective, this shortcoming could be translated into Okere's
unique contribution to philosophy as a whole. It is his commitment to the
universality of the philosophical enterprise. It is here that he distinguishes himself in a remarkable way from some other African thinkers
who contributed to the debate on the possibility of African philosophy.
Hountondji comes to mind readily in this regard. He defines African
philosophy as "a set of texts, specifically the set of texts written by
Africans and described as philosophical by their authors themselves."[44]
After demolishing ethnophilosophy as enunciated by Tempels, he
proposes a new way in which African philosophy can exist, *"au sens
d'une littérature produite par des Africains et traitant de problèmes
philosophiques."*[45] That is, as a literature produced by Africans concerning philosophical problems. So for Hountondji, *Bantu philosophy* does
not qualify as African Philosophy while Kagame's *La Philosophie
Bantu-Rwandaise de l'etre* qualifies because it is written by an African.
So while Okere emphasizes philosophical method and rigor as a condition for valid African philosophy, Hountondji replaces them with the

nationality of the author. For Okere, a work with such an orientation can hardly qualify as philosophy. For him, philosophy is hermeneutics. He states clearly the practical implication of this. It is that philosophy "is not an abstract science; it is a statement of meaning by a person committed to life and to reality and eager to relate himself to life and reality ..." To do philosophy, therefore, is to interpret one's culture. For us, black African philosophers it means "familiarity and identification" with our culture. The advantage of this identification is that it enables us "to articulate authentically at that ultimate level of meaning which is properly the philosophical, the peculiar understanding of life and reality embedded in our culture." It is in this way that "a culture can speak by itself, of itself, and for itself." This is both a self-interpretation and a self-assertion. According to Okere, it "is no doubt the best way to restore self-confidence to a humiliated culture." [46]

Notes

[1] Henri Maurier, *Philosophie de l'afrique noire,* Anthropos-Institut e.V., 1985, p. 16.

[2] Henri Maurier, "Do we have an African Philosophy?" in Richard A. Wright (ed.) *African Philosophy* An *Introduction*, New York: University Press of America, 1984, p.26.

[3] Ibid., p.28.

[4] Ibid., p.31.

[5] Ibid., p.35.

[6] *Philosophie de l'afrique noire*, pp.73-74.

[7] Ibid., p.16.

[8] Ibid., p. 17.

[9] Mogobe B. Ramose, *African Philosophy through Ubuntu,* Harere: Mond Books, 2002, p. 34.

[10] Ibid.,

[11] Ibid., p. 35.

[12] Ibid.,

[13] Paulin J, Hountondji, *African Philosophy, Myth and Reality* trans. Henri Evans, London: Hutchinson University Library for Africa, 1983, p. 34.

[14] Ibid., p. 45.

[15] Ibid., p. 51.

[16] Ibid., p. 62.

[17] Ibid., p. 63.

[18] P.O. Bodunrin, "The Question of African Philosophy" in Richard A. Wright (ed.), African Philosophy, New York: University Press of America,3rd. Ed. pp.11- 12.

[19] Ibid., p. 13.

[20] Ibid., p. 10.

[21] Ibid., p. 14.

[22] Ibid., p. 19.

[23] Theophilus Okere, *African Philosophy, a Historico-Hermeneutical Investigation of the Conditions of its Possibility*, Lanham: University Press of America, 1983, p. 15.

[24] Bernard Stevens, *Cours d'Initiation A la Philosophie,* Louvain-La-Neuve: Ciaco, 1986, p. 11.

[25] Theophilus Okere, *African Philosophy*, p. 20.

[26] Ibid., p. 21.

[27] Ibid., p. 22.

[28] Ibid., p. 24.

[29] Ibid., p. 25.

[30] Loc. Cit.

[31] Ibid., p. 36

[32] Ibid., p. 37.

[33] Ibid., pp. 50-51

[34] Martin Heidegger, *Being and Time,* p. 188.

[35] Ibid., p. 193.

[36] Theophilus Okere, *African Philosophy*, p. 53.

[37] Ibid., p.54.

[38] Ibid., p. 72.

[39] Ibid., p. 65.

[40] Ibid., p. 64.

[41] Ibid., p. 65.

[42] Ibid., p. 65.

[43] Ibid., p. 115.

[44] Paulin J. Hountondji, *African Philosophy,* p. 33.

[45] Paulin J. Hountondji, *Sur la "Philosophie Africaine,"* Paris: Francois Maspero, 1977, p.41

[46] Theophilus Okere, *African Philosophy,* p.128.

7

Philosophy: A Particularist Interpretation With Universal Appeal

M.B. Ramose

1. Introduction

Time and fate seem to be companions that often compel the human being to ask basic questions about the individual self. Quite often many human beings pose questions such as the following: Why was I born at all? Why is it that I was born exactly at that particular time? Where do I come from and, where am I going? Perhaps time is a wise human invention to try and make sense of the questions posed. Without the illusion of time it might be impossible to know who I am. And once I do not know who I am then I might have to conclude that I exist only by chance. Because of the contingency of my existence it is unnecessary to bother about my destiny or fate. I simply must accept that if there is no satisfactory answer to the question, "where do I come from" then there is no need to be concerned about where I am going either. Fate, like time, is a wise human invention to give meaning to the question of identity and change.

The preceding questions as well as the wise inventions that go together with them may be interpreted in many different ways. For example, the question where do I come from and, where am I going may be considered to be geographical. It may be just an inquiry about the location and identity of a place. The map as a product of geography may be of particular importance in this inquiry. Coupled with the question concerning the exact date of birth, it may also be construed as an actuarial question decisive in determining insurance risks. In this essay, all three questions are construed as philosophical. From this perspective, it is no wonder that Theophilus Okere, in his long and glittering journey as a philosopher born in Nigeria, found it fitting to be editor of the book, *Identity and Change, Nigerian Philosophical Studies 1.*[1]

Thirteen years before he edited the book referred to above, Okere manifested his interest in the philosophical question of identity and change. This happened with the publication of his book on African philosophy.[2] It is therefore fitting, in my appreciation of Okere's illustrious voyage as a philosopher, to reflect upon his thinking on the identity of African philosophy in the continual flux of change in the African condition.

2. Identity

The experience and concept of identity has been a matter of particular philosophical interest. In everyday life the meaning of identity seems rather obvious, for example, in talk about "identity papers." For Okere it is necessary to define and describe the identity of "philosophy" and, in particular "African philosophy". Interestingly, he moves along two paths in fulfilling this necessity. The one path is the philosophical. Along this path he engages in an in-depth and extensive investigation into the meaning of "philosophy." The second path is the everyday life. In this path he takes the meaning of the term "Africa" for granted. It is as if everybody understands and accepts the meaning of the term. But this is not the case. Many scholars have and continue to probe into the meaning of the term "Africa". In order to fill the void created by Okere's omission to inquire into the meaning of the term "Africa", it is fitting to focus briefly on the meaning of the term.

In the chapter with the significant title, "The universe according to Europe" Ali Mazrui investigates the origin and meaning of the term "Africa". He concedes that the term might be of Semitic and Greco-Roman origin. But the

> application of the name in more recent centuries has been due almost entirely to western Europe. ... we should question Europe's decisions about boundaries of Africa and the identity of Africans. ... We have to accept the continental definition as presently defined internationally. But I personally regard the present boundaries of Africa as not only arbitrary but artificially conceived by European geographers in a former era of European dominance. For the purpose of this book I accept the Red Sea

as one of Africa's boundaries but I do so decidedly under protest.[3]

Indeed "Europe's decisions about boundaries of Africa and the identity of Africans" should be questioned on political and ethical grounds. Imposing a name on a people without their consent is politically unjustified. It is an invitation to the rejection of the name. If the name is accepted at all it will be so "under protest". Although many post-colonial countries have not expressly rejected the name Africa, some have deliberately reverted to indigenous names which are considered to be consistent with their sense of identity. We know, for example, of Botswana and no longer Bechuanaland. Similarly, we have Namibia instead of South West Africa and, Zimbabwe. Ethically, it is unfair and unjust to alter and distort the identity of another without legitimate and sufficient cause for doing so. This reversion to names that the indigenous peoples of a community identify with shows the importance that they attach to their culture and history. According to this sense of identity, the cultural-historical name takes priority over the name Africa. The latter still remains part of their identity but at a secondary level. On this basis, the continual questioning of "Europe's decisions about boundaries of Africa and the identity of Africans" remains a legitimate political and ethical necessity. This, however, is not always without pain and suffering as the experience of the struggle for Biafra in Nigeria shows. It is apparent that for the indigenous peoples conquered in the unjust wars waged by the Romans and under the umbrella of colonization, their identity is deeply embedded in their history and culture. Accordingly, African philosophy cannot dispense with the history of Africa in general and, in particular the history of philosophy. In this connection Osuagwu argues as follows.

> To a certain extent we are rewriting history, to set the defective aspects of the historical status quo aright, so that the authentic image and genuine roles of Africans by birth as by other associations or qualifications will properly and honourably appear. This is only being true and just to history made by Africans as by others within and without Africa. In conducting their historical essay, African philosophers want to rectify the historical prejudices of negation, indifference, severance and oblivion that have plagued African philosophy in the hands of European devil's advocates and their African accomplices. African historical

investigations in philosophy go beyond defense, confrontations and corrections. They are also authentic projects and exercises in genuine scientific construction of African philosophy concerning the diverse matters of its identity and difference ..." [4]

Furthermore, the political and ethical legitimacy of the interrogation of the term "Africa" becomes apparent in the debate concerning the substitution of the term "Africa" with Afrika. In the first place the replacement of the term "Africa" with Afrika is the seizure of initiative by the indigenous conquered peoples of the continent to reconstruct their history from their own perspective. It is not the denial of the Greek presence and the Roman conquest of the northern part of the continent. On the contrary, it is the integration of this experience into the history of "Africa" as understood by the indigenous conquered peoples of the continent. Nkrumah writes,

> In the new African renaissance, we place great emphasis on the presentation of history. Our history needs to be written as the history of our society, not as the story of European adventure. African society must be treated as enjoying its own integrity; its history must be a mirror of that society, and the European contact history must find its place in this history only as an African experience, even if as a crucial one. That is to say, the European contact needs to be assessed and judged from the point of view of the principles animating African society, and from the point of view of the harmony and progress of this society. [5]

This process of historical reconstruction is an integral part of the definition of the identity of the indigenous conquered peoples. Seen from this perspective, the debate on the replacement of "Africa" with Afrika is much more than a struggle for the correct spelling of the term. Part of the argument in this connection is that Afrika is a Ki-Swahili term denoting the indigenous peoples of equatorial East "Afrika". According to this view, the term may be used to refer to the whole continent since it originates from the black humus soil of the continent. The same argument obviously applies to the view that the term exists albeit with a different spelling in the Berber language. [6]

No doubt the spelling of the term in Ki-Swahili is clothed in the attire of the Roman alphabet. Does indigenous Africa not have its own forms of re-presenting thought, that is, art, music and writing, for example? The conventional scientific view that Africa did not have writing is based upon a questionable knowledge of African history. At the same time it is founded upon a restricted interpretation of writing. This interpretation is philosophically questionable as Derrida's "On Grammatology" has shown. The question whether or not "c" or "k" is the correct spelling is decided primarily by phonetic considerations. It is not decided on the basis of semantics. But once the latter is invoked in the context of the culture and history of the continent then it becomes apparent that the struggle for the meaning of the term "Afrika" is underpinned by fundamental political and ethical considerations. As such it is much more than the quest for scientific sophistication in philology.

In the light of the foregoing it is suggested that Okere should have devoted some attention to the meaning of the term "Africa"/ "Afrika" precisely because the term is one of the key words in the title of his book "African philosophy" published in 1983. Doing so, is not simply a question of satisfying academic curiosity. It is, in the first place a political and ethical imperative. This imperative applies to West Africa as well because "For an understanding of mid-twentieth-century Africa, both the Islamic and the western intrusions need detailed examination. …The Africa of today has grown out of the trials of the past, and the wisdom of Africa's new leadership is rooted in the experience and intellectual discrimination of those earlier leaders who first encountered Europe on West Africa's shores". It is this encounter with European intrusions on the one hand and Arab invasions in Africa on the other that have bestowed upon its peoples the triple heritage[8] of indigenous traditional Africa, Westernisation and Islamisation. Okere is himself aware of this triple heritage and emphasizes its crucial importance for the construction of contemporary African philosophy. According to him,

> To a greater or lesser extent, the African today is a living confluence of cultural rivers, the major rivers being, on the one hand, the traditional culture with its various tributaries of religion, social structure, language, values and world view, and, on the other hand, the Christian-Western culture with its own tributaries. For many other Africans, Islam consti-tutes a third major factor.[9]

Compliance with the political ethical imperative to inquire into the meaning of the term "Africa" is consistent with the indigenous Africans' quest to construct an African identity on their own terms. This is one of the bright threads that shine through Okere's philosophy. According to him,

> Any honest discussion of African culture today must face again the question of its existence and identity. By the question of existence I do not mean the racist question of whether Africans have any worthwhile culture of which to boast; nor by the question of identity do I mean whether there is unity of culture in Africa. Rather, here the question of the existence and identity of African culture is that of finding out what we mean when we use the phrase 'African culture'. What do we affirm or deny? Is it something that has identifiable boundaries in time and space; and does it have the same boundaries for the historian as for the philosopher, the cultural anthropologist, the scientist and the artist? ... what is its definition in the literal sense of its '*fines*' or limits? [10]

3. Bounded Reasoning

Another reason for questioning Europe's decisions about the boundaries of Africa and the identity of Africans is philosophical. It is the question of the definition of the boundaries, the 'fines' or 'limits' of the identity of Africans and their philosophy. Philosophically, there is a close connection between place and identity. In a sense, one cannot define one's identity adequately without reference to place in the ontological sense. "To be man is to have an existential 'place' but this 'place' must become the house of our Being in which our ontological dimension, our being here, unfolds and finds fulfillment. 'Place' places us both horizontally and vertically; it is the dimension of our ontological and existential uniqueness."[11] 'Place' then is our 'house'; our space of dwelling. The coincidence of place and space means that our ontological being requires a concrete 'house' which must be turned into a home as our place of dwelling. Being housed in a home is the possibility condition for the construction of identity. Without a home understood as the coincidence of place, space and time within boundaries it is not possible to construct an identity. This is because a home is by definition a place and space in time contained within boundaries. The erection of boundaries is necessary for the construction of the identity of the "I". Even "God" however, conceived, needs at least one boundary, namely, the separation between creator and creature. Without this line of demarcation the identity of "creator" and "creature" will be fused into a oneness. "God" cannot be "God" without the boundary between creator and creature. The erasure of this boundary is the obliteration of creator and creature. The result of such obliteration is an ontological oneness.

The criteria for the self-knowledge and the identity of such a oneness will be different from those of beings whose construction of their identity is predicated on the erection of boundaries. Bounded reasoning then is the reasoning that proceeds from the premise that in order to define and have one's identity, it is ontologically necessary to erect at least one boundary, namely, the boundary between "I" and the rest of whatever "it" might be. My place and space within a particular time are contemporaneously the inscription and the description of my identity. This is possible only if "I" situate myself in a particular place in space. By so doing, I recognize the existential boundary between myself and the rest of "it". This existential boundary is an ontological imposition that we are all condemned to live with. Ontology imposes upon us the necessity to recognize that we are housed and, within the boundaries of that house we must construct a home; an identity. This is the thought underlying Okere's understanding of philosophy in terms of the text and the context. It is to a consideration of this that we now turn.

4. Culture: Context and Text

I have already stated that in his search for African philosophy, Okere investigates the meaning of the term philosophy. The investigation is important to establish the meaning and purpose of African philosophy today. In pursuit of this purpose Okere argues that the seedbed of philosophy is the "non-philosophical". The "non-philosophical" or, non-philosophy is the existential condition out of which philosophy grows. Three years earlier than Okere's African Philosophy, Enrique Dussel espoused a similar thesis in his Spanish book, *Filosofía de la liberación*. In the English translation published in 1985 Dussel's thesis is that "Philosophy, when it is really philosophy and not sophistry or ideology, does not ponder philosophy. It does not ponder philosophical texts, except as a pedagogical propaedeutic to provide itself with interpretive categories. Philosophy ponders the *nonphilosophical*; the reality. But because it involves reflection on its own reality, it sets out from what already is, from its own world, its own system, its own space."[12] The concurrence of both philosophers on this point is significant because each one of them writes and speaks from the experience of colonization, "civilization", christianisation, oppression and exploitation. They speak from the experience of the so-called Third World, that is, the world created mainly by Westernising Europe as an expression of her desire to hold on to her racism by inventing an artificial vertical relationship between herself and the formerly colonized peoples. Okere argues against this contrived inhuman relationship. He focuses upon the "intolerance" of Christianity in general and, in particular that of the Roman Catholic Church. In this connection he suggests that

> the fourth century Athanasian Creed provides an insight into the spirit and mood of a church very early in history, infected by the Greek virus which demotes the Good and extols the True as the basic category of religion. Presuming already to know the truth and have it all, it thus paves the way for future ages of arrogance and intolerance *vis a vis* other cultures. ... Africans were generally regarded and treated as savages whose true humanity and spirituality was in question and whose culture had obviously nothing to offer. The Christian and ecclesiastical racism that initiated and encouraged both the slave trade and colonization was given more fillip by Darwin. The *mission civilizatrice* of Christian Europre's colonial imperialism and the *mission evangelizatrice* of Europe's Christian church become confounded. In such an atmosphere there could be little or no respect for the culture of the 'primitives'. Their indigenous religion was condemned as idolatry; their Gods were but demons or fetishes; their ancestors were lost souls, having lived and died outside the Church; their feasts and ceremonies were all idolatrous and pagan; their dances were immoral; their diviners were sorcerers; their medicine was magic and quackery; their languages were hopelessly tone-infested cacophonies, while their names were unpronounceable gibberish for which the canonized names of European canonized saints had to be substituted. All was one irredeemable *massa damnata*. With such a consistently intolerant and uncompromising attitude and, worse still, the imbibing of this attitude by its African faithful, Christianity continues to be an inhibitory factor in the process of retaining the Africanness of modern African culture and developing a via media or a

neo-African way of life."[14]

The preceding paragraph is intended to show that for Okere, the experience and concept of philosophy is inconceivable without a context. Context is the possibility condition for the identification and reading of a text. On this reasoning, culture is the indispensable context of philosophy. Consonant with this reasoning, Okere defines culture and, in particular, African culture in the following terms. "Culture today in Africa, as any time and anywhere, means total historical experience without denial or suppression of past or present, a dynamic unity of ancient and modern, a two-headed continuum with one head plunged into the immensity of the immemorial past, and the other as firmly and deeply immersed in the contemporary here and now."[15] This, by Okere's own admission, is a "total and holistic view of culture". One point that emerges rather indirectly from Okere's definition of culture is that memory is an integral part, an indispensable element of the concept of culture. Part of the reason why memory is an integral part of culture is that memory preserves both the experience and concept of identity. Without memory the idea of personal identity is conceptually empty and philosophically blind. It is worth pondering why, in some of his philosophical thought, David Hume devoted some time to write on the topic of personal identity. Alongside this it is pertinent to consider that Mazrui in a text published after Okere's book, African Philosophy, posits the following rhetorical question: "Can there be African identity without *an African memory*?"[16] Okere himself raises this question indirectly in the sense that he posits it as a problem in the search for a definition of African philosophy. He states:

> …..let us state the problem. Generally, one can say that philosophy in the West has been essentially a continuation of Greek philosophy. But Greek philosophy itself derived from and grew up within a given cultural complex, and despite its great age and many wanderings, carries unmistakable marks of its national identity. It is tempting, therefore, and perhaps legitimate to ask if this same Greek-born western philosophy ought to be the only valid philosophy for other cultures significantly different from the Greek culture or whether philosophy is so related and dependent on its cultural universe that each genuine philosophy would have to grown and evolve from its particular culture. If the latter is the

case, then philosophy in black Africa would have to emerge from the cultural context of black Africa, nay, in Africa philosophy would have to be homegrown if it is to be philosophy.[17]

Okere's demand that African philosophy should be "homegrown" is an endorsement of the view that philosophy like any other scientific or academic discipline is, in the first place, concrete and particular. Concrete in the sense that it must arise from actual experience at a particular place within a particular time; particular in the sense that concreteness does, ontologically, require the erection of boundaries that make the construction of identity possible and meaningful. On this reasoning, Okere clearly advocates particularity in and of philosophy. He certainly is far from endorsing particularism. Support for this is found in his definition of philosophy and his implicit call for dialogue between African and other non-African philosophies. We turn first to his definition of philosophy.

Having identified context as the indispensable precondition for philosophy, Okere then proffers the following definition of philosophy. "… philosophy, strictly speaking, is a special form of the march of reason in its age-old dialectics with reality, distinct from all the other intellectual forms that ape or resemble it. … all philosophy is tainted by historicity, a historicity which brings to light the place of culture. It is as much the fundamental relativity of all philosophy as the dependence of every philosophy on its cultural background that comes clearly to light … More than that, one has to say that it is only within the framework of a certain culture that one can understand or philosophize."[18] Okere's insistence on the particularity the "fundamental relativity of all philosophy" and its "dependence … on its cultural background" of all philosophy is ontologically grounded. It is a response to the ontological imperative to build a home once one is thrown into a house, that is, once one is situated in a "place". His response is the recognition of the necessity to comply with the ontological exigency to build a home for oneself. It is a philosophical statement that ontology does not offer homelessness as an alternative to being-a-human-being-in-the-world. This ontological condition is not a creation of Okere. Nor does he use it to construct an ideology. In this sense Okere is not advocating particularism when he insists on the particularity of all philosophy.

His call for dialogue between African and other non-African philosophies is evidenced by his challenge to the individualist private character of christian morality. The importance of his challenge lies in the fact that he proposes African religion as an "alternative" that could enrich Christian morality. As he put it: "… I wish to present a different approach to the problem from the point of view of African religion and suggest that if Christianity could graft this element of corporate responsibility into what is a very impressive heritage, it could exert greater influence for good in the public life of the world community."[19] In this connection Okere argues that the poverty of Christian Morality is to be found in the fact that the individual is educated to uphold the view that morality is a private matter. The translation of this into practice often spelled disaster for both the agents and the victims. The "privatization of morality" in this way has, according to Okere, opened the way to many preventable "crimes" in the public sphere, for example, " (a) The Atlantic Slave Trade which entailed the degradation of fellow human beings of the black race to mere chattel and objects of merchandise, a trade carried on for centuries by Christian peoples and nations with moral impunity and, at times with ecclesiastical blessing. (b) Colonialism that is the usurpation of the freedom and sovereignty of weaker peoples; the violence, the wars and the ethnocides that made possible colonial occupation; the partition and sharing of whole continents such as Africa like a cake among Christian states."[20] Indeed private morality has often served as a subterfuge to deny responsibility for one's actions. It has, also, made it possible to canonize private devils on account of the sanctity of their public lives.

> The implied indictment of the Christian religion on its failure as represented by these evils of the public life is not to say that some Christians or even the Christian leadership were in complicity or did not protest evil. Often enough they did, if often belatedly. Rather, that these crimes took place at all in a Christian dispensation, that they were perpetrated by Christians who might pass for saints in their private lives, that is the tragedy. Also, it is bad enough that any one of these crimes took place by way of a strange exception, but that so many-and even more-happened in the very bosom of Christianity must indicate a serious absence of the Christian code at this level of events.[21]

Okere's point goes beyond identifying the "crimes". It is pertinently to invite and effect an enriching corrective by replacing the individualist privacy of christian morality with the "corporate responsibility" of traditional African religion. This surely, is an implicit statement on the necessity for dialogue between African and non-African philosophies and cultures. It goes without saying that for this to happen the cultural boundaries erected out of ontological necessity must be permeable. It follows then that Okere is advocating neither particularism nor parochialism. His is an appeal to universality constituted from multiple concrete particularities. Only in this way can philosophy become a text ready to be spoken or read and then interpreted.

5. From culture to philosophy

Okere's argument that philosophy is culture-bound rests upon a strong ontological foundation. He is however careful to add that culture by itself is not by necessity philosophy. It is therefore necessary to make a deliberate transition from culture to philosophy. Accordingly, he posits the thesis that "Black Africans, having their own cultures, can have their own proper philosophies by driving and elaborating them from their own cultures. But it is not enough to have a culture in order to have a philosophy. A mediation, a passage from culture to philosophy is necessary."[22]

In his elaboration on the above thesis Okere considers if some of the specific writings of Hountondji, Kagame and Mbiti really qualify as African philosophy. Generally, the representation and discussion of these authors in the 1983 book provide rather limited information and depth of discussion concerning their respective positions. This representation tends to give the impression that Okere makes sweeping statements and provides rather thin evidence for his arguments in relation to each of the authors. In view of his emphasis on culture as the mother of philosophy, it is curious that Okere does not include Kwasi Wiredu, the author of Philosophy and an African Culture, among his interlocutors.[23] It must be noted, though, that Wiredu's book was published in 1980 while Okere's Doctoral dissertation was completed already in 1971.[24] It is salutary to note that the source from which Okere's discussion on these African philosophers is drawn, namely, his Doctoral dissertation contains much more elaborate and fair discussions of the authors mentioned. Against this background it is understandable that Okere engages in the search for the "passage" that is, the method through which Africa could make the transition from culture to philosophy. After a careful study of Gadamer, Heidegger and Paul Ricoeur, among others, Okere concludes that hermeneutics is the appropriate method for transition from culture to philosophy.

> ... African philosophies are possible. Philosophy is an effort at self understanding, a giving of meaning to one's own world and existence. It is always 'my' philosophy in other words, a first-person effort. ... To open the envelope is to expose what is implied in it, the letter. Philosophical reflection is the process of explicitation, an uncovering, a disclosure, an unfolding of the meaning and sense implied in those objectivations of life which are symbols. Reflection means *implicita explicare* making the implicit, explicit. African cultures have their own symbols pregnant with meaning. A reflection on these symbols with a view to making the implicit meanings explicit would constitute African philosophy.[25]

True to his definition of African philosophy and hermeneutics as its method, Okere explores the meaning of Igbo names. He certainly is not alone along this route. Some of his former students have made his definition and method of philosophy heard in far away Leuven in Belgium. They have presented their Masters research work and their Doctoral dissertation precisely on the particularity of Igbo culture made explicit through the hermeneutical method. Anthony Njoku's work, "Speaking names: naming as speech among the Igbos of Southern Nigeria" is one among the many examples available. Through a happy coincidence the wind of Okere's understanding of African philosophy and its optimal method evidently dropped the seeds of his thinking beyond Nigeria. His philosophical depth comes also to the fore in his essay on "the structure of the self in Igbo". This style and focus of African philosophy is echoed in Gbadegesin's essay, Eniyan: the Yoruba concept of a person and Kwame Gyekye's "Person and community in African thought". In the southernmost tip of the African continent the present writer through the publication of his "African philosophy through ubuntu" is also treading along the same path as Okere. So it is then that the Okere commission of inquiry into African philosophy is well under way and producing fruit. The Okere commission of inquiry into African philosophy is inscribed in the following irrevocable and memorable words.

> ... it is recommended that one should go back to one's own roots and sources. The sources, the headwater region of creative and original thought, are one's own culture. No familiarity with the foreign and borrowed element can suffice for the articulation of something so deep-felt as one's understanding of one's self and one's world. It is not only a question of fruitlessness when one undertakes to think foreign to oneself. It is also a moral question of being honest and true to one's self.[26]

6. Conclusion

There is no doubt that Okere has made a great and lasting contribution to African philosophy. It is fitting to warn you, dear Professor Okere, that your retirement shall not be an easy one. Permit me to assure that without your prior consent we consider ourselves privileged to call on you ex tempore. This is because it is certain that we will continue to draw from your wisdom as tread along the path of African philosophy that you have charted so lucidly and vigorous. Our gratitude to you shall therefore be in the form of interminable consultations. Please take that is a live expression of our gratitude and laudation for a work well done.

Notes

[1] Okere, T., (ed.), *Identity and Change, Nigerian Philosophical Studies* , Washington D.C.: Paideia Publishers, 1996.

[2] Okere, T., *African Philosophy, A historico-hermeneutical investigation of the conditions of its possibility,* Lanham: University Press of America, 1983.

[3] Mazrui, A.A., *The Africans*, London: BBC Publications, 1986, pp. 25, 29 and 38.

[4] Osuagwu, I.M., *African Historical Reconstruction*, Volume 1, Owerri: Assumpta Press, 1999, p. 25.

[5] Nkrumah, K., *Consciencism*, London: Panaf Books Ltd., 1979, p. 63.

[6] *Encyclopaedia Britannica* Volume 1, Chicago: William Benton Publisher,

1974, p. 117.

[7] July, R.W., *The Origins of Modern African Thought*, London: Faber and Faber, 1968, pp. 19-20.

[8] Mazrui, A.A., "Post-colonial society and Africa's triple heritage of Law," *Indigenous, Islamic and Western tendencies, in Enlightenment, Rights and Revolution*, (ed.) MacCormick and Bankowski, Z., Aberdeen: Aberdeen University Press Aberdeen, 1989, pp. 252 254.

[9] Okere, T., "African culture: the past and the present as an indivisible whole," in *Identity and Change*, (ed.) Okere, T., Washington: Paideia Publishers Washington D. C., 1996, p. 10.

[10] Ibid., p. 14.

[11] Heidegger, M., *The Question of Being*, London: Vision Press Limited, 1956, p. 25.

[12] Dussel, E., *Philosophy of Liberation*, (trans.) Martinez, A. and Morkovsky Christine, New York: Orbis Books, 1985, p. 3, emphasis added.

[13] Parkinson, F., *The Philosophy of International Relations*, London: Sage Publications Inc., 1977, p. 24.

[14] Okere, T., "African culture: the past and the present as an indivisible whole," p. 21-22

[15] Ibid., 23-24.

[16] Mazrui, A.A., *The Africans*, p. 76.

[17] Okere, T., *African Philosophy, A historico-hermeneuticalInvestigation of the conditions of its possibility,* Lanham: University Press of America, 1983, p. x-xi

[18] Ibid., pp. ix, xiii.

[19] Okere, T., The poverty of Christian individualist morality and an African alternative, in *Identity and Change*, op. cit., p. 123

[20] Ibid., p. 120.

[21] Loc. Cit.

[22] Okere, T. *African Philosophy*, p. xiv.

[23] Wiredu, K., *Philosophy and an African Culture*, Cambridge: Cambridge University Press, 1980.

[24] Okere, T., "Can there be an African philosophy? A hermeneutical investigation with special reference to Igbo culture," Doctoral dissertation presented to the Catholic University of Louvain, Belgium, 1971.

[25] Okere, T., *African Philosophy*, pp. 114-115

[26] Ibid., 118-119.

8

Okere on the Self
A Hermeneutical Approach to an Ontological Question

Godfrey Igwebuike Onah

1. Introduction

The most fundamental philosophical problem is also the most difficult: Who am I? This fact has been attested to by many philosophers and philosophical traditions, from the Ancient Egyptian Mystery System to contemporary Existentialist and Postmodern thinkers. The centrality of self-knowledge to the entire philosophical enterprise, though made popular in Greek philosophy by Socrates, was first found in Egyptian philosophy. The Egyptian Mysteries taught that self-knowledge was the basis of all true knowledge.[1] Socrates repeated the same teaching in a way that would, perhaps, have been regarded as plagiarism in modern scholarship. Kant reduced all philosophical questions to the anthropological question: What is man? And Heidegger argues that the knowledge of the human being (*Dasein*) is the key to the knowledge of Being as such, given that the human being is the only being capable of asking the question about Being. But it is precisely here that the difficulty concerning self-knowledge lies, at least in part. When the human being is both the question and the questioner, the line separating the object and the subject of knowledge disappears and objectivity tends to be swallowed up in subjectivity. Though this need not necessarily imply subjectivism, the risk thereof is significantly increased. Little wonder, then, that despite the enormous amount of progress registered in his knowledge of the objective world and in his knowledge of some aspects of his being, man's comprehensive knowledge of himself does not seem to have advanced beyond the most elementary and is often fragmentary. Sometimes, the problem is even further compounded by the very mode in which the question is posed. It is not always clear whether the anthropological question should be posed as a "what is?" question or as a "who is?" question. That is why the question of method is not an otiose question in philosophy, especially in the philosophy of human nature. It often happens that the proposed answers to the question "what or who is man?" are contradictory, even within the same philosophical tradition or philosophical school.

Be that as it may, the anthropological question cannot be postponed in philosophy. For to inquire about the ultimate nature of anything at all is to inquire about the ultimate nature of the inquirer. This, I think, is the basic meaning of Kant's position on the four questions of philosophy. Even when the human being is not the explicit theme of a philosophical reflection, man's self-knowledge still remains the ultimate aim of every philosophy (and perhaps of every human knowledge). Those thoughts of a philosopher or a philosophical tradition that are more explicitly anthropological are often only clearer articulations of the ideas underlying and underpinning other supposedly non-anthropological thoughts.

In the history of western philosophy, the human being became an explicit theme of philosophical reflection only gradually. It is common for historians of western philosophy to describe the period of Ancient Greek and Roman philosophy as "cosmocentric," the period of Christian Medieval philosophy as "theocentric" and the periods of modern and contemporary philosophy as "anthropocentric." But these qualifications can be misleading in at least two ways. First, they may give the impression that earlier philosophies studied the physical world and God, but not man. In the light of what was said earlier, the human being is always at the centre of the philosophical enterprise, even when he is not the direct material object of study. Second, one may think that the anthropologies of the later periods are clearer, more complete and more solidly founded than the earlier ones. On the contrary, despite the claims of anthropocentrism, later philosophies of human nature have offered more confused and confusing ideas of the human being than the earlier ones. These later ones, which often lack the solid metaphysical foundations of the earlier philosophies, have even sometimes doubted the existence of a human nature common to all human beings.

Contemporary African philosophy has been struggling with how to make sense of its double heritage. On the one hand, it enjoys the rich heritage of African traditional thought and culture and African philosophy. On the other hand, it is also a co-heir of the Western philosophical tradition, since most of the protagonists of contemporary African philosophy are trained in the academic philosophical tradition of the West. Like earlier philosophical thoughts in the West, traditional African thought often did not explicitly thematise the problem of the human being.[2] Nevertheless, a careful examination easily reveals the wealth of material relating to the philosophy of human nature in such thoughts. Theophilus Okere, like a few other contemporary African philosophers, has undertaken such a careful examination of the traditional thought of an African people, the Igbo, in an attempt to discover what philosophy of human nature is contained in this thought. In this essay we shall evaluate the result of Okere's inquiry in the wider context of the contemporary philosophical debate on human nature. To show the peculiarity of Okere's interpretations of traditional Igbo thought, some of his conclusions will be compared with those of at least one other African philosopher with a similar cultural background, Ifeanyi Menkiti. However, before proceeding with our examination of the outcome of Okere's inquiry, it would be useful, first of all, to examine his method of inquiry, since, as it has already been noted, the question of method is not an idle one in philosophy.

2. The Problem of Method

Philosophy seems to enjoy the reputation of posing more problems than it actually solves. Even the very issue of its method is itself a problem. Unlike what obtains in many other forms of human knowledge, philosophers do not agree (perhaps they do not even need to agree) on the method or methods to be used in their inquiry. The maieutic method of Socrates, the Aristotelian method of introspection, the methodic doubt of Descartes, the critical method, the dialectical method, the phenomenological method, the analytic method, philosophical hermeneutics… these are only a few of the many that have been proposed and pursued by philosophers in history. In his first major publication on African philosophy, Okere denounced what he regarded as the "false routes" hitherto followed by many in the quest for African philosophy. In his opinion, "the search for an African philosophy has not yet yielded very satisfactory results... [because the search] has been pursued along false routes."[3] The "false routes" to which Okere refers here are the methods of inquiry. He criticizes authors like Placide Tempels, Alexis Kagame and John Mbiti for making "facile assumptions" on the relationship between African culture and African philosophy. These authors, according to Okere, do not make sufficient distinctions between the nature of culture and of philosophy. Consequently, they gloss over the mediation that must take place between them before an African philosophy can emerge from an African culture. He argues that although philosophy is culture-bound, culture *as such* is not philosophy. Taking the inspiration from the works of Heidegger, Gadamer and Ricoeur, Okere opts for the hermeneutical method in the quest for African philosophy. He affirms in unequivocal terms: "It is *only* within the context of hermeneutics that African culture can give birth to African philosophy."[4] This affirmation has several implications. Here we shall underline only two of them because of their importance in the proper understanding of Okere's reflections on the self within the context of Igbo culture.

One implication of the affirmation that we would like to underline, which is not so obvious to some Western philosophers (Hegel, for instance), is the contextual character of every philosophy. Philosophy is culture-bound not only in Africa but *everywhere. Every philosophy* bears the indelible stamp of the culture within which it is nurtured. Okere agrees with Hiedegger's view, according to which "all philosophy is an interpretative explication of one's own symbolic world, of one's culture, which is already a prior understanding of Being."[5] Any claim to universality on the part of a philosophy or of a philosopher ought to be balanced with the recognition at the same time of the cultural context of the philosophy or the philosopher. Failure to do this exposes a particular philosophy or philosopher to the risk of absolutism and totalitarianism.

The other implication of the affirmation, one not so obvious to some earlier African philosophers (for example, the three whom Okere criticizes in his book), is the individual character of philosophy.

Although culture, within which philosophy is nurtured, is a collective product, that reflection of it that is philosophy is basically an individual enterprise. "Philosophy," Okere writes, "is not a collective project. It is only when a collective culture is labored on by an 'I' that the philosophical signification appears.... The authentic philosophical project is undertaken by an 'I' from within his culture."[6] If one bears these two implications of the hermeneutical option in mind, one may better appreciate the similarities and the differences between different philosophical traditions and between different philosophers within the same tradition. We shall return to this point later.

Within the hermeneutical method, Okere keeps both phenomenology and ontology together as two moments of the same inquiry. This is particularly important in the study of human nature. On the one hand, the phenomenological approach seeks to gain preliminary understanding of the human being through an interpretation (hermeneutics) of his manifestations. On the other hand, ontology seeks to deepen this interpretation in order to arrive at Being as it is manifested in the human being. Without arriving at this foundation of the human being, philosophy will never be able to provide a unified explanation of the various manifestations which are readily observable at the phenomenological level. In this regard Heidegger affirms: "The phenomenology of Dasein is a *hermeneutic*.... Philosophy is universal phenomenological ontology, and takes its departure from the hermeneutic of Dasein."[7]

Of special importance in the hermeneutical method is language. Whichever way one may define culture, language (even in the sense of tongue) remains a fundamental element. Consequently, Okere suggests the attentive interpretation of the cultural symbols expressed in language as a valid method of doing (African) philosophy. And it is to language that he turns when in a later essay he seeks to work out a concept of the self from the raw materials of Igbo traditional thought.

3. The Self as the Basic Unit of Identity and Autonomy

The first thing that Okere points out in his analysis of the Igbo word for self, "*onwe*," is that its root is the verb "*inwe*", which means to own or to possess. He then relates this to some dialectical variations of *onwe*, namely, "*ike*" and "*ogwe*," both of which refer to the most fundamental basis of an individual being. From this he concludes that the self is that to which ownership of a thing, actions, feelings, sentiments or attributes can be ascribed. Thus "myself" or "*onwe m*" would literally mean "he who owns me."[8] This implies that a self has attributes, can be source of actions, and so on. In what would sound like a tautology, one could say that self-possession is the first characteristic of the self. But such tautologies are old in philosophical discourse as when classical metaphysicians say that being is or that being is being. Okere offers the following working definition of the self:

> *Onwe*... roughly meaning self, is the core subject of identity, perduring and enduring all human experience. It is not describable and has no name and no function except as the ultimate author of all the functions of the individual, the carrier of all experience. It is the link between the experiences of yesterday and today, the basis of that proprietorship by which these fleeting multitudes of experience are one and are mine.[9]

At first sight, this may look like a restatement of Hume's solution to the problem of personal identity[10] or, at best, a version of the Kantian primordial "I think", which accompanies all our representations and accounts for the unity of our experiences.[11] Needless to say, however, that in Okere's analysis, there is no tincture of the scepticism of Hume. And, despite the reference to the unity of experiences both in Kant and in Okere, the latter's concept of the self is radically different from the Kantian primordial "I think." This is because whereas the Kantian "I think" is an epistemological category, Okere's self or *onwe* is essentially a metaphysical or, to be more precise, an *ontological* category. The self, as the *core subject of identity*, is, first and foremost, the *subjectum* of which other things can be predicated but which cannot be predicated of anything else; the *substratum* (not in the Lockean sense), the irreducible foundation of being, in which other characteristics, including consciousness or knowledge, inhere. It is the "trunk" (as the dialectical variation *ogwe* suggests), to which other qualities are, as it were, attached. The self is the "ultimate subject of all attributions."[12] It is first the basis of the unity of being, the basis of ontological identity, before being the basis of the unity of consciousness or of epistemological identity.

It would therefore seem safe to conclude that in Okere's view the self is a *substance*. In traditional Aristotelian metaphysics, a substance is that which exists in itself and not in another. The following passage from W. Norris Clarke presents a good summary of the conception of substance in Aristotelian-Thomistic metaphysics:

> There are four basic points to note about this conception of substance as the primary instance of real being: (1) it has the aptitude to exists *in itself* and not as a part of any other being; (2) it is the unifying center of all the various attributes and properties that belong to it at any one moment; (3) [it is] ...the abiding, unifying center of the being across time; (4) it has an intrinsic dynamic orientation toward self-expressive action, toward self-communication with others, as the crown of its perfection.[13]

Substance is the primary instance of real being and the first principle of being is identity. In designating the self as the basic unit of identity and as the ultimate author of the functions of the individual, Okere carries on a metaphysical tradition whose roots cut across cultural barriers. Although he never uses the term "substance" to refer to the self, the reference to ontological self-possession and identity shows that for him the self is not a process, a relation or a quality, but a substance that is capable of undergoing a process, entering into a relation and possessing qualities, in as much as *it is in itself* and *possesses itself.*

Besides being the basic unit of identity, the self is also the basic unit of autonomy. This is equally contained in the idea of self-possession. To own oneself is to belong to no one else but oneself to be free, to be autonomous.[14] This identification of freedom with autonomy ought not be exaggerated, for it is not understood in the Greek (or Kantian) sense of being one's own law-giver. It rather points to that nature of the self whereby an individual is regarded as the ultimate moral source (even if not always the ultimate metaphysical source) of his decisions and actions. There is something about Igbo traditional thought that makes absolutism next to impossible. Chinua Achebe has correctly observed that "nothing is *totally* anything in Igbo thinking; everything is a question of measure and degree."[15] Within this context, freedom and autonomy, whether ontological or moral, would also be a question of measure and degree. Inattention to this fact may have led some scholars to attributing some exaggerated positions to Igbo traditional thought. When therefore Okere says of the self that it is not owned,[16] this ought not imply a denial of the nature of the human self as belonging to a social group.

It is only after having established the nature of the self as a substance that Okere goes on to give a descriptive concept of the self. The various aspects of the self: or spirit, *chi*, heart, body, and so on, are presented not as separate or separable parts of the self but as its attributions and functions. Our author owns up that figuring out the complex relationship between these attributes and functions among themselves and between all or each of them and the self is one of the most difficult challenges of an anthropology that draws its inspiration from Igbo culture.

Of primary importance are the spiritual aspects of the self. Several elements are involved here. The term "*muo*" or spirit in Igbo language is used to refer to both the immaterial element in the human being and to other immaterial non-human beings, including deities. "This indicates," according to Okere, "that man is thought of as sharing in some way in the peculiar being of spirits. Despite appearances, man is therefore part spirit." Among the various attributes of the spirit as expressed in language are life, thought, reflection, will, memory, and understanding. It is the principle of life and thought in all their forms. It likens man to the divine.

Very closely related to *muo* is the personal "*chi*," a term which defies translation into any Western language and can only be broadly described. Okere regards it as an enigmatic but crucial principle and offers this descriptive definition:

> The Igbo *Chi* is the divine double or personal guardian and protector that is variously conceived as part of God in man, or a divine part in man, but presiding essentially over the individual as he or she works out his or her destiny.... It is also part of the individual's identity and is seen as the prime moving force and principle of individualism in Igbo culture. As such it is strictly personal, indivisible, not shared or sharable with others.[17]

In a similar descriptive manner Achebe says: "In a general way we may visualise a person's *chi* as his other identity in spiritland his *spirit being* complementing his terrestrial *human being*."[18] *Chi* is at the same time divine and strictly personal, that is, unique to the individual. It is a kind of unique manifestation of God's creative power, "a personified and unique manifestation of the creative essence."[19] The fact that the same term is also used for God suggests the close link that exists between the individual human being and God in Igbo traditional thought. There is something more than the merely visible in the human being. There is something divine in him and something sacred about him. Elaborating this point Okere writes:

> The shared community of the name *Chi* in Chi, Chukwu, Chineke and Ezechitoke or Chukwu Okike, which links the personal god of the individual with the supreme God to the exclusion of all other so-called gods, seems to point to a very special and exclusive relationship between the individual and his creator. The divine in man is hinted at, as is a certain indwelling of God in the individual. The transcendent in man is also suggested, as is his subordination to his divine guardian.[20]

This divine in man is the ontological basis of the dignity and uniqueness of every human being, even the infant, the criminal and the mentally sick. An offence against a disadvantaged person is regarded as an affront to his *chi*.

The idea of freedom and autonomy to which we referred above cannot be fully understood if removed from the context of the role of *chi* in the individual's life. The broad outlines of a man's destiny is thought to be negotiated between the individual and his *chi* at the moment of creation and thereafter fixed. During his terrestrial existence, therefore, the individual is expected to work out the details of this pre-agreed plan, under the strict supervision of his *chi*. This pre-agreed plan is regarded as his destiny, which, though hidden from the human being, is always somehow ascertainable through some religious and social institutions and practices. Neither the individual nor his *chi* is absolutely fixed in this delicate relationship in which personal freedom and destiny are played out. By way of summary, Okere gives the three basic meanings of *chi* as follows: "(1) A divine force… unique to the individual,… and constitutive of the individual…. (2) A guardian , resident deity, deputizing for the Supreme God… God's double within the individual…. (3) …the principle of destiny as well as of fortune."[21]

Another constitutive element of the self is the heart, *"obi."* Although simple vocabulary may give the impression that this is a material element, the heart does seem to be more a spiritual element than a material one, for it is the inner source of morality in the individual. Neither *muo* nor *chi* is commended or blamed for the individual's moral acts, but his *obi*. The body is also morally neutral, except as the external agent of the intentions nurtured in the heart. The spirit (*muo*) may contemplate an action, the body may execute it and *chi* may approve of its execution. But it is always to the good or bad, virtuous or wicked heart (*obi oma* or *obi ojoo*) that the goodness or the badness of a moral act is ultimately attributed. This makes it more a spiritual than a material faculty.

The body is evidently the material aspect of the self, which, nevertheless, has a complex and intimate relationship with the spiritual aspects. It is sometimes metaphorically used to represent the self in its concrete external manifestations. It also plays an indispensable role as the medium through which the individual is inserted within a given community. This insertion within a community is expressed in terms of blood relation or consanguinity, and often lived out in the form of physical proximity and interaction.

Though not one of its constitutive elements like the others, the community is, nevertheless, a determinant factor in the concept of the self within the context of Igbo traditional thought. Okere puts it aptly:

> If we have been looking at the structure of the kernel of the self, one must immediately add that this hard core is surrounded by a thicker layer of enveloping relationships…. Even though one can be thought of as a unit and in abstraction from any thing else, in fact, the self is never alone. The individual is never a pure, isolated individual…. This is why in this culture, the self is a congenitally communitarian self, incapable of being, existing and really unthinkable except in the complex of relations of the community.[22]

It is within the community of other closely related selves that each individual self attains its perfection. Beginning from the members of one's own family, to all the members of a traditional community, the individual self lives out its identity and autonomy in relation. The "I-We" relation is an indispensable mediator of personal identity and autonomy.

The metaphors of the "core" or "kernel" of the self and the "layer of enveloping relationships" permit Okere to safeguard the two important poles of the self, namely, the substance-pole and the relations-pole. While defending the importance of the web of relations in the full understanding of the self, he does not thereby suggest that it is these relations that constitute the self. The self exists *in itself*, though not in isolation, but in relation with others in a community of selves. It is often said that the Igbo and in general the African concept of the self or person is social, so social that it is sometimes contrasted with what is supposed to be the Western "static" notion of the individual substance. In his account of the structure of the self, Okere deliberately avoids all forms of comparison between the concept of the self which emerges from his interpretation of Igbo culture and some other concepts of the self, whether Western or Eastern. His conclusions show the limits (and sometimes even the futility) of all such comparisons, for there is no uniformity in the concepts of the self nurtured within any single cultural context.

In the Western philosophical tradition, earlier concepts of the self were substantialist and metaphysically stable. From the time of Hume, however, this substantialist and metaphysically stable concept of the self was slowly replaced by a concept of the self as a process or as a relation, through a gradual distortion of the meaning of substance in philosophy. First came Kant's metaphysical scepticism. Then followed the Hegelian assimilation (*Aufhebung*) of substance in the subject and the assumption of the primacy of the category of becoming over that of being. Charles Darwin's evolutionism has had a tremendous impact on later philosophical thought. By the time the Existentialists and the Postmodernists appeared on the scene, it had become a common assumption in philosophy that "the Self is not a substance but a lived relation to that which situates it; that this relation is and only could be an internal relation... that that which situates the Self which shall be called the situating Other enters into the very ontological constitution of the Self."[23] Thus, many contemporary philosophers understand substance as static and as excluding of relation. Consequently, they seek to define the self in terms of relation and process and not in terms of substantiality and individuality. One of the strongest defences of the evolutionary and relational concept of the self is found in George Herbert Mead.[24] But as W. Norris Clarke has ably shown, a proper understanding of the classical notion of substance highlights its dynamic relational dimension and sees being as substance-in-relation.[25] One does not therefore need to deny substantiality to the self in order to defend its relational character.

The "processual" and relational view of the self was also proposed by Ifeanyi Menkiti from the context of African (Igbo) traditional thought.[26] We shall now examine this view briefly in order to show how it differs from Okere's view, irrespective of the fact that both authors share the same cultural background.

4. Menkiti's Dilemma and Okere's Proposal

Before outlining the basic elements in Menkiti's view of the person,[27] it may help to draw attention to a dilemma which he mentions in a later essay, but which was, probably, already weighing heavily on his thoughts as he wrote the earlier one. He states:

> A philosopher, having put on one side common sense, the sense that is held in common regarding the things that are in the world, and having put on the other side metaphysics, whose understanding is also about the things in the world, soon notices a dilemma crashing in on him. The dilemma has to do with the gap, the discontinuity in the discourse issuing from the two types of understanding.[28]

Faced with the dilemma resulting from the difference between common sense knowledge (which he also calls traditional thought) and metaphysical thought, a dilemma that is so serious as to give rise to a "cognitive war" within the metaphysician, Menkiti seeks a way out by suggesting that there isn't after all a discontinuity between the two modes of understanding but rather only a different kind of metaphysical thinking in Africa. He argues that the two understandings are so continuous that one can talk of "traditional African metaphysics", and he cites the understanding of the person as an illustration. The only thing the metaphysician needs to do is to abandon all forms of supernaturalism and ground his metaphysical thinking empirically.[29] Much can be said concerning this concept of "traditional African metaphysics" and the way in which Menkiti resolves his dilemma. But let us move on to his concept of the person, not only because he cites it as an illustration of the resolution of the dilemma, but also because it is more directly related to our discussion here.

There are three basic tenets of his doctrine of the human being. First, the human being is not defined abstractly but by reference to a community. Second, one *is not* originally a person at conception or at birth, but gradually *becomes* one through a process of incorporation into the community and also *ceases to be* a person with time after death. Third, since one becomes a person only gradually, it follows that all human beings are not ontologically equal since some are "more" persons than others. For instance, infants and anti-social persons would be "less" persons than socially integrated adults. Those who are only apparently persons but in reality are not so are, according to Menkiti, referred to as "it" in African societies. He describes this concept of the person as "maximal" in contrast with what he regards as the "minimal" concept in Western philosophy. He also argues that this "maximal" concept of the person is shared by all African societies.

This concept of the person, though attractive for its effort to safeguard the social dimension of life so important in African societies, is replete with difficulties. Let us start with its description as "maximal." A definition or a concept is by its very nature minimal, for it seeks to extract that which is common to all the members of a genus. A "maximal" concept or definition would be a contradiction in terms, for when considering the *maximum* that each individual member of a specie can attain in its development, it would be difficult to fix the boundaries, which is what definition (*definitio*) is all about. It does seem that in Menkiti's anthropology there is a conflation of the concept of the person with its perfection. What he describes may well represent a *fully developed* person. But one has to *be* a person first before *becoming* a fully developed person.

Another difficulty with this concept of the person is that it denies the fundamental ontological equality of all human beings. Many aspects of traditional life in many African societies (the Igbo in particular) demonstrate exactly the contrary. There is, yes, a strong social dimension in the concept of the person in Igbo traditional thought. This does not, however, imply the denial of some fundamental ontological basis which belongs to every individual human being, irrespective of his or her social status. When a human being is said "not to be a human being," such a statement is largely metaphorical. Infants and insane persons, for instance, may be excluded from some social responsibilities, but this does not deny them the basic dignity they deserve as human beings, as one who deliberately kills an infant or a mad person would definitely discover. Moral valuations, strong as they are in such traditional thoughts, do not equate to ontological valuations.

With regard to Menkiti's "it-argument," it suffices to point out the linguistic difficulties contained therein. In Igbo, for instance, the same pronoun (*o*) stands for he, she and it. Only from the context can one tell whether the statement "*o di ndu*" means "he is alive," "she is alive," or "it is alive." It is not clear on what basis Menkiti would claim that that statement referred to a child should be translated "*it* is alive." What is clear is that a child is never referred to as a "thing" (*ihe* or *ife*) in Igbo, except perhaps in the extreme case of parents who have suffered so many successive infant deaths that they believe a reference to a newly born child as a "thing" could deceive the *ogbanje* spirit, thought to be responsible for such deaths, into leaving the child alone.

Could it be that Menkiti never really got out of his dilemma? Did he merely deny its existence and thought that it was resolved? In Okere's view, as we have already seen, there is a difference between culture and philosophy. Traditional thought or world-view is part of a culture and metaphysics is a special branch of philosophy. This being the case, the difference between traditional thought or popular wisdom and philosophy cannot be papered over by the mere addition of the adjective "traditional" to metaphysics. If, therefore, as Menkiti suggests, there is a discontinuity between common sense knowledge and knowledge obtained through metaphysical reflection, such a discontinuity would still exist between traditional African thought and African philosophy or African metaphysics. According to Okere, it is precisely such a discontinuity that necessitates the mediation of personal interpretation, a hermeneutic, of traditional common sense knowledge before a philosophy could emerge therefrom. Such a hermeneutic would enable the philosopher to isolate the different strands that make up traditional thought, sift them, decode those of them that need to be decoded, rearrange them... before he can attempt the production of a *personal* philosophy from traditional thought. To assume, as Menkiti does, that "metaphysical understanding in traditional African thought so neatly dove-tails with the regular understanding of physical nature that the two understandings ought to be seen as forming one continuous order of understanding,"[30] would confound issues rather than clarify them. And a philosopher who makes such an assumption may find himself or herself in a similar dilemma as Menkiti's. But if one accepts Okere's proposal, at least one will enjoy the freedom of presenting one's personal philosophy, instead of remaining in the straight-jacket of one who arrogates to one's self the unrealistic position of being the philosophical spokesperson of an entire people or, worse still, of an entire continent.

5. Conclusion

The philosophical problem of being and becoming, permanence or identity and change, is a perennial one. It is one of the central problems of classical ontology, that is, of the metaphysics of being. Like every fundamental problem of ontology, it touches every branch of philosophy. This problem becomes more complex in the philosophy of human nature, that is, when it is directly posed about the human being. Whereas some philosophers admire the doctrine of permanence in the style of Parmenides, others are more attracted to the constant flux theory of Heraclitus; while still some others try to maintain a delicate balance between the two extremes. As has already been noted in this essay, many contemporary philosophers seem more inclined towards the constant flux hypothesis about the self. The thoughts of Okere on the self that we have examined here show that he steers a middle course. On the one hand, he defends the existence of an ontologically constituted "hard core" of the self. On the other hand, he equally acknowledges the importance of a complex network of relations through which the self develops as it strives towards the perfection that belongs to its nature. He arrives at these conclusions through a careful reading and interpretation of Igbo language and traditional thought. The advantage of this position over some other positions that see the self only as a process or as a relation is that it safeguards the two important poles of the self and of personal identity. The following remark by Leke Adeofe is relevant here:

> Any credible theory of personal identity must be metaphysically and socially stable, and the two forms of stability must be interconnected.... Metaphysical stability helps to explain the unity of the self, so to speak, that makes personal identity possible. Social stability helps to explain our socialised existence, our belief systems, social character, and projects of value that seem to make our lives meaningful.[31]

Having suggested to African philosophers in his first major philosophical work what route to follow in order to produce thoughts that are both truly philosophical and authentically African, Okere in his later works takes his own suggestion seriously. Using the method of interpretation of culture, he proposes philosophical thoughts that are culturally nurtured, ontologically grounded, and universally relevant. Without attempting any forced analogies between Igbo traditional thought and Western philosophy, he shows how in the common search for the truth, philosophers who start from different cultural backgrounds can still meet each other at various points of the search, and, hopefully, also at the point of arrival.

Notes

[1] See George G. M. James, *Stolen Legacy: Greek Philosophy Is Stolen Egyptian Philosophy*, Trenton, NJ, Africa World Press, 1992, p. 88.

[2] This observation is aware of Kwasi Wiredu's advice on the right way to compare African thought with Western thought. See K. (J. E.) Wiredu, "How not to Compare African Thought with Western Thought," in Richard A. Wright (ed.), *African Philosophy: An Introduction*, Third Edition, Lanham: University Press of America, 1984, pp. 146-162. There is no implied comparison here between traditional African thought and the Ancient Greek and Medieval philosophies in the Western

tradition.

[3] Theophilus Okere, *African Philosophy: A Historico-Hermeneutical Investigation of the Conditions of its Possibility*, Lanham: University Press of America, 1983, p. 11. It is to be noted that this observation was made more than twenty years ago.

[4] Ibid., p. 15. Emphasis added.

[5] Ibid., p. 116.

[6] Ibid., p. xv.

[7] Martin Heidegger, *Being and Time*, trans. John Macquarrie & Edward Robinson, Oxford: Basil Blackwell, 1962, p. 62.

[8] Theophilus Okere, "The Structure of the Self in Igbo Thought," in Theophilus Okere (ed.), *Identity and Change: Nigerian Philosophical Studies*, I, Washington D. C., Paideia, 1996, p. 151.

[9] Ibid., p.152.

[10] Cf. David Hume, *A Treatise of Human Nature*, London: Penguin Books, 1987, Book I, Part IV, Section 6.

[11] Cf. Immanuel Kant, *Critique of Pure Reason*, trans. Norman Kemp Smith, New York: St Martin's Press, 1965, B 131, pp. 152-153.

[12] "The Structure of the Self," p. 161.

[13] W. Norris Clarke, *Explorations in Metaphysics: BeingGodPerson*, Notre Dame: University of Notre Dame Press, 1994, p. 105.

[14] "The Structure of the Self," p. 152.

[15] Chinua Achebe, *Morning Yet on Creation Day*, London: Heinemann, 1975, p. 97.

[16] "The Structure of the Self," p. 152.

[17] Ibid., p. 156.

[18] Chinua Achebe, *Morning Yet on Creation Day*, p. 93.

[19] Ibid., p. 99.

[20] Theophilus Okere, "Names as Building Blocks of an African Philosophy," in Theophilus Okere (ed.), *Identity and Change*, p. 143. This is not the right place to go over the debate about the names for God in Igbo. Suffice it to say that many of such names contain the word "*Chi*" as part of their root and that in many other compound words, especially in names, *Chi* stands for God. For further discussion on the issue see Achebe's essay, "Chi in Igbo Cosmology," in his *Morning Yet on Creation Day*, pp. 93-103; Christopher U. M. Ezekwugo, *Chi: The True God in Igbo Religion*, Pontifical Institute of Philosophy and Theology, Alwaye, Kerala, 1987.

[21] "The Structure of the Self," p. 156.

[22] Ibid., pp.159-160.

[23] William A. Shearson, "The Common Assumptions of Existentialist Philosophy," *International Philosophical Quartely*, 15 (1975) 2, pp. 137-8, quoted in Desmond Connell, *Essays in Metaphysics*, Four Courts Press, Dublin, 1996, p. 25.

[24] See George H. Mead, *Mind, Self, and Society: From the Standpoint of a Social*

Behaviorist, ed. Charles W. Morris, Chicago: University of Chicago Press, 1974.
[25] See W. Norris Clarke, *Explorations in Metaphysics*, pp.102-122.
[26] See Ifeanyi A. Menkiti, "Person and Community in African Traditional Thought," in Richard A. Wright (ed.), *African Philosophy*, pp. 171-181.
[27] Okere prefers the term "self" to the term "person" which Menkiti uses. In some other context it may be necessary to make a distinction between the two terms. Irrespective of the difference in terminologies, however, both authors are concerned with the same human reality examined within the context of an African culture.
[28] I. A. Menkiti, "Physical and Metaphysical Understanding: Nature, Agency, and Causation in African Traditional Thought," in Lee M. Brown (ed.), *African Philosophy: New and Traditional Perspectives*, Oxford: Oxford University Press, 2004, p. 107.
[29] Ibid., pp. 108-109.
[30] Ibid., p. 108.
[31] Leke Adeofe, "Personal Identity in African Metaphysics," in Lee M. Brown (ed.), *African Philosophy*, pp. 80-81.

9

Philosophy vs Hermeneutics
Between Ruinance and Enowing

Innocent Enweh

> This is certainly for philosophy the most revolutionary result of
> the hermeneutical movement. Apart from teaching Us how best
> to read and understand ancient authors, and apart from offering
> US a magnificent anatomy of the art of philosophising, it
> becomes the Magna Carta of all those of other cultures who aim
> to build up a philosophical tradition which will be more than a
> mere footnote on the pages of Greek and Western philosophy.[1]

1. A Flash Back on Heidegger: Martin Heidegger considers the
question of Being as the most fundamental of all questions. He demonstrates the primacy and priority of this question in three respects,
namely, that it is the broadest of all questions, the most profound of all
questions and the most original of all questions.[2] For Heidegger doing
philosophy means asking "'Why are beings at all instead of nothing?'
Actually asking this means venturing to exhaust, to question thoroughly,
the inexhaustible wealth of this question, by unveiling what it demands
that we question. Whenever such a venture occurs, there is philosophy."[3]
Philosophy here is synonymous with ontology. But with Heidegger,
ontology takes a new twist in a hermeneutic mutation of phenomenology. Pulling hermeneutics out of the sphere of communication, as it was
traditionally known to be, and radicalising phenomenology in a hermeneutic of facticity in which the task of phenomenology lies in unveiling
that which gives itself only in self-concealment, Heidegger proposes a
fundamental ontology grounded in Daseinsanalytik.[4] Dasein is essentially Being- in-the world. It is in being-relation which constitutes the

structure or framework of its understanding (self-understanding and understanding of the world around). Dasein's self-understanding is achieved in self-interpretation. Heidegger tells us that self-understanding is a third moment in all understanding. Understanding is an existential, that is, a categorical and basic determinant of our being-in-the world. The role of understanding is central to the hermeneutic of existence. Michael Gelven gives three reasons why understanding is crucial to the existential analytic:

(1)It provides an account, within the existential analytic, of how Dasein is aware of possibilities; (2) It provides the basis of Heidegger's theory of interpretation; and (3) It provides the basis for Heidegger's theory of freedom, which is developed as a central theme in *Of Essence of Ground* (*Vom Wesen des Grundes*), a work published two years after *Being and Time*.[5]

According to Heidegger, it is interpretation that completes understanding. "In it the understanding appropriates understandingly that which is understood. It becomes itself. Such interpretation is grounded existentially in understanding; the latter does not arise from the former. Nor is interpretation the acquiring of information about what is understood; it is rather the working-out of possibilities projected in understanding."[6] The interdependence of knowledge of the parts and knowledge of the whole that has been a theme in hermeneutic reflection takes a new significance in Heidegger. This is because according to him the fore-structures provide for a preliminary understanding of both whole as well as parts. In explaining this circle he mentions three essential ingredients of any interpretation. Every interpretation is grounded in a fore-having, foresight, and fore-conception.[7] Okere's appropriation of Heidegger centres on the latter's elaboration of the fore-going thesis. By insight or oversight Okere's elaboration of Heidegger's hermeneutic circle, radicalised it to near absurdity. Sifting out the specificity of Okere's thought from a twenty-six paged chapter saturated with a mass of echoes from Heidegger entails a hermeneutical midwifery that consists in fully unfolding that which was realized through Okere by means of a truly engaged attack on him. If Heidegger is correct in saying that "interpretation is not the acknowledgment of what has been understood, but rather the development of possibilities projected in understanding,"[8] then my rehearsal of what Okere wrote down will be as much idle talk, the ruinance of philosophy, as Okere's abundant citation of Heidegger in the name of allowing the author to speak for himself. We are bound to go beyond the obvious un-discussed assumption, what "stands there"[9] to evaluating the fruitfulness or legitimacy of his appropriation present in the "unsaid;" in this way we mobilise the author's insight and our intuition for the enowing (event) of a philosophical hermeneutics that is cultural revendication.

2. Insight and Oversight

Philosophical reflection on Okere's work is a Herculean task for more than one reason. The three philosophers - Martin Heidegger, Hans-Georg Gadamer, and Paul Ricoeur - that Okere selected for discussion on hermeneutics and philosophy come under the phenomenological current. It is difficult to determine from the sequence of Okere's treatment of these authors what his priority is. He presents the authors in the following order, Ricoeur, Heidegger, and Gadamer. The fact of treating Ricoeur before Heidegger and Gadamer shows that historical precedence is not under consideration. Surely the arrangement is not alphabetical, nor is it easy to claim that it is based on preference in terms of degree of relevance. If the degree of relevance were to be the criterion, how can we determine whether the sequence of arrangement is in ascending or descending order? Or could it be that the sequence is a matter of convenience? What the intention of our author is in this wise remains veiled. But it appears from the overall purpose of the work that the concern of our author is to provide a method through which philosophy is to emerge in Africa. It is therefore in this context that we are situating the entry of Heidegger into the dialogue of Okere's thought. This choice is no salvo to other difficulties that the text presents. Okere's uncritical adoption of his philosophers' views makes it hard for us to determine which philosopher plays more prominent role in his view of hermeneutics. The three philosophers he studied have each a view distinct and different from the other, and so it will be unrealistic to imagine that they enjoy equal merit in Okere's work. If in Okere's thinking the three philosophers complement one another, then it should have been shown clearly how, where, and to what extent they constitute an integral philosophical position in his work. The most curious of all the difficulties stem from the lack of analysis in his exposition of the views of philosophers under reference. The impression is that all that was said by the philosophers he refers to harmonise freely, yet we know that they differ in principle on account of which each enjoy a certain degree of originality in his idea of hermeneutics. One may ask, what informs Okere's silence over these apparently irreconcilable views? If we must attempt harmonizing the three views adopted by Okere it appears the only solution is resort to Okere's original intention as it is expressed in patches of link-up ideas intended by him to help re-align his readers' mind to the pertinence of a given philosopher under discussion to his main objective. In this regard we find three possible ways of understanding Okere's use of Heidegger.[10]

2:1. First Reading: Transformation and Opposition.

Understanding Okere's appropriation of Heidegger requires considering the introduction of Heidegger as a way to elaborating on Ricoeur's thought. Okere expressly states in the [11]Introduction that he intends "to complement the three stages of Ricoeur with the great insights of Heidegger and Gadamer." Ricoeur accepts the role of method in his hermeneutics but Heidegger shows aversion for method. For Heidegger "Method follows what is in fact the utmost corruption and degeneration of a way."[12] Elsewhere he writes: "Idle methodological programs ruin science."[13] He finds rigorous methodology insufficient and detrimental to the message of philosophy. His only discourse on method is destruction of Descartes who sees in method the best ally of philosophical enterprise. He prefers to speak in terms of way rather than method. In a word he is anti-method. He associates the use of method with the natural sciences rather than the human sciences. The natural sciences objectify reality and create a dichotomy between the subject and the object. Heidegger objects to this attitude of science in his critique of traditional epistemology. Against the objectification of the world, Heidegger proffers the view that Dasein and the world are internally related, and it is impossible to conceive of the world as a meaningful referential structure without considering Dasein. The point at issue here is that since Heidegger rejects the idea of method, it is most probable that Okere's insertion of Heidegger's hermeneutics as one of the methods of doing philosophy - that is doing philosophy understood in terms of transiting from culture to philosophy through methodologico-hermeneutical mediation - must have come as a result of Ricoeur's influence. Okere much against Heidegger's style accepts the use of method in philosophical enterprise, and hermeneutics is the method he considers most appropriate. In his exposition of Ricoeur's hermeneutics Okere outlines the different stages[14] in the passage from culture to philosophy. We estimate that it is against this background that he introduces Heidegger. The question of Being and the circle of Sein and Dasein are perceived from the point of view of history and thus re-inscribed into culture. Finitude, facticity, and being historically situated are presented here as characteristics of culture. Okere takes a step back from the Being question into culture. From this point he differs from Heidegger. It is culture that is to be questioned and man is the questioner. The ontological analysis of Dasein gives way to a hermeneutics of culture.   Transforming Heidegger's notion of "the World" into an anthropological concept, Okere interprets it as culture. This transformation permits the separation of culture from the subject who reflects on culture.[15] It is a return to the epistemological approach. While Heidegger separated philosophy from science, Okere prefers maintaining a dialogue between philosophy and science. This permits a critical perspective in hermeneutics and a possible development of questions of method with respect to the historical sciences. As a complementary thesis to

Ricoeur's the structure of interpretation remains the same - phenomenological, hermeneutical and reflective stages - only that the hermeneutical stage metamorphoses into hermeneutical as-structure and fore-structure and interpretation is super-ceded by reflective activity.

2:2. Second Reading: Transposition and Separation.

In the first reading Okere aims at re-reading some of the key concepts in Heidegger with a view to opposing himself to Heidegger. In the second reading the effort is at radicalising the concepts employed by Heidegger and insisting on the same line of approach, namely, the denial of method and the quest for ultimate foundation, and the dissolution of the problem of dichotomy between the subject and its world. Bearing in mind his main focus, which is culture as the lieu from which philosophy emerges, Okere conceives culture as constitutive of the reference-complex of which Heidegger speaks about in his theory of meaning. Here hermeneutics is not so much considered a method of philosophy as a way of philosophy. Hermeneutics of culture coincides with philosophy itself for the emergence of philosophy is contemporaneous with the dynamics of hermeneutics. In place of ontological analysis of Dasein he initiates an ontological analysis of culture. Plunging into the hermeneutic circle, he confers on culture the role of pre-suppositions in the work of interpretation. In his own words:

> The very basis of interpretation shows that it works only with pre-suppositions - in our own context, with the framework of a certain culture. The Vorhabe - the acquis prealable - the prior acquisition - represents the entire cultural heritage and tradition of the interpreter, a heritage which not only furnishes the material to be interpreted but the background to the interpretation.[16]

However, the ambiguity in Okere's employment of the concept of culture ridicules hermeneutics and imprisons it in a choking vicious circle. Culture is seen to play the role of Dasein's world, the "as-structure" and the "fore-structure" thereby constituting hermeneutics a revendication of culture. All is culture, all begins with culture and all ends with culture. In effect culture is the subject and object of hermeneutics, the how of hermeneutics, and the presuppositions of hermeneutics such that one is left to wonder whether interpretation will in reality be able to make explicit what is already in the culture in the form of possibilities. Leaving it to culture to interpret itself deprives man of his place in the hermeneutic enterprise. Culture becomes a self-contemplating and an unquestionable monad. Questioning gives way to contemplation of culture and all that is left to man is poetic intuition. With the death of reflection, what is left of philosophy is absolute relativism.

The interpretation we are exposing here is the ineluctable consequence of Okere's identification of As-Structure (Understanding) and Fore-Structure (or what he describes as three foundation of interpretation) with culture. With this identification we are only left with a Dasein that must wait on culture to reveal itself. As it were, this is a hang over from the first reading of Heidegger in which culture is read in an objective way. It is total vision based on "intuition." It is immediate seeing deprived of all forms of interpretation. It is a return to a vision of the object as absolute and immutable. It is a re-introduction of the view that objects in the external world are independent of the subject. Thus Okere insists on the hermeneutical responsibility of culture in the following words:

> Moreover, the very act of meaning-giving consists in building up, out of the elements of one's environment, a complex of references and relationships. Therefore man's ultimate interpretation, his philosophy will be necessarily historical and culture-bound, articulated relatively to his environment and world. His environment will prescribe the terminology, provoke the questions and predetermine the answers.[17]

While Heidegger speaks of Dasein as the being that poses the question of meaning and confers meaning on its world, Okere speaks of culture as provoking the question and furnishing the answers. Since culture is its own interpreter, interpretation is no longer the responsibility of Dasein. It simply belongs to Dasein to intuit the self-interpretation of culture made manifest in culture itself. Culture manifests itself to Dasein that in turn contemplates it or intuits it. Here hermeneutics takes a new turn. It is the description of the self-manifestation of culture as present in intuition. Hermeneutics becomes phenomenology understood as re-description of the phenomenon of culture. It could be said that while Heidegger proposes phenomenological hermeneutics, Okere advocates re-descriptive phenomenology. But it needs to be added immediately that hermeneutics as Okere uses it has neither to do with the art of avoiding misunderstanding (Schleiermacher), of understanding (Gadamer) nor with interpretation of existence (Heidegger). It is pure and simple a re-description of objects as they present themselves in "intuition." Dasein has only a linguistic role to play, namely, the articulation of what is present in "vision." It may be useful to consider the role Okere gives to language in hermeneutics. We find it strange to see Okere place language in the context of fore-structure of understanding, particularly, in fore-concept (Vorgriff). He writes:

> The Vorgriff (the Griff is obviously taken from German idea "grasp" expressed in Begriff) shows that the interpretation of the object is already prejudiced by the existing conceptual apparatus of the interpreter. Here the role of language becomes obvious. It carries with it a predisposition in terms of concepts which already dictate the orientation and possibilities of the new interpretation."

In *Being and Time* Heidegger presents language alongside understanding and state-of-mind as the constitutive ways of being "there," that is, as Dasein's modes of being-in-the world. Language is a mode independent and distinct from Understanding within which Vorgriff (fore-concept) is found as constitutive of the dynamics of interpretation. That Okere locates language within one of the modes of Dasein's being-in-the world, rather than allowing it a place as a distinct mode, compounds the confusion in his appropriation of Heidegger. The most that can be said of his insertion of language in fore-concept is that it is suggestive of the role of language in later Heidegger in which Dasein's primary access to Being is and through language, the result being that language becomes the site for the event of truth. Understood in terms of later Heidegger, the insertion of language in Vorgriff would mean dissolution of the structure of interpretation.

2.3. Third Reading: Affinity in Distinction

A third possible reading of Heidegger in Okere is to see the latter's effort as that of remaining close to Heidegger while projecting a distinct thesis. He extends the notion of Dasein's World to include culture. In this way philosophy, which has assumed the place of Dasein, is seen to be in internal relation with its culture. The structure of interpretation, (the fore-structure), is suppressed as culture shows it's ubiquitous presence in the sphere of understanding so that what remains of understanding is the as-structure. Philosophy is left with two modes of being-in (herme-neutics and language) with language integrated into the structure of hermeneutics. In this sense every understanding is language-bound. Philosophy understands, that is, interprets its culture linguistically. Language becomes the expression of what is already present in the hermeneutics. Philosophy understands its culture in and through language. But the difficulty with this interpretation is that it makes no place for the possibility of error in understanding. It assumes all the merits and demerits of Heidegger's hermeneutics.

3. The Limits of Philosophy: Finitude, Facticity and Historicity

Okere in his exposition of Heidegger's fundamental ontology aims at two things: (a) "to see very clearly how culture and philosophy are related, and how philosophy evolves from culture"[18] (b) "how the fundamental historicity of man affects all his efforts at meaning-giving, rendering them inescapably contextual and culture-bound."[19] The first two of these objectives we have tried to explore in part two of this reflection. Although we have no explicit consideration to the relationship between culture and philosophy, we have offered three possible ways of reading Okere's mind with respect to how philosophy can emerge from a culture. Here our interest is to highlight his understanding of the limitations of philosophy on the grounds of which he insists on the radical relativity of philosophy. In this connection he writes, "The radical relativity of all question of Being, of all giving of meaning to reality, in other words of all philosophy, is seen from a closer look at Heidegger's Daseinsanalytik."[20] It needs to be remarked that at this point Okere's simply echoes Heidegger since the latter had argued, based on Kantian influence on him with respect to the question of finitude, that philosophy is man's expression of his finitude; that it is man's way of feeling at home in a world into which be found himself thrown. Since man is limited and restricted, as a consequence, philosophy as human activity is incomplete and finite. Philosophy cannot have a full grasp of reality at once, nor could man through a dialectic play of one opinion against another arrive at a view that is true in "itself." No view we arrive at is the view. There are bound to be multiplicity of possible views at all times. Okere takes off from this perception of the nature of philosophy and goes to see in the structure of the Being question the restricted nature of philosophy. That every question has its point of departure (context) and orientation (aim) smacks of the relative nature of every question. Like the questioner, the question is historically bound. Since philosophical questions are so conditioned, philosophy is ineluctably historical, limited and relative. In short to understand human Dasein is to understand the being of philosophy.

One may ask, how come it that Okere insists so much on adapting the logic of Heidegger's fundamental ontology to reflections on hermeneutics of culture? What role does the establishment of the relative and finite nature of philosophy play in making philosophy emerge out of culture after all? In Heidegger the question was not so much philosophy and culture as philosophy and human existence. We may not be able to answer these questions but it appears Okere is by this gesture making philosophy to take the place of Dasein as he had already, as we explicated above, made culture to replace Dasein's world. While for Heidegger the Being that was the issue is Dasein, for Okere it is philosophy. One can as well say that he is proposing an ontology whose object is an epistemic being. It is the question of the being of philosophy, African philosophy. The being of philosophy at issue is the being of possibility. Raising the question of the possibility of African philosophy means the raising of the question of the being of philosophy from the angle of the possible. The question of the possibility of philosophy is the question of the condition of being of philosophy as possibility. The being of philosophy is being-possible insofar as it is not yet made explicit by hermeneutics, but it is insofar as it is in understanding waiting to be "explicitated" in interpretation. It is and it is not. Here the notion of facticity finds its relevance. It could be said that philosophy is pre-possessed (factical) in the understanding. Philosophy stands originally within a factical. In Okere the factical is ruinance: the questionability of Tempels and Mbiti. Although the intention to confront embodies a power that discloses and illuminates, understanding the sense of philosophy from a special and temporal restriction is the path to dilettantism. Philosophy is confined to its history, and doing philosophy becomes research: seeking answers rather than raising questions. It is not by recourse to some sort of validation of "its possessions or possessive possibilities" as Okere tends to do in his work that criticism historically illumines. Refusal to seek accreditation does not imply that philosophy is devoid of presupposition. In Heidegger facticity designates the character of the being of "human" Dasein. In his own words, "his expression means: in each case "this" Dasein in its being-there for a while at the particular .... insofar as it is, in the character of its being, there' in the manner of being ... , Dasein is there for itself in the "how" of its ownmost being."[21] Adapted to Okere's thought facticity applies to philosophy and the ownmost being of philosophy is a how of philosophising, "an indication which points to a possible path of beingawakeful." Here we are face to face with what is precisely, namely possibility, "and only in its temporally particular, there," its being "there" for a while."[22] In the awhileness of temporal particularity, philosophy is African philosophy as possibility. In its public manner of having been interpreted in the today, the specific categories of philosophy would include ethnic, collective, linguistic, critical tendencies. The awhileness of philosophy as possibility is linked to historicity. We do know from Heidegger that historicity is rooted in temporality. "The Being of Dasein finds its meaning in temporality. But temporality is at the same time the condition of the possibility of historicity as a temporal mode of being of Dasein itself, regardless of whether and how it is a being 'in time.'"[23] Dasein is constituted in its occurrence' by historicity. History itself is grounded in historicity. Dasein is its past, and this, in a double sense: he bears his past in his present and 'in the manner of its being which' on each occasion 'occurs out of its future. In effect "Dasein grows into a customary interpretation of itself and grows up in that interpretation."[24] Its past besides following after it, 'always already goes ahead of it.' Applied to philosophy this mode of being, historicity of the possible, tarries on with its past, and its very past always goes ahead of it. The possibility of (African) philosophy is as and what it already was.

4. Final Impression

In the foregoing reflection we have, besides allowing ourselves to be guided by the 'said' and the 'unsaid' of the passage under consideration, remained faithful to Okere's original intention which is the coming-to be of (African) philosophy. Our author's concern is an attempt to think the enactment of philosophy without reducing such enactment to what already was. Such philosophy must fulfil the traditional understanding of philosophy, but should be sufficiently unique to bear African stamp while transcending the claims of Tempels and Mbiti. Conceived in a given culture, its birth must be 'mid-wifed' by hermeneutics. It is concerned with the happening of what can be, and as such a concern with the coming to be of what is not. In it hermeneutics is stretched to its limits: a guide in a path yet unthread becomes the path beyond which nothing is expected. Hermeneutics, as Okere conceives it, is African philosophy as African philosophy awaits enactment in hermeneutics. Okere thinks a new departure in which the topography is culture, the itinerary is hermeneutics, and the mission is philosophy. Somewhere between the ruin and the enactment lies the elusiveness that Okere makes the subject of philosophical reflection. He claims an authoritative interpretation of what (African) philosophy is or ought to be, yet he insists on the radical relativity of philosophy. His stubborn insistence on the priority of finitude questions the relevance of transcendence and holds out a closed philosophy, however the "translatability" of language provides a leeway for possible dialogue and transcendence, Okere's claim that true philosophy operates at the level of universal seems to be contradicted by his idea of the radical relativity of all philosophy. In his account, his predecessors were incapable of installing thoughts that transcend their ethnic and linguistic origins. True philosophy must be distinguished from ethnic wisdom. He writes: To have an authentic African philosophy, there is need ... to seek the meaning of the totality of reality.... Over and above this intention and project, the questions of life and reality must be pitched at a certain level, at the level of universality and the answer must attempt to find a meaning for the totality at the level of the totality, at the level of ultimacy.[25] But strange enough, Okere pretends to find in Heidegger a veritable method of attaining this model of philosophy. But the truth is that Heidegger is the most outstanding critic of this model of "Western rationalism." By his manifesto, just sited above, Okere classes himself with the Cartesian tradition. It is thus difficult to see from his presentation of Heidegger how he reconcileled the seeming contradiction in insisting with equal strength on Cartesian model of philosophy on one hand, and on the post-modern emphasis on historicity and relativity of truth (represented here by Heidegger) on the other. For pretending to realise his Cartesian project by recourse to historicism (as found in his reading of Heidegger), he could be called a new Dilthey. However, he does not seem to have quite succeeded in this wise for want of analysis of essential and important concepts. Certainly, some philosophical currents fascinated him but he was too enthusiastic to allow a critical encounter with these currents before engaging in his philosophical project. Judged by the goal be set for himself, it is difficult to see how Heidegger's hermeneutics has helped him. However, should the introduction of Heidegger to his thought be considered independently, then some degree of philosophical rigour and precision would be needed to polish his insight. In Okere the enactment, the enowing, of (African) philosophy is a passion and a struggle. We consider the Olympian role he assigns to hermeneutics and culture the mark of the singularity of his thought. Where he writes in whisper, Heidegger shouts so that he can push the latter's thought into new expression. Little wonder he freely transposes Dasein into philosophy, Dasein's world into culture, and sees in Being-in' a justification for "the relativity of all giving of meaning and all interpretation." When in exposing the temporality and historicity of Dasein he sees a connection with the role of tradition and culture in all understanding and especially in philosophical understanding, it is not very clear whether he is simply echoing Gadamer or coming up with fresh insight. For him, culture and hermeneutics characterise philosophy itself according to object and method of treatment. In this regard he marks himself out, inaugurating a hermeneutic of culture which shut in its own circle remains a re-description of prejudices. In short, hermeneutics is cultural revendication: "That a culture is understood and interpreted means that this culture is re-assumed, re-appropriated, retrieved, and made to live again by a new and creative act done in the first person."[26] However, one may apply himself to reading Okere, one thing is evident, namely, that the tension in his work is symptomatic of the tension in the understanding of consciousness. Okere hopes to come to philosophy by matching his project with, in order to distinguish himself from, those of western philosophers. The West has defined philosophy, and what is expected of the rest of us is to apply ourselves to this definition. Yet, among the West we find people, Heidegger for one, who questioned the reduction of philosophy (love of wisdom) to science that is about calculation and measurement. While Okere remains in labour of philosophy, expecting hermeneutics to play the birth attendant, we are faced with three options, namely, to gratify ourselves like the proverbial tortoise that expressed joy at seeing his wife's spit; or like the proverbial wasp adopt another's child for our own; or perhaps like the good mother nurse the child in our bosom not worrying about whether it has a roman nose or hazel eyes.

Notes

[1] Okere, T, *African Philosophy: A Historico-Hermeneutical Investigation of the Conditions of its Possibility*, Lanham: 1983, p. 54. This comment which concludes our author's exposition of Heidegger's philosophy is in my humble opinion the highest tribute a philosopher," as far as I know, has paid to another philosopher in the history of philosophy. Okere can as well declare: Heidegger has spoken and the cause is finished! This essay is a commentary on Okere's appropriation of Heidegger's hermeneutical approach. Our reflection is on chapter three of the book African Philosophy. It is with great pleasure that I accept the invitation to comment on Okere's work for I count him, after St. Augustine, as one of my primary influences on the path of philosophy.

[2] Heidegger, M, *Introduction to Metaphysics*, New Translation by Grefory Fried and Ricbard Polt, London: 2000, pp. 2-4

[3] Heidegger, M. Ibid., p. 8.

[4] Heidegger in his lecture Ontology - *The Hermeneutics of Facticity*, translated by John van Buren (Bloomington & Indianapolis: 1999) notes that he employs the concept ontology only in terms of reference to a questioning and defining which is directed to being as such (p. 1) and since phenomenology directs the investigation and defines the questioning of what is the theme of ontology (pp. *53-80),* "Ontology is only possible as phenomenology" and the phenomenology of Dasein is hermeneutics in its most original sense Heidegger, M, 'The Task of a Destructuring of the History of Ontology' in Martin Stasse (editor), *Philosophical and Political Writings*, London: 2003, pp. 48-67; also, *Being and Time*, translated by John Maquarrie & Edward Robinson (Oxford: 2000), p.60). Gens, J.-C in his annotation in Heidegger, M, *Les conferences de Cassel*, 1925, Paris: 2003, pp.76-91 offers useful information on how the hermeneutic of Dasein replaces the classical hermeneutical question in Heidegger's lectures from 1923 to 1925.

[5] Gelven, M, Heidegger's *Being and Time*, Illinois: 1989, p. 86.

[6] Heidegger, M, *Being and Time*, p. 189.

[7] Enweh, Innocent 1, "Truth and Interpretation: The Hermeneutics of Heidegger and

Gadamer," p. 7, an unpublished DEA project, UCL, Louvain-la-Neuve (June, 2003).

[8] Idle Talk" (1927) in *Philosophical and Political Writings*, p. 242.

[9] Heidegger, M, Being and Time, p. 192.

[10] It is most probable that Okere did not understand Heidegger's phenomenological hermeneutics. This misunderstanding of his destroys what is authentic in Heidegger. But it is in this very destruction of what is authentic in Heidegger that lies what is fruitful and legitimate in Okere's thought. I n this regard he is authentically heideggerian. This is for the simply reason that according to Heidegger an authentic interpretation will require a destruction of the traditional categories and concepts. It is Dasein appropriating for itself what tradition offers. This is what Heidegger himself did in his call for the destruction of philosophical tradition and the rethinking of philosophical question. Okere in destroying what Heidegger represents beats for himself a new path in philosophical hermeneutics.

[11] Okere, T, *African Philosophy*, p. xiv.

[12] Heidegger, M, *On the Way to Language*, translated by Peter D. Hertz New York: 1982, p. 91

[13] Heidegger, M, Ontology - *The Hermeneutics of Facticity*, p. 35. [14] Okere, T, *African Philosophy*, p. 7-18

[14] Okere, T, *African Philosophy*, p. 7-18.

[15] Ibid. pp. 46-48.

[16] Ibid., p. 53.

[17] Ibid., p. 54.

[18] Ibid., p. 32.

[19] Ibid., p. 32.

[20] Ibid., p. 41.

[21] Heidegger, M, Ontology - *The Hermeneutics of Facticity*, p.5

[22] Ibid., p. 24.

[23] Heidegger, M, "The Task of a Destructuring of the History of Ontology, 1927" in *Philosophical and Political Writings*, p. 49.

[24] Loc. Cit.

[25] Ibid., p. 10.

[26] Okere, T, *African Philosophy*, p. xiv-xv. [27] Okere, T, *African Philosophy*, p. Xv.

10

Can there be an African Philosophy of Science?
An Appeal to the Hermeneutical

Everistus Ekweke

1. Introduction

The enterprise of science should be simple and succinct. It "is supposed to be a faithful description of the real world."[1] A description of the world must not be understood as an irrelative exercise that thrives in an absolute uniformity. It is true the world is one. It is also true the one world has various components and there are contextualized explanations behind the so-called faithful description of the same "one world." An epistemic approach to the world in the sense of investigation appeals to knowledge in the general sense of the word. But this investigative appetite becomes more apt when one respects the contextual as well as the respective aspects of the world. This would be recognition of the world as some holistic constitution expressed by some unity in diversity. In this wise, the world becomes a constitution, an epistemic macrocosm that recognizes its own respective micro-concepts that are the "initial condition,"[2] for this macrocosm. And so our approach in this paper will be a hermeneutical one. This is an exercise that is interested in the meaning of some respective things in the "one world"

The respective things in the world include the endeavour that is called natural science. Some choose to call it exact science and some others call it real science; while some still call it science of nature. However, what we are talking about is a researched appreciation of nature writ large. Even in this area of human natural activity there is also some sense of hermeneutics; there is an aspect of interpretative meaning where culture and *status quo* combine to hew out a paradigmatic

"Weltanschauung" from a network of some traditional ethos. In this sense, culture; tradition, meaning, ethics (a thing that is metaphysically elastic between life and death), paradigms, micro-world-views and more, are intricately interwoven. There is a pre-meditated effort by the *"Homo-Sapiens"* to live in and at the same time transcend the mere ephemeral exigencies of his space and of his time. By so doing, he engages in an examined appreciation of his space. He also investigates the nature of his time, questioning and being satisfied or not with the asymmetry or seeming thermodynamism of the same time. This is characteristic of time.

Our suggestion would be that this characteristic stands science in good stead as it is a hermeneutical category. It is an element in the study of nature that wants to identify with meaning and interpretation in their specific regards. Meaning makes sense and interpretation translates this sense into some praxis. And praxis is communicatively cinematic. For it is thermo-mutative (that is of events and of circumstances) where curiosity is the watch word.

If we are permitted to use the ilk of the European interpretation of science as an example, we can point towards a divergent group of variegated interpretations. From Greek antiquity, there have been variant views about the interpretation of the nature and the constituents of science. The Milesians talked about specific fundamental substances that were the primary constituents of what we refer to today as science. Thales insisted that water is the fundamental substance. For Anaximenes, the last pupil of the Milesian school, it is "air."[3] This shows that since European nay Greek antiquity, this divergence of opinion and or interpretation has been going on. One of the turning points in the interpretation of science in the sense of the behaviour of the constituents (nature) of this same science finds expression in the fate of physics today. For the Newtonian interpretation of reality, which proved a good guide[4] is now seemingly obsolete. The so called new physics is preferred since, for modern physicists it promises most firmly established ideas[5] in comparison with what could be referred to as "Old Physics." Einstein a major actor in the issue of the new physics presents counter intuitive notions of space and time, thanks to his relativity theory.[6] And since this is a current issue *In physics, it attracts particular attention. Or in...* what is referred to as the "Chemical revolution," there is the story of the phlogiston[7] theory of combustion. The seventeenth century scientist George Ernst Stahl made the proposition that in the process of the burning or the rusting of a material, a substance called phlogiston is being given off. This seemed plausible. But, when Lavoisier, the French Scientist brandished his *"principle Oxygene"*[8] he could prove that combustion and rusting involve something that is taken from the air. This thing is called Oxygen. According to scientists of the chemical world, the later proves more plausible than the former.

This is just an example. It shows how important interpretations are. Even, in the same area of research and scientific endeavour there is still the need for interpretative clarity. This exercise makes for a crystal understanding and subsequent acceptance of the happenstances in a given *status quo*. This is as much important in history, events, culture as well as in science, philosophy and general *"Weltanschauung."*

2. Hermeneutics: The Interpretative Option

An exclusive and precise intellecto-literary definition of hermeneutics is scarcely a facile option. For it is originally tied to a given scientific study of the Bible affecting Judeo-Christian specific interpretations as regards the fundamental understanding of their sacred scriptures. Be this as it may, "hermeneutics" is of "hermeneutic." And hermeneutic is closely related to the "hermeneut." In this order, the hermeneut (that means the Gk. "hermeneutes"; from the verb „hermeneuein") is an interpreter with particular reference to the early Church. "Hermeneutic or hermeneutical" as the case may be is the adjective of "hermeneut." It is the Greek "hermeneutes." The difference in spelling here is scarcely consequent. But, it means "of interpretation." Its verb is (in Greek), "hermeuein" as we have seen earlier; and it means to interpret. It also means to translate. The Greek word "hermeneus" as related to "hermeneutic" also means interpreter. Following from this the hermeneutical is interpretative. "Hermeneutics" which adds only an "S" to the word "hermeneutic" is an applied explanatory element of the later. It becomes therefore, the study of the methodological principles of interpretation. In certain specific quarters (which is very necessary to mention here) hermeneutics is of exegesis (a scientific approach to the Bible)[9] That is why it is said to be the study of the general principles of

Biblical interpretation.[10]

All the above indicate that hermeneutics concerns interpretation. It is also of the meaning of meaning itself. Hermeneutics enlists the services of explanation with the aim of shading sufficient light on the significance of a word or a proposition.

Theophilus Okere is a foremost hermeneutical philosopher. His main area of emphasis is the roles of philosophy, culture, tradition and ethics among peoples in the sense of interpretation. His particular area of study in this regard is Africa where interpretation is an urgent intellectual preoccupation in the face of structural "misunderstandings" from both home and abroad. However, Okere has taken time to trace a solid, albeit cursory, history of hermeneutics. And as we have hinted above, he has made sufficient reference to the Bible of the exegetical[11] culture implicating interpretation and scholarship. But, he never stopped at this. He has gone further to contextualize hermeneutics. His is the kind of hermeneutics that mediates between culture and philosophy. For him, it is necessary to put hermeneutics "in perspective in relation to culture on the one hand and philosophy on the other."[12] It is in this same line of thought that he (Okere) maintains that the African thinking has to be explanatorily made explicit through the hermeneutical approach. That is why he insists that a study of hermeneutics in such a contextual perspective "…will perhaps show more easily and clearly that it is only within the context of hermeneutics that African culture can give birth to African philosophy."[13] Thus, Okere has put a far too wide horizon of hermeneutic into a context. Okere's context is the African cultural context. The African culture when hermeneutically interpreted can appeal to our thought category and produce an African philosophy. In this sense the meaning and interpretation of culture becomes germane in an ontological approach to the African thought process. And for Okere this exercise will produce a philosophy truly African and truly traditionally African.

With the aid of the contextual and the perspectively philosophical, we have cursorily discovered Okere's interest in hermeneutics. We, therefore, intend to toe the same path as does Okere without an overly parroting of his thoughts in this regard. Our context is science and our perspective is the philosophically African. This will help us to do a faster reflection asking whether there can be an African philosophy of science.

3.   Philosophy of Science and the African: A Hermeneutical Procedure

Our reflection has a task of responding to the question: Can there be an African philosophy of science? One could ask, how can one pose this question? Yes. One can ask this because of our African chequered history that seems to have an undulating kind of progress. This question is asked because our African authentic thought category has been cajoled and jeopardized by other cultures. These cultures believe - and it has been working for them - that their own is paradigm of excellence and by this decimal the African has none. But those who uphold this tend to forget that Paulin Hountondji's famous "decollage conceptual"[14] has a lot of objective truth in it. And that is why he writes concerning this thus: "The decollage conceptual to say the truth, has always been realized. All men think by concepts, under all the heavens, in all civilizations, even if they integrate mythological sequences in their discourses (like Parmenides, Plato, Confucius, Hegel, Nietzsche, Kagame et. al.) or even if the discourse rests, in its totality, on fragile ideological foundations from which the scientific vigilance must liberate it at every instance." African civilizations from this point of view, are not exceptions to the rule. The African conceptions are as well thought out and as well eclectic as other conceptions. They rightly differ from other ones when they emphasize certain concepts that run at variance with theirs. This claim is true of philosophy and its allied disciplines such as literature, ethnology and anthropology. It is equally true of both science and hermeneutics.

Philosophy itself, among other things, is an exercise in thought processing. It has a system that accommodates both the particular and the universal in their ontological rights; where ontological refers to the quiddity of specific beings, and or entities. Philosophy is, following from this, all embracing. Masolo,[15] while making reference to Hountondji points out the intricate characteristics of philosophy. Philosophy is an activity. Even though it has a system of operation, it is not itself a system. Philosophy finds expression and transcends itself in history. This is mostly the case as philosophy professionally carries out its activity. By so doing philosophy transcends systems and appeals to the relationship existing between its exteriority and also its interiority. By so doing a confident and peculiar synthesis of continuity and opposition is established. And for Houndondji this is an operation in a dialectical relation in strict sense.[16] Philosophy therefore thrives in a dialectical synthesis that is all embracing. Philosophical reflections spread both inwards and outwards; radiating thought processes that seek for the ultimate meaning of things in their species and in their genera.

In our context philosophy relates well, therefore, to both science and hermeneutics. It relates well to axiomatic systems of methods of a structural nature. It also relates well to theories of meaning where interpretative explanations are only necessary.

Science itself is a discipline that is widely acclaimed as being methodically adequate especially when it has to do with the empirically observational. A referential approach to the word science would concern the functioning of the society where an ordered approach to operations is implicated. In this case, science is used in the sense of the scientific that means order, study or procedure towards achieving a set goal. Thus science could be applied to politics, sociology, economics, military logistics, and history like disciplines. If we take recourse to the western appreciation of science, science in the empirical sense becomes an indispensable discipline nay the king of them all. Their reason is that science for them reveals hidden nature. According to this mentality we cannot have access to the true nature of reality except when science uses its prestigious key to unlock this deep unreachable recesses of nature. They indicate this claim making reference to the history of empirical science where theories have been adopted, rejected and readopted, made reference to and sometimes superseded by new ones.

The successive development about the cosmological theories of the universe is a glaring example. The West believes that it is thanks to science and its empiricity that this progress in knowledge has been achieved in the same vein they make a lot of reference to quantum physics which contemporarily is related to the Einsteinan principles of relativity.[17] One of the claims of the relativity principle was the argument that time and space did not exist from eternity. And it is this idea that brought about the conception of the Big Bang,[18] in which a philosophically and empirically constructed theory tells the story of a cosmological origin of the universe. With this theory which tells of a universe in continuous expansion where a myriad of galaxies fly away from each other at unimaginable speed. Thus a history of the universe is retold. The universe advances from the Laplacian[19] static universe to a universe in a dynamic state. A universe in a dynamic state is the Big Bang type, the constituents of which are an astro-physical complex structure that comprise *inter alia* the evolution of stars, the death of stars, the galaxies with their complex nature; the presence of the galactic and super-galactic black holes which are the fate of stars and galaxies when they seem to have died out.

Our exemplary story, albeit cursory, of the history of the universe put in science - particularly astrophysics - is to expose how important the West holds science. For them the importance of a scientific paradigm finds expression in its evolutionary and or developmental significance. The aspect of science that they emphasize is the empirical. They hail it for its capacity for prediction that has more than 80% functional success. Its axioms,[20] method paradigms[21] are very close to an adequate description of nature, of reality as it is. And these fashion their arguments for the progress of the same science.

One would now ask what African's own appreciation of science is. This question would include what the African has which could be referred to as science. As we have hinted above, even though science *"stricta dicta"* is a special discipline, it falls into a general approach to knowledge and the acquisition of it, when put into the myth and reality dialectic of life which extends between birth and death, between blossom and corruption, science becomes not only a way of life but also a philosophy of action that sufficiently implicates history. Concerning the foregoing and relating it to development, Hounondji posits that:

> if the development of philosophy is in some way a function of the development of the sciences, then African philosophy cannot be separated from African science and we shall never have, in Africa, a philosophy in the strict sense, a philosophy articulated as an endless search, until we have produced, in Africa, a history of science, a history of the sciences. Philosophical practice, that peculiar form of theoretical practice that is called philosophy, is inseparable from that other form of

theoretical practice called science.[22]

This means that both philosophy and science are developmental categories. This holds and could mean that the way the African is doing philosophy, so should Africa also fabricate a device with which it will do science and subsequently do a philosophy of it. This however, does not mean that the African should necessarily borrow a doing of science that is western. The reason for this suggestion is that the African and the European or the westerner do not have the same scientific history. They do not even share the same origin, strictly speaking, of thought and of philosophy. The African should therefore engage in a methodic thought process that is both truly African and truly historical of Africa.

Despite Houtondji's fears that Africa has no history of science, we can say Africa has one. We should not forget that Africa is today documentarily known as the cradle of all civilizations.[23] These civilizations range from industry to history through science to technology and culture. One can rightly say this because there was a time when Africa was the focus of the world. In the West African region for instance, some evidence expose some advanced civilization in history and technology. Even people from some Asian and European countries imported materials of advanced technology from Africa, including the area Nigeria now occupies. Spectacular developments were noticed culturally and historically in such areas in Nigeria and West Africa like Ife, the Northern part of Ghana, Bankori, in the South of Mali and the Niger Delta areas between Benin and the Camerouns.[24]

The above means that the doubt about the possibility of an African philosophy of science is misdirected. For the materials for this exercise are available. Further evidence of the existence of these materials abound. It has been reported that in the Igbo-Ukwu area of Igboland the science and technology of metals which date back to 500 B. C.[25] was evident. Incidentally, this technology lasted about two and a half centuries and its original forms disappeared into some unbridled facts of history. This happened not without reasons beyond which the people of that age could not exercise any control. Talbot also reports the existence of iron work which flourished in many part of Igboland[26] in Nigeria from very early times. Documents also show that:

> The technology of iron smelting was fully developed along the Nsukka - Udi axis. Settlements were dotted with furnaces up to six to ten feet high. Casting with bronze reached its Zenith by A. D. 900 in Awka area. Nkwerre later became another ironwork centre. Enugu and Ika towns had boundaries here and there, and the raw materials of iron ore copper lead, hard charcoal, latente and clay were mined in different locations in the Igbo culture area.[27]

This points to elements of science and technology evident in the Igbo area of Nigeria. Once again these are raw materials for thinking in both science and technology. Be this as it may, Okafor has a structural presentation of iron smelting in Africa. For him: African bloomery iron smelting was distinguished by three characteristics: the direct production of medium carbon steels direct from the furnace; preheated draught arrangements; and the development of shaft furnaces with self-induced draught.[28] But "inspite of these ... achievements and this level of technical sophistication, it is not surprising that the industry gradually declined, at different rates in different areas, in the face of cheap steel imported from the blast furnaces of Europe."[29] This researched evidence exposes a lot of ideas about the fates of general history in Africa. It refers more particularly to the facticity of science and technology in Africa. For reasons that border on either African's inability to forge its own system of progress or an abuse of its complacent hospitality to its visitors, the present state of its science leaves much to be desired.

Without being apologetic, it is only necessary to make reference to the relationship that Africa had with the West. The dramatic and complicated history of contact and contamination with the West still affects our growth significantly. As Kanneh remarks, "'Africa,' already 'invented' by western systems of control and yet resisting any total interpretation, can only be approached through "impure" modes of analysis, which refer both to absolute self-reflexibility and a notion of difference."[30] Thus this relationship with the West may have their so called advantages. But we like to submit that the same relationship had made the West not only to interpret Africa wrongly but has presented Africa, even to Africans as a fundamental historical disappointment. The African had already begun to say no to this. Even some westerners like Taylor and Kuhn[31] have emphasized that the understanding of people's action should be predicated on a hermeneutical approach that is normally interpretation laden. The interpretation involved should differ systematically from culture to culture. This advice to the West by the westerners to be appropriated in the hermeneutics especially with regard to the culture of other people is timely for us at this juncture. T. Okere, an avowed hemme[32] neut of culture and philosophy, agrees with an appropriate interpretation of particular cultures and philosophies in their specific traditional rights. Here philosophy is adequately employed so that mistakes in logic and meaning would as much as possible be eliminated. Science and the philosophy of it will not be left out in this exercise.

It is in the light of the above that we would invite Okere who posits that "the individual is determined by his past and present and inserted into historical situation which is his culture. Man's interpretation of reality-which is philosophy is first of all based on interpretation of himself and thus will necessarily be coloured by this insertion. It is by relating the elements of culture to himself that one creates and constitutes meaning and becomes a philosopher. The relation of culture to philosophy is explained from the structural constitution of man."[33]

As we would like to borrow Okere's hermeneutic idea of relating culture to philosophy as coming from man's structural constitution, we also want to accept Hountondji's advice. As we said above while bringing in one of Hountondji's ideas, both philosophy and science have to work together to avail to Africa the right hermeneutics it needs to properly interprete its culture and its thought.

An African philosophy of science would be existing already when we have considered our general and scientific history - while not forgetting our culture - add hermeneutic components to it. This attitude will help us not to joke with this serious matter. We can ask Africa some specific questions on the "how" and the "why" of our scientific and technological complacency. What, for instance, happened to the iron smelting endeavor of some parts of the lgboland of South Eastern Nigeria. By asking this question we do not intend to tie Africa to the apron string of western scientific and analytic paradigms that constitute growth in western science. Africa can make its own discoveries to improve on its own experience of the world. Capra shares this idea while commenting on western physics and Eastern mystics. He says: "It seems then that Eastern mysticism and western philosophy went through similar revolutionary experience which led them to completely new ways of seeing the world. ..., the European physicist, Niels Bohr Indian mystic Sri Aurobindo both express the depth and the radical character of this experience.[34] This explains that in our world of variegated experience and culture both philosophy and culture engage our world view in a worth while hermeneutics. This calls us to order in the sense of approaching reality as it is and allowing it to speak to us in a manner that suits it. Thus can we, armed with a hermeneutic, cultural, philosophical and scientific ear listen it to and approach specific situation while giving them adequate and specific interpretations and meaning. This is a genuine way through which we can do a philosophy of science truly scientific and truly philosophical of Africa.

4. Conclusion

As we conclude this text, it is worth while to listen to one of Okere's submissions that every African should be proud to accept. "The main practical conclusion one can draw from all this is that philosophy is no abstract science; it is a statement of meaning by a person committed to life and to reality and eager to relate himself to Life and reality .... Doing Philosophy is to creatively interpret one's culture. For black African philosophers it will mean familiarity and identification with their culture .... It is thus that a culture can speak by itself, of itself and for itself." This self interpretation is also a self-assertion, it is no doubt the best way to restore self-confidence to a humiliated culture. When it comes to doing philosophy of any sort, this is Okere's stand. "Culture," "familiarity" "self interpretation," "self-assertion" and of course, "hermeneutics" are the key or operative expressions that feature in Okere's thought. As we conclude this text, we moderately re-appropriate this thought of Okere in both philosophy and science because it is worth the while.

Our submission, therefore, is that an African philosophy of science has to put into consideration the issue of history, culture, origins, authenticity and hermeneutics, in its system of operation. For the West, a philosophy of science criticizes scientific submissions with particular reference to theories. In Africa philosophy of science must not occupy itself with the kind of thing that worries the westerner. It has to ask ultimate questions about the attitude of scientific programme in Africa. Why, for instance, does it take time to transfer a culturally based theoretical myth to practical components of reality in nature, which for the African could be called science. Why, for instance, do our scientific endeavours get nipped in the bud? If we discover the reason what efforts are we making to eliminate these teething errors? Such questions are necessary in the critical philosophical enterprise towards the exigencies of science in both the micro and macro levels of intellectual endeavour.

In summary, we have adopted a non- definition approach in our text. That is why we have given a descriptive meaning of our key concepts in this presentation. Our submissions show that science should be succinct in its attempt to reveal nature as it is. We have also admitted that this enterprise of science should be as microcosmic as it should also be macrocosmic. A hermeneutical approach to perspectives in both science and philosophy should only be necessary in philosophy of science with particular reference to an Africa philosophy of science. Our submission has explored the western categories of scientific research, while not asking Africa to absolutely do it the western way. We have also referred to hermeneutics, traced its intellectual origins and discovered its interpretative powers with particular reference to exegesis, philosophy, culture; and even added that it plays roles in philosophy of science. Okere's particular interest in hermeneutics has convinced us that culture and philosophy work together in a worthwhile socio-intellectual enterprise. The enterprise of philosophy when rightly carried out should appeal to contextualized cultures and use hermeneutics in its operations. Our thinking has necessitated our recourse to the aspect of the philosophy of science that should be used by the African. Once again we have enlisted the services of hermeneutics as we employed philosophy, science and the African thought processes to make our suggestions as regards the possibility of an African philosophy of science.

Following from these, we have taken an excursion, just for instance, to the western aspects of science as well as their approach to the philosophy of it. We have discovered that their system implicates hermeneutics as they historically and paradigmatically assess their scientific lots. And this has stood them in good stead over the centuries. Our attitude is not to ask the African to emulate this. Ours is a suggestion that requests an authentic, contextualized hermeneutic, an original approach which could borrow a leaf from other cultures that have experienced successes in this regard. This is incidentally in line with Okere's suggestions when he says; "In the matter of an African philosophy, by Africans, fear has also been expressed of the temptation and the danger of the search for originality or the cultivation of difference. Too late such fears, and in vain, since if philosophy is philosophy at all, it is fatally condemned to certain originality and a certain difference based on the originality and difference imposed by its cultural background.[35] Therefore, our approach to an African philosophy of science, has to be original. This originality should have to fearlessly implicate culture, tradition, history, the sense of difference, background while enlisting the services of some hermeneutic characteristics. This task is contemporarily germane as we should strike a difference between the other's own interpretations of what we (Africans) are and our self assertion in respect of what we Africans really are.

Notes

[1] Paul DAVIES And John GRIBBIN, *The Matter Myth,* London: Penguin books,1991, p.14

[2] Cf. Karl POPPER, *The logic of Scientific Discovery*, London: Unwin Hymann   ,1990, pp.100-101   see also: Evaristus EKWEKE, *Falsifiability, Science and rogress in Popper with a Contextual African Example*, Brussels: Edition societe ouverte,2001, p.1 36

[3] Steven WEINBERG, *Dreams of a Final Theory,* New York: Pantheon Books, 1993 P.7

[4] Paul DAVIES and John GRIBBIN, *The matter myth,op.cit.p.18*
[5] Ibid.,p.19
[6] Ibid.,p.19; see also Ilya PRIGOGINE, et al., *L'Homme face a la science* Paris: Criterion,1992, p.19

Everistus Ekweke **207**

[7] Ilya PRIGOGINE, et.al., op. cit. p.19

[8] Paul THAGARD, *Conceitual Revolutions*, New Jersey: rinceton University Press, 1993, pp.33-40

[9] In the Encyclopedia Britannica, it is said that a hermeneutics is "the study of the general principles of biblical interpretation. For both Jews and Christians throughout their histories, the primary purpose of hermeneutics, and of the exegetical methods employed in interpretation, has been to discover the truths and values of the .... In the history of biblical interpretation, four major types of hermeneutics have emerged: the literal, moral, allegorical and analogical." In the first type of hermeneutics - the literal - emphasis is laid on „plain meaning," appealing to grammar and contexts in history The second - the moral - takes care of the ethical imports of the biblical accounts giving US lessons there from. The third -allegorical - simply interprets the narratives. And the fourth -the anagogical-occupies itself with the mystical, interpreting the bible with the view of prefiguring the life to come. However, „in the modern as in other periods shifts in hermeneutical emphasis reflected broader academic and philosophical trends; historical, - critical, existential and structural interpretation have figured prominently during the $_{20}$th century. On the non academic level, the interpretation of prophetic and apocalyptic biblical material in terms of present day events remains a vigorous pursuit in some circles." (Peter NORTON, et.al, (eds), The New Encyclopedia Britannica, vol.5,(Chicago,1994), pp.874-875

[10] Philip BABCOCK, (ed.), *Webster's Third New International Dictionary*, Chicago: Merriam -Webster Inc., 1986, p.1059

[11] Exegesis/Exegetical : A scientific study of the bible , revealing the meaning of things, using history, background study, environmental considerations , and the truth of respective circumstances. These implicate happenstances that border on a dearer understanding of the texts of the Holy Writ; involving persons and groups, culture, tradition and general ethos.

[12] Theophilus OKERE, *African Philopsophy: A Historico-Hermeneutical investigation of the conditions of its possibility*, New York: University press of America, 1983, p. 15

[13] Ibid., p. 15

[14] Paulin, HOUNTONDJI, "Remarques sur la philosophie afrIcaine contemporaine" Diogene,71(1970)p.139. See D. A. Mosob, *African Philosophy in Search of Identity*, Edinburg: *1994,* p. 198. The literary translation of this is „Conceptual take -off'. The ideological meaning suggests a philosophy of action that seeks to be objective,

ecclectic and civilizational: especially of Africa.p.1 98
[15] D.A. MASOLO, op. cit., p.1 99
[16] Paulin HOUNTONDJI, *African Philosophy: Myth and Reality,* London : Hutchinson,1983, p.87
[17] The theory of relativity was a turning pomt in the empirically scientific modern Europe. Having successfully proved   more plausible than the classical mechanics of the Newtonian dispensation , it set out to solve a lot of problems bordering especially on physics and allied disciplines. Thus „in addition to satisfying the intellectual cravings of the scientists of the day, the theory of relativity was to make completely new and fantastic predictions which were to culminate in the dawn of atomic age. The theory of relativity consists of two main parts the special (or restricted) theory of relativity and the general theory of relativity. The special theory was presented by Einstein in 1905 and the General theory in *1916".* (cf. James A. Coleman , Relativity for the Layman , London: Penguin books, 1 990, p.44
[18] Trinh Xuan THUAN, *La melodie secrete,* Paris: Editions Gallimard,1991, pp.145-1 52
[19] Ilya PRIGOGINE,et.al, *L'homme face a la science,* op.cit., P.13
[20] Karl POPPER, *The logic of scientific Discoverv,* op.cit.,pp.71-75
[21] Thomas 5. KUHN, *The Structure of Scientific Revolutions,* Chicago: University of Chicago Press, 1970, p.83ff.
[22] D.A. MASOLO, *African philosophy in Search of Identity,* op. cit., p. 199
[23] Eugene E. UZUKWU, *A Listening church, Autonomy and Communication in African Churches,* New York: Orbis Books, 1996, p. 32.
[24] Evaristus E. EKWEKE, "Nigeria in Western Ideology of Democracy: Any possibility of An African alternative," Amamihe: (2003) p. 62. Journal of Applied philosophy.
[25] Micheal A. NWACHUKWU, „Beyond Technuzu: Reflection on Igbo Perception and Practice (Ahiajoku lecture 2003,) p.9.
[26] A. TALBOT, *The peoples of Southern Nigeria,* London: Frank can 1969, pp. 336-336.
[27] Micheal A. NWACHUKWU, Beyond Teknuzu: op.cit, P. 9-10.
[28] E.O OKAFOR, *New Evidence of Early lron-smelting from South Eastern Nigeria".* (1993) (Quoted in Ahiajoku 2003) p. 11.Technology", (Ahiajoku lecture)
[29] Ibid.,P.11.
[30] Kadiatu KANNEH, *African Identities,* London: Routleadge, 1998 P.29
[31] Thomas 5. KUHN, *The Road since Structure,* Chicago: The University of Chicago press, 2000, pp. 218-219.

[32] Theophilus OKERE, *African Philosophy*, Op. cit. P. 16

[33] Ibid., p. 16.

[34] Fritjof CAPRA, *The Tao of physics*, London: Flamings, 1992, p. 62.

[35] Ibid., p. 128.

11

Okere, Igbo Names and African Philosophy

M. F. Asiegbu

1. Introduction

Not until 20th century analytic philosophy came to focus on "how words hook onto the world"[1] do proper names constitute an enormous philosophical problem. If words acquire their meaning by standing for items in the world, then words are labels, tags, or symbols. Words mean what they signify because they stand for, represent, denote, name, or even refer to objects in the world.[2] This is the basic idea of the Referential Theory of Linguistic Meaning. Quite attractive, apparently obvious and definitely commonsensical, this theory claims that words relate to the extra linguistic world by means of reference. On this view, a proper name is identical with its bearer. If a proper name were to mean anything, it would mean nothing but its semantic referent. Proper names are meaningful in so far as they stand for objects in the world. "Hilary Clinton," for instance, refers to the person Clinton; while a general term like "cat" picks out cats. Sentences are meaningful when they reflect the state of affairs they depict. Thus, a competent speaker of a language is able to grasp sentences in the language once s/he knows what the component words in a sentence represent.

Consider sentence (1): "Marion Jones won five gold medals at 2004 Olympics in Athens." Should an interlocutor claim not to grasp the meaning of "… won five gold medals at 2004 Olympics," one would say that s/he was ignorant of English language. S/he would be displaying ignorance of history, geography or sport should s/he fail to grasp the reference to "Marion Jones" and "Athens." Rarely would one suggest that s/he did not understand what "Marion Jones" or "Athens" means. Indeed, if names have meaning, it would be the case that whoever fails to grasp the meaning of "Marion Jones" or "Athens" will not understand sentence (1). But this is not the case! Actually, proper names like Marion Jones and Athens often times do not form an essential part of dictionary entries. It is not even an omission leaving out proper names in such entries. If proper names have meaning, what are they? A good number of African writers would agree with J. S. Mill[3] that proper names have denotation but would dispute his view that proper names do not have connation. These thinkers do not just refer to any proper name; they mean African proper names. These names are not just labels; they are also meaningful.

Running through nearly all works on African names is the conviction that African names are laden with meaning. For such works, meaning is a distinctive mark of African names. These works create the impression that African proper names are meaningful is a cultural trait. Were this particularity of African proper names not considered an African cultural trait, it would not have motivated most works on African proper names. Hence, *African* names are not only meaningful, these studies further leave their audience with the view that proper names of *American* and *European* origins, at least, differ from African proper names by being *meaningless*.[4] Thus, to bear an African proper name is equivalent to bearing a name suffused with meaning unlike most European/American proper names!

Consider some of these studies of Igbo names. Grouped into twelve categories, Ubahakwe in *Igbo Names: their Structure and Meanings,* studies the pattern, and meanings of an enormous list of Igbo personal names. With an additional list of 4,500 Igbo personal names, names entirely unknown to Ubahakwe, Ebeogu[5] claims he has improved significantly on Ubahakwe's collection. The different categories into which these thinkers have grouped Igbo personal names are instructive for a proposed African philosophy.[6] A recently concluded study of Yoruba names,[7] lists as many as 20, 000 Yoruba names with their meanings and pronunciation. About such studies, we may note, at least, three particularly interesting conclusions. Firstly, while a cardinal issue for names of non-African origin, the problem of reference is merely considered secondary for African names. There is more to *African* names than mere identity tags! Meaning is this plus feature. Secondly, the issue of meaning as a marked characteristic of African names becomes primary. In this regard, it is common to come across African studies that rely heavily on African names, as if making a reference to African names substitutes good reasons for one's case. Lastly, in what seems to be an insightful remark, whose impact Ebeogu is unaware of, Ebeogu criticizes Ubahakwe's work, observing that all Igbo personal names are abbreviations of whole sentences; or they are themselves phrases. In his words, Igbo personal names are "contractions from either phrases or full sentences they include noun phrases, positive statements, questions and requests, and conditional sentences."[8] In other words, these names are definite descriptions or abbreviations of descriptions, Ebeogu seems to maintain.

My intention is to show, contrary to the view held by Okere and other thinkers, that the Referential theory has a powerful grip on the Igbo. These thinkers are not only definitely mistaken about the influence of this theory; if they reject it, they do so for some non-obvious reasons. Nonetheless, I do agree with Okere that philosophy is culture-bound; that it involves an individual reinterpreting his culture. That Igbo proper names could provide one of the essential means of doing it is the issue. We shall examine, therefore, whether Igbo names would serve this purpose.

Majority of thinkers also glory in specifying the possible meanings of Igbo proper names. They maintain that the meaning of these proper names afford one a lee way to Igbo thought pattern and worldview. Okere does exactly this and more. Although Okere discusses Igbo names, following largely the pattern of study prevalent in works on African names, his purpose is different. His study of Igbo names is an attempt to expose what resources and working materials Igbo names provide for an eventual African philosophy. Much as he does not depart from the prevalent works, which privilege the issue of meaning over the reference of names, he recognizes, nonetheless, the double role of Igbo names: they function as identification marks or tags and also are imbued with meaning. Nonetheless, he urges for a closer attention to the meanings of these names, influenced, as he is, by his vision of African philosophy. But for his methodological presuppositions, Okere would not be defending the pre-eminence of meaning of Igbo names over their reference. This is, in fact, the view we shall defend all through this work. To prove his case, Okere relies on the social significance of Igbo names.

Hidden in his view of names is a misunderstanding that allows him the luxury of arguing for the priority of meaning over reference of names. This misconception imbedded in his arguments is the view that 'foreign' names do refer only just because they are meaningless. Were they imbued with meaning, these names would function in the same manner as Igbo personal names. The pre-eminence of meaning to reference seems to result as an answer to the question, is reference all there is to names? Given his goal, Okere insists that there is more to Igbo proper names than meets the eye.

By minimizing the importance of reference, Okere appears to suggest either that reference of names is hardly topical and problematic, if at all; or he creates the impression that there is a ready solution to the issue of reference of names. Thus, the question to which he needs to respond is this: if meaning, what happens to reference? Is the problem of the reference of names resolved or does such a problem not arise for Igbo names? Contrary to Okere's view, we shall argue that reference is the primary role of any kind of names. Okere never set out to discuss names for their own sake. If anything, he has an eye to something greater to generate an African philosophy via a study of Igbo proper names. Any assessment of Okere's work[9] would take into consideration this ultimate purpose. Eventually, one recognizes that Okere continues, in his article,[10] his previous preoccupation in his book.[11] While he does not develop any African philosophy through names, he gives important hints and points out possible routes to such a philosophy. His firm conviction is that once a philosophy does not arise from one's cultural roots, it is yet to become one. This is valid for all philosophies as it is mostly for an African philosophy. For this reason, we find it important enough to source a solution to the problem of reference from within African culture. Such an undertaking would be true of Okere's original purpose and insight.

2. The Powerful Influence of the Referential Theory

The Referential theory[12] is one whose powerful grip over people comes alive in the unsuspecting way people apply it in their day-to-day activities. Since the bearer of a name is both its meaning and referent, to know a person's name is to exercise power over the individual. Spell cast on people succeed, it is believed, once the magician is in possession of the person's name. To abuse a person's name is an affront on the name's bearer. Some religions refuse to make public a god's name for fear of blasphemy. Any disrespectful use of a deity's name is considered, in some religions, not just a mistake but even sinful. Often times, children bear names of virtues in the hope that they will imitate the graces in question.[13] Indeed, a proper name is a person's most precious possession. This view, I shall show, draws from the social significance of names in Igbo culture. It entails portraying the relationship between names and fame, names and personality, names and womenfolk. At the end of it all, I shall insist that none of these relationships faces down the problem of reference of names.

Name and Existence

It is the case that an object, a person, or even a pet is generally associated with a name. If people spend time to choose names for their pets and hobbies, it is the case that a human being cannot exist without a name. This development seems to point to the fact that a name essentially makes a person.[14] The Genesis legend of creation assumes that God's creative act was completed only when every Dick and Harry got named! (Gen. 2: 18 23) 'Bringing into being' came to mean 'calling them by name' (Is. 40: 26). If, for the Igbo, a person's descendants perpetuate his lineage posthumously in his name, then to cut off his name is to kill the person; to put an end to his existence. For we live even in our names.

Name and Fame

There is some relationship between a name and reputation. A famous man has a name to defend. And who hasn't! Following a person's exploits, deeds, and achievements, especially when these gain wide acclaim, the person becomes reputed for them all. This person's name is dear to him and is often defended at all costs! His achievements and mighty deeds become an extended part of his personality. As one would express it, these exploits become "his name writ large."[15] In this line, a 'name' is coterminous with 'reputation.' In this respect, a 'name' easily translates 'renown,' 'glory,' and even 'fame,' for instance.[16] One seeks to carve a name for oneself by one's deeds. Hence, a good name is worth a whole life-time of service and good deeds than an instantly momentary reputation that dies away as it arises. This reality is nowhere more evident than in Igbo culture.

Without a name, a person in an Igbo community is worse off than a penniless nobody in a society where the cult of riches holds enormous sway. As good as a dead man, this nameless Igbo resembles an *'efulefu',* one "who sold his machete and wore the scabbard to battle."[17] In the traditional society, acquisition of names (and so fame) depends largely on one's achievements and exploits. This view is proven true in the case of Okonkwo, Achebe's principal character.[18] Okonkwo of the nine villages of Umuofia, whose exploits and success in life have carved out into a living legend, proves true this claim. Already a great wrestler at eighteen and a titled man at thirty-eight, Okonkwo boasts of two barns and husbands a family of three wives and eight children. With five human heads, he is a great warrior. He cuts a radically different figure from his father Unoka. In Okonkwo's eyes, Unoka, a rather carefree, indolent and irresponsible man, is a disaster. All through the fabric of Umuofia society, the reprehensible memory of Unoka, unlike Okonkwo the son, has spread like a stain. In fact, Unoka is much like the strange wine-taper Obiako who eventually gave up his trade; or again like Okonkwo's son Nwoye who became a convert to the new religion, Christianity.[19] The trio - Unoka, Obiako, and Nwoye have no name to defend in the eyes of Umuofia.[20]

Had Unoka lived well into a revered old age, led an exemplary moral life, seared a male child (he did Okonkwo), and finally became honoured with a second burial celebration, he would become an ances-tor.[21] Ancestor status is the greatest name one could acquire in Igbo culture. Unfortunately, Unoka could not make it. Towards the tail end of his life, he caught an abominable illness that denied him any burial.

What Okonkwo feared he had lost with Nwoye's conversion to Christianity was exactly the ancestral status.[22] But his lineage would remain as far as other male children of his did not follow Nwoye's example.[23] Okonkwo left behind him a reputable memory of great exploits and achievements, crammed full into a brief period of his life than 'most men who live the allotted span can dream of'.

Men like Okonkwo take on sobriquets whose meanings are pointers to great deeds and achievements. 'Ome ka Agu' one who behaves like a lion. This name likens its bearer to a lion, just to show that he is meant for great deeds. 'Akunyili' alludes to the cult of wealth very much rife in Igbo society. 'Nwokeadinjo' epitomizes the phenomenon of male chauvinism in the society. These sobriquets are as widespread as there are men. In a society, which prices men's achievements and mighty deeds high, these sobriquets, more often than not, come to replace the names people received at childhood. Sometimes, people tend to retain the sobriquets than the person's name. Generally, people acquire these sobriquets either as a result of their behavior, their virtues (e. g. generosity), or as ideals set for themselves. In terms of this last role, sobriquets function as a programme of life, one to which people look up to.

Name and Personality

Suppose you bear an ugly, disagreeable, and detestable name like 'Dutroux' or your name has hardly any meaning like 'Gwnyed,' in what way does it affect your personality, if at all? Consider that interesting question of Esau about his brother, Jacob: "Is he not rightly named Jacob? For he has supplanted me these two times" (Gen. 27: 36), thus giving credence to the view that name influences and perhaps determines a person's personality. If this is accepted, then a name wields power over a person's future, his ambition, hopes, and expectations. In fact, one would say that a name constrains its bearer to comply to its import; to configure his existence, his life to what essence a name expresses. "Nabal" is a case in point. This name is interesting for its bearer conforms to the expressed meaning. The husband of Abigail, whom the warlord David later took as wife, made excuses for Nabal, her husband. 'As his name is, so is he; Nabal (meaning fool) is his name, and folly is with him." (I Sam. 25:25). Here the character defines the person.

Just as a change of a person's name supposedly changes his character, so also a grasp of a person's name gives one mastery over the person. To succeed in his bid to harm a person, a *dibia ogwu,* amongst other demands, requests for the victim's name.[24] Invoking a person's name also entails coming under the authority and the protection of the invoked name. This is the import of the supplication, 'only let us be called by your name' (Is. 4:1), the common prayer invoking God's name and demanding him to act!

Name and Womenfolk

If one were to sexualize achievements and mighty deeds in Igbo society, one would typify them as male. Men rather than women are associated with great achievements. If men immortalize their names through these exploits, women as well as children remain unsung all life through. Unknown, they fade away into silence as if they never walked the earth. Although their role may not compare to the male role in the society, one underestimates the power of women to one's risk. The Earth goddess *Ani* is largely instrumental to Okonkwo's downfall. The Igbo legend voices an ancient belief in feminine strength and puts in perspective the dialectics of male and female power. Achebe writes,

> In the beginning Power rampaged through our world, naked. So the Almighty, looking at his creation through the round undying eye of the Sun, saw and pondered and finally decided to send his daughter, Idemili, to bear witness to the moral nature of authority by wrapping around Power's rude waist a loincloth of peace and modesty.[25]

The female role in the society goes hand in hand with feminine power. Since the female folk lives in the shadow of their men folk, the traditional society attributes to the women folk the role of "intervening only when everything else has failed … like the women in the Sembene film who pick up the spears abandoned by their defeated men folk…." The women are "the court of last resort … {which is} too far too late."[26] The female folk the 'second class citizens,'[27] in addition to some men who are unable to hold down work, the poor and the marginalized do remain nameless and hence faceless in Igbo community. Feminist movements crusade for the betterment of the lot of women in Igbo society today, a society that, in some cases, holds down the rights of women as it once did in the traditional society. As Achebe graphically presents them, women fill the same role in traditional society as in the contemporary one: 'the role of a fire-brigade after the house has caught fire and been virtually consumed.'[28] A catalogue of female names does not reflect the male features that achievements, mighty deeds, and exploits exemplify! Feminists are wont to put down this phenomenon to male chauvinism. Such names as Oduenyi Elephant's tusk, Akwugo - Eagle's nest, Nwaekuruele - Beauty beholden, are deemed feminine,[29] making the stock of feminine names. The Referential theory, as shown above, is not down and out, although African writers tend to neglect it, relegating it to a second place. Even for Okere, Igbo proper names are primarily statements of meaning.

3. Proper Names as Statements of Meaning

Okere makes much of the claim that Igbo names are a means of record-ing events in the life of a community, or a family, and an individual could make use of it to write his life history.[30] He sees these names as "lasting memorials;" they are "immemorial history." Nonetheless, the signifi-cance of Igbo names as history, in my view, is fundamental to the role of names in the culture devoid of scientific technique for recording history. In the wake of the abundant opportunities to get educated, unlike yesteryears when only few set out in quest of the "golden fleece," the role of Igbo proper names as records of events and history will soon be over. If Igbo names are 'statements of meaning,'[31] the type of meaning in question will differ from the presumed meaning of 'foreign names' like Rita, Augustine, and Aristotle. While the meaning of these names consists in the descriptions with which one associates these names, the meaning of Igbo names derives from the circumstances and the lan-guage itself. The names are not associated with any descriptions at all. 'Ezebuilo,' 'Onwuneme,' 'Amaka' for instance, derive from Igbo lan-guage. Okere's argument that Igbo names are statements of meaning arises principally from the circumstances surrounding a name.

Consider the name, 'Ekene,' which abbreviates 'Ekene dili

Chukwu,' meaning 'Thanks be to God.' A grand father thanks God for letting him live to see his first grand-son. Enshrined in this name is the story of a family of a man and a woman to whom were born five ladies and four boys. After the first two young men took to the Catholic priesthood, the father of the family kept alive the hope of taking in his own hands a grandson. The father of the family celebrates the family's gratitude in the name of the grandson.

Consider also the name 'Onwuma.' Achebe typifies, by this name, the lot and agony of a mother of ten children, all of whom but one died in early childhood.[32] What a source of unbounded joy and a 'crowning glory' a child is to a woman in Igbo culture! And what a horrible nightmare the woman Ekwefi knew as she buried all nine children! Achebe reports the woman's story vividly, bringing out the attributions of various names. He writes thus,

> The naming ceremony after seven market weeks became an empty ritual. Her deepening despair found expression in the names she gave her children. One of them was a pathetic cry, Onwumbiko 'Death, I implore you.' But Death took no notice; Onwumbiko died in his fifteenth month. The next was a girl, Ozoemena 'May it not happen again.' She died in her eleventh month and two others after her. Ekwefi then became defiant and called her next child Onwuma 'Death may please himself.' And he did.[33]

This grave account of the personal lot of an Igbo woman concisely captures an individual's thoughtful reflection on death and her reaction to this dreadful phenomenon. In Igbo culture, one does 'plead' even with death; one 'prays' death to stem her havocs, as the name 'Ozoemena.' This encompasses a world of attitudes and relationships. It might take several dimensions. In the case of a repeater child, one presents some appeasing sacrifice, consisting of those things that children are prone to, like toys, teddy bear, and chocolate foodstuffs to the spirits who torture the woman.[34] Such elements, as are described above, Okere argues, are praepadeutic to an African philosophy conceived through the meaning of Igbo proper names. The circumstances, events, and in fact history of a proper name, are a part and parcel of Igbo proper names. If these names abbreviate whole sentences and noun phrases, it is because of their bid to capture circumstances leading up to them.

4. Igbo Names: Noun-phrases and Abbreviations of Whole Sentences

Above, we remarked that Igbo names are abbreviations of whole sentences. They are also noun phrases. For this reason, one could easily view them as descriptions rather than genuine proper names. As a result, they become subject to the difficulties that 'foreign' names face. A few examples are appropriate to establish our view.

Name	Syntactic Format
Nnanna	Nna nke nna
Afamefuna	Afa m efuna
Umunnakwe	O buru n'umu nna ekwe
Ekene	Ekene dili Chukwu
Tansi	Tabansi
Maaka	Madu ka

The above names are, therefore, short forms of sentences. As abbreviations of sentences, they are not really genuine proper names. Abbreviations of sentences they are, no doubt, but does this feature make them descriptions much like 'foreign' names such as 'Aristotle?' Some differences exist between 'Ekene,' for instance, and 'Aristotle.' While 'Ekene' abbreviates a whole sentence, 'Aristotle,' translates a number of descriptions, like 'the student of Plato,' 'the Stagirite philosopher,' 'the teacher of Alexander the Great.' Thus considered, 'Ekene' is not a description but an abbreviation of an entire sentence. But is this the peculiar feature to which Okere and other thinkers refer? If so, how do they resolve the problem of the reference of 'Ekene?' From another perspective, 'Ekene,' an abbreviation is in itself a complete sentence. In addition to being a short form of "Ekene dili Chukwu,' Ekene may stand for salutation, as the rendition of the greeting, "Hail, Joseph." In Igbo, it translates as, 'Ekene, Joseph.' Such Igbo names are not widespread. There arises a problem of interpretation here. Of the two possible meanings of 'Ekene,' which one does a speaker mean when he refers with the name, 'Ekene.'? A study of the meaning of Igbo proper names does not resolve this ambiguity.

5. Is Meaning a peculiar feature of Igbo Proper Names?

Meaningful 'foreign' names are not, like Igbo names, a result of individuals' profound reflection on their world, the human condition, people's successes and failures, or even the record of a family/community's past events. They are no 'reservoirs' of meaning. It would seem the case that this view of Okere's about the meanings of 'foreign' names is true.

If Peter means "rock," and Stephen stands for 'wreathe' (from the Greek Stephanos), Laurentius (Lawrence) means 'laurel,' and Linda 'pretty,' what does Paul mean if not "small," since Paul the apostle was small of stature! 'Mels' is a curious Russian name that seeks to combine the names of Marx, Engels, Lenin, and Stalin. Indeed, one can consider it an acronym of these historical figures. Sooner, it may come to mean these personalities just mentioned. Where 'Boucher,' 'Boulanger,' and 'Masson,' name three different professions, could they be said to mean 'butcher,' 'baker,' and 'mason,' when they name different individuals respectively? Consider 'Roux,' 'Leroux,' 'Roussel,' or even 'Rousseau,' all of which are variants of the term 'red;' do not these names mean 'red?' 'Fitzgerald,' and 'Dickson,' are patronymic names, formed as they are, from the suffix 'son' as in the case of Dickson, or the prefix 'Fitz,' as in 'Fitzgerald,' The 'Fitz' is an ancient Norman French word, 'fis' that, in modern French, is *'fils'* meaning 'son.' As there is Dickson, so also are there Harrison, Nixon, Robertson, Gibson and others. Does it make any difference if you go by the name 'Orgetorix' meaning 'King of killers,' 'Plato' 'broad' (of shoulders), or Godfrey (same as Geoffrey) 'divine peace?'[35]

Compare these names and their meanings with Igbo names. Omenuko Provider in times of need; Ezeasogu A king who is not afraid of war; Jaamike- Acknowledge my mighty deeds;Ummunnakwe Would that the patrilineage were in accord; Ikemba   The people's Ambassador. Dikedioramma the great man, the beloved of his people. The literal meanings of these Igbo names, Okere would urge, are completely different from the meanings of their foreign counterparts. The difference between these two naming systems, Okere suggests, is that the naming system of the Igbo is tied up with the culture and indeed with the entire worldview of that culture. Unlike the 'foreign names', Igbo names exemplify a system of naming that ensures a link between the past and the present; between the world of the living and the dead. Despite the appeal of the foreign system of naming, the naming system of the Igbo lives on. Even the Zeitgeist of modernity has not eclipsed it. It not only resists these changes and pressures, but especially, it is "a self-renewing magisterium."[36]

Thus, names like 'Plato,' 'Godfrey,' 'Harrison,' as seen above, are meaningful. What, however, are the meanings of names like Augustine, Moses, Rita, and lemon? One discovers that the achievements associated with personalities, who bore these names, give their meaning. These achievements typify their deeds. Augustine, for instance, refers to the saint who authored the *Confessions* and the *City of God*. The son of Anna, a saint just as his mother, he was the Bishop of Hippo and defended the faith through his writings. He has at least 60 works to his credit. By Moses, one means to refer to the leader of the Israelites; who fled Egypt; the brother of Aaron .... Rita would mean the cloistered lady who received a thorn from Jesus' crown; a wonder worker whose cult is widespread in Europe. Similarly, Aristotle would mean the teacher of Alexander; the student of Plato; the ancient philosopher.... For a natural term like 'lemon', one lists its properties $P_1....P_n$.[37] These properties give the meaning of the common term lemon.

In Okere's view, when we say that Igbo names are meaningful, we do not intend the achievements associated with some great names. After we run down the list of achievements of Moses; and outlined the works of Augustine of Hippo; or even related the history of Aristotle and his peripatetic school; in fact after we narrated the devout life of Rita, we are yet to give the meaning of those names. Compare the achievements ascribed to these great names with some Igbo names like Ezebuilo, Ekene, Uzuakpundu, Ezimma, and Onwuma. Unlike the foreign names, the meaning of these Igbo names derives from Igbo language and the circumstances attendant upon the person's birth. One need not recourse to the achievements of the bearers of these names to specify their meanings. If one wishes to compare some meaningful European names to Igbo names, one has to select names whose meanings are given in the language. Such names as Steinbrecher (one who breaks stones), Baker (who bakes bread), Fox (a cunning wild animal) Rabbit (name of a domestic animal), Livingstone (a stone that is alive) seem to compare with some Igbo names. A close look at these names shows that Steinbrecher, Baker, Livingstone, Fox (if it stands for cunning), Lamb (if it stands for gentleness) would stand on the same platform as the Igbo names Ezimma, Onwuma, Ezebuilo, Uzuakpundu, and Ekene. But Rabbit, David, Augustine, Rita, Moses, Aristotle would not! In themselves, these names are not meaningful. For what could for instance be the meaning of Augustine, Moses, Rita, for example. Any attempt to stipulate the meaning of these names succeeds in describing exceptional deeds ascribed to them. There is, thus, some story associated with great names. These stories, in a large measure, make attributions to these names and so presumably become their 'meanings.' This is the difference on which Okere and other thinkers insist.

However, if UNESCO's view about the danger facing Igbo language in the next hundred years is true, then Okere's bid for an African philosophy via Igbo proper names will end up in a blind alley. So also is the euphoria about the meaning of Igbo proper names. Foreign influences on Igbo people and their culture seem to vindicate UNESCO's remark.[38]

6. Foreign Influences: Bane of African Philosophy via Igbo Names

The effect of foreign influences on Igbo names casts a somber shadow over Okere's view that Igbo names are 'statements of meaning,' and hence capable of providing the much required elements for an African philosophy. In Igbo land, the colonial masters forcibly attributed English names to individuals. The least of the reasons for this is to obviate the language difficulty that the colonial masters faced. Thus, it became fashionable to bear such names as John, Augustine, Amando, Rita, Theresa and many others, all of which are non-Igbo. In so doing, the colonial masters set up a practice that carved a niche in the lifestyle of the Igbo. These 'strange' names marked those employees in the service of the colonial masters. Replacing the Igbo names, the 'meaningless names' also imported an entirely new problem into the study of Igbo names the problem of meaning of English names.

With the advent of Christianity, such 'English names' became common as names of patron saints chosen at baptism. Isichei, for one, decries this requirement at the celebration of baptism, where the candidate is obliged to drop his vernacular name in preference to the 'meaningless name' like 'Augustine.'[39] Not until the 70s/80s could candidates at baptism opt for theophoric vernacular proper names at baptism with/without the English names of patron saints. About the same period, and in a related attitude, Mobutu Sese Seko replaced his country's name Congo with Zaire and required his countrymen to follow suit in giving preference to personal names in vernacular. Ever since, Mobutu's *authenticité (authenticity)* has caught up with nearly all Africans.

The harsh economic reality of developing economies in Africa has facilitated a migration to Europe and America in search of better times. The effect of such a sojourn, when it becomes long, is a gradual loss of the indigenous culture and language. Parents name their children, in some cases, after the ideals of the society where they reside. This is the reason for the widespread of the celebrity names. With the gradual loss of the mother tongue, children bear, as their surname, the first name of their fathers. Hence, it is common to meet Chijioke David and Uche Paul, for those parents who still retain some attachment to their roots. Nonetheless Kingsley Moses and Faustina Stephen are equally Igbo! When the latter brand of names prevails, Okere's insistence on meaning as a special feature of Igbo names ends up in a blind alley.

7. Conclusion

As a linguistic category, Igbo proper names, Okere admits, serve two purposes: more than reference, Igbo names are meaning-laden. If one is in search of constituents for an African philosophy, Igbo names, in virtue of their meanings, are eligible components for such a philosophy. In as much as philosophy implies a rational reflection on the symbols of one's culture, an African philosophy via Igbo names is possible.[40] In themselves, these names encode years of profound rational reflection on life, and the world; they exemplify, in different ways, the categories and concepts through which the Igbo perceive and grasp reality. Through names, one could readily glimpse a gamut of attitudes, values, and reactions of the Igbo to events and the world. Unlike 'foreign' meaningless names, which are the butt of village jokes, Igbo names do not fail to express a message, identify a heart's desire, isolate some grief for a lost one, nurse some future hopes, or even grieve for a jilted love. Igbo names attest to the different perceptions and perspectives to reality, persuasions, beliefs, and convictions of people in life.

In this regard, Okere typifies Igbo names as 'statements of meaning.' If *the bishop of Hippo* and *the author of the 'Confessions,'* identify 'Augustine' to recount these deeds of Augustine is not, for Okere, to give the meaning of the name 'Augustine.' After one lists the properties of a thing, or the descriptions associated with a name, one has not drawn out the meaning of a proper name. This is the difference to which Okere refers when he ridicules 'foreign' names like Wolf, Sheppard, Baker and others as meaning-laden names. This difference permits him to claim that meaning is a peculiar characteristic of Igbo proper names.

Are meaning-laden names peculiar to Igbo culture? 'Nabal' is a typical Hebrew name. With all the significance of this name, once in history there was a man whose personality conformed to the meaning of the name. As the man, so the name: the name means 'foolishness' and a greater fool than the bearer, there is not. 1Sam. 25:25. Other Hebrew names like 'Jesus,' 'Immanuel,' 'Isaiah' are suffused with literal meaning deriving from the language. These names, the meanings of which are not attributions associated with reputed individuals who once bore them, resemble Igbo names. While such a phenomenon may not be wholly lacking among other cultures, meaning-laden names are not a characteristic of Igbo names only. Rather, the Igbo attach greater importance to these names than do other cultures. This is why Okere privileges names of this culture as essential elements for an African philosophy.

The significance of Okere's perception of Igbo names as 'statements of meaning' does not derive from his readiness to elaborate an African philosophy which benefits from the philosophic import of Igbo names. Neither does he intend to sponsor any current of thought dealing on Igbo names. Rather, his major contribution lies in the methodological presuppositions of his paper. Philosophy, Okere believes, is undoubtedly an individual enterprise; it implies an individual engaged in a reasoned interpretation of his culture. While there can be no collective philosophy unless one understands thereby a collection of individual efforts at philosophizing, such individual discourse of one's culture requires a spark of a genius for such philosophies to arise. Okere's view about the sources of African philosophy primarily underlies his major thesis about Igbo names. If he sees Igbo names as bricks for constructing African philosophy, it is because he insists that it is inappropriate laying down any rule about the sources of African philosophy. An uninformed and untrained villager, much in the like of the pre-Socratics, could provide as good a philosophy as any celebrated university professor of African philosophy. One could provide a deeply profound philosophical reflection as the other. He inclines towards the view that publication and literacy are necessary for typing an African philosopher. Yet, one need not make them an indispensable criterion since there might be as many an African philosopher as there are villagers who evince profound philosophical views.[42] In consequence of this view, one is wont to understand Okere's view on Igbo names as an attempt to prove his view that African philosophy can arise from "some unrecorded, inglorious Socrates, some unsung Plato's and Aristotle's blooming unknown in an unappreciative environment."[43]

The principal role of names in a language is one of reference. Names serve to refer. Okere minimizes this view so as to showcase his preferred understanding of Igbo names as 'statements of meaning.' But Igbo names do sustain the two usages. While Okere does not deny the referential use of names, he gives pre-eminence to the fact that Igbo names are pregnant with meaning. He defends this view with an eye to elaborating an African philosophy. Yet, he fails to note that such a philosophy could arise from a discussion of the referential use of Igbo names. Okere's strong point aims to show that one may successfully get to an African philosophy through a study of the meaning of these names. Indeed, a necessary step to such a philosophy consists in "teasing out" the meaning that these names possess. When one investigates Okere's assertion, one finds out that he puts weight on the social significance of Igbo names within the culture.

Because Okere lays strong emphasis on Igbo culture, he omits the descriptive use of Igbo names. In this case, a miss by an inch is as good as by a mile!

Notes

[1] Conceived as a sequel to Russell's *History of Western Philosoph*, London: Routledge, Repr. 1995, Ayer's *Philosophy in the Twentieth Century* London: Weidenfeld and Nicolson, 1982, is a disappointing attempt to typify this century's philosophy. The major failure of Ayer's work consists in its inability to acknowledge the basic problem of the 20th Century Analytic Philosophy: "how words 'hook onto' the world," H. Putnam, "After Empiricism," in *Realism with a Human Face*. J. Conant (ed/introduction), Cambridge: Harvard University Press, 1992, pp. 43 53. To characterise this century's philosophy without giving adequate consideration to this problem is a disservice to philosophy itself. In this regard, Ayer's work fails to achieve its goal.

[2] W. G. Lycan, *Philosophy of Language. A Contemporary Introduction.* London: Routledge, 2000, pp. 4-5.

[3] In contrast to the Referential theory, proper names, Mill writes, "denote the individuals who are called by them; but they do not indicate or imply any attribute as belonging to these individuals." J. S. Mill, *A System of Logic.* E. Nagel (ed), New York: Hafner Publishing Company, 1950, chapter ii, section, 5). Mill thus disputes the Referential theory's determination of meaning by means of reference. For he claims that proper names have a singular purpose: they are denotative.

[4] Ibadan: Daystar Press, 1981, pp. 101 102.

[5] E. Ebeogu, "Igbo Proper Names in Nigerian Literature Written in English," *InternationalFolklorReview*7 (1990), pp. 148 153.

[6] These categories show the range of field that such an African philosophy may cover. They include Gods and Deities, The Good and the Virtuous, Kinship, Natural Phenomenon, Social Concepts, The Calendar, Titles, Evil and Non-virtuous, Natural and Physical Objects, Parts of the Body, Material Assets, and Occupations. For these categories, see E. Ubahakwe, *Igbo Names: their Structure and their Meanings,* Ibadan: Daystar Press, 1981, pp. 101 102.

[7] Lagos: West African Book Publishers, 2003.

[8] E. Ebeogu, "Onomastics and the Igbo Tradition of Politics," *African Languages and* Cultures 6 (2) (1993), pp. 133 146.

[9] T. Okere, "Names as Building Blocks of an African Philosophy," *Identity and Change: Nigerian Philosophical Studies I,* (1996), pp. 133 149.

[10] Ibid.

[11] T. Okere, *African Philosophy. A Historico-Hermeneutical Investigation of the Conditions of its Possibility.* Lanham: University Press of America, 1983.

[13] But the theory leaves much to be desired. Suppose words functioned like proper names, by picking out the individuals they denote; it would be impossible to formulate grammatical sentences. Moreover, if all there is to meaning is reference,

then the Referential Theory will record immense success. In that case, two terms, which possess the same semantic referent, will not differ in meaning. But "John Paul II" does not mean "the Pope." What an embarrassment this is for a theory claiming that words are meaningful because they refer to items in the world!

[14] A. J. Ayer, *The Concept of a Person and Other Essays.* London: Macmillan, 1973, pp. 129 161.

[15] E. E. Uzukwu, *Worship as Body Language. Introduction to Christian worship: An African Orientation.* Collegeville, Minnesota: The Liturgical Press, 1997, pp. 274-280.

[16] R. Abba, "Name," in *The Interpreter's Dictionary of the Bible. An Illustrated Encyclopaedia.* G. A. Buttrick (ed), Nashville: Abingdon Press, 1982, pp. 500 508.

[17] Ibid., p. 502.

[18] C. Achebe, *Things Fall Apart.* Op. Cit., p. 3ff.

[19] Ibid.

[20] Ibid., p. 16. In search of the causes of his failure, Obiako's response to the Oracle makes him into the like of Nwoye were Okonkwo to view his "cursed" son Nwoye, who "is not worth fighting for." (See C. Achebe, *Things Fall Apart.* Op. Cit., p. 112*)* To the Oracle's statement, "Your dead father wants you to sacrifice a goat to him." Obiako replied, "Ask my dead father if he ever had a fowl when he was alive."

[21] For the story of Okonkwo and the personage mentioned here, see C. Achebe, *Things Fall Apart.* Op. Cit.

[22] The statement aims at itemising the conditions for ancestral status. The 'mysterious' swelling Unoka's claims to ancestral status became a dashed

[23] The more Okonkwo thought of his future life as an ancestor, the bleaker it seemed to him. If, at Okonkwo's death, other sons of his followed Nwoye's footsteps, Okonkwo would not only lose the necessary second burial rites, he might also be subjected to the same lot as the unsung individuals thrown into the evil forest.

[24] One's lineage could continue without a good memory eventually. We shall not delve into the relationship between lineage, good memory, and a name.

[25] Cf M. F. Asiegbu, *Dibia Ogwu,* Unpublished Term Paper, B. M. S. Enugu, 1985.

[26] C. Achebe, *Anthills of the Savannah.* Op. Cit., p. 97.

[27] Ibid., p. 87.

[28] B. Emecheta, *Second Class Citizen.* New York: G. Braziller, 1974/1997.

[29] C. Achebe, *Anthills of the Savannah.* Op. Cit., p. 92.

[30] The major question about these names is whether they are in the same category as negative existential since their bearers are faceless unless they have some outstanding achievements to their credit.

[31] T. Okere, "Names as Building Blocks of an African Philosophy," *Identity and Change: Nigerian Philosophical Studies I,* (1996), pp. 133 149. In so far as the names preserve the lore of an individual experience, a family's life-history, or the events happening in a community, they are historical records.

[32] T. Okere, "Names as Building Blocks of an African Philosophy," Op. Cit., pp. 133 149.

[33] C. Achebe, *Things Fall Apart.* London: Penguin Books, 1958/2001, p. 56.

[34] Ibid., p. 56.

[35] A study of these series of relationships, the phenomenon of re-incarnation and a repeater child, as well as certain rituals associated with them such as unearthing a repeater child's *iyi-uwa* falls outside the scope of this work.

[36] Cf "Name," in *The New Encyclopaedia Britannica.* 8, 1768/1985, pp.493 494.

[37] T. Okere, "Names as Building Blocks of an African Philosophy," Op. Cit., p. 148.

[38] Cf H. Putnam, "Is Semantics Possible?" in *Mind, Language and Reality. Philosophical Papers 2.* Cambridge: Cambridge University Press, 1993, 139 152. For the meaning of the natural kind term 'lemon', the conjunction of the properties of lemon render the meaning of lemon. If the properties in question comprise P_1, P_2 ... Pn, and whatever possesses these properties exemplifies a lemon, then a conjunction of these properties defines a lemon. In such a case, it is the intension of the term 'lemon' that defines a lemon. It determines what the extension of a lemon is. While a theorist argues that a conjunction of the properties determines a term, a cluster theorist maintains that a cluster of properties associated with a term determines the extension of the term.

[39] Cf C. Moseley and R. E. Asher, *Atlas of the World's Languages.* New York: Routledge, 1994; S. A. Wurm and T. Baumann, *Atlas of the World's Languages in Danger of Disappearing.* Paris: Unesco, 2001.

[40] E. Isichei, *The Igbo People and the Europeans: The Genesis of a Relationship To 1906.* London: Faber and Faber, 1973, p. 92. One may equally contrast Isichei's view with the anxious concerns of some pastors who refuse baptism to their flock because they preferred vernacular names to 'meaningless names'. We shall not be dealing with the pastoral dimension of the problem of names.

[41] T. Okere, *African Philosophy. A Historico-Hermeneutical Investigation of the Conditions of its Possibility.* Lanham: University Press of America, 1983, chapter two.

[42] T. Okere, "Names as Building Blocks of an African Philosophy," in *Identity and Change. Nigerian Philosophical Studies 1.* T. Okere, (ed)., Washington, D. C.: The Council for Research in Values and Philosophy, 1996, pp. 133 150. This article makes the debate about the origin of African philosophy important to Okere's discussion of Igbo names.

[43] T. Okere, *African Philosophy: A Historico-Hermeneutical Investigation of the Conditions of Its Possibility.* Op. Cit.

[44] Loc. Cit.

12

An Evaluation of Theophilus Okere's Conception of the Place of African Traditional Values in Contemporary African Societies

J.C.A Agbakoba

1. Introduction

The purpose of this paper is to examine and evaluate Theophilus Okere's perspective in respect of the aftermath of the culture shock in African, that is the powerful intrusion of foreign (particularly western) culture in Africa via the agency of colonization and imperialism (in the political sphere); Capitalism (in the economic sphere); Christianisation and Westernization (in the ideological sphere). Okere's work under consideration, it should be noted deals primarily with religion and Christianization considered as principles purveyors of values which have implications for not only spirituality and morality, but political, economic and social life as well. The aftermath of this culture-shock refers to the more or less indelible deposits of beliefs, values, organizational patterns, contacts, knowledge and other major cultural elements left by the intrusion of the West in Africa, which have become principal factors in the development (and underdevelopment as the case may be) of African societies and how Africans are grappling with, adapting and/or adopting these deposits.

    A look at Okere's work, "the Assumption of African values as Christian Values" shows that he belongs to the general pattern of intellectual response to the culture shock which we may designate the patriotic-romantic response. In this paper, we shall show the features of the patriotic-romantic response and evaluate them, especially in respect of providing direction and purpose to Africans in the aftermath of the culture-shock; and in doing this, we shall compare and contrast the patriotic-romantic response with alternative forms of response to the culture-shock in Africa, notably what we may call the patriotic-realist response and the assimilationist response.

The patriotic-romantic response is a strand of the nationalist response to foreign influences and domination in Africa. Generally, the nationalist response is strongly tied to the issue of the African person's identity: freedom, authentic humanity, equality with persons from the other races that make up humanity. When Europeans came to take hold of Africa, Africans experienced deep culture-shocks, elements of which are: (1) Politically, Africa was quickly overrun militarily; completely new and hitherto unanticipated politically units were formed; and completely new and radically different forms of administration were imposed on her. (2) New economic systems which featured such things as replacement of trade by barter in some places with monetary transactions, introduction of new forms of money, individual ownership of property and capitalism, plantation agriculture, were introduced. (3) Culturally, Christianity came with a lot more strength than was the case in earlier attempts at evangelization and consequently made enormous strides in displacing and replacing the traditional African religion and worldview; new forms of education and socialization were introduced.

A particularly distasteful aspect of this experience was that Europeans conceived and spread the view that Africans had no history, philosophy, culture, and even no state in some cases; and consequently, Europeans had taken on the onerous burden of civilizing the African with the civilization process conceived as the replacement as much as possible of everything in traditional Africa. This denigration of African culture was handy in accomplishing the dark purposes of Europeans in the continent, for it became a strong ideological weapon in the exploitation, humiliation and racism that was visited on Africans.

In dealing with this problem, it appears that many Africans thought (and still think) that if the apparent ideological justification for denigration of the African person is trashed, the exploitation, humiliation and racism that it justified will disappear. This is the underlying assumption of the patriotic-romantic approach. It, consequently, seeks to preserve and promote African identity and accomplishment (civilization) based on traditional African culture and worldview. This approach is nationalistic (hence its patriotic element) and traditionalist, for it holds that the traditional African society was more or less blissful and should be recaptured unadulterated as much as possible or that certain aspects of the traditional life and society (that is of traditionality) are values in themselves that are worth retaining in the contemporary setting (hence the romantic element in this approach).[1] As an intellectual movement, the patrioticromanticist methodology is mainly descriptive; they seek to describe the traditional values, beliefs etc and show how they link up with one another to form a coherent system of meaning (an internally consistent and meaningful system).[2]

2. The Patriotic Romanticism of Okere

In this section we shall present the evidence that shows that Okere belongs to the patriotic-romantic school. In Okere's work under consideration there is quite some equivocation and ambivalence that apparently could make one place Okere, in more than one of the schools of thought mentioned above. In what follows below we shall itemize the apparently contradictory statements and try to resolve them.

Statement 1:

> Are the history, the ideas and ideals, the aspirations and achievements, the collective experience of our people simply worth nothing to a religion that now claims our allegiance exclusively? This is too hard to believe. African Christians have been brought up to despise and renounce the old traditional religion. But what is being offered in its place is totally foreign, developed in every detail by outsiders. The choice put to them seems unfair to accept this foreign made product or to return to the traditional religion which, however, discredited, has the authentic stamp of a self and home made article. For however poorly made, if it is self-made then it is truly one's own.[3]

Statement 2:

The assumption of African values as Christian values is a peculiar aspect of the general problem of indegenisation. But here it is not a question merely of making Christianity acceptable to the African but rather of making African values acceptable to Christianity, of fermenting them with the leaven of the gospel and incorporating them into the value scheme of people who are as genuinely Christian as they are African.[4]

Statement 3:

At any rate, Africans in opting for autonomy today have also opted for all its risks and it is becoming clear that modern Africa would rather be content with a less perfect religion in which however they can recognize their cultural contribution, than with an impeccably Orthodox Christianity where every item has been regulated and prescribed from overseas.[5]

Statement 4

Not all African values will need to be revived, promoted or Christianized. There is need for a certain discrimination of values. Some values are fatally tied down to structures that are either anachronistic or for some reason no longer acceptable, for there is also such a thing as the evolution of values… other values are not only more permanent in time but seem destined for a more universal vocation eventually being accepted beyond their time and place of birth. Of such values some are indifferent to the ethos of the gospel but can be ennobled and baptized with its spirit, while yet others are as it were already *naturaliter Christiana* and capable of enriching the so far one-sidely European interpretation of the gospel.[6]

Statement No 1 shows a clear preference for indegenous products, for things African and a certain parity of all indegenous products considered as the products of a given people. We can see in this Okere's nationalism and hence the patriotic aspect of his approach.

In statement No 2, Okere can be understood as saying that African values have to be transformed by Christianity. This is more or less the view of the patriotic realists, which hold generally that the spirit of those traditional values that, are amenable to Christianity and which were expressed in and through beliefs, practices and social relations germane to the traditional setting should be given its proper meaning and significance within Christianity and should be expressed in and through beliefs, practices and social relations germane to the contemporary African setting.

Statement No 3 is an ultra-nationalist position with the racial chauvinism and ethnocentrism that goes with it; it is a position that denies the existence or accessibility of objective truths. Okere of course, recognizes that this might be "the reverse side of the coin of ethnocentrism with which we have often reproached Europe"[7] To justify his inclination towards this position, he relies on the following arguments:

1.   There must be reciprocal influence between the pristine Christian message and a receiving culture; " for any given people the gospel will influence the culture as certainly as the culture will influence the gospel".[8]

2.   When a people receive the gospel they are challenged to indegenize it that is to make it their own- their own experience and this they can only do by interpreting the gospel in the light of their own experience. Thus he writes: "The reception of the gospel cannot, but be hermeneutical. There will be no understanding of the gospel except from the context of the people's previous understanding of themselves. A culture can receive the Christian message only on its own terms."[9]

An assessment of the above justification will have to depend heavily on the existence of an essence of Christianity and our attitude towards such an essence, particularly whether one holds or does not hold that it could be modified by way of adulteration or increase in perfection. If the essence of Christianity cannot be modified then the reciprocal influence between it and a receiving culture will be such that, on the part of the receiving culture, there will be transformation that will make it as much as possible to be after the image of the essence of Christianity. This will apparently engender substantial and essential changes in the receiving culture both in terms of the range, meaning and significance of values, beliefs, ideas and concepts that is cognitively and practically, in terms of the forms of social relations, social practices and institutions. On the path of Christianity, the influence will not lead to any substantial or essential changes but rather to Christianity's maneuverability, that is, its ability to communicate its essence in various challenging cultural situations.

If, however, a person holds that the essence of Christianity can be modified then the reciprocal influence between Christianity and a receiving culture could involve the modification of the essence of Christianity as well as that of the receiving culture. It is not clear at all whether Okere holds the first type of reciprocal influence or the latter type. However, there are reasons to think that he would opt for the latter: if " an impeccable orthodox Christianity" that reflects the essence of Christianity is less palatable than " a less perfect religion (in case), a Christianity that compromises the essence of Christianity, then Okere accepts the modification of the essence of Christianity - the terms on which a culture accepts Christianity will include the modification of the essence of Christianity and the argument for this can only be that, there is no objective truth.

In addition, Okere's argument cannot get him out of the charge of racial chauvinism and ethnocentrism. This is because the only way one can justify racial chauvinism and ethnocentrism that overrides or denies objective truth is by demonstrating convincingly that truth and perfection are not objective but relative, hence Christianity has no essence, at least not one that can be known; the ultimate epistemological basis of the hermeneutics upon which he based his argument would have to be epistemological relativism. Okere espousal of relativism, however does not accomplish this. Okere expresses a certain type of ontological relativism. For him a value is relative because it is referential, that is, it belongs to someone and always must belong to someone: "every value is a value for someone."[10] But this does not mean that "what is good for Europe is necessarily not good also for African but rather .... a value has its raison d'etre in its original context of relevance. Its initial *locus standi*, from where then it can have or acquire universal validity."[11]

One thing that strikes one immediately with Okere's conception of the relativity of values above is that he does not make any explicit distinction between the ontological composition of a value and its formal composition (or structure). Let us illustrate this. A society may hold that spanking is good for erring children. The ontological composition of this value is the act of spanking a child. The formal composition of this value lies in the structure of the relationship between the child and people and/or things that the act of spanking seeks to represent and/or seeks to establish. For example, a boy may break the windowpane of a neighbour with a stone for no other reason than mischief. Such a child's father may spank him for breaching the reciprocal relationship that exist (or should exist) between the boy and his family and their neighbour, that is, the sort of social contract in the neighbourhood that is meant to ensure the mutual well-being of the families in the neighbourhood. The formal composition of the value lies in the level of consistency contained in the social contract of the neighbourhood as well as in the relationship between the father and the son, which is contained in what may be described as family contract: the reciprocal relationship between members of a family, which is composed of duties, responsibilities, obligations, etc. The boy in this context may be guilty of breaking the structure of the consistency that should characterize the relationship between the neighbours and between him and his father who may have been a dutiful and responsible father and who may have ordered him to stay away from mischief. It is important to note that people from another society may desire the structure of consistency (that is the formal composition) that informs the spanking of children in this neighbourhood namely, the formal composition of the social contract and " family contract" in this neighbourhood; but they may not desire the act of spanking of children itself, that is the ontological composition (which they may consider an ancient and outmoded pedagogic value for which they have a better substitute); in which case they may borrow the formal composition of this value but then cloak it, in a different ontological composition.

Given the above distinction, it should be clear that the idea that a value should first originate in the context of its *initial locus standi* and then acquire universal validity can at best pertain only to the ontological composition of a value   that is the specific material for the institutionalization of a given formal composition and how that specific institutionalization spreads and the extent to which it spreads (if it does spread) over the world. On the contrary, when we consider the formal composition of a value, we are at once discussing the structure of the consistency (or inconsistency as the case may be) that characterizes a value; we are therefore discussing its essential nature; this is not something it can acquire along the line, it is rather what it essentially is. We can determine the structure of consistency of a value by looking at its horizon of consistency that is, the degree to which it holds or is meant to hold in space, in time, objectively (that is, impartially, across the subject-object divide; this requires logical analysis that should be done independent of the nature of the material composition for the institutionalization of a value; except of course, if one wants to look at the pattern of consistency that arises as a result of a combination of values (that is, the internal consistency of a system of values).

Okere no where states the points that may lead to argument for the non-existence of objective truth or the existence of only relation truth such as the denial of the basic principle of non-contradiction upon which all forms of logic depend or the denial of cross cultural understanding and knowledge all he asserts is that the ontological composition of a value takes place in a given social setting, after which this composition may spread to other parts (and perhaps every part) of the world. This assertion cannot free him from the charge of racial chauvinism and ethnocentrism, for the bite of this charge lies in the denial of objective truth even though one knows or suspects that it is objective truth; in favour of an untruth (falsehood) that apparently serves one's race or ethnic group better in given situation. Okere then appear as an Ultra-nationalist with all that goes with this view in spite of his attempts to get himself out of this position.

In statement No. 4. Okere states that there are African values that are by nature Christian values and should therefore move simply from the Traditional African Religion and setting into Christianity and the Christian setting in Africa and outside Africa; these values include liberation/salvation, the extended family, communalism, republicanism, tolerance (we shall examine these values in details shortly).

Okere here shows himself to be a romantic. There are traditional values that should pass from the traditional setting without modification; it is simply a matter of transplanting those values and they will again begin to thrive and spread the bliss, which they used to give out in the traditional setting. This, of course, is highly problematic, for it not only glosses over the question of the meaning and significance of such values within the new system they may find themselves and they cohere (or do not cohere) with other values of the new system, but it also ignores the role of political and economic factors in the existence and character of values.

What then can be said about classifying Okere? In the first place, statement No. 2. that holds out the possibility of patriotic-realism is not pursued by Okere. Secondly Ultra-nationalism and patriotic-romanticism do not conflict fundamentally. The difference between the two schools lies in the fact that the patriotic - romantic believes (even if erroneously) that the values that they are promoting can be demonstrated on an objective basis to be superior (including being more sound) than contending values; while the ultra-Nationalist has no such respect for objective truth. There is, however, a pathway from patriotic-romanticism to ultra-nationalism: if the patriotic-romanticist fails to demonstrate the truth of his/her claims, he/she might slip over to Ultra-Nationalism in order to maintain commitment to the values he/she is espousing. Okere, one should say is a patriotic- romanticist, otherwise he would have devoted his considerable intellect to defending a thor-ough- going relativism. However, it seems he left the door to Ultra-Nationalism open. What will Okere do if the patriotic-romanticism he espouses is shown to be untenable as we intend to do in the next section? Will he slip over to Ultra-nationalism. The answer is not certain.

3. Inculturation and the Aftermath of the Culture shock

In order for us to appreciate what happens after radically different cultures including especially belief system and values collide, we have to address the following questions: is there a new dominant culture? What is the nature of the dominant culture that emerges? What is the basis of its subsequent development? What options are there for the subordinated and, perhaps, also withering culture? To answer these questions we need to properly account for the nature of social and cultural changes and the mechanism of such changes, including especially how a society adopts and/ or adapts a value, belief, practice, whether they are internally generated or externally generated. Let us now see how Okere addresses these questions in respect of religion and values.

First, we should note that Okere does not posit these questions in the above manner in his work, however, some of them, at least are implicit and there are implicit answers to them. The answers to above questions, respectively are: Okere thinks apparently that Christianity has gained dominance over African traditional religion, at least in large areas including southern Nigeria. For him the problem is how to imbue this ascendant Christianity with elements from the traditional system or simply, how to indegenize (inculturate) it. Okere does not provide an analysis of the nature of Christianity nor that of African traditional religion; he apparently presumes that the reader understands the nature of these two religions; this, however, cannot be taken for granted; indeed if such an analysis was done-especially if it incorporates analysis of the formal and ontological composition of the two religions the possibility (or impossibility) of the sort of cultural exchange he envisaged would have been much clearer. Okere holds that elements of the traditional values (not just the outward appearance of the traditional system) should be infused into Christianity in African, at least. These responses present fundamental problems. Let us look at them starting with the African values that he suggests should be incorporated into Christianity.

The first value he mentions is liberation/Salvation. This in a nutshell is the liberation of Africa from the status of being "the underdog of the world"; from "underdevelopment, exploitation, oppression, subjugation."[12] This value desire and struggle for liberation cannot be said to be a traditional African value. People from various types of cultures, all over the world, have cherished this value at some time or the other. Okere rightly does not say it is a traditional African value, but if it is not a traditional African value then what makes it an African value? It seems that the only way we can say that it is an African value is if we say that liberation is a value of all socially conscious and vital people that are oppressed and exploited. Africans, at the moment are socially con-scious, vital oppressed and exploited. Therefore, Africans have libera-tion as one of their key values. This means that this value will be shared, as indeed, other people, notably Latin American peoples and some

Asian countries, share it. There is nothing specifically African about it a value as indeed anything is best designated by the thing(s), peculiar to it; to say something is African demands that such a thing be peculiarly African.

The next value Okere mentions is the extended family because it is " an ideal frame work for practicing the virtue of fraternal love".[13] Again, like liberation, the extended family is not a peculiarly African institution or value; it existed in societies and still exists in some societies outside Africa. In addition, it is in no way necessarily helpful in making the individual acquire universal love; rather it may constitute a stumbling block to an individuals' progress in this direction. This is because the problem of acquiring universal love is the problem of bridging the in-group out-group divide (1-you; we they divide). Many individuals can be easily indifferent to the fate of people outside his/her in-group. Since a person's identity (or self hood) includes such a persons personal identity (P1) - that is his/her idiosyncratic self - and such a person's social identity (SI) - that is, the widening circle of social groups he/she may belong to, including the family, extended family, clan, nation, religious associations, professional associations - the problem is how to get the individual to respect the personhood of people who do not belong to groups that makeup his/her social identity. A person who touches the circle of people he should show fraternal love at the level of the extended family has actually done very little and is likely to be a treat to the development of a tribe or nation.[14]

The same is the case with communalism, for communalism is the extended family writ larger. Okere cherishes communalism not only as a framework for practicing cooperation but also espousing the notion of corporate responsibility. Again communalism is not peculiar to Africa. Communities at a certain level of technological development across the globe operate in a communalistic manner hence Marx held that it marked a certain mode of production with concomitant social relations of production and super structural ideas and institutions.

Secondly, the key thing about corporate responsibility is that it requires that a member of a collectivity police activities of other members in order to ensure that they do not err; it extends the responsibility of an individual for the wrong doing of others on the grounds that the individual ought to speak and correct other members by all available means to prevent them from error or continuing in error. Viewed in this way corporate responsibility is not opposed to individual responsibility, rather it extends it. Consequently, it will be hypocritical to concentrate on corporate responsibility without taking care of ones own individual responsibility first (one will be policing others while being perfectly open to the same sin and crime, that is while not minding the log in ones own eye); and it will be constricting the individuals role in the upkeep of his/her communities morality if people concentrate on individual responsibility conceived in terms of the crimes and sins the individual commits or does not commit. Corporate responsibility, which in effect could be said to be holding a person responsible for a good act which should have prevented one's co-member of a collective erring (that is making such an act a sin or crime) is not peculiarly African; Africans have not practiced it in the past more than other people of the world nor are they doing so more than peoples in the present. Indeed, our problem today stems in part from our having a much lower sense of corporate responsibility than is required to operate successfully in our contemporary world.

This problem stems largely from the fact that we have been unable to maintain in the modern world the essence of communalism, the idea that "we were individual within a community" that "we took care of the community and the community took care of us".[15] But other people notably the Japanese have been able to move this idea into the modern setting by making it the basis of their modern business corporations (companies). Companies carter for the individual's (employee's) welfare including offering such things as employment for life, payment for marriages, funeral costs holiday, etc. In return they get loyalty and hardwork from employees. Nothing stops us from doing this here except the ease with which cheating and fraud is perpetrated, which inturn breeds a deep sense of distrust and disloyalty. The communalism that Okere speaks of cannot survive for long in the current economic setting; for as we employ higher levels of technology, traditional communalism will increasingly disappear; the sense of cooperation, however, can be retained in a different social and economic setting if we have the appropriate values, as the Japanese example shows, but alas, we lack the necessary values. The realist approach to this issue is to work for the development of values that will make for cooperation in the contemporary setting; not the hankering after a past that cannot be revived or one the revival of which will make a society less competitive and more open to external domination the ideology of African communalism in Nyerere's Tanzania, for example, left a legacy of poverty and a globally uncompetitive economy which the people will have to address, if they want increase in their well being. (It should be noted that on the positive side it left a legacy of accountability).

The fourth value Okere talks about is republicanism in political arrangements; he recommends that the Church adopt this. Again republicanism is not a specifically African value. And it seems that it is not recommendable for spiritual organizations. This is because such organizations are based on intuitive knowledge (both the revealed and non- revealed types). Such knowledge and understanding is available to only a few persons usually; others have to believe the claims of such persons by faith. Absolute authority in the assertion and defense of such claims is important, for, otherwise, people who have had nothing revealed to them and who may have no understanding will begin to advance modifications that will move such spiritual organization away from its spirit and purpose. Republicanism here will certainly bring this about because it involves the consensus of opinion of a large number of persons (ideally all believers) yet revelation insight and profound understanding are given to a few. It is for this reason that Russell who though was an atheist could perceive and assert that in less than 200 years time a good many of the current Churches would have disappeared, but the Catholic Church will remain on account of its mode of organization. Republicanism is neither specifically African, nor is it likely to aid the course of Christianity in Africa and the world generally. Okere's reason for desiring it is simply to have something that exists in Africa for a change; it is not based on the merits of this value; a case of patriotism gone awry or is it ultra- nationalism?

Finally, Okere recommends tolerance in religious matters, this value he says "has become typical of Africa due mainly to the extreme cultural and religious pluralism present in Black Africa".[16] If we are to go by the data of religious conflicts (the frequent riots arson and plunder in the northern part of Nigeria due to ChristianMuslims conflicts; the riots, in coastal Tanzania, Kenya and northern Ghana for the same reasons; the war in Ivory coast due largely to the perceived maginalization of the Muslims of the north) then Okere will be hard put to account for the existence of the tolerance that he asserts. On the contrary it appears that religious intolerance occurs in Africa, as in other parts of the world where people of different religions - particularly these belonging to the Abrahamic religions - Christianity, Judaism and Islam - exist in large numbers and are compelled by some reason or the other to live in close proximity. The term "African religious tolerance" does not seem to have any objective backing. Africa has generated neither the factual nor theoretical basis in the establishment of such a claim. This time we are talking of something that is not only not specifically African but also non-existent. This is perhaps romanticism gone awry; there is therefore nothing to say further about it except that Okere might wish to develop the theoretical basis for the existence and spread of such a value.

The problems discussed above - of talking about more general values as if they are specifically African; of disregard for this political and economic context in which a given value may thrive; of patriotism and romanticism gone awry, etc arise because of the theoretical basis from which Okere advances.

First, there is no clear conception of a cultural system as a system of values that constitute an integrated whole, consisting of supreme beliefs and values, from which other beliefs and values are derived directly or indirectly; he has a more fragmented than holistic view of cultural systems. Consequently, for him values can be held independent of the major systems of society notably, the economic and political systems; there is thus some sort of value compartmentalization.

In reality, the value system is holistic and hierarchical. It interacts with and influences other systems of society - economic, political, etc, and is inturn influenced by them. This interaction is such that the value system generates values and perspective that can enable people at any given time to adjust to and or transform the other system of society. But in doing this the supreme beliefs and values do not change; rather, they, by way of logical unfoldment, produce derivative values or license compatible values that accord with the task of providing meaning, direction and purpose to contemporaneous societies. They, thus, constitute the nodal organizing principles of society. When they change there is a cultural revolution; such as Africa is experiencing following its culture - shock and the ascendancy of Christianity. The criteria for determining African values that should be adopted by Christianity and the emerging Christian culture in Africa are that such values should be specifically African, relevant to the socio-economic survival and development of contemporary African societies and derivable from the supreme beliefs and values of Christianity. Okere's recommendations do not meet these criteria in one way or the other.

Let us note here that the assimilationist programme is doomed for a major reason it shares with the patriotic-romanticist, namely: a disregard for the relevance of a value to the social, economic and political life of a people especially in respect of the concrete life-situation of a people. The assimilationist absorbs foreign values without question and thereby undermines the survival and development potentials of the African.

Finally, let us note that the threat to the survival of Christianity which Okere noted, which may come as a result of the failures of indegenization of Christianity, can be averted not so much by the romanticist programme, but by the generation of relevant values (whether they are from traditional sources or not) by the logical unfoldment of the Christian potentials. This is a process that demands creativity and assiduity from African Christians. It may as well be that Africans did not do this in the past, for the non-proselytizing nature of the centuries - old Christianity in Ethiopia may be accounted for at least in part, by Christianity's adjustment to this environment; in which much of its essence and driving force was lost.

Notes

[1]. See Olusegun Oladipo, *The Idea of African Philosophy*, Revised edition, Ibadan: Hope Publications, 1998, pp 13-50

[2]. Ibid, 29 50

[3]. Theophilus Okere "The Assumption of African Values as Christian Values " in *Lucerna*, NO1, Vol.1 July-December 1978, p.10

[4]. Ibid p.9

[5]. Ibid p.10

[6]. Ibid p.11

[7]. Ibid p.10

[8]. Ibid

[9]. Ibid

[10].Ibid p.6

[11].Ibid

[12].Ibid pp 11-12

[13].Ibid p.12

[14]. See J.C Ekei *Justice in Communalism* Lagos: Realm Communications Ltd, 2001. He asserts that, " it is therefore an illusion to think that the positive benefits of communalism are no longer relevant today with a high rate of urbanization, and modernization. The contrary is rather the case. Granted it is no longer forceful as it is in the traditional setting, it nevertheless finds new expressions through other organs as town unions, social clubs, village, and family meetings, basic communities and other forms of society in contemporary urban setting". These town unions, clubs, etc have a very negative effect in the development of national consciousness and they aid the destruction of the economy and the institutions of the state by promoting nepotism, clannishness, ethnicity etc in the national institutions of African states.

[15]. Theophilus Okere, Op cit pp 12-13, Here he quoted J. Nyerere's apt description of the essence of Communalism.

[16]. Ibid p.14

13

Proverbs as Sources of African Philosophy

Cletus Umezinwa

1. Introduction

The issue of the African Philosophy has become a hobbyhorse for contemporary African thinkers. The discussion on it has been tethered around the status of African philosophy. In his detailed and classical contribution to this discussion in the early 1970s, T. Okere affirms that African philosophy is possible.[1] In an attempt to explain what he means, he makes a distinction between culture and philosophy. And he describes culture as non-philosophy or traditional wisdom. And recently he refers to it as "popular philosophy."[2] Okere believes that culture or popular philosophy and formal philosophy or philosophy in the strict sense are not the same. However, for him, they are symbiotically related because every philosophy in the strict sense must develop and flourish from non-philosophy or traditional culture. From this he argues that since the Africans have their indigenous culture there is a possibility of developing African philosophy from it. The condition for its possibility is simply because the Africans have their culture.

Like Okere, Wiredu also makes a similar distinction between traditional philosophy (African traditional worldview) and African philosophy.[3] He believes that the traditional philosophy can be studied in its own right but rejects the idea of developing contemporary African philosophy from it ; traditional philosophy is simply "a stock of originally unwritten proverbs, maxims, usages."[4] For him, African philosophy should be based on current African experience.[5]

Wiredu's position is evidently in contradistinction to that of

Okere. The latter believes that Africans are not insular; they are not isolated from the rest of the world. Africans have their traditional philosophy just like every race on earth. And if other peoples developed their philosophies from their cultures or traditional philosophies, there is no reason why African Philosophy should not follow the same line.

In this essay, we wish to emphasize how an aspect of culture, namely, language, but more specifically, how proverbs existing in traditional African languages are being used to develop African philosophy. Indeed many contemporary African philosophers have already begun to make serious researches in philosophy and to consolidate their findings not only with etymological analysis, but also and more importantly, with proverbs. Proverbs "are the most important aspect of the language."[6] And "It is in proverbs that we find the remains of the oldest forms of African religious and philosophical wisdom."[7] Proverbs are the defining features of African languages.

Greek philosophy developed from its cultural background. Proverbs, for example, were used extensively in building philosophical theories and sustaining philosophical claims. Proverbs were used as litmus tests for many philosophical assertions especially in politics and ethics; they served as indices for identifying the authenticity of philosophical claims. Let us see a few examples of this in Greek philosophy.

2. Greek Philosophers and Proverbs

Many of the known ancient formal Greek Philosophers anchored a good number of their political and ethical theories on proverbs. Plato and Aristotle are in the vanguard in this respect. Their works are interspersed with a good dose of proverbs. They were inserted at appropriate places in order to give credibility to claims.

In the *Republic*, for instance, Plato proposes the common ownership of property and wives for the guardians.[8] He argues that such arrangement would help these guardians not to have divided loyalties, one for their private interests, the other for the public but rather to channel their entire energies towards the promotion of the public good.[9] To buttress the view that the common ownership of property is the best political system he cites a proverb "All things in common between friends"[10] This is a saying that Timaeus attributes to Pythagoras as the originator[11] but it has become accepted as a proverb. Plato and Aristotle designate it as such.[12]

In the *Politics*, Aristotle subjects Plato's call for communal ownership of property to severe criticisms. He prefers rather to subscribe to private ownership of property since this would promote the practice of two virtues: liberality and temperance.[13] Nevertheless, he maintains that even though things should be privately owned, they should be disposed for common good. He cites the same proverb noted above as unimpeachable evidence to boost his qualified sense of common use of property.[14]

Aristotle further employs this same proverb to serve as a basis for his claim that friendship exists to the extent that people own things in common.[15] This means that those who have many things in common are friendlier to themselves than those who have less. Based on this conclusion that is founded on a proverb, Aristotle denies friendship between a master and a slave "for a master and a slave have nothing in common: a slave is a living tool, just as a tool is an inanimate slave."[16]

There are two other proverbs that were also deployed during the transitional period of traditional Greek philosophy to formal philosophy. They are "like is dear to like" and "the opposites are dear to one another." These proverbs are diametrically opposed; one is the obverse of the other. Aristotle mentions them as proverbs and attributes the former to Empedocles as the source and the latter to Heraclitus as the originator.[17]

The importance of proverbs in the enhancement of a philosophical theory appears again prominently in Plato's attempt to use the above two opposing proverbs to determine what it is that brings about true and lasting friendship. To find this out he proceeds by making a claim that perfect friendship can exist between people who are good.[18] He tries to espouse this conviction with the proverb: "Like is dear to like." From his intensive and abstruse questioning, he finds out that the proverb is incapable of sustaining the claim. He tries to salvage the claim with the other proverb, namely, "the opposites are dear to one another" and ends up in abysmal failure. At the end of the dialogue on friendship, Socrates tells his interlocutors, Lysis and Menexenus " …we believe we are friends of one another but what a friend is, we have not yet succeeded in discovering."[20] Whether Plato has any other motive for arguing the way he did, the point is that the treatise is inconclusive. If the proverbs have bolstered his claim the result could have been otherwise than it is.

Aristotle is more elaborate in his treatise on friendship. And so he has no difficulty in drawing support from these two proverbs to sustain his tenets. For him, friendship is divided into two major parts, on the one hand that existing between the equals and on the other that which exists between those who are unequal.[21] Equal friendship exists between those who are good, or useful or pleasant to themselves. Because they are equal and alike, friendship thrives between them. Since the good expect something good, the useful something useful and the pleasant something pleasant, they are attracted to each other whenever they find their respective objects of love. And so, Aristotle avers, "Amity consists in equality and similarity, especially the similarity of those who are alike in virtue."[22] Thus, Empedocle's proverb supports and is supported by Aristotle's theory on equal friendship. Even Aquinas would affirm this conclusion for he says: "Likeness, properly speaking, is a cause of love"[23]

Heraclitus' own proverb, on the other hand lends support to Aristotle's claim that friendship can exist between unequals. This type of friendship exists mostly between the rich and the poor, the ruler and the subject, the parents and their children. This is the friendship of the opposites. In this kind of friendship, what the friends expect from each other is not the same. What the poor expects from the rich is not the same as what the rich expects from the poor. They have different needs. And their attempt to solve them draws them together to form friendship. What the one lacks, the other complements. It is utility, therefore, that makes the friendship of the opposites possible.[24]

Other instances abound where proverbs are culled up to buttress a point. Writing on education, Plato says that the education of the mind and character of a child should precede his physical training. And also he holds that caution should be exercised with regard to what a child is taught for childhood is an impressionable period in a person's life. Any mistake at this stage could have incalculable effects. Plato underscores this point with a Greek saying "the first step…is always what matters."[25] Aristotle cites the same saying in another context to support his view that it is good to remove *ab initio* all things that can bring about revolution in the state.[26]

Plato, again, employs a proverb at a very suitable place to register a point while constructing his political system. This is seen when he argues that women should have equal rights and opportunity with their men counterparts. Women, for instance, should be included into the class of the Guardians. He argues that this arrangement would be to the benefit of the state. He greases the cog of his argument by citing a proverb, which says: "For it is and will always be the best of saying that what benefits us is fair, what harms us is shameful.[27] Plato uses proverbs therefore to serve as building blocks for his ethical and political claims.

In general, the Greek philosophers during the period of transition from traditional philosophy to formal philosophy did not begin to philosophise with raw materials drawn from outside their cultural experience especially in matters relating to ethics and politics. They always took off from the elements or understanding existing in their culture. In discussing happiness, for instance, Aristotle brings together various concepts that are used by the Greeks to designate happiness, namely, virtue, prudence, wisdom and pleasure. In his reflection, he accepts that, while each of these concepts has something to do with happiness, none is totally right and none is totally wrong.[28] He develops his own version of happiness not from abstract but rather from these raw materials already present in his culture. The same is true of his treatise on friendship. The various kinds of friendship - utility, pleasure and good friendships - were there already in Greek culture before he began philosophising. What he did was simply to give "a functional distinction between different kinds of friendship. But he did not legislate a verbal distinction arbitrarily restricting the usage of 'friendship' to one favoured kind of association. ...Aristotle had a healthy respect for ordinary usage."[29]

Thus, we see that the great masters in Greek philosophy set a historic step when they profusely employed proverbs to serve as bulwark to their philosophical claims. Let us now see Okere's efforts to develop African Philosophy from African culture.

3. Okere and African Philosophy

Africans have resources, like the Greeks, from which they can develop the philosophy that they can call their own. Endless debates over the status of African philosophy are rather superfluous. It is preposterous to continue to engage in such a venture that does not lead to any meaningful progress. Okere was involved in these debates. However, he has abandoned them, doing philosophy now in the African way. He has reflected on the Igbo concepts of the Self (*Onwe),* Names and Justice from the African background.

In his treatises on Igbo Self and Names, he employs a hermeneutical approach that is centred on etymological derivation of the meaning of words as well as on the explication of idiomatic expressions or wise sayings encoded or shrouded in Igbo language. It is through this method that he was able to state authoritatively that "Onwe" is the ensemble of personhood whereas "muo" (spirit) and "obi" (heart) are various aspects or manifestations of the self. [30]

With regard to names, Okere says that Igbo names go beyond mere identification. For him, African names, nay Igbo names are resource materials from which one may know what they believe with regard to God, man, life, death, destiny, historical events and interpersonal relationships. According to Okere "...Igbo names always bear a message, a meaning, a history, a record or prayer. This is also to say that they embody a rich mine of information on the people's reflection and considered comment on life and reality. They provide a window into the Igbo world of values as well as their peculiar conceptual apparatus for dealing with life." [31]

What is fascinating is that Okere arrives at his conclusions on the Self and names through careful reflections on the words, sayings, attitudes and beliefs of the Igbo. He is convinced of the validity and effectiveness of this method for he believes that: "A sustained reflection on Igbo language and grammar will not only bring to light the way the people organize their universe, it will also show that language is its verbal system." [32]

On the Igbo concept of justice, Okere presents what this means from the standpoint of his distaste of using foreign ethics to solve African problems. For him, the many and diverse problems and tensions that are presently gripping and crippling the African nations cannot be resolved by recourse to the western adage, "If you want peace, prepare for war." This principle, which characterises the history of the West, has supplanted the African way of managing crises. For the African, Okere maintains, justice and peace are congruous terms; indeed they are symbiotically related,[33] and consequently, there is no need of war in order to achieve peace.

To confront Africa's problem of war and violence, Okere calls for a return to the principle of justice and peace. To demonstrate how this is Africa's heritage, he goes into the etymological consideration of justice and peace. He arrives at the conclusion that "peace is justice and justice is peace."

Even though he accepts that etymological analysis may be very useful especially with regard to Igbo words, he admits that generally it is fraught with difficulties. And so, he goes beyond mere articulation of the provenance of words to the use of proverbs to confirm the Igbo notion of justice. For him, proverbs are the foundation upon which justice rests. He states this emphatically:

> "…what the Igbo understand as Justice, … are expressed here in the four of the most quoted aphorisms in Igbo ethics. *Egbo bere, ugo bere, nke si ibe ya ebela nku kwaa ya* (let the kite perch, let the eagle perch. Whichever would not let the other perch should have his wings broken). *Onye anwuna ma ibe ya efula.* (Let one not die and let one's neighbour not be missing). *Ya bara onye bara onye.* (Let there be profit for the one and let there be profit for the other. *Emee nwanyi etu emere ibe ya, obi adi ya mma* (If a woman is treated as her fellow women are treated, then will she be happy).[34]

Hence, in the discussion of these themes, Igbo self, names and justice, there is a deliberate paradigmatic effort by Okere to philosophise from African context. While he does not consider traditional wisdom as philosophy in the strict sense, he, nevertheless, draws from it. Traditional philosophy stands foursquare behind his conclusions as we have just seen.

4. The foundational role of proverbs in African Philosophy

Besides Okere, there are attempts by some Africans to go beyond the theoretical status of African philosophy to actually doing philosophy. Wiredu, for instance, discussed the question of truth from two perspectives. On the one hand, he took his bearing from the western philosophy and on the other hand, he flagged off from the African points of view. His discussion of truth from the western background was a continuation of his undergraduate and postgraduate studies of Berkeley's principle of "Esse est percipi."[35] It is a principle, which he tried unsuccessfully to deny but which he later found to be irrefutable. It is from this that he developed his controversial description of truth as an opinion.[36] Here is an African using western instrument to state his case on truth. However, this position has been given virulent attacks by Omoregbe and Blocker.[37]

From the African perspective, Wiredu maintains that truth in Akan is associated primarily with morality and not with cognition.[38] He comes to this conclusion from his analysis of the Akan word 'nokware'. Furthermore, Wiredu maintains that for the Akan, there is no single word for truth. According to him, 'what is so', in Akan language, is what the English regard as truth. Wiredu also says that the distinction between truth and fact in English does not exist for the Akan people. All these claims are products of his reflection on Akan language. But Wiredu fails to use proverbs to substantiate his claims. By so doing he has left them on precarious positions. This is a chink in his armour. And this has made him liable to criticisms. Bedu-Addo, for example, attacks his claim that for the Akan truth has primarily a moral connotation.[39]

Nevertheless, the argument Bedu-Addo uses to establish his case against Wiredu is flabby since it can be subjected to the same rigorous linguistic analysis. The reason for this is because there is evolution in the significance of word; as the years roll by they acquire additional significance different from the original meaning. And to argue for or against a point of view from etymology can be contentious since those embroiled in the argument could be drawing their respective significance from different historical understandings of the same word. Etymology as analytic instrument, when compared with proverbs, does not achieve much in terms of philosophical elucidations. This is because the meaning embedded in proverbs does not easily change over time. Hence proverbs are of paramount importance in the substantiation of philosophical claims. Bedu Addo's rejection of Wiredu's conjunction of truth with morality could have been more meaningful if he had sustained his counter claim with proverbs instead of engaging in the same etymological interpretation, which had made Wiredu's position odious.

However, it is to be noted that, in another context, Wiredu moored his elucidation of a concept on proverbs. In his argument that consensus as an ideology is of African heritage, he has recourse to proverbs. To substantiate his point he takes the Ashantis as a place where the idea of consensus is derived from their sayings: "There is ...no problem of human relations that cannot be resolved by dialogue" and again "One head does not hold council."[40] To argue in this way is a welcome shift from Wiredu who had refused to accept that African philosophy should take its bearing from traditional philosophy.

Udo Etuk is another contemporary thinker who manifests indeed the importance of proverbs in building up African philosophy. In his essay on African Logic,[41] Etuk argues that just as there are diverse forms of philosophy Chinese, British and American there are also various forms of logic. Logic is a very important aspect of any specie of philosophy. Hence, if there is African philosophy, there is *ipso facto* African logic. For Udo Etuk, African logic is distinct from western Logic. According to him, African logic is a kind of logic in which "status" plays a significant part. He gives example of this logic as follows:

> If anyone cut another person's palm fruits, then he will pay this fine.
> S has cut another person's palm fruits.
> But given the two premises, it does not follow that:
> S must pay this fine;
> Because the status of the person intervenes:
> But S is a grandchild of this community.
> Therefore, S will not pay this fine.[42]

This kind of logical setting is certainly different from western kind of logical formulation. However what is interesting is that Etuk upholds the validity of this logic with an adage from Ibibio community.[43] Igbo logic supports Etuk's categorisation of African logic as distinct from the western logic. The Igbo would say *Ahu ihe ka ubi eree oba or ahu nze ebee okwu* (When something that is greater than farm is seen, the barn is sold or when a titled man comes in, there is a break in speech). This is the logical mindset of the Africans. It could be found in other cultures but it is preponderant in Africa.

The use of proverbs by contemporary African thinkers is fast becoming *a la mode*. This is because of the lucidity, lustre and credence they add to philosophical claims. Opata, for instance, enumerates attributes of truth among the Igbo as self explanatory, indestructible, etc. He cites proverbs to prove the validity of these attributes beyond reasonable doubts.[44] In a similar vein, Oguejiofor enumerates the qualities that exist in Igbo friendship as "trust, openness, understanding, tolerance, generosity and sincerity." What is interesting again is that he confirms this list with Igbo proverbs.[45] To designate the Yoruba people as not aggressive but rather temperate people, Oladipo has recourse to the Yoruba proverbs to argue for his case.[46]

Some African philosophers, who discuss African themes from African perspectives, employ proverbs in order to overthrow the points of view that they do not endorse. Oguejiofor, for instance, uses a proverb to challenge Umezinwa's position that friendship among the Igbo is based on utility. Umezinwa has maintained that all forms of friendship, such as that between the good, as well as that between the pleasant, as found in the *Nichomachean Ethics,* are all interpreted by the Igbo in terms of utility.[47] Oguejiofor argues that this view is mistaken; friendship is not always based on utility. He supports his position with Igbo proverb *"Ezi enyi ka ego."*[48] Similar use of proverb was made by Onah to challenge Wiredu's biological basis for common humanity. Wiredu rejects the ontological nature of *okra* among the Akan people as the basis of equality among human beings. He subscribes rather to common biology than to this. Onah argues against Wiredu with an argument that uses a proverb. He maintains "…the common humanity of all, the universality of the one human family, is based on the *Okra*, which is equal in all human beings and at all times because it transcends the biological. It is clear that all brains are not as equal as all *okra* are supposed to be. The traditional Akan are well aware of this fact, which is documented in the proverb: '*Ti nyinaa sa, na emu asam nyapa* all heads are alike, but not all their contents are alike."[49] With the support of this proverb Onah's position is clear enough and it shows that *Okra* is better than Wiredu's biological argument in providing the raison d'etre for "the common humanity of all.

There are however indeed objections that can be made in recommending proverbs to serve as fortresses to philosophical claims. First, a proverb may not be widely known and there is a possibility that one may compose a proverb on the spur of the moment and use it as unimpeachable evidence to make his case. Secondly, there may be proverbs that are contraries. And this may make an argument appear inconclusive. Owolabi rejects Wiredu and Gyekye's use of proverbs to support their claim that Africans have democratic value - consensus. For him this is logically unacceptable. In his words: "...African proverbs are numerous and at times opposing and contradictory. Just as we have proverbs to defend democracy so do we have many to defend autocracy."[50]

The above objections are real but they are not insurmountable. First, a proverb that supports the conclusion of a philosophical reflection should be one that is generally known by the people. The Igbo proverb *Egbe bere ugo bere*- for example is widely known in Igbo land and is accepted as a moral principle. It is such proverbs as this that could be relevant in the substantiation of a point. The second difficulty, which concerns the existence of contrary proverbs, can be overcome or surmounted by situating them in their appropriate contexts. Earlier we saw how Aristotle applied two contrary proverbs in his treatise on friendship.

5. Conclusion

From the foregoing, it is evident that Okere has been proved right that African Philosophy is possible. The fact that the contemporary African philosophers, wittingly or otherwise, are reclining on culture to sustain their philosophical claims shows that it is possible to have African philosophy that is built from African culture or non philosophy or specifically from proverbs. Africans should not underrate their proverbs because their forebears uttered them so many years ago. The Greek proverb, "what benefits us is fair, what harms us is shameful," was uttered many centuries ago. But it retains its force to this day. The emergence of Christianity with its emphasis on love has not vitiated the force of this proverb. Indeed, it seems to be the underlying conviction that characterises the way the Americans and the western countries relate to the rest of the world. Africans should not shy away from using their cultural heritage to develop the philosophy that will address their problems. To do otherwise is to neglect the historical force of development.

Notes

[1] Okere, T., *African Philosophy*, London: University Press, p.xiv.
[2] T. Okere., "Introduction" in *Identity and Change* ed by T. Okere, Washington d.C.: Paideia Publishers, 1996, p.1.
[3] Wiredu, K, *Philosophy and African Culture*, London: Cambridge University Press, 1980, p.36.
[4] *Ibid.*, p.29.
[5] *Ibid.*, p.36.
[6] Nwala, T.U., *Igbo Philosophy*, Ikeja: Literamed Publications, 1985, p.96.
[7] Mbiti, J.S., *African religions and Philosophy*, London: Heinemann, 1982, p.67.
[8] *Rep.* 416^d, 457^d.
[9] *Rep.* 464^{c-d}.
[10] *Rep.* 424^a.
[11] Diogenes Laertius, *Lives of Eminent Philosophers*, VIII, 10.
[12] *Rep.* 424^a; *NE*, VIII, ix, 1159^b, 1.
[13] *Pol.* II, ii, 1263^b, 7
[14] *Pol.* II, ii, 1263^a, 4
[15] *NE*, VIII, ix, 1159^a, 1.
[16] *NE*, VIII, xi, 1161^b.
[17] *NE*, VIII, i, 1155^b, 6.
[18] *Lysis*, 214D.
[19] *Lysis*, 215 A C.
[20] *Lysis* 223 B.
[21] Cf *NE*, VIII, vi, 1158^b 7 - vii, 2.
[22] *NE*, VIII, viii, 1159^b, 5.
[23] *ST*, I-II, 27, 3.
[24] *NE*, VIII, viii, 1159^b, 6.
[25] *Rep.* 377^b.
[26] *Pol.*, V, iii, 1303^b, 2.
[27] *Rep.* 457^b

[28] *NE*, I, viii, 1098[b], 6-7.

[29] Fortenbaugh, W.W., "Aristotle's Analysis of Friendship: Function an Analogy, Resemblance, and Focal Meaning" in *Phronesis,* vol. XX, n° 1 (1975), p.51.

[30] Okere, T., "The Structure of the Self in Igbo Thought" in *Identity and Change*, ed. by T. Okere, Washington: Paideia Publishers, 1996, p.160-161.

[31] Okere, T., "Names as Building Blocks of an African Philosophy" in *Identity and Change*, ed by T. Okere *op.cit.*, p.133.

[32] Okere, T., *African Philosophy*, *op.cit.*, p.121.

[33] Okere, T, "Egbe bere Ugo bere: An African Concept of Justice and peace", p.11.

[34] *Ibid.,* p.9. Okere considers the Igbo saying "Egbe bere ugo bere, nke si ibe ya ebela nkukwaa ya" as that which "most aptly enunciates the principle of the human rights of every human" (Okere. T., "Human Rights and Democratisation in West Africa" in *Church and Democracy in West Africa* ed. by F. Nwaigbo et al, Portharcourt: CIWA Publications, 2003, p.34).

[35] Wiredu, K, *Philosophy and African Culture*, *op.cit.*, p.114.

[36] *Ibid.*, p.115.

[37] Omoregbe, J.I., "African Philosophy: Yesterday and Today" in *Philosophy in Africa*, ed. by P.O. Bodunri p.12; Blocker, G., "Wiredu's Notion of Truth" in *Philosophy in Africa*, pp.63-66.

[38] Wiredu, K., "The Concept of Truth in the Akan Language" in *Philosophy in Africa*, p.43.

[39] Bedu-Addo, J.T., "On the Concept of Truth in Akan" in *Philosophy in Africa*, pp.68-84.

[40] Wiredu, K, *Conceptual Decolonization in African Philosophy,* Ibadan: Hope Publications, 1995, p.57.

[41] Etuk, U., "The Possibility of African Logic" in *The Third Way in African Philosophy* ed by O. Oladipo, Ibadan: Hope Publications, 2002.

[42] *Ibid.*, p.112.

[43] *Ibid.*, p113.

[44] Opata, D.U., *Essays on Igbo World View*, p. 84-85.

[45] Oguejiofor, J, "Friendship in St Augustine and in Igbo Traditional Thought" in *Amor Amicitiae On the Love that is Friendship*, Leuven: Peeters Publishers, 2004, pp.330-332.

[46] Oladipo, O., "Rethinking Yoruba World-View and Ideas of Life" in *The Third Way in African Philosophy,* ed. by O. Oladipo, Ibadan: Hope Publications, 2002, p.160.

[47] Umezinwa, C., *The Pre-eminence of Friendship over Justice in Aristotle's Philosophy*, Unpublished Thesis, 2001.

[48] Oguejiofor, J., "Friendship in St Augustine and in Igbo Traditional Thought" in *Amor Amicitiae On the Love that is Friendship*, *op.cit.*, p.329.

[49] Onah, G., "The Universal and the Particular in Wiredu's Philosophy of Human

Nature" in *The Third Way in African Philosophy*, p.84.

[50] Owolabi, K.A., "Can the past salvage the future? Indigenous democracy and the quest for sustainable democratic governance in Africa" in *Philosophy, Democracy and Responsible Governance in Africa*, ed. by J. Oguejiofor, Munster: Lit, 2003, p.436.

14

Mutato nomine, de nobis historia narratur?
About Intercultural Philosophy

Marco Massoni

Philosophies have to be attentive to each other. It is in the mutuality of dialogue or, better still, a polylogue among cultures speaking through their philosophies that the hope of lasting understanding lies.

(Theophilus Okere, 2004)

Masters I like to call those from whom I keep on learning, even and far beyond the very first meeting, be it either a book or a personal encounter. This is the case of Theophilus Okere, whom I had the privilege to meet as well as the pleasure to read some of his writings. In the last decade the international philosophical debate has been giving importance, among the other things to the urgent necessity of rethinking globally the different traditions from an intercultural perspective, that is to say, not making any new discipline up, but rather, a remarkable and necessary re-orientation of philosophies. In particular I am referring to the Japanese philosophers Tetsuro Watsuji and Kitaro Nishida, the last tendency of the thought of Raimon Panikkar, the *Overlapping Theory* of Ram Adhar Mall, the *Dialogical Model* of Heinz Kimmerle, the *Polylogical Approach* of Franz Wimmer, the radical transformation of the Philosophy of Liberation into an intercultural philosophy proposed by Raúl Fornet-Betancourt, the philosophy of interculturality as understood by Giovanni Leghissa, along with some other contributions of similar range plus some other essays belonging to the area of comparative philosophy, not to mention the whole debate and its bibliography concerning African philosophy, whose bibliographical references I will limit exclusively to the work of Tsenay Serequeberhan, who takes inspiration from the philosophy of Theophilus Okere. Please, note that on purpose I do not intend here to dig into details of the above mentioned philosophers[1] apart from Mall, whom I was given the opportunity to deepen my knowledge of during my doctoral studies in Germany and whose guidelines on intercultural philosophy I wish to present in this paper. My intention is *sic et simpliciter* to discuss some crucial points in regards of the possibility of developing an intercultural philosophical orientation from Theophilus Okere.[2] As he himself says:

> The dialogue among cultures could be carried on in many ways, but philosophy seems to be particularly suited to the task of achieving human understanding. It makes the same assumptions for all. It works with common reason and reason alone, making no appeal to any other authority but reason, an ability that is shared by all men.

Intercultural philosophy - right because the promise of philosophy for intercultural dialogue can be seen equally clearly in its well known function as a clarifier of ideas, words and concepts can be considered the international movement that nowadays collects the most critical energies of the philosophical engagement. It tends to close with the classical paradigms and, without emphasising any particular conceptual scheme, goes towards a transformation of all the philosophical traditions, by diverting every ethnocentrism through dialogue. To the *'intercultural dialogical reason'* thinking means *'to perform solidarity by means of arguing'*, in accordance with an appropriate assertion of Raúl Fornet-Betancourt, which has to be alternative to the uniformity of an overwhelming global rationality, that in principle accuses of irrationality whomever and whatever stands against it.

Thus intercultural philosophy has not the shape of a philosophy *of* several cultures, rather it reveals itself, when we consider it as a philosophy *in* different cultures. In fact intercultural philosophy wants to be an alternative to multi-culturalism, trans-culturalism and cross-cultural studies, due to the idea that philosophical reflections are supposed to be born in several places and in various ways. That means not going towards the goal for cultures to live or to survive one next to the other, but on the contrary towards a reciprocal melting among cultures.

Always according to Okere:

> Hitherto nearly everyone has been listening to the philosophy of one cultural tradition. It is now time for every culture to listen carefully to every other culture, as it is the questioning and wonderment that constitute the core of the philosophy project.

Merely from a descriptive outlook I have to realise that within the contemporary debate concerning the intercultural philosophy we sometimes run across the distinction between the attempt of building universal models of rationality on the one hand and considering the otherness as the object of the science on the other hand. The former will be related to the theories of communication of both Apel and Habermas with all their implications and limits we are all aware of the latter will focus on Ethnology and Anthropology. Personally I do not feel comfortable with any of these approaches, for the very simple reason that both are strictly congenital insiders of western metaphysics, although presumably not yet so adequately understood. Anyhow I put off further explanations to future studies.

Again with Okere:

> For philosophy to serve as mediator and honest broker between cultures, it must have accurate information and intimate knowledge of those cultures in order first to get a sympathetic insight into them. This is the only way to be aware both of the real similarities and the real differences there are among cultures.

Another concern would be that of being able to give the right importance to the way we outline the representation of the otherness: each concrete relation with the other undergoes several mediations that are not easily being mastered by the bearers involved. Consequently, we face the necessity of a critical discourse that has to pay attention to the commencement of the rhetorical procedures representative of the common sense, but also distinctive of those scientific disciplines whose function should be to legitimize specific inclusion and exclusion of the other.

The process of constitution of intercultural plural identity is being developed through a process that is simultaneously of appropriation and expropriation, according to which elements originally belonging to the self migrate towards the other. However, one tries his best to maintain a distance from the hermeneutical tools he uses to depict a meaningful horizon, which is to be able to neutralise his action exactly in its immediate aftermath. Synthetically, one has to keep distance from every possible one-way, unifying and reassuring refuge.

Besides, the chore of intercultural philosophy is also a critical and meta-linguistic activity in respect of the other human sciences as a whole, in order to stress the problems of an effective communication between different traditions. That may occur, provided that he who undertakes such assignment is not considered as a transcendental subject that would attempt to identify himself with a superior universal reason. In doing so he would lift with no reason a specific point of view far above all the others and possibly dominate them. The risk that we had better not run again is avoiding to keep on being sons of the West only *(mutato nomine, de nobis historia narratur)*.

> Until recently the West has monopolised philosophical reflection in such a way that philosophical enterprise seems unthinkable outside the categories forged by the West.

In order to appropriately carry on an intercultural philosophical praxis, trying to extrapolate from its own isolation one's philosophical tradition and confronting it with other traditions of thinking in terms of a *"creative cross-pollination of ideas that would lead to intercultural understanding,"* is not enough. That is because the subjects should also be able to suspend their operating categories and, what is more important, to put aside both their own identities and their belonging to a *determined* context which, at the same time, *determines* them as such. Being committed to a project of intercultural philosophy means being able to abandon our universalist expectations, modifying our conceptual languages and schemes. Moreover, we have to eliminate somehow those elements that preclude hosting the otherness: not an easy task, but crucial. Let us now report what Okere writes about culture and philosophy:

> Culture is the foundation of philosophy: without the background there could be no foreground. [...] Culture provides the horizon and the objection of life, whereas philosophy is its interpretation. [...] Philosophy and culture are heterogeneous.
>
> Philosophy is not a cultural universal, not to be presumed a priori to be a part of every other culture. [...] Each philosophy - within and by means of its historicity, relativity and limits, is the self-interpretation of a culture. The environment of the author will prescribe the terminology, provoke the questions and predetermine the answers. [...] Philosophy is not a general world-view of a people and language and thought are not so related that a philosophy can be directly deducted from a language [...] On the one hand a *Weltanschauung* is not philosophy, not even a «collective» one, in that it describes a popular and traditional image recounting the story of the origin and the actual functioning of the *Status Quo*, whatever it might be. It is indeed a statement of fact and is accepted as such by the community. Philosophy on the other hand is essentially an individual enterprise and is often *mise-en-cause*, and a radical questioning of the collective image.

Okere is right, when he says that many western philosophers Plato, Hegel and Heidegger, for instance were radically influenced from non-philosophical, pre-philosophical or even anti-philosophical elements, belonging to the realm of culture, for the development of their ideas and systems. That happened, and still happens, because any philosophical discourse as a whole bears some implicit prejudgements and precomprehensions, delineating the background, from which every effective philosophical discourse is being nourished.

    Such non-philosophical elements have evidently been remarked in Gadamer's *hermeneutical circle*, for which thinking means facing the past. Solely the idea of critically coming up to terms with the tradition - called *horizon* in Serequeberhan and *locus philosophicus* or *pre-*

philosophical elements of culture in Okere - can legitimize the possibility of existence and developing of any African philosophy. From an intercultural perspective, I would say, Okere looks attentively at the pivotal focus granted to the *'Vorurteil'*, otherwise named *historical a priori,* or symbol, in which *'tout a été deja dit.'* According to the influence of Ricoeur on Okere, philosophy can be seen as a reflection on symbols. More precisely philosophical reflection, in terms of *implicita explicare,* is the process of explication of the meaning implied in these objectivations of life, namely symbols. Therefore, every act of comprehension that we do, especially when directed towards the other, will be as meaningful as much we can put into play our prejudices, although such an attempt will never end nor come up to conclusion once and for all.

> Total reflection is impossible to finite beings. [...] Total rationalism is impossible in philosophy, in fact for any reflection some data have to be taken initially for granted, without proof, and as it were by decree. They have to be believed or, as is rather more often the case subconsciously presumed, at any rate, unquestioned. [...] The existence of non-philosophy, therefore, is justified by the impossibility of total rationalism. It is concession to human finitude.

What is also outstanding is the success of Okere in keeping the peculiarity of philosophy, without declining it into the *Kulturwissenschaften.*

About African Philosophy:Tsenay Serequeberhan[3]

> The possibility of an African Philosophy raises the question of the validity and universality of truth and of the communicability of cultures and their respective philosophies. Is truth relative? It seems this conclusion is inevitable [...], but is this relativity such that mutual understanding is impossible? This need not be. [...] According to Gadamer, the limits that our culture imposes on us are also the condition of possibility of our recognising what does not belong to this culture as other and thus something to be understood. (Theophilus Okere)

The Eritrean philosopher Tsenay Serequeberhan has based several ideas

on the suggestions of Okere principally in regards of the relationship between historicity and philosophical reflection.
According to Okere:

> We shall look at Hermeneutics as an epistemological tool, a method of mediation, and of making the passage between culture as lived and culture as reflected.

He believes that the African philosophical hermeneutics is fully aware of starting its progress from being placed in a distinctive historical and social context. Hence it pleads its assumption and the truth of its lived presence. Such truth is precisely its own self-representation at the service of the hopes and expectations of the history of Africans.

> For the African philosopher African culture is not to be limited to the distant past, but must take in the full diapason of Africa's experience, the totality of its past in the fullness of its present consciousness.

Serequeberhan names *Horizon*[4] the lived experience and calls *Discourse* its philosophical fore-grounded outcomes; philosophy assesses its *reflexive* and *reflective* discourse pertaining to a historical, cultural and political *milieu*. The hermeneutical peculiarity of contemporary African Philosophy thus consists of the interplay between horizon and discourse, the former designating the historical and hermeneutical domain within whose limits philosophy arises and the latter appointing the inner references of the actual conditions of existence made possible thanks to the horizon itself. Here becomes visible how African Philosophy is, and it could not be something other than this, a hermeneutical endeavour, even when its interpreters are not thoroughly aware of it: thinking out of unusual ideas and taking historicity out of the cage are the main commitments.
With Okere we could affirm that:

> No familiarity with the foreign and borrowed element can suffice for the articulation of something so deep felt as one's understanding of one's self and one's world.

One is allowed to reply to the accusation that carrying on hermeneutical positions in regards of either African Philosophy or Intercultural Philosophy means still being embedded to the West, observing that any place, Africa or Europe or any other *topos*, has exactly the same right and the same dignity to develop its own philosophical understanding and their implications. In fact whatever ontological wandering within the borders of the European Modernity can also rightfully being set even from within the ontic frontiers of other cultures, according to Serequeberhan or, with Mall: since the general concept of philosophy possesses a universal connotation over and above its particular, adjectival qualifications, then we are allowed to speak of Interculturality. It is a matter of fact that Hermeneutics born in the West and Hermeneutics being adopted from elsewhere than the West are two phenomena sharing the same effort of theoretical reconstruction of the meaning of their own lived heritages.

> Philosophy ultimately is not poetry or narrative history, or descriptive phenomenology, but rather a discourse on the being of things. It is a statement with an ontological bias, a statement of how things are in themselves: an ontology. Rather than ontology, it was Hermeneutics that rescued philosophy from itself and enabled it to take the first step to act as a bridge among cultures and peoples, it did this by reminding philosophy of its own cultural origins and clearing the ground about its prejudgements, originating biases, initial and abiding interests and unconscious presuppositions. Once philosophy becomes fully aware of its own cultural background and its limits, its strengths and perhaps also of its weaknesses, it will be in a position to appreciate statements, ideas and philosophies from other cultures and ultimately generate a dialogue among ontologies and philosophies. In so doing, it creates a forum for understanding cultures and for seeing the rich pluralism as well as the basic compatibility of cultures.

The thought of Serequeberhan, inspired by Okere, provides the key for the development of African philosophy, which being legitimized by the hermeneutical circle would produce an incisive *Kehre* to Intercultural Philosophy.

> We should already distinguish the reality of philosophy from the promise of philosophy; the one dealing with philosophy as we have known it in history, and in the history of intercultural relations on the

one hand and on the other, the promise it holds, the great hope which is pregnant with, the as yet unachieved potential of philosophy.

In view of the fact that Okere[5] criticises *"the project to make the West the measure of all things"* and the overpowering westernisation of the world, by way of the uncontrolled expansion of its values - individualism, materialism, democracy and capitalism - I take the liberty to mention the proposal introduced by the Italian philosopher Giacomo Marramao.[6] He reads the globalisation not purely as the phenomenon of the worldwide westernisation, but more precisely in terms of 'Passageway towards the West' *(Passaggio a Occidente)*. This interpretation is a sort of compulsory path for all cultures - bar none - in the direction of the Modernity: in a manner of speaking, a transit approaching what the West is meant to be. Furthermore, such binding movement is destined to provoke the deepest metamorphoses in the codes of conduct either for the so-called 'other' societies or for the same western civilisation. Marramao goes deeper: western metaphysics has been ceaselessly thinking not only about the *identity*, but also about the *difference*, constantly conceived in terms of unity, as if it were the critical point through which it has always been impossible to detect Being. Contrasting with Mall's overlapping theory that, under the light of Wittgenstein works analogically on the family of similarities by rejecting both the two extremes of whole identity and of radical difference, Marramao welcomes the *conflict of identities*, by means of which the sound recognition of differences can take place. Subsequently, even in Apel and Habermas we can effortlessly locate some residual metaphysical items, especially when their theories of communication are being applied between/among different cultures, because their approaches try to work on what those cultures should have in common rather than focusing on their differences.

About Intercultural Philosophy: Ram Adhar Mall

The foreignness of the other: the alien, or the other, is given to us before our attempt at understanding the other. (Ram Adhar Mall)

We can consider culture as the shaping of a specific and durable form of life *(Lebensform)* in the analysis of men with nature and with other cultures. There are several philosophies either intra-culturally or inter-culturally. The *inter-cultural* view is not essentially different from the *intra-cultural* one, because there are also various scientific, ethical and political models within the same culture.

Heidegger pointed out that Being has different ways of showing itself, manifestating its truth according to various cultures. Philosophy becomes a disposition towards man as such *'Anthropos qua Anthropos'*, presenting itself as *'orthafte Ortlosigkeit'*, *topical* and *a-topical* at the same time. In this way the intercultural approach frees from the narrowness of any cultural outlook.

The reciprocal relationships of our time with regards to cultures, philosophies, religions and political worldviews have another quality compared to those of the past, as we are living a *de facto* existing hermeneutical situation and, for example, it is not the case that Europe seems to be surprised of the fact of being interpreted itself by non-Europeans. Mall believes that a crucial dialogue is to be given via the following issues: the self-understanding of Europe within Europe, the European understanding of non-European cultures, religions and philosophies, the development of non-European cultural circles, the understanding of Europe via non-European cultures.[7] In such situation the main question remains who understands whom, how and why. When we try to understand others, we meet to differ and differ to meet, as the other is also experienced by us through its resistance to our determination to assimilate it.

Hermeneutics assuming as pattern the model of identity increases by two its process for the comprehension of the other. The purpose to understand and to be understood is joined together as two sides of the same coin.

The concept of *analogy* on the one hand used to indicate the incommensurability between God and his creation and on the other hand used to show the necessity of putting God and his creatures side by side. Although God and his creation do not belong to the same species, Mall's use of analogy refers to features, which do belong to the same species. From an intercultural point of view, then, analogy may be seen as a notion that does not underline a total identity or a whole difference, which reminds the *overlaps*, in regards of Wittgenstein's central theme of the *Family Similarity*. Thus, Analogy is the similarity of relations among things and events, which are or could be different. The diversity of the other can be reached, without reducing it or neglecting it.[8] The hermeneutical subject of the analogical hermeneutics thus does not play his role next to any empirical, cultural and historical issue.

According to Mall we can define either what intercultural philosophy is or what intercultural philosophy is not: intercultural philosophy is not the name of a specific philosophical convention, be it European or non-European; it is topical and, nonetheless, a-topical (in other words *localised* and *spotless*); it is not an eclecticism of different philosophical traditions; it is not a mere formal-logical abstraction; it is not just a reaction or a comprehensive understanding facing the *de facto* pluralistic scene in contemporary worldwide context of cultures; it is neither an esthetical practice nor an exotic-naïve interest for what is not European; it is not a place for compensation; it is not a subsidiary of Postmodernity, even though it benefits from its repercussions. It is incorrect to think that intercultural philosophy is just a trendy expression in the wake of post-modern thinking and necessitated by today's global context. Despite the liberal pluralism common to both intercultural philosophy and post-modern thinking, the phenomenon of intercultural thinking, far from being an outcome of Postmodernity, exists in its own right beyond mere temporality, historicity and contextuality. Last but not least there is no trans-cultural philosophy as well.

The prefix 'inter' shows an in progress space-in-between in accordance with the Wittgenstein's notion of family similarity. Those who stay at the crossroad of different cultures and live the transmission together with the translation of the forms of life and of the linguistic games, they also directly witness the urgency, the difficulty and the need of an intercultural understanding.

Always according to Mall, intercultural philosophy is the name of a spiritual and philosophical attitude that accompanies, like a shadow, all the characters of a *philosophia perennis* - which has to be seen just as a regulative idea - and prevents from looking at them as standing positions; it resides in different cultures, but it also transcends their narrow limits, it doesn't have one mother tongue, as it is polylingual. Intercultural philosophy shows conflicts bound with exigency to overcome them; it is a sign of an emancipation process; it means also to look at the need to start shaping and conceiving the new from the ground; it rejects the mighty tendency to globalise just a single philosophy, religion, culture or political vision; it supports the idea of unity without uniformity *(Einheit ohne Einheitlichkeit)*; it calls the one by several names; it sees all the philosophies as actually diverse, but not so radically different as not to be signposts towards true philosophy; it aims at a transformation of philosophy beyond its own mono-cultural viewpoint; it is also a necessary condition for the possibility of any comparative philosophy; it depicts a philosophical model that gives confidence to the general possibility of using the notion of philosophy by admitting the variety of philosophical centres and origins. Intercultural philosophy states the contingent aspect existing within the framework and from the standpoint of the way Europe has been coping with the non-European realities: as a matter of fact is it due to a historical contingency that there has been an *Orientalismus* rather than an *Okzidentalismus.*

From a philosophical point of view it is so wrong to define a philosophical truth only through a particular tradition as to describe any specific tradition by means of a philosophical truth, whereas from a theological point of view, inter-religiousness, that is not to be considered as a religion one can belong to, is just another name for interculturality. Finally, from a political point of view, interculturality is another way of saying a pluralistic-democratic-republican line, inasmuch as also the political truth is not granted to any particular group, class or party alone.

As far as Gadamer is concerned, even though we cannot completely avoid the hermeneutic circle, nevertheless we have to take care not to dogmatize it. In fact, those who take the hermeneutic circle to be our philosophical fate fail to avoid a repetition of self-understanding in the name of understanding the other. For this reason intercultural philosophy rejects the idea of a hermeneutics of identity that is intolerant of difference. Those who talk about the radical other claim the truth for themselves and underrate the importance and virtue of relativism and pluralism. Before getting deeper in the implications of Wittgenstein's philosophy in the approach of Mall, let us have a look at what Okere says about him:

> The language-game theory confirms that it is the context
> that determines meaning and intelligibility. […] Historicity

underlines the fact that all philosophy is fundamentally finite. According to Wittgenstein no meaning is comprehensible except by the help of a definition, that is, by the imposition of limits or rules.

Wittgenstein's context dependency not only concerns the linguistic expressions, but also the actions and the other behaviours. As said by Winch,[9] Wittgenstein conceives cultures as forms of life entirely diverse from one another, a statement that leads to a strong *relativism* (i.e. Incommensurability). In addition to it, always according to Winch, there are absolute cultures, so that, in order to understand another culture, it is necessary to internalise the linguistic games of the other and nearly disregard that we were bearing in mind linguistic games as such. Differently, as stated by Bernstein, if the incommensurability is also intra-cultural, then both translation and transmission within the same culture are, by and large, a linguistic problem. Nevertheless, even though contexts may vary, they remain bound to a generic term-context, and subsequently they become commensurable. The main question for the intercultural communication, therefore, is not *if*, rather *how* we understand a foreign culture, even if a completely different linguistic game is being played; and also: how communication and discourse can be possible, without consensus?

Since Wittgenstein believes that being able to think of a logically perfect ideal language is not possible anymore, we have to admit the internal pluralistic nature of the language itself. If language consists of different linguistic groups that cannot be reduced one to another, although bound together by reason of a closer or a more remote family similarity, then language shall not be considered as a rigid and unchanging unity; rather it will be perceived as a dynamic variety or multiplicity of free Linguistic Games, which are partially similar and partially different among them. So what we observe is a complicated net of resemblances crossing and overlapping each other. It also goes without saying that, in doing so, we are clearly leaded to a non-ontological philosophy.

If we admit that no absolute text and no absolute interpretation are given, and if we also admit that ethics, religion, art and culture are merely a matter of interpretation, then we come to realise that no intercultural philosophy can arise, starting from a pure, single ego. To some extent it would rather turn out from the different behaviours of the human beings, belonging to specific cultural systems. Since these cultures are not to be considered as monads, the recognition of the enormous variety of interpretations does not direct us to a not tying relativism, rather to a biologically, anthropologically and socially conditioned one.

Mall reminds us that in order to understand a foreign culture, ethnology has adopted two different methods: on the one hand the *emic* approach and on the other hand the *ethic* approach. Whereas the former seeks to describe its object along with its behaviour from within its own contexts, categories and rules, the latter tries to do the same by means of scientific hypothesis and theories in relation to a specific object of study. According to what is being said, western Orientalism,[11] for instance, would demonstrate the arrogant and inappropriate claim to understand some foreign cultures and its forms of life, merely through metaphysical and objective representations of what and how we believe they should be and look like. Wittgenstein in his critical *Bemerkungen über Frazers Golden Bough*[12] evidently supports the emic methodology rather than the ethic, accusing Frazer to bring into play a theory of identity, particularly when he explains the exotic and unfamiliar activities in such a realistic way, to assume languages as if they were natural facts. The causal explanation is not for later Wittgenstein adequate at all in relation to the idea of a comparative cultural philosophy, anthropology and interculturality. Should cultures, philosophies and religions be so utterly dissimilar and absolutely unrelated that we could not even figure the same general concept out, then we could not even be able firstly to conceive such difference nor secondly to express ourselves about it.

As far as contextuality and family similarity thesis are concerned, both *relativism* and *universalism* seem to have been badly constructed. It is so either because in contrast to Okere - philosophical questions are not always culturally dependent, as Relativism affirms, or because a specific cultural factor is not to be given an all-purpose meaning, like Universalism asserts. Mall's concept of *analogous hermeneutics* is guided by the intercultural conviction that one truth can be said under different names, which bears wide resemblance to Wittgenstein's deepest insight into family similarity. In fact Mall rejects either the identity notion, because it does not make room for diversities, or the radical relativism, as it heavily depends on a radical difference, leaving no space for overlapping features among cultures. Against any ethnocentric absolutisms and supremacist views carried out by radical relativism, Mall encourages the idea of an *egalitarian universalism* that acknowledges different cultures and philosophies as equal.

Wittgenstein describes the world language *(Weltsprache)* not as the name of a single phenomenon called 'world language.' He explains it as the name of the class of an unlimited number of linguistic games, which are bound by the family similarity, beyond any whole identity and beyond any radical difference. Just as world language is not the name of a real language that is identified as such, analogically intercultural philosophy is not the name of a specific philosophical tradition as such, but represents an attitude, an orientation.

The idea of Game *(Spiel)* for Wittgenstein is a concept with indistinct edges *(Begriff mit verschwommenen Rändern),* in the sense of a reserve of interpretation. According to Wittgenstein there is only the Unity in view of the Variety *(Einheit angesichts der Vielfalt)*: the idea of the overlapping family similarity is this Unity in front of the Variety beyond the both illusions of a total identity and of a whole difference.

Notes

[1] Franz Martin Wimmer, *Interkulturelle Philosophie. Geschichte und Theorie*, Bd. 1, Wien: Passagen 1990.
ID., *Globalität und Philosophie: Studien zur Interkulturalität*, Wien: 2003.
ID., *Interkulturelle Philosophie. Eine Einführung*, UTB, Wien 2003.
Tetsuro Watsuji, *Fudo - Wind und Erde. Der Zusammenhang zwischen Klima und Kultur*, Darmstadt: Wissenschaftliche Buchgesellschaft 1992.
Raúl Fornet-Betancourt, *Filosofía intercultural*, Universidad Pontificia de México, 1994.
ID., *Interculturalidad y globalización. Ejercicios de crítica filosófica intercultural en el contexto de la globalización neoliberal*, Frankfurt: 2000.
ID., *Transformación intercultural de la filosofía*, Bilbao: 2001.
ID., *Zur interkulturellen Transformation der Philosophie in Lateinamerika*, Frankfurt: 2002.
Ram Adhar Mall, *Philosophie im Vergleich der Kulturen. Interkulturelle*

Philosophie - eine neue Orientierung, Darmstadt: Wissenschaftliche Buchgesellschaft, 1995.

ID., *Essays zur Religionsphilosophie und Religionswissenschaft. Eine Dialogorientierte und Interkulturelle Perspektive,* Nordhausen: Traugott-Bautz, 2004.

Kitaro Nishida, *Logik des Ortes. Der Anfang der modernen Philosophie in Japan,* Darmstadt: Wissenschaftliche Buchgesellschaft ,1999.

Heinz Kimmerle, *Interkulturelle Philosophie zur Einführung,* Hamburg: Junius, 2002.

ID., *Die Dimension des Interkulturellen,* Rodopi, Amsterdam 1994.

Raimon Panikkar, *Pace e interculturalità. Una riflessione filosofica,* Milan: Jaca Book, 2002.

Giovanni Leghissa, *L'archivio delle culture. È possibile una filosofia dell'interculturalità?,* in «Aut Aut», 307-308, Milan 2002.

Giangiorgio Pasqualotto, *East & West. Identità e dialogo interculturale,* Marsilio, Venice: 2003.

Filomeno Lopes, *Filosofia senza feticci. Risposte interdisciplinari al dramma umano del XXI secolo,* Rome: Edizioni Associate, 2003 Cristopher Durt, Wahrheit und Toleranz aus interkultureller Perspektive Auf der Suche nach gemeinsam Handlungweisen, Munich 2004 (not published yet).

[2] Theophilus Okere, *African Philosophy. A Historico-Hermeneutical Investigation of the Conditions of its Possibility,* Lanham: University Press of America, 1983.

ID., African Culture: The Past and the Present as an Indivisible Whole - Names as Building Blocks of an African Philosophy - The Structure of the Self in Igbo Thought, in Theophilus Okere (eds.), Identity and Change, Nigerian Philosophical Studies, I (in Cultural heritage and contemporary change series II. Africa, volume 3) Washington 1996.

[3] Marco Massoni, *Tsenay Serequeberhan: un'ermeneutica della filosofia africana. La filosofia nel contesto africano attuale. Orizzonte e discorso,* in Lidia Procesi (eds.), *Prospettive di filosofia africana,* Rome: Edizioni Associate, 2001.

[4] Tsenay Serequeberhan, *Hermeneutics of African Philosophy. Horizon and Discourse,* New York: Routledge,1994.

[5] Theophilus Okere, *Philosophy and Intercultural Dialogue,* paper presented on March 2004 during the conference entitled «*Dialogo interculturale in un mondo globalizzato, ma sempre più polarizzato: il ruolo della filosofia, della scienza e del cristianesimo»,* organised by the *Istituto per lo Studio della Non Credenza della Religione e delle Culture* (ISA) at the Vatican University Urbaniana, Rome.

[6] Giacomo Marramao, *Passaggio ad occidente. Filosofia e globalizzazione,* Turin: Bollati Boringhieri, 2003.

[7] Filomeno Lopes, *Terzomondialità. Riflessioni sulla comunicazione interperiferica,*Turin: L'Harmattan Italia, 1997.

[8] Dilthey: «Die Auslegung wäre unmöglich, wenn die Lebensäußerungen gänzlich fremd wären. Sie wäre unnötig, wenn die ihnen nichts fremd wäre» (W. Dilthey, Gesammelete Werke, Bd. 7, Göttingen: 1973, S. 225).

[9] P. Winch, *Ethics and Action*, London: 1972.

[10] R. J. Bernstein, *Beyond Objectivism and Realtivism: Science, Hermeneutics and Praxis*, Philadelphia:1983.

[11] Edward W. Said, *Orientalism,* New York: Routledge & Kegan Paul, 1978.

[12] Ludwig Wittgenstein, *Bemerkungen über Frazers Golden Bough*, in Klagge & Nordmann (eds.) *Philosophical Occasions: 1912-1951*, Indianapolis & Cambridge: Hacket, 1993.

15

Identity and Change in African Culture
The Case of African Women

Aweto Pauline Ogho

1. Introduction: Concepts and Misconcepts

While identity may simply be defined as what a thing is, that is to say, its sameness, Philosophy would generally take the trouble of adding the word "quod." In this way, identity is no longer simply what a thing is, but "that" which makes a thing what it is and nothing else. On the other hand, change is the process by which a thing becomes different, becomes "other", is transformed, transfigured, transplanted, no longer the same.

It will not be out of place to sustain that the juxtaposition of the concepts of identity and change as qualifying elements of the same reality in itself contains elements of intrinsic contradiction. In other words, the question, simply formulated is, "How can something be the same and at the same time different?" This contradiction constitutes but an instance in the myriad of contradictions, otherwise known as dualism, (one and many, being and becoming, substance and accident etc) typical not only of the origin but also of the development and dialectic of western philosophical thought and history.

Likewise, the concept of culture cannot be clearly and distinctly defined without running into some ambiguity. Culture on the one hand could be defined as a distinctive characteristic of the human person within a social set up and, consequently, belonging to the realm of collectivity. Paradoxically a person "distinguished" from others through the acquisition of specific skills, knowledge and ability is also said to be a person of culture. In this way, culture connotes a human person in the realm of individuality, in other words, that which makes him or her "stand out" and excluded from the group or collectivity.

The fruits of an individualistic concept of culture have no roots in Africa and African thought, rather the collective conception is raised almost to the level of a god. If culture is a collective affair, what about Philosophy?

"Africa" as a word and the reality it depicts is the apex of contradiction. Historically, one cannot, without discomfort talk of Africa without specifying "which" and "what" Africa is the object in question: Is it the pre-colonial (sometimes referred to as primitive or primordial Africa, which, tripped off every negative connotation could be termed Africa uncontaminated and uncompromised), or the colonial or post-colonial Africa? This triplication of identity is often reduced to duplication into traditional and modern. The conflict arising from their co-existence, continuity and discontinuity is the catalyst and justification for a polarized Africa.

While she may claim to be the cradle of civilization, that which was conceived and delivered on her soil not only did not continue to grow there, but never embarked on a return journey to its legitimate roots, after this same "good" achieved its highest level of development and achievement. It is almost impossible to talk about Africa today without certain adjectives which are slowly becoming synonymous with the continent as a whole. Africa today is often accompanied and identified with AIDS, poverty, tribal wars, genocide and so on. With disposition in natural resources one wonders why she is always permanently "developing" and "under-developed", in spite of having contributed in no small measure to those societies which today refer to themselves as advanced industrial and technological societies. What is even the more vexing about Africa as a bond and bundle of contradiction is that basic human needs such as food and shelter are yet to be massively addressed. Even though religion and religiosity are attributed to Africans as a second nature, one cannot bridge the gap between extreme religiosity, collective morality and the high rate of corruption, crime and egotism which have no practical bearing with what is theoretically claimed collectively.

In such a situation of confusion, contradiction and dilemma on which the continent as a whole is hanging, the issue of the condition of women seem to be out of place and irrelevant. Like the continent itself, African women are hanging in the balance between tradition and modernity. The importation of feminist values and disvalues, unfounded, unconnected and contrary to African ideas of femininity and womanhood, has given rise to a new form of "women's war" which has no bearing, in terms of aims, interest and development with the historical Aba Women's Riot of 1929, in Nigeria.

There is no universal application of womanhood, a concept which is historically and culturally determined. In this way, the same concept of womanhood (apart from biological disposition to bear children) cannot be applied to the African woman in the same rule and measure as her western counterpart. Again there is no concept such as a common enemy or oppressor, which, again, is culturally determined with an economic base and a handful of superstructures. While the oppressor of the western woman today is the "world of men" and her only worry is how to penetrate that world, and not only be part of it but also rule it at the expense of excluding the domestic and family sphere from her immediate priorities, the enemy of the African woman today is a continent that is permanently under-developed, without the possibility in the nearest future of attaining full development and self-determination.

At this point, the questions that readily come to mind are: Who and what is the African woman today? How has identity and change in African culture affected her? How has the polarization of the continent affected her concept of womanhood? Is it really still possible to talk about authentic African claims after so much pollution from the outside world? With what legitimacy could one talk of a pure race of African women amidst all forms and figures of Africanized women and Westernized women? Is the definition of her identity to be found in traditional Africa with dignified womanhood and complementarity, where women, though separated and excluded from the male world had their powers, self-determination and fulfilment as wives and mothers, or in today's polarized womanhood? Which model of emancipation can be proposed and applied to today's women in Africa? Is it a sort of "better life project", aimed at improving their conditions in order to better cope with the precariousness of day-to-day living and survival with the ultimate dream of bringing them to self determination with the possibility of choice through education, responsible (and not traditionally imposed) motherhood and self consciousness, proposable to the majority, or the elitist model of assorted feminisms imported from various parts of the universe, with records of failure, incompatible with African values and proposable to a minority? These are some of the questions this article sets out to answer.

2. African Philosophy and Culture

Though the underlying background of this write up is identity and change in African culture as related to women, a reference to Philosophy and its relevance to culture would not be out of place. In fact:

> Philosophy is a unique cultural form and despite affinities, is not to be confused with other forms such as myth, Weltanschauung and religion. But it grows out of a cultural background and depends on it. Discovering and studying this relationship will also be the condition for the development of a black African philosophy[1]

According to Okere, even though there is the need to investigate the relationship between culture ("the horizon and objection of life") and philosophy (the hermeneutics or interpretation of culture), culture in the final analysis is distinct from philosophy, since it constitutes "non-philosophy."[2] He proposes the thesis that non-philosophy can also become philosophy through the mediation of Hermeneutics.[3]

Culture as "non-philosophy" (philosophy being the "self interpretation of culture"[4]) is defined by the author, among other things in the following way;

> Our concept of culture includes not only the way we lived yesterday, but the way we live today; not only the heritage of our ancestors, but also that of our contemporaries. Above all, it emphasizes the meeting of the old and new, the impact made on the ancestral heritage by the colonial experience and its tributary forms of culture contact religion, morality and values.....But today's African culture is neither the romanticized, pre-colonial Neanderthal museum piece arrested in its development and fossilized in its authentic purity, nor is it yet the much vaunted one dimensional culture which the West relentlessly has continued to foist upon the rest of the world. Any African culture

surviving today, as indeed any flesh and blood African, is a complex mix of old and new.[5]

Though Okere conceives of African culture as a "complex mix of old and new", he does not buy the idea of its division into traditional and modern, which he holds to be "essentially an academic abstraction"[6] Consequently, African culture is made up of the "past and present as an indivisible whole", but then, in the process of interaction between the past and the present, a new cultural situation is created, in the words of the author;

> .....the old culture as something separate, intact and retrievable is no longer valid for the individual African as constitutive of his universe; it has been forever affected; that any contemporary individual African inherits all the elements of his cultural history from past to present; ... that the fusion, amalgamation or juxtaposition of these elements forms a new tertium quid, ... that this tertium quid is not identical in every individual since one must allow for individual creative freedom, and that this creative freedom is a freedom to modify, choose or to withhold commitment to any element, but at any rate involves some reactions to such elements.[7]

In other words, African culture is not a collective affair where the individual is negated but the same individual's capability and possibility through the exercise of freedom to appropriate a mix of the old and new, thereby creating his or her personal *tertium quid*, personal because it is not one dimensionally valid for all. Again, a personalistic, individualistic and non collective view is what the author has of African philosophy, since "philosophy, on the other hand, is an individual enterprise and is often a mise-en cause and a radical questioning of the collective image."[8]

This distinction and opposition between philosophy and *Weltanschauung* is indispensable not only for the understanding and definition of African philosophy and culture but also goes a long way to unfold age-long errors, misconceptions and wrong syllogisms as applies to various realities of the African continent. This distinction will also lead to the understanding that what has been trafficked and counterfeited for the identity of African women today is a simple *Weltanschauung*, the African world-view of the *Status quo* of women. The historical alternative is a "philosophy" of African women, essentially "an individual enterprise and a radical questioning of the collective image." The logical conclusion of the situation so created is not far- fetched; the amalgamation of the old and new will necessarily give birth to a new *tertium quid*, that is to say, an individualistic and personalistic approach to the African universe of women.

3. Identity of the African Woman

It is common to refer to African women as a generalized and homogeneous subject, stripped of every form of particularity. But it will be proper to recognize the underlying differences that cut across the generic umbrella of womanhood. Such differences are determined by elements such as the geographical area of provenience (rural, urban) culture, customs, tradition, religion, economic independence and education, to mention but a few. While it is generally assumed that African women have no right to property ownership, it is not surprising to know that certain remote and sometimes unknown tribes and culture allow women this right.

On the other hand, it will be an impossible enterprise to consider every single African woman, tribe, culture, tradition and so on, in order to arrive at a fictitious scientific and legitimate claim of the use of the term "African women" in homogeneity. Equilibrium could be found in the recognition and acceptance of diversifications, in order to arrive at some unificatory factors, such as, for instance, belonging to, and sharing the common experience of womanhood as defined by African traditions. A cross cultural and intercontinental definition of womanhood has been historically bound to the domestic sphere. The two key words that have always accompanied such definition in every time and place are marriage and maternity, giving rise to the role of wife and mother.

Though marriage and maternity do not always go together in some societies, especially in the West, where the woman can freely choose marriage without maternity, maternity without marriage, none or both of them, in a variety of "options", womanhood in Africa is meaningless without both. In a way, African women do not often choose to get married, they are simply expected to do so as some sort of natural or rather traditional obligation. In the same way, the question of choice is of little or no relevance to the issue of maternity, which is not only a biological, natural and traditional obligation but also the logical sequence and consequence of marriage. According to Mbiti:

> In some African societies, marriage is not fully recognized or consummated until the wife has given birth. First pregnancy becomes, therefore, the final seal of marriage, the sign of complete integration of the woman into her husband's family and kinship circle. Unhappy is the woman who fails to get children for, whatever other qualities she might possess, her failure to bear children is worse than committing genocide; she has become the dead end of human life, not only for the genealogical line but also for herself .... The fault may not be her own, but this does not excuse her in the eyes of the society ... the childless wife bears a scar which nothing can erase. She will suffer for this, her own relatives will suffer for this; and it will be an irreparable humiliation for which there is no source of comfort in traditional life.[9]

The indispensability of childbearing in marriage could be considered by the fact that the "greatest single cause" of divorce and separation is sterility or barrenness A connected issue is that of polygamy, a widely diffused practice not only in traditional but also in modern day Africa;

> The custom fits well into the social structure of traditional life, and into the thinking of the people, serving many useful purposes.....the more wives a man has the more children he is likely to have, and the more children the stronger the power of 'immortality' in that family ... .he is 'reborn' in the multitude of his descendant ... such a man has the attitude that the more we are the bigger I am. Children are the glory of marriage, and the more there are of them the greater the glory."[11]

Apart from fitting into traditional life, polygamy is not often uncon-nected with barrenness of the first wife or with her one -dimensional production or reproduction of only female children. Since all women in childbearing age with the capability to do so should do so until this is no longer possible naturally and biologically with the arrival of menopause, the issue of the number of children a woman should actually bear in spite of her infinite potentiality becomes superfluous and in fact no issue at all. The question of demography or rather absence of demography and family planning programme in Africa seems to be for major concern of all to the exclusion of the very subject concerned. Children are considered to be gifts from above and the decision not to welcome them is often not considered to depend on human intervention. Most women in Africa bear a dozen of children, not because of carelessness, stupidity or ignorance but because their attitude is simply that of being receptive to some natural and divine disposition, in a way beyond their choice, control and sometimes comprehension.

4. Identity as Role and Relation

One unique particularity of the African concept of identity, especially with regard to sex and gender, is its link with role and relation. In other words, traditional Africa has an elastic concept of gender, in contrast to its rigid Western conception. In effect, this means that while there is a delineated demarcation between male and female role, function and relation in a one-way circulation model of action and interaction, in the African concept, such a demarcation is not absolute but instead allows for some degree of elasticity. Consequently, traditional Africa has records of women who played the role of men, in relation, not only to women but also to men. In such circumstances, it is not only possible in many African societies to talk of "male daughters and female husbands"; it is also possible for a woman who did not biologically generate a child to be a mother. It is to be added that the term mother is not only limited to the relation with biologically generated children but also in various degree to different members of the family and the tribe as well. Often, the mother is also mother to her own husband, in the same way as the husband could also fondly "daddy" his own wife. Needless to say, the ideas expressed here are unromantic and constitute incomprehensible language to the foreign ear.

In a polygamous family where the first wife is barren, she could "marry" another wife for the husband. Sometimes, the first wife, with age, consolidates her position as "mother" to subsequent wives, while it is not uncommon to see a harem of wives live like "sisters". Children born by subsequent wives are also children of the first wife. This idea is better expressed by Mbiti, though in male application:

> The brother, who inherits the wife and children of his deceased relative, performs all the duties of a husband and father. The children born after this inheritance generally belong to the deceased man; though in some societies they belong to the 'new' father. In some societies if a son dies before he has been married, the parents arrange for him to get married 'in absentia', so that the dead man is not cut off from the chain of life. It may not matter much about the biological link; it is the mystical link in the chain of life which is supreme and most important ... .Children may therefore be born long after the person died physically.[12]

The supremacy of the "mystical link" above the "biological link" throws more light on the African concept of identity, especially with regard to gender, as linked to role and relation. It is not unusual to hear Africans referring to themselves as brothers and sisters when, in reality the only thing they have in common is colour, without the minimal reference to biological or even tribal link. A woman may conveniently "marry" other women without being male biologically and therefore without the possibility of being a husband. The idea of female husband is therefore a symbolic and mystical link in terms of role and relation. In most African societies, a woman does not only get married to the husband but to his entire family or even kinship. In effect, she becomes wife of the entire group, women inclusive. This idea of marrying the entire household may be the reason behind the woman not being simply wife (in relation to the husband) but a "housewife", that is to say, in relation not only to the day-to-day duties in the immediate household and home, but also in relation to the entire family of the husband in question.

This specific characteristic of defining identity in reference to role and relation is not always positive. In its negative undertones, when a woman is only the wife of so and so and the mother of so and so, often their names are completely forgotten. It is misleading and reductionist to identify women exclusively as wives and mothers and nothing else. Remaining within the domestic sphere is often taken to mean "doing nothing at home", but a careful consideration of the day-to-day activities of the housewife shows that she works round the clock and handles more clock and handles more than twenty activities and mansions daily, while the man only goes out and handles one mansion alone the whole day. The only difference apparently is simply the fact that the man "goes out" and his fatigue is financially remunerated, while the woman stays at home, do more job and receive no recognition whatsoever. Today, the idea of housewife is almost obsolete as most women especially in the urban areas equally work outside the family for money. This novelty should be addressed as a determining factor in gender equality and fair play, a novelty instigated by waves of change in the identity of African women.

5. Change in the Identity of the African Woman

In addressing identity and change in the African cultural spectrum Okere writes

> It is of this altered culture or mixed salad of old and new that we can legitimatelyspeak when we talk of African culture today. This present culture is an amalgam of the sum total of all its part: pre-colonial, ancient past; the experience of the slave trade, colonization and independence; the present multi-lingual, multi-ethnic form of political co-existence, the massive urbanization, industrialization and neo-colonial exploitation; the religious pluralism, exposure to modern education and growing capitalism; the growing mass poverty, consumerism and corruption; the mass urban unemployment and the deserted village syndrome. All the factors and elements labelled new, imported and foreign are part of the present culture.[13]

The nature of this article will not allow an in-depth consideration of how these changes affect the world of women. It is for this same reason that the question of their identity was limited to that tradition-ally defined as wives and mothers. Since this sphere was limited to the family, changes in there identity will consequently be considered in relation to changes in the family or how change in African culture has affected traditional African family set up.

The first in a series of changes is what Okere refers to as "mas-sive urbanization" and "the deserted village syndrome." Migration from the rural set up of the villages towards the cities is done for the sole purpose of the search for greener "pastures without" often putting other factors into consideration. For instance, while some women day-dream about the excitement of leaving the village and its typical forms of enslavement such as farming, firewood and water fetching, they often forget the new forms of slavery attached to city life. While it is possible for women in rural areas to remain housewives, this is almost impossible for most women in urban areas where the cost of living is more elevated. Most probably, urbanization marks the meeting point between the experience of African women as working wives and mothers and women from other parts of the world.

Urbanization has a major role to play in the westernization of African family system, with the nuclear family model prevailing over the extended family model. In the words of Mbiti:

> The size of the family is shrinking from the traditional 'extended' family concept to one in which the parents and their children constitute the family in the modern sense of the word .... The fact of children and young people having to live away from home in order to attend schools or universities tends to weaken family solidarity. The education of children is increasingly being passed on from parents and the community to teachers and schools where it becomes more of book learning as an end in itself that on education which prepares the young for mature life and future careers.[14]

Urbanization also introduced a new concept of neighbourhood, exigencies of hygiene and forced family planning, without adequate preparation and methodology. While women in traditional Africa passively welcomed every pregnancy and birth as natural and divine without protest, modern African women, with the constraints and imposition of new styles of city dilemma are gradually being conscious that they can no longer have all the children in their potentiality.

Among other things, Mbiti identifies the transition of marriage as a community affair to an individual affair, the diffusion of mixed and intertribal marriages and especially family instability as some of the major changes.[15] This "family instability" leads to family duplication in terms of geographical separation of families, especially where only the father migrate to the city. This,

> Creates great strains on the emotional, psychological, sexual
> and marital life of husband and wife. In addition, the children
> grow up without a father at home, so that the image of the father
> is simply someone existing in a distant town from where he
> occasionally sends them money for clothes and school fees, and
> comes home once a year or every two years. For the wife, the
> husband is simply a person who descends upon her once a year or
> less often, to quench her sexual passion, fertilize her and
> disappear like a frogman. He hardly shares in the daily responsi-
> bilities and concerns of raising a family. The wife is both mother
> and father to the children.[16]

Another consequence of modern city life is prostitution, "found in every
African city and town, this being an economic necessity or convenience
for women since it helps them to earn some money, find somewhere to
live and meet some of the demands of city life."[17] This phenomenon,
which started as an "economic necessity" for women and an indispensable good for men who are constrained to live far away from their wives,
has within these last years assumed an international dimension as the
twenty-first century slavery. The continuous trafficking and smuggling
of young African women and girls, (especially from Nigeria, Ghana,
Sierra Leone, Ivory Coast) to Europe for sexual exploitation is a phenomenal development in the last decade which has eaten into the roots of
the dignity and identity of African womanhood. Today, one of the
challenges facing African women, especially on the international arena,
is that of restoring their identity through a rediscovery of authentic
values of femininity.

6. Identity and Change as Continuity

In referring to the past and present of African culture as an indivisible
whole, Okere holds that it is not possible to choose either only the
modern or the traditional. The option he presents is that of accepting
both of them in the spectrum of continuity, for him,

> The first option is only theoretical....To choose only the

traditional for instance, one would have to live in monastic isolation where only the circumstances of traditional life prevail. But there is no such oasis or cast iron laboratory, disinfected, deodorized, anaesthetized and insulated from outside influence. To be born at all, to survive and live in our world today is to be exposed to a wide range of extra-traditional conditions of living.[18]

In application to the cultural identity of women, it goes without saying that pure traditionalism is obsolete, constituting some sort of "monastic isolation", which all along has been "infected", somewhere, somehow, along the line of history. These "extra-traditional conditions of living" which today's women in Africa have to reckon with, is the focal point of reference when defining their role and identity. While traditional life confines them to the domestic sphere and that alone, modern life presents them with a myriad of models, some of which are even contradictory, going as it were, against the basic claims of tradition.

The various movements for the liberation and emancipation of women which originated in the West started off with some innocent claims that women should not just be wives and mothers, since they have equal rights to work with men. (Though it would be more proper to say that modern impositions of the conditions of living have made it impossible for women to remain at home, since their economic contribution is both vital and necessary). This assertion of equal rights gradually paved the way for parity between men and women or equal opportunities for both. Today, the issue of equal opportunity has not only driven so many women to tough competition with men but has also, to a large extent, given rise to their wanting to dominate men, in some sort of role reversal. What is even the more frustrating is that these women, in wanting to be men are no longer women. They live on their careers as managers and directors but often at the price of renouncing marriage and maternity.

Which way then for women in Africa today? The answer is not far-fetched; while it is not possible for them to live in the conditions of their pure past as dictated by tradition or identify, with some waves of modernity, the only alternative is that of fusion, the continuity of the past and present as an indivisible whole, that *tertium quid* proposed by Okere which is nothing other than a personal and individual appropriation of the elements of the surrounding culture, freely modifiable according to individual creativity.

7. African Feminism as Elitism

"One is bound to use the expression 'African culture' with more than a thousand qualifications."[19] These words of Okere could be appropriated with regard to term "feminism," an expression used to denote the claims that women should have equal rights and status with men. From this simple and apparently harmless affirmation so many destructive superstructures have been constructed. From the feministic model of those whose reason to be is that of replacing men, it takes but a step further to arrive at those who are out there to destroy the world of men, depicting an inexistent world made up of only women, where men are useful only for their reproductive contribution to the human race. Most recently, even this contribution seem to have been substituted in some scientific laboratory in Japan, where a female rabbit was reproduced without male contribution.

Obviously, feminism, in all its forms, degrees and modes of manifestation, is a one-dimensional choice, that is to say, of the new, to the detriment of the old, of modernity, at the expense and agony of tradition; a choice, which in reality is only theoretical and not applicable in day to day living. While "a regress to the old would be a march into cultural limbo and into the veritable *musée de l'homme,*"[20] a complete break from the old in order to embrace the new is equally impossible since the new will often refer to the old at one point in time or another. This point is clear with Okere's illustration with a Nigerian child, who cannot be "disinfected, deodorized, anaesthetized and insulated from outside influence" (that is to say, modernity), and at the same time be protected from tradition:

> By the end of this encounter with the institutions of church and school, and thanks to a mixed dose of indoctrination, instruction, brain-washing and the programmatic devaluation of his own culture, the cultural purity of the adolescent's native tradition has been substantially compromised compromised but not quite obliterated, because the resilience of the traditional culture is still evident in the very name(s) the child bears, the badge of circumcision, the facial scarification or other tribal mark with

which he has been stamped and the relevance of the ancient institutions of family village.[21]

To say that traditional the identity of the African woman has been compromised and to some extent contaminated by extra-traditional values is to say the obvious. However, extreme or leftist feminism, which proposes the negation of womanhood and femininity in pursuit of other forms of self- affirmation, realization and autonomy outside the defined canons of tradition and nature is not applicable and cannot be transplanted into the African soil. This is so because the social, moral and especially economic presuppositions indispensable for feminist claims are more or less absent.

In the first place, the social status of women in Africa is often inseparable from their marital status. Some women even accept to be second or third wives only to be socially accepted and recognised in the society. One of the traditional columns in some major Nigerian newspapers is that of the change of name, the formula is unmistakable as Nigerian women and girls sign off their father's name in order to assume their new identity defined in relation to their bond with another male figure.

Women in Africa are not just considered as human beings; they should also be in the position to prove to be so by being fertile and reproductive. We have seen how Mbiti described the fate of sterile women in African societies, even though they may not be in any way responsible for their sterility, their innocence does not make them irresponsible. Apparently the choice of conscious and responsible sterility proposed by feminists in favour of other self indulgent interests is completely estranged from modes of existence in this part of the globe.

For women to be completely independent from men, they must have arrived at some level of economic autonomy. Economic autonomy of women, when not in collaboration and contribution to the family and completely severed from the male world is often not viewed with favour. In fact tradition has it that women should not be completely independent, as they often depend on men, in other words, women are not educated to be autonomous, they are not prepared and taught to be on their own, to stand on their own feet and fend for themselves, their only dream is to get married, possibly to wealthy men who would be able to "maintain" them, often, to love a woman in most African societies is synonymous with "caring" for her, and such care is mainly manifested and measured in terms of the amount of money he gives her. Most African women will not forbid their husbands from going to other women as long as he still cares for them economically, problems actually begin when this economic attention begins to deviate. This way of tying women to men and not making them autonomous is sometimes disastrous as some women, especially at the death of the partner find themselves alone. It is only at this point that one could talk of them "trying" to fend for themselves and their children, and this is no easy task at all, as they have to do so unprepared, starting from nowhere. This shock would have been spared if women, right from the start were not completely and exclusively dependent on men.

Again the idea of "equality" between men and women is in itself problematic and only theoretical, consequently not possible in actual life. To be equal according to Oxford's dictionary is to be the same in size, amount, value, rank etc, to be identical or similar or to have the same ability in strength and courage. The question of equality between men and women is superfluous in Africa and is no point of debate at all for both men and women. Rather than a sterile pursuit of equality, actual and factual life situations present men and women in their diversity and the need of both parties to complement one another. The strength of African women today lies in the fact that they have comfortably, without stress accepted this diversity and complemented men whenever and wherever possible. Even in their fight for more visibility, their projects have always been in view of walking side by side with men, not behind them and above all not in front of them, they never imagined a world without them, they do not intend to replace them as a race in extinction.

8. Conclusion; A Womanist for Africa

The term womanist is freely coined for the purpose of this paper to depict the real situational needs and identity of African women today, in contrast to the projection of false need and identity attributed a priori to the same subject in question without a concrete consideration of the surrounding cultural spectrum.

It is pure feminist imperialism to import and apply models of western liberation and emancipation to African women who do not and cannot share the same dreams and aspirations. Any project for their liberation and emancipation must take off from the African soil, spear-headed by the same women and above all, in line with traditional canons of womanhood.

Women today in Africa are faced with a chain of standing and pressing needs. One of such is economic, which is not a question of living, living well and living better as Whitehead proposed but simply that of survival, in other words, most women in today's Africa are not living but surviving. The vital and basic needs of food and shelter are not at the reach of all, especially women. Until such needs are met, talks about self realization will find no concrete application.

For the majority of African women, the issue in question cannot be liberation and emancipation but a "better life project," which will help them improve their conditions of living.

A fundamental issue to be addressed as an indispensable ingredient is education as an instrument of self consciousness and autonomy. Education here should not be taken for "adult" education or the numberless mass mobilized evening lessons geared towards literacy, but the process of schooling which begins from childhood. Most African societies excluded women from going to school for obvious reasons which can no longer be acceptable in today's world. Most probably, it is only in education that one can really talk about equal opportunities for men and women, the claim that women's education ends in the kitchen is no longer an excuse as women need education even to be in the kitchen.

Education is therefore the key issue and the point of departure, it should not be limited to basic education but should extend to the mini-mum level necessary for basic economic independence or at least the potentiality to be so. The point being made here is that there is the need to make a qualitative leap from the consideration of women as a group of indispensable parasites who need to depend on men for their survival to their being considered as individuals capable of independence and autonomous existence, with or without men folk. To do this, women need to be acquainted with the necessary instruments, the first, basic and most important being education.

The introduction of education into the world of women in Africa would go a long way to revolutionize their role and identity in the society. One of such consequences would be the postponement of the age of marriage and childbearing and logically also of the number of children to be borne. Without going through the process of education, girls go into marriage and automatically become women jumping through adolescence between the ages of 15 and 17 and with that, ignite the process of childbearing which only ends at menopause, say around the age of 45.

With education, the age of childbearing is moved forward, ideally women should also be given the opportunity to begin their autonomy before going into marriage. In this way, the historical alternative being proposed here is that women in Africa should not get married before the age of 25 to 30, they should settle down with themselves before they traditionally settle down with men. In other words, they should consciously go into marriage as free and autonomous individuals and not do so because they cannot survive otherwise, marriage should be a point of departure, not a port of arrival.

The idea of women entering into marriage as autonomous individuals will contribute in no small measure to changing the traditional view of "selling" or giving women away as "goods" as fixed prices to the best bargainer. Again when women become self sufficient, marriage and maternity will no longer be considered as traditional obligations without alternative, but free, mature and responsible choice of every woman as an individual.

A correlated issue regarding the changing roles of men and women in the society is collaboration in the domestic sphere. Even though this may appear foreign and far from the African reality, it is a question to be addressed insofar as women no longer stay at home alone. The point is that since women now "go out" of the home to work for money and contribute economically (a role traditionally played only by men) men also have to "come into" the home and collaborate with women in running the home (a role played exclusively by women).

In reality, this idea will find no application in Africa within the next decades, thanks to the conception of women not only as mothers to their children but also to their husbands as well, so that while the children with time grow and leave the home for studies or marriage, the husband remains the eternal baby to be curdled. The role of African women as mothers to their husbands constitutes a main obstacle towards gender equality in domestic collaboration.

For an effective change of attitude, women have a major role to play, especially in their education of their male children and their perception of malefemale role and relationship. It may not be out of place to affirm that men are who they are today, thanks to who women as mothers have brought them up to be. A man whose mother never protected from domestic chores will have no problem in collaborating with his wife in the home after marriage.

In a word, Women in Africa today need independence and freedom to choose and to be. They should not continue to remain passively tied to tradition but be conscious of themselves as persons and individuals and as such with inalienable rights to self determination and freedom, "freedom to modify, choose or to withhold commitment to any element, but at any rate involves some reaction to such elements."[22]

In conclusion, a complete liberation and emancipation of African women is utopian. However, before diving into the traditional principles which characterized the fight for women's freedom in other parts of the world, it may be necessary to see if these ideologies could be applied in the typical circumstances surrounding women in Africa. Perhaps the emancipation of African women may not be a revolution but a gradual adaptation to the new roles which universal femininity has established for the woman's world.

Notes

[1]. Theophilus Okere, *African Philosophy, A Historico-Hermeneutical Investigation of the Conditions of its Possibility,* Lantham,: University Press of America, 1983, p.i

[2] Ibid., p. xii "For several reasons these efforts are totally inadequate to justify the titles they claim as African philosophy in any authentic sense of the word. But their most fatal disability is the confused understanding of what philosophy is. It is precisely by reflecting on what actually constitutes philosophy in contrast to what is non-philosophy, that is culture, that one clearly sees that what we are dealing with is a problem of hermeneutics"

[3] Ibid., p.11 "What is philosophy in the first place, and what is not philosophy? How does non-philosophy become philosophy? What is culture and what is philosophy?

What aspect of culture is philosophy? What can happen to culture so that it brings forth philosophy? To ask such questions is to get to the heart of the problem of Hermeneutics"

4 Ibid., p.xii

5 Theophilus Okere, (ed) *Identity and Change; Nigerian Philosophical Studies 1*, Washington D.C.: 1996, p .9

6 Ibid., p.10

7 Ibid., p. 18

8 Theophilus Okere, *African Philosophy*, Op. Cit., p.7

9 John. S. Mbiti, *African religions and Philosophy,* London: Heinemann, 1969, p.110.

10 Cf. Ibid., p.145

11 Ibid., p.142

12 Ibid., p.144

13 Theophilus Okere, *Identity and Change*, op. cit., p.14

14 John. S.Mbiti, op. cit., p. 225

15 Cf. Ibid., p.226.

16 Ibid., p. 226.

17 Ibid., p. 226

18 Theophilus Okere, *Identity and Change*, Op Cit., p. 9 10.

19 Ibid., p. 16

20 Ibid., p. 19

21 Ibid., p. 10

122 Ibid., P.18

16

Globalization as Dialogue of Culture
From Conflict to Convergence

George F. McLean

1. Introduction

Human rights are first of all a matter of dignity and respect due to the human person as such, and hence to every and any human person. They are classified into three, reflecting their progressive articulation in the United Nations declarations: negative as rejecting actions that violate human dignity, e.g., torture; positive as affirming the goods to which all humans should have access, e.g., food, work and education; and cultural as extending to the spiritual dimension integral to the full development of human beings.

This latter group takes on special interest as we enter a global age in which people intersect and interact, not only along with their cultures, but in terms of these cultures. Thus, to treat the theoretical foundation of human rights as the progress of the sense of person in a global age we must look at the nature of the interaction of cultures and civilizations.

This would appear to require two steps which will be the structure of this presentation Part I provides the bases by considering the opening of human awareness of subjectivity in the last half of the last century and the access this provides for appreciating the nature and formation of cultures. Part II takes up the relations between civilizations, especially in their religious roots, for which it will be necessary to study: (a) the new global unity and a proportionate mode of thinking this unity (Nicholas of Cusa), (b) the way in which this is differentiated from within by each culture in its process of self-definition and transformation (analogy of proper proportionality), and (c) the relation between these cultural traditions and civilizations (the notions of participation and analogy of attribution).

2. Subjectivity, Cultures and Civilizations

The Opening of Subjectivity

In 1900, Whitehead later wrote, that he thought that physics was complete as a science and that only some details remained to be worked out. At the time atoms were considered the smallest building blocks of the physical world. During the succeeding century, however, physicists broke into the atom and managed in that radically new and totally unknown dimension to work out the yet more basic components of the atom and their interrelations. The result was a total transformation of physics and radically new human capabilities for transforming the physical world from this more basic level.

What would it mean, we might ask then, if we could discover not merely the interior make up of the lonely atom, but that of the human being? And what if this understanding could not merely have been for the human, but for the inner constitution and operation of the life of human consciousness with its capacities for creative freedom and social interaction?

This indeed is precisely what has happened in the last century. It explains why we are able now to talk of cultures and face the issue of intercultural relations in newly tragic, yet potentially hopeful, ways.

The history of this development might be traced back politically to Masaryk, the Protestant founder of Czechoslovakia. He sent off the young Jewish scholar, Edmund Husserl, for studies in Vienna with the small gift of a writing box and the large gift of an introduction to Franz Brentano. From his Catholic heritage, Brentano was sensitive to Aristotle's notion of intentionality or the inner directedness of the human mind and heart. This had been honed by centuries of experience in the interior spiritual life, classically described in *The Spiritual Combat* by Lorenzo Scupoli, with its great coterie of the giants of the Catholic spiritual tradition from Augustine to St. Theresa of Avila.[1]

Later in his search for the foundations of arithmetic, Husserl was led ineluctably to the essential operation of human consciousness. Where objectively the number 3 may consist of three units, arithmetic is rather a matter of being able to hold these three simultaneously and to manipulate them through patterns of relationships.

But where some had classified this as psychology and interpreted it in the external objective categories of the sciences, Husserl, by following with great acuity the notion of intentionality received from Brentano, was able to discover the distinctive character of human consciousness and develop a pattern of techniques for uncovering it or bringing it to light as indicated by the etymology of the term 'phenomenology': phe (light)-nomen-ology.

The difficulty with this, consisted not in its brilliant accomplishment, but in its being only part, if an essential one, of the understanding of human consciousness. For if human consciousness were left to itself then it would be a consciousness of consciousness, ricocheting back and forth as in a hall of mirrors and thereby entrapping the human spirit in itself. It was the accomplishment of his successor, Martin Heidegger, to open Husserl's phenomenology to the metaphysical level where the work of human consciousness could be appreciated as the emergence of being into time. In this light the work of human consciousness was no longer a matter of private dreams or even of mere objective correspondence; rather truth was an unveiling of being from, via, and as the work of human consciousness.[2]

Heidegger's successor, Hans-Georg Gadamer, was able to appreciate this in its yet broader character as not solely that of an isolated consciousness, but rather of the human person as born in, and of, a family and raised in a community with its distinctive symbol system, language and history. To this he responded with the development of a historical hermeneutics as a process of interpretation of this conscious evolution of communities which, writ large, are cultures[3] and written yet more broadly are the civilizations which Huntington describes as the largest "we".[4]

The Development of Cultures and Civilizations

Let us briefly review once again this emergence of being as culture in the human person and in the community described at greater length above. To do this we must note briefly the character of being by returning to the early Greek philosopher, Parmenides, the first to identify being. In his famous *Poem* he identified a basic rule for thinking about being, namely that it is never to be confused with, or reduced to, nonbeing.[5] This is apparent in more overt terms through our experience of our inability to annihilate anything even a rock when crushed will always leave a remainder. But being not only resists non being, it is active and, as can be seen in plant life, when given the conditions will grow, flower and bear fruit in pursuit of its proper *perfection* (i.e., to make [*facere*] through and through [*per*]). At the animal level these functions are carried out in a conscious manner: the animal seeks out its sustenance and defends its life, even ferociously when necessary.

All of this is present in the human person, who adds self-consciousness and self-determination. When to this is added the imagination, the human person is able to work out endless ways of responding to the environment, physical, social and spiritual, in pursuit of self-realization or perfection at all these levels.

In the light of this emergence of being in the complex unities which are human persons and communities, it is possible now to garner a deeper sense of the reality that is culture. If it be true that the human person and community as self-conscious and imaginative have multiple, almost limitless ways of pursing their perfection, then it becomes necessary to set priorities, that is, to give greater weight to some than to others. Etymologically, to weigh more (*valere*) is the root of 'value'. This might be a matter of external objects of preference, but here it is especially of those more internal and spiritual qualities which shape our action.

In turn, a pattern of values and actions will develop a set of special capabilities or strengths (*virtus*, whence "*virtue*"). Virtues interlock with values in a mutually reinforce symbiosis that progressively shapes the overall context of personal and social life. Concretely, this is the way children can be raised or cultivated; hence the term "*culture*" as the way to cultivate the soul.

But, of course, circumstances change; new challenges and opportunities arise. Hence the culture is under continued reevaluation by each generation which must decide what to pass on to its children and how to adapt it in order that it be life giving for them. The content of this continued process of testing over time, reevaluation, adaptation, application, and passing on (*tradere*) is termed the "*tradition*".

A cultural tradition is marked then by three characteristics:

- First, it is fundamentally a creative work of freedom. As freedom is the inner exercise of the unique human existence, it is a unique expression of the life of a people as consciously lived and freely committed. This then needs to be understood as it were from within as one's deepest life commitment.

- Second, as it is the only real possibility available to a person or people for a life of meaning and dignity for themselves and their children, nothing will be defended more rightly or more fiercely when necessary.

- Third, as a culture is the effect of the exercise of human freedom exercised consciously at the level of spirit, it can be said rightly that culture is the place where the Spirit of a people dwells. The cultural heritage of a people is the proper effect of the work of the Spirit with and through them; it is the cumulative result of divine providence leading the people through history.

3.   Global Unity

The new global reality is essentially a new awareness of unity. This emerged visually with the landing of the astronauts on the moon in 1969. What they found there was uninteresting. But what they did there was striking, namely expand the human consciousness to the earth as a whole a single globe, round and beautiful.

Since then we have moved inexorably in this wholistic direction. Gradually we have begun to appreciate the environment as one, so that all human planning must take into account the effect which the project will have on the overall ecology, local, national and global. With the end of the cold war, this has become true in the economy as it has organized itself as a single world system; in politics as the various regional and overarching unities have developed; and in informatics as a single perspective on the world is increasingly disseminated and assimilated.

The coordinated impact of all these dimensions constitutes a change of horizon which is not only quantitative and incremental, but qualitative. Life is being lived differently, indeed globally, in our day.

This means that new thinking is required for this new age. Modern times during the previous four centuries were rightly called the age of reason as all was reduced thereto; it was indeed hegemony of a rationalism. To begin this all was excluded (Locke's blank tablet),[6] placed under doubt (Descartes),[7] or simply smashed (Bacon's idols[8]) in order to rebuild with clear and distinct concepts. These concepts are univocous, universal and necessary; from them all unique difference and hence freedom has been removed. In this processes of analysis in search of the basic components and their synthesis, the focus is on the parts and their interrelations; their synthesis as a whole eludes one's grasp. In these terms it is possible to carry on negotiations to determine which part will be forfeited for what other, but the sense of the whole corresponding to the organic character of a culture, civilization or globe is simply not available. Dialogue between civilizations is simply not possible.

To these processes of discursive reasoning is contrasted, *intellection* or understanding by which one grasps a whole, in terms of which its parts are then appreciated. Rice[9] contrasts the two as the experiences of walking through a valley, on the one hand, in which one first encounters each object one by one and then assembles them, and seeing all from a hill top, on the other hand, in which all is seen as a whole and the parts are seen in their inter-relations. Intellection is a distinct act of human consciousness which we need to renew and whose practice we need to refresh in our day.

In this light Nicholas of Cusa speaks of four levels of unity:[10]

1. the simple unity of any individual being,
2. a complex unity assembling multiple simple individuals,
3. a global whole with its diversity about which we are directly interested here, and
4. the absolute unity of God himself.

Globalization directs our attention to 2 and 3, but as we shall see not without the engagement of 1 and 4.

As we noted above the development of human technological capabilities now urges upon us environmental concerns. We have to think of the impact on the overall ecology of the use of rivers for expelling industrial chemistry, or of the use of carbohydrates as fuel upon the ability of the ozon-sphere to protect us from the radiation of the sun.

When now we think in the contemporary terms of globalization the earlier thought of Nicholas of Cusa finds new application. This appears when we consider globalizaiton not only as a matter of a single economic or political system (hard power) but also as a matter of information and communication (soft power). Here hermeneutics is called upon to play a special role. What hermeneutics suggests is not an imposition of an abstract universal which would omit the unique differences characteristic and indeed essential to the various cultures, nor is it a simple transfer of a component from one culture to another. As in medicine the challenge is the way an organic reality rejects any addition from an alien sources and how this can be overcome.

Hence, hermeneutics looks rather for an inner transformation of a culture, stimulated by seeing desirable elements in other cultures, but achieved precisely by drawing creatively upon one's own cultural resources.

Note that this respects the freedom and cultural identity of a people. It does not simply adjust their culture according to the international or world economic and political dictates, but works to adjust the economic and political order according to what the people want to be and to become or more probably to achieve a proper accommodation between the two.

Nicholas of Cusa, who often is described as the last of the medievals and the first of the moderns, considered *intellection* of the whole as the key to understanding. That is, to think in terms of the whole and to retain this as the basis of the meaning of all the particular components of the whole, which then are appreciated precisely as contractions or limited realizations of the whole: the whole as contracted to this or that. This echoes, in reverse, the classical notion of participation, not in its meaning as *mimesis* or image, but rather in its sense that the multiple images never exhaust the whole.

This has two immediate implications for Cusa. First, the multiple are complementary one to the other, for the other is that contraction of the whole which I fail to realize myself but which -- thinking always in terms of the whole -- my meaning requires. Second, the multiples are therefore essentially related one to the other. Just as the father is such only through the son and vice versa, the very definition of the one includes the reality of the other. This, rather than conflict and competition, can be the basis for human cooperation in a global age.

4. Pluralism and the Convergence of Civilization

As works of creative human freedom cultural traditions are differentiated from within. They are similar as being pursuits of their own perfection in their own way. The similarity here is had not by omitting or abstracting elements in order to achieve sameness or univocity between cultures, or by lessening the fervor with which each pursues their own perfection and in their own way, but rather in the vigor of the pursuit of perfection by the many peoples each in their own manner.

This reflects the seeming paradox that as free, distinct and unique they are similar in the very uniqueness and distinctiveness of their free pursuit of perfection. How is this to be understood?

Cultural Differentiation from Within: Analogy of Proper Proportionality

Cornelio Fabro concludes the second of his two major studies of participation[11] with a chapter on analogy, which he describes as the language of participation. To look further into the nature of relationships between cultures, it will be helpful to employ the tools of analogy and the long discussions on its nature and multiple modes.

What is salient for us is that analogy is first of all contrasted to univocity. Univocous terms have always and only the same meaning. It is the strength of science to proceed exclusively by this manner of term; as a result the conclusions are not only exact, but necessary and universal in application. Such terms are obtained by omitting what is unique to each. This is acceptable in the realm of things or objects. But cultures, as we have seen, are effectively the cumulative freedom of a people. Freedom, in turn, is precisely and essentially a unique affirmation of a being, expressing in turn the uniqueness of its author. It has been the tragedy of the past that this uniqueness has been suppressed and lost. It is the hope of the future that abstractive processes can now be supplemented by other modes of knowledge sensitive to the uniqueness of cultures. Hence for work on culture and their relationships we need to move to another type of term, not univocous but analogous.

Beside univocity there is another type of predication, namely, equivocity, in which what is predicated is simply different in each case. This has a number of types. In one the same term happens to be used of two things only by accident without any relation between them. Thus, the term 'pen' is used for an instrument for writing and for a place for holding pigs. But, of course, the cases of equivocity which are of interest to us are those where the same term is used intentionally.

One is the analogy of attribution or a "three term" analogy.[12] Here a term is applied to two or more cases due to the fact that each is dependent upon the same one reality as its cause. The perfection exists formally only in the one cause or primary analogate, but the name is applied to the others inasmuch as they depend upon that one. Typically this is the case of healthy as applied to food and to a scalpel.

Another type of analogy is that of proper proportionality or a "four term" analogy. This consists of at least two proportions which realities are not identical or equal to each other, but are similar only in the proportion that each represents within itself, i.e., in the relations of B to A and of D to C

$$A{:}B :: C{:}D$$

Note that this is not metaphor in which what is real is only one of the proportions, of which the other proportion is only illustrative (the real smile on the face being described by an imaginary sun on the valley, or vice versa). In contrast, here in the analogy of proper proportionality both proportions are real.

In the effort to analyze the nature of the analogy of proportionality in the early 1930s in the face of the totalitarian threats of the times, it was seen necessary to underline the fact that this was not a halfway point between univocity in which all were the same and equivocity in which all were simply different, for if the uniqueness of each were not assured from the beginninig, Penido found, it could not later be regained.[13]

Hence the definition of this analogy as somewhat the same and some-what different was rejected. Instead it was emphasized that this was in fact a matter of equivocity in which the two analogates were first of all simply different or eqivocous. Thus, each element is distinct in the analogy:

$$
\frac{\text{the existence of A}}{\text{the essence of A}} \; :: \; \frac{\text{the existence of B}}{\text{the essence of B}}
$$

There is nothing of A in B, neither its existence nor its essence.

This is important for cultures as the products and bearers of human freedom in all of its uniqueness. One is simply not the same as the other in any part. Yet in the midst of the differences the two are some-what the same in that each is a relation of its existence to its essence or an actuation of essence by its own proportionate existence. They are differentiated from their deepest principles, yet both are somewhat the same as realizations of existence, each in their own way.

When applied to culture as works of human freedom it can be seen that each culture is differentiated from its deepest origin, that is, in the very nature of its arising from human freedom. Their degree of sameness lies in each culture being a unique way of striving after its own perfection. Consequently, attenuating the exercise of what is proper to my culture or religion is not a way of relating to, being more cohesive with, or being one with other cultures or religions. Rather, it is precisely in the uniquely personal exercise of one's freedom, i.e., in the total pursuit of one's realization, perfection and fulfilment according to one's own culture, that we are alike. As free humans are similar precisely in and by their free exercise of being by which they are at once most nique in themselves and most distinctive vis- a-vis others.

Convergence of Civilizations: Analogy of Attribution

There is a danger here rightly noted by Prof. Gyekye,[14] namely, that by so stressing the uniqueness and diversity of the many cultures and locating this in the vigorous pursuit of perfection in one's own terms that each might be trapped in isolation in their own culture, that one's life might be simply incommensurable with other cultures, and that one would be unable to comprehend other cultures or work together with them.

In the four term analogy of proper proportionality it is necessary to assure that each pair, while not equal or identical (univocous) with the other, nonetheless does have real similarity to the others. For this we need to call upon another type of analogy, the 3 term analogy of attribution, by which two are similar by their causal relation to a third on which they both depend. Here the proper perfection being considered is in the third, i.e., in the one upon which the others depend. This is the creative power of the divine source on which all depend, and which is unique to the absolute One in which all participate. This is the one in the *pros hen* analogy of being in Aristotle[15] or the *mimesis* of Plato. But because Plato and Aristotle were working in terms of substance as form this participation was in an identity of kind: it explained things in terms of their species, the perpetuation of which was their final purpose.

In the subsequent development of appreciation of existence in the tradition from the early Church Fathers and the medieval Islamic, Jewish and Christian philosophers this came to be seen as a matter not only of formal participation, but of intensive existential participation as developed by Cornelio Fabro.[16]

What is essential in this existential, transcendental or metaphysical realization of participation is not that each is a replication of the same form in an identity of kind. Rather each is an actual realization of being according to the exercise of freedom that has come to constitute this as a unique culture. Yet each is similar in being related to the one cause on which each depends. Hence there is a similarity in each of the effects of the absolute one in that each depends for its being on the One Creator, source or efficient cause.

If now we reverse the type of causality in order to speak in terms, not of the efficient cause or source, but of final cause, end or goal something very interesting emerges that is especially appropriate to the issue of cultures. Cultures are ways of cultivating the soul, i.e., ways in which one's good or perfection can most appropriately be pursued.

When this is deepened to religions, which S. Huntington notes are the basis of civilizations and hence of cultures, as the specific relation (re-ligatio or 'binding back', as an etymology of 'religion') to the one God, then we find that each religion is totally distinct yet convergent in its direction to the One. In this case, it is not only that the religions are analogous by a proportion of proportions, but that all, while coming each from a distinct quarter, converge because they tend toward the same Goal.

In this light, the danger of a relativism in which each is incommensurable and incomprehensible to the other falls away and does so in the very distinctiveness of the pursuit by each of the one divine. Rather than being simply isolated from, and against one another, they are both unique and convergent in their deepest search for perfection and self realization. From this follows a founded hope, namely, that the more the cultures approach the one goal of their pilgrimages the more they will be able to appreciate the significance and complementarity of each other. The cultures will be natively cooperative with one another precisely to the degree that they advance in their own realization.

5.   Conclusion

In this way our global age opens new hopes:

First, as seen in terms enriched by human subjectivity the various cultures can be read from within and thereby seen, as with Heidegger's *dasein*, as the mega manifestations of Being in time.

Second, cultural traditions as the cumulative freedom of a people are unique to the life project of each and are to be protected and promoted.

Third, employing Cusa's ability to think in terms of the whole, the many cultures come to be seen as complementary and interrelated one with another.

Fourth, in order to explore this in greater depth the analogy of proper proportionality enables one to appreciate something truly amazing and unexpected, namely, that it is in the very distinctive and unique pursuits of the good by each culture they are similar. This is not in some formal abstraction cut off from life or applied univocously to the destruction of the multiple cultures. Hence, Christians can appreciate and admire the single minded adhesion to the One by Moslems and are able to do so through their own unique experience of devotion to the divine.

Fifth, the mutual appreciation of cultures in their most basic pursuits is clarified by means of the analogy of attribution taken in terms of final causality as each culture pursues its perfection. The image which forms is that of Isaias in which all peoples of the earth are on convergent pilgrimages to the Holy Mountain, where God will be all in all.

Notes

[1] Lorenzo Scupoli, *The Spiritual Combat* (London: Burns, Oates and Wasbowine, 1935); Augustine, *Confessions* (New York: Knopf, 2001); and Teresa of Avila, *Interiror Castle* (Garden City, N.J.: Image Books, 1961).
[2] Martin Heidegger, *Being and Time* (Albany: SUNY, 1996).
[3] Hans-Georg Gadamer, *Truth and Method* (New York: Crossroads, 1989).
[4] Samuel Huntington, *The Clash of Civilizations and the Remaking of the World Order,* New York: Simon and Schuster, 1996.
[5] Fragments 3 and 6 in G.F. McLean and P. Aspell *Readings in Ancient Western Philosophy,* Englewood Cliffs, N.J.: Practice Hall, 1970, p. 40.
[6] John Locke, *An Essay Concerning Human Understanding ,*New York: Collier, 1965.
[7] René Descartes, *Meditation on First Philosophy,* trans E.S. Haldane and G.R.T. Ross, Cambridge: Cambridge University Press, 1911.
[8] Francis Bacon, *Novum Organum,* New York: Library of Liberal Arts, 1960.
[9] Eugene Rice, "Nicholas of Cusa's Idea of Wisdom," *Traditio,* 13 (1957), 358.
[10] David de Leonardis, *Ethical Implication of Unity and the Divine in Nicholas of Cusa* Washington, D.C.: The Council for Research in Values and Philosophy, 1998, pp. 47-50.
[11] Cornelio Fabro, *Participation et Causalité selon S. Tomas d'Aquin,* Louvain: Université Catholique de Louvain, 1961, and *La nozione metafisica di partecipazione secondo S. Tommaso d'Aquino,* Torino: Societa editrice internazionale, 1950.
[12] See J. Ramirez, P.O. "De analogia secundum doctrinam Aristotelico-thomisticam," *Ciencia tomista,* 24 (1921), 34-38.
[13] See M.T.-L. Penido, *Le role de l'analogie en theologie dogmatique,* Paris: Vrin, 1931, pp. 37-40, 53-57; cf. St. Thomas Aquinas, *Summa*

theologiae, I, q. 16, a. 6.

[14] Kwame Gyekye, *Beyond Cultures: Perceiving a Common Humanity: Ghanian Philosophical Studies, III*, Washington, D.C.: The Council for Research in Values and Philosophy, 2004.

[15] Joseph Owens, *The Doctrine of Being in the Aristotelian Metaphysics,* Toronto: Pontifical Institute of Medieval Studies, 1978.

[16] Cornelio Fabro, *Participation.*

17

Prejudice In Okere
Universality In Contextualism

Augustine Oburota

1. Introduction

T. Okere is known for persistently researching on the meeting point between culture and philosophy. Having posed the question *Can There Be An African Philosophy?*, he has been seeking the answer, re-posing the question and elaborating on his results. 'Every philosophy has its roots in a particular culture', is a key premise in his philosophy. While openly recognizing the place of culture in philosophy, as well as the role of philosophy in culture, he insists on the importance of cross-cultural thinking. Every philosophy has its cultural base, its context, and there is always a connection between brands of philosophy - the idea of the universal within culture.

With the historicist tendencies in his works, today Okere is highly placed among the hermeneutic theorists. We intend here to take a cursory look at the place of 'Prejudice' in his thought. It is one of the major concepts for achieving his aim, and we observe that he employed the teachings of other great philosophers like Heidegger, Ricoeur and Gadamer, to mention but some, in his search for the cultural roots of philosophy. Like his fellow hermeneutic theorists, he can be accused of relativism or even irrationalism. However, his emphasis is that truth can be looked at from various perspectives, just as one culture varies from another. He retains the vital place of rationality in philosophy, and this he tries to show even as he argues for perspectivism.

2. Hermeneutics in Heidegger

Heidegger's hermeneutics lays less emphasis on the theory of interpretation, and more on an ontological theory of the human being in the world, otherwise known as *Dasein. Dasein* literally means 'Being-there', 'Being-in-the-world.' Standing for humans, *Dasein* is a being that understands itself only in relationship with the world. It determines its own being, as well as the being of the world: 'If no Dasein exists, no world is "there" either'.[1] Individuals get their proper designation and define themselves from their relationship to and with others. This explains the fact of 'being-there' of the *Dasein,* indeed not only being there, but also what we shall become in the future.

   Dasein's other meaning is Being in interpretation. Understanding is an element of *Dasein* upon which interpretation stands. Understanding means applying what we know to our particular context. When we do so, then we are engaged in interpretation. Existential understanding includes the following: fore-having (*vorhabe*), fore-seeing (*vorsicht*), and fore-understanding (*vorgriff*). They make up *Dasein*'s pre-understanding or pre-rationality. *Dasein* interprets the world all of the above.

   Therefore, in its being-in-the-world *Dasein* is not a *tabula rasa*. Rather, it exists already with its three elements of pre-understanding. These pre-conceived ideas make up *Dasein*'s being and its understanding of its place in the world. In encountering the world, *Dasein* attributes a certain significance in an attempt to understand and live in the world. Sometimes its preconceived understanding may not be the same as the world encountered. In that case, a new understanding evolves through such an encounter. To be in the world is, therefore, to increase one's wealth of understanding both qualitatively and quantitatively, a continuous broadening of horizon. Moreover, as the horizon of understanding expands, the better the quality of the meaning and the self-realization acquired.

3. Prejudice, *Vorurteil*, in Hermeneutics

'Nobody speaks from nowhere' is a very common aphorism used to portray the perspectivity that foreshadows all attempts to best express our ideas. This common everyday saying has an equivalent in philosophy that has caused the flow of much ink - Prejudice. Our experiences colour our understanding of this world, and this is the fact Gadamer specifies as 'Prejudice'. The intention of the speaker, the understanding of the listener, the context of the speech act, all these are factors that determine the meaning of what is being expressed in speech, in writing, in worldview. Our thoughts are not free of prejudice. People always talk from their various presuppositions.

According to Aristotle, not even the words we utter are identical with our thoughts. Words convey thoughts in such a way that thoughts are at risk of being misrepresented by words. It was for this reason that classical Greece took the science of rhetoric very seriously, and much later the Church fathers, like Tertulllian, Clement of Alexandria, Origen, etc, were oriented towards the application of hermeneutics, not intending to prove, but to make intelligible the mysteries of the Christian faith. In the medieval times, Anselm would see theology as 'faith seeking understanding'. The Holy Spirit was the source of all truth and understanding. In line with this, the Reformers would turn to the Bible (*sola scriptura*), and embrace individual interpretation of the scriptures, supposedly led by the Spirit of course.

For Heidegger, the prejudicial nature of thought already mentioned is highly remarkable. People's preconceived ideas contribute greatly to their knowledge of the world. This implies a surer understanding and appreciation of otherness. Heidegger as a phenomenologist was only trying to lay bare the reality of the world. His was not necessarily an exercise in praise of prejudice. It means that one must reckon with the dangers inherent in one's effort at understanding the world.

The renowned father of philosophical hermeneutics, Hans-Georg Gadamer, would continue in the tradition of Descartes, using hermeneutics to continue the search for real knowledge or truth. He introduced the idea of *sensus communis* to stand for Bacon's *alia ratio philosophandi*, 'another way of philosophizing. Knowledge is not contained in the universals alone. Even art and aesthetics, though subjective, contain the truth as well. They do not follow the rules of the universals, but go by the subjective way of judgment or taste. Furthermore, for Gadamer, Being is language, 'Being that can be understood is language'.[2] Hermeneutics is then said to be both ontological and universal. He calls hermeneutics a 'universal aspect of philosophy'. Through a discipline of questioning and inquiring the truth can be reached.

4. Okere's Hermeneutics

Okere is a crusader of hermeneutics of culture, with a lot of influence from Heidegger, Gadamer and Ricoeur. Okere's perspectivism projects the hermeneutic theory into sociology and anthropology. For him, culture has a truth content. Just as culture underlies our thought pattern, and there is pluralism of culture, so too there is no one and only criterion for attaining the truth or that is the basis of truth, of values and of meaning. Rather, there are alternative doctrines and alternative instrumentalities.

Metaphorically, all this means that our understanding is beclouded by lived experiences, our culture or accumulated worldview. For Okere, this is a given or a constant that constrains one to be really more careful in the attempt to interpret the world. This kind of thinking makes the study of one's culture, one's own thinking, necessary for a better understanding of the world. This also is known to be the major task of phenomenology. We are required to seek the reason for various rationalities and values in the different, sometimes contradicting, foundational worldviews.

It is remarkable that Okere does not deny the truth content of the classical world or other philosophical schools, for he makes use of the classical authors like Plato and Aristotle, and of medieval authors like Augustine, Anselm and Aquinas, and many others. His grouse with Western philosophy in general is that it has an unnecessary bias for system-building. However, with hermeneutics, there is the recognition of perspectivity in knowledge, otherwise known as prejudice. Hermeneutics has rescued philosophy from itself and enabled it to take the first step to act as a bridge among cultures and peoples, says Okere. Hermeneutics did this by reminding philosophy of its own cultural origins and clearing the ground about its prejudgments, its originating biases, its initial and abiding interests and unconscious presuppositions. In his search for African philosophy, he makes recourse to hermeneutics as foundational: 'It is only within the context of hermeneutics that African culture can give birth to African philosophy.'[3]

5. Universality as Diversity

Okere holds that philosophy is relevant in intercultural dialogue, especially if we consider philosophy's role as a clarifier of ideas, words and concepts. Philosophy helps in the understanding of the words used in describing and explaining reality, as well as facilitates analysis of the concepts applied.

Philosophy's use of logical reasoning is called for as well in intercultural dialogue. This will help in a pluralistic world with its many differences of worldviews and opinions. According to Okere, because the concern of philosophy is that of ultimacy, and ultimacy is the search of all cultures, the role of philosophy is believed to be relevant not only at all times, but also in all cultures. This is what one could call universality as diversity. Here indeed lies his answer to the pertinent question 'what is the basis of plurality of rationality?' As K. Wiredu would argue: 'suppose there were no cultural universals. Then intercultural communication would be impossible. But there is intercultural communication. Therefore, there are cultural universals'.[4] In other words, there may be the same material object of philosophy but various formal objects. The various formal objects are also the various systems of reasoning. Okere calls for a less rigid philosophical tradition.

Okere's philosophy is very much against system-building, and opens up an avenue of questions and answers that are undogmatic and open-ended, 'a reasoned choice among many plausible answers'. Okere's choice tends towards the doctrines of Plato and Aquinas, as opposed to that of Kant and Hegel, as Okere himself would acknowledge. He shared something in common with Schleiermacher who emphasized the role of reason, even as he upheld and developed the hermeneutic theory.[5] Okere can be seen to be tending towards deconstructionism, very much in line with Derrida's critical theory. He says: 'though a philosopher comes into being by reflection on some difficulty of his day, he does not resolve it by building a closed and self-contained system of explanation.'[6]

Okere's method tends to uphold the primacy of philosophical anthropology. While the role of ontology in philosophy would widen the gap between theory and praxis, having little or nothing to do with cultures, on the contrary, philosophy should encourage intercultural exchange. This gives much credit to philosophical anthropology. Such a philosophy would highlight the great importance of friendship and cooperation, as did the Stoics and the Epicureans, as well as emphasize great respect for the Other, as did Protagoras and as is done by existentialists today. Like Heidegger and Gadamer, Okere would lay bare the primary role culture plays in philosophy. In all, Okere would recognize that whether we begin with the universal method or particular experience, each has a fair share of its own problematic.

6. Where then lies the peculiarity of Okere?

Okere's weight bears very much on the argument that even as philosophy pursues the ultimate and the objective, truth conveys itself in various objective thoughts and languages. The task of the philosopher would be to acknowledge and study the various ways of expression of truth, appreciate them, and emphasize ways they could be appropriated socially and politically for the advancement of peace in the world.

We are speaking from perspectives and prejudices. People should learn to reflect on one another's reflections and perspectives. Philosophy in this case would contribute to world peace and social order. Praxis, for Okere is an essential task of philosophy. Realizing how tied to culture philosophy is, it follows that the practical implication of philosophical discourse is a task for all true philosophies and philosophers.

Perhaps Okere's greatest contribution to philosophy is his clarion call to take philosophy to its roots culture: 'philosophy and culture (a) are heterogeneous and (b) must be mediated by preliminary hermeneutical work which comprises various levels'.[7] This great link between philosophy and culture shows the limits of philosophy: 'the essential historicity of man, the fact that he is born into and limited within culture from which limits he can soar, though always in a limited way.'[8]

7. Assessing Okere on Prejudice

There are philosophies, yet philosophy is one. One of the main problems posed by Okere's stance in seeking philosophical truth in culture or in a particular lived experience is that of making truth, meaning and values historically conditioned. Culture is dynamic and subject to time and change. As in Gadamer, the context determines the rationality of discourse. Plausibility, therefore, is time bound. This is where the difficulty lies. One smells relativism. There is a problem of how to justify the philosophy of a particular culture or lived experience as philosophy at all.

There is also the problem of ambiguity and falsehood. How does one determine the truth-value of different and conflicting lived experiences? What if alternative doctrines on a particular philosophical question differ to the point of incompatibility and contradiction?

However, the fact remains that not all contexts may contain the optimal truth, for Heidegger, for Gadamer, as well as for Okere. Some contexts are more justifiable than others. Any truth founded on culture may be proved wrong in another historically conditioned context. For Okere, it would be the task of a true philosopher to subject one's reasoning to continual examination. This gives philosophy its glory, that is, creativity in rationality. Philosophy remains in this case an on-going, open, quest indeed.

When Gadamer speaks of prejudice, he does not in any way mean to make truth relativistic. Rather he speaks within the circle of properly educated minds that can subject the world to rigorous rational investigation. Okere likewise would prefer to be accused of perspectivism, instead of relativism. His views transcend relativism in the sense that he advocates openness to other schools of thought and to the better alternative. As already noted above, his idea of philosophy leaves no room for a self-contained system, no place for relativism. The limitations of philosophy apply to each and every system. This is the contribution of hermeneutics. Hermeneutics being an applied knowledge like ethics, it is not epistemic and has no 'unchanging regularity' [9] like mathematics.

Though one would have expected Okere to have embarked on a more detailed critique of particular experience and hermeneutics itself, it is clear in his thoughts that not even these alternatives are considered perfect in searching for the truth. Moreover, he does not do away with regulative standards. He still acknowledges the significant roles of precision, coherence and conformity in the machinery of reasoning. He only raises the prospect of more alternatives than the traditional reasoning. Today, this way of looking at philosophy remains quite trendy with the popularity of phenomenology, hermeneutics and existentialism. Even in logic, there are schools that advocate less rigidity and more pluralism.[10]

8. Conclusion

It is quite easy to detect traces of Heideggerian thoughts everywhere in Okere such as sameness and difference, pluralism and subjectivity, as well as alterity or otherness. In adopting such an approach to philosophy, Okere would not escape the criticism held by some that in the face of their apparent failure in world civilization, African philosophers tend to opt for a reconciliatory stance. It is said that pluralism is the hiding place for African thinkers who feel that the mistake of the West has been to project their particular worldviews as a universal law.

Indeed, pluralism tends to accommodate both the orientation of Africans towards tradition and towards Westerner's pursuit of modernity. Looking at Okere's hermeneutics of culture, there is an emphasis on culture as the seat of thought and action. Culture here is not to refer mainly to the past. It is rather one's own situation in life, including one's past. It has to do with the *nova et vetera*, a phrase Okere loves to use frequently.

There is no gainsaying that Okere achieved his aim of arguing for an African philosophy. There cannot be one single philosophical system. This is clear if we believe as did Okere that philosophy is coloured by culture. Prejudice holds the key to philosophical pluralism. Okere would prolong this fact further into interhuman relationship, using it to advocate for peace in the world. There remain, however, possible dangers of falling into philosophical indifferentism and potential reduction of philosophy to mere sociology.

Notes

[1] M. Heidegger *Being and Time* J. Maquarrie & E. Robinson (Tr.), Oxford: Blackwell, 1962-1996, p.417.

[2] H-G Gadamer, *Truth and Method*, London: Sheed and Ward, 1989, 2nd Ed., p.474.

[3] T. Okere *African Philosophy A Historico-Hermeneutical Investigation of the Conditions of its Possibility*, New York: Univ. Press, 1983, p.15.

[4] K. Wiredu *Cultural Universal and Particulars An African Perspective*. Bloomington: Indiana Univ. Press, 1996, p.21.

[5] cf. Schleiermacher *Hermeneutics and Criticism*, 1808.

[6] T. Okere, *African Philosophy…* p.84.

[7] Ibid.

[8] Ibid. p.59.

[9] cf. J.C. Weinsheimer *Gadamer's Hermeneutics A Reading of* Truth and Method. London: Yale Univ. Press, 1985.

[10] See for instance N. Rescher's *Many-value Logic*, New York: McGraw-Hill, 1969.

18

The Challenges of African Moral Heritage
The Igbo Case

John Chukwuemeka Ekei

1. Introduction

Naturally, it is better to introduce this intellectual excursion by asking a basic question on whether the Africans actually possess a morality, or better still, a moral philosophy from where we can stand to talk of her moral heritage. In other words, is there a moral heritage in Africa? And if there is, what is it? A seeming skeptical question at the very beginning of this seeming direct paper may as well demand a certain amount of courage. For there are many scholars especially among Africans who will likely not accept anything short of affirmative answer with regard to Africa possessing its moral heritage like the rest of the world. Again, the way the topic is captioned seems to favor even taking the positive reply as a fiat, to a point of leaning to Gadamar's inclination that an answer is suggested in every expressed question[1]. That not withstanding, there is, I think, something in Bertrand Russell's conviction that philosophical questions help to increase the interest of the world, and show the strangeness and wonder lying in the ordinary things taken for granted in our daily life[2]. In other words, the *challenges* of African moral values presuppose the existence, or to be precise, a primary determination of the existence of such moral values. Another problem may be to find out, "which" African moral heritage are we talking about. Who are the Africans, to begin with? Does it mean those living at present in Africa or those in Diasporas or both of them? Since Africa is often reported in many quarters as multicultural and heterogeneous in constitution, which of these diversities is referred to? What import is the concept "African" in African moral heritage? Which of its epoch is in focus, traditional, modern, or contemporary? What qualifies as African moral heritage, and what does not? Not of least importance, of course, is a question of basic canons, measurement or parameters to be employed in assessing what can be regarded as African moral heritage? Or does every cultural material in Africa qualify as its moral heritage? Assuming finally that, Africa has a moral heritage, what are the possible challenges facing it? These and more are some of the questions bordering our overall discussions.[3]

2. Morality in Africa

It is not out of place here, to recall the skepticism that across the years trailed any discussion on whether the Africans or its part as the Igbo tribe of Nigeria possessed what could be called 'morals or morality.' Leo Frobenius was not alone in regarding the entire Negroes as those with no moral heritage.[4] Again, after many years of service in Nigeria during the colonial era, Lord Lugard referred to the people of southern part of Nigeria as those with no system of ethics and no principles of conduct.[5] In his book, *Among the Ibos of Nigeria,* G.T. Basden affirmed that "The word 'morality' has no significance in Ibo (Igbo) vocabulary; and where the natives have remained untouched by outside influence there is nothing exactly corresponding to the social evil of European life."[6] In less emphatic terms, I. A Correia admitted that African-Igbo have a moral heritage, but he reduced it to 'the lowest grade of moral consciousness.' These negative views seemed to have arisen at the time, due to little or no appreciation of the impact of cultural relativity on people's way of lives as well as a seeming lack of understanding of the participatory and perspective nature of what we generally consider as 'truth,' or something 'worthwhile,' as 'proper,' 'allowed,' 'approved' or 'legitimate.' That the word morality has no significance in Igbo vocabulary as reported by Basden implies a judgment of some sort. In this case, it is a judgment of meaning and value. In other words, it implies a value judgment.

Like every value, "it is essentially referential and contextual;

that is, every value is a value for someone or for some people."[7] In other words, values are to some extent culturally determined. Consequently, the concept 'significance,''value,'or 'meaning' is a relative term, "not because what is good for Europe is necessarily not also good for Africa but because a value (or significance) has its raison d'etre in its original context of relevance … from where then it can have or acquire universal validity."[8] All this comes to demonstrate that what is considered a value in Europe may not necessarily be regarded as value in African. And in the same way, what is taken, as a value in Africa may not necessarily be seen as a value in Europe or America.

It then follows that the mistakes of the early critics of Africa stems from an implicit problem of confusing two different cultural mindsets: the African and the European. While the word morality has no significance in Igbo vocabulary, judging from western - Basden's mindsets, it possesses significance and meaning to African- Igbo mindsets. The underlying differences border on the import of cultural relativity coupled with noticeable ideological differences. So, different cultures and environments can account for the existence of different moral concepts, interpretations and expressions. The same thing can be said of African culture vis-a-vis the western para types. Being different continental environments and cultural groups, for that matter, they invariably produce different moral features and exigencies. Hence, it is an illusion to judge one continental cultural group with the moral paradigms of the other as G.T. Basden and other critics of Africa had done.

(a) Morality and Culture in Africa

K.C. Anyanwu rightly defines culture as "a common living experience shared by a *particular* people."[9] In other words, every group of people in a particular environment shares a peculiar experience in life brought about by the unique environment in which they live. In fact, it is this environment that determines the type of experience a given people shares. If a person can really reflect on the enormous contributions his environment has made in his manner of thinking, of perceiving, of acting out what he has actually thought out, the story will be different! If only he can equally imagine how a given circumstance brought about by that particular environment has tremendously shaped and affected his attitude to life, his mode of giving interpretations to his day-to-day encounter with life, he would better appreciate the place of culture in fashioning what is considered the "good" or the "evil"! It is therefore not surprising that particular environment necessarily defines to a large extent, the mode of behavior as well as the detailed application of such moral notions as good and evil, approved and disapproved, moral and immoral.

There is no doubt that uniformity exists in the use of concepts regarding moral or immoral issues. But its detailed interpretations, significance and meaning are often culturally determined. In other words, do not kill is unarguably a universal moral norm accepted by all cultures but why it is considered wrong to kill, including the excusing circumstances are often culturally determined.

In other words, the "culture of a people (*including their moral outlook*) cannot be separated from human experience, and it is this experience that produces it"[10] By "experience", according to Montagu is meant, "anything an individual or group of individuals has undergone or lived, perceived or sensed."[11] What they perceive in common within that given environment constitute their basic vision or their worldview. And this worldview consists of the "complex of beliefs, habits, laws, customs and tradition of a people." It embodies "the overall vision a people has about the reality, the universe, life and existence, their attitude to life and to things in general."[12] It includes the way they approve human conduct and why they assess it that way and not the other way. In fact, it is in that freedom to evaluate experiences in a particular manner as against other available options that makes a people unique. Here, the uniqueness touches not only on the way they conceive and interpret the world around them but also on how they behave in different circumstances of their lives.

This diversity in human evaluation and character of actions is perhaps, what the early critics on Africa failed to appreciate. "Due to differences of human experiences as well as the differences in its interpretation, there are differences in cultures."[13] In fact, the implication of this submission is far reaching: It means that culture determines who the people are. It also shapes and reshapes them in such a way that they exhibit certain peculiar traits, which can be known and appreciated from the cultural standpoint. Hence, to understand a people is to understand their culture that shapes them as unique people. It means that for the West or westerners to understand and appreciate African moral values is for them to understand the African unique environment and peculiar experience from which African unique morality and moral values emanate. In other words, if African moral exigencies and behavior can be likened to a drama or play, then their unique environment and common living experience become a prompter that influences their (moral) actions and behavior from within.

It then follows that "due to the plurality of cultures and the different interpretations of experience as noted above, it is impossible to look for the One Truth about the meaning of life, (of morality, of laws, of politics) and of the world in any culture."[14] In place of considering any given culture as sole culture with absolute, universal and standard features; intercultural participation and mutual cultural dialogue are preferred in the search for the one truth of man and his world. Following this understanding, western, Chinese, and African systems of morality become from cultural stand points, different perspectives of understanding human conduct and behavior.

(b) Africa as Unity in Diversity

We have seen the impact of different cultures on the evolution of different worldviews including different moral experiences, actions and behaviors. We have equally argued that from cultural standpoints, each of these moral experiences and expressions provides its unique and satisfactory ways of articulating and solving problems as well as resolving enigmas arising from moral dimensions of peoples' lives. In other words, because of diversity in people's experiences and expressions, there is no way of believing that   different cultures will produce just one unilateral way of looking at morality, or of considering what is 'good' and 'evil' in their environments.

Now, in our own case, looking at Africa as a continent can it be justified to believe that it shares only one common moral heritage in spite of its multiethnic compositions and diversities? What exactly entitles us, in the first place, to talk about African moral heritage, when Africa has various cultural groups? Here, Richard A. Wright puts it more directly, "Given the fact that there are over forty (40) different countries in Africa, each with a number of different language groups (Ghana, For example has ninety five (95) distinct language groups), there could not be such a thing as African moral heritage (African philosophy) if at all, it would be "African moral heritages" ("African philosophies")."[15] Perhaps, Wright is not the only scholar who has made this observation concerning Africa. What seems rather, peculiar about his remark is his ability to dramatize his findings with concrete data. African ethnic and cultural diversities, not withstanding, 'they have deep underlying affinities' as Kwasi Wiredu observes, 'running through these cultures,'[16] which justify speaking of African moral heritage. It is necessary therefore to locate and examine those underlying affinities running through African cultures, especially as they concern her specific moral values, up to the point of being considered her valued heritage.

3. Existence of African Moral Values and Heritage

If a value is a value for somebody, or at least, a value for a group of people, it means that, in its broadest sense, a value is that, which everybody and every people irrespective of time and place can boast of. In other words, every group of people has what they consider a value; and whether it is appreciated as a value by a different group of people is immaterial in this case. Here, a value is considered as something relative; relative to the person group whose value it is. Hence, different persons or groups can talk of their respective values in life; justifying the often-quoted proverb that one person's meat is another person's poison. That notwithstanding, some values cut across different cultures to the level of possessing a universal acceptance. A ready example, in this category is '*life*.' It is almost a moral certitude that everybody and every culture, no matter how preliterate appreciates the objective value of life. Our consideration of African moral heritage will necessarily cut across these two senses of value. It is in fact, on the basis that some moral elements in Africa possess some objective moral worth or significance (value) that they are ipso facto considered good enough to be inherited as heritage.

　　Again, not everything inherited and preserved as a heritage in Africa qualifies as her moral heritage. In fact, there are different kinds of

African heritage. There are, for instance, African religious heritage, African artistic heritage, African legal heritage, and African musical heritage. Then, what specific values in Africa qualify as African moral heritage? The question can simply be answered by saying that they are those African values that possess certain moral implications in the lives of the people. G.J. Warnock articulates the basis of morality as "human predicament", which is fraught with great limitations and is, ever liable to go badly, if the conscious actions of the rational beings are not forth coming. In other words, he defines the general object of moral evaluation as that which "…must be to contribute in some respects, by way of the actions of rational beings, to the amelioration of the human predicament - that is of the conditions in which these rational beings, humans, actually find themselves."[17] He narrowed down what he considers as human predicament into five basic factors, namely; "limited resources, limited information, and limited intelligence". Others are "limited rationality, and limited sympathies."[18] Of all these limiting factors, Warnock judges limited sympathies as the most critical and the most crucial in making human condition very miserable and unbearable. Hence, he considers it as a chief preoccupation of morality to expand human limited sympathies in the society.

On another note, Austin Fagothey, conceives the basis of morals or morality as "happiness,"[19] which is ultimately anchored on the last end of man, in the possession of God. He judges the means to this end as "the human act or voluntary human conduct."[20] He conceives morality as the quality in human acts by which we call them right or wrong, good or evil. In other words, "it is a common term covering the goodness or badness of a human act without specifying which of the two is meant."[21] In our own case, African moral heritage means those good moral values, which help, in one way or the other in the amelioration of the ugly human condition. That is, African moral values should contribute to the promotion of human welfare in Africa and even beyond as the world is ever becoming a unified village in many respects.

However, what should be regarded as African moral heritage, just by that very fact, should painstakingly be differentiated from religion or African religious heritage. Just as the observation rightly made by Wiredu in the case of Akan, African moral values are not founded on African religion and they are not part of it.

Traditional moral thinking on the foundations of morality is

> refreshingly non-super naturalistic. …anyone who reflects on
> our traditional ways of speaking about morality is bound to be
> struck by the preoccupation with human welfare: What is
> morally good is what befits a human being; it is what is decent for
> man what brings dignity, respect, contentment, prosperity, joy,
> to man and his community.[22]

The point being made here is that morality, even in traditional Africa is not founded on religion but on human rational efforts as to what is conducive to human welfare. So, when talking about African moral heritage, our attention will be directed to those entire valued heritage in (traditional) Africa that emanated principally from human articulations and reflections aimed at bringing far reaching improvements in cushioning his ugly situations.

And since these values are culturally rooted, in the sense that they are *prima faciae* relative to a particular culture, they are equally dynamic as the culture that embraces them. In other words, values are open to cultural changes involving innovation, social acceptance, selective elimination and final integration. So, when we talk of African moral heritage in the present day context, it will be utterly naïve to restrict our thinking to merely African traditional moral values alone. This is because what could have been known as traditional values must have integrated new values in one-way or the other. It is this apparent transformation or adaptation of values that brings about the issue of "challenges" as we shall soon examine. Meanwhile, in the consideration of African moral heritage, her unique worldviews assume a pride of place.

(a) African Worldview as a Source of Moral Heritage

Our effort so far, has been to demonstrate that "values" and "heritage" are always considered in a context of culture or a people's way of life, action and behavior. There is a way in which a people's values can be seen as a product of their unique worldviews. Here, we consider worldview in terms of "a complex of belief, habits, laws, customs and traditions of a people."[23] It includes the overall pictures, which a people possess about the universe, life and existence in general. The worldview of a people embodies all their estimations concerning what they consider good, proper, and worthwhile as well as the contrasts of all they consider evil, improper, or not worthwhile.   Basically, the Igbo and African worldview in general incorporates two essential beliefs:

- *The unity of all things, in so far as they are,*
    (Involving the integration of supernatural, animate, and inanimate Beings), and
- *An ordered relationship among all these beings in the universe,*[24]
    (Including the harmonious interaction of these Beings, their coexistence, and c-ooperations),

It means that the philosophy of "unity" and "ordered relationship" is an African basic moral vision, from which his other concrete exigencies as extended family practice, communalism, consensus democracy, and participation flow as from a source. It is also from this understanding that the African sense of collective responsibility and brotherhood as well as his vision of humanism emanate as from a root. In other words, African worldview as we rightly mentioned before plays the role of a moral prompter, providing the needed guide and force to human actions and behavior as the case may be.

Hence, we consider the African moral heritage in toto as a veritable off shoot of its cherished worldviews. This invaluable role of a people's vision, is what V.C, Uchendu has in mind when, in reference to its significance, reveals that: "To know how a people view the world around them is to understand how they evaluate life and how they evaluate life provides them with a character of action". From this, it is easily understandable why the nature of people's worldview determines the quality of their action and behavior, their beliefs and, attitudes. In other words, if the people's world vision is good in a particular area, their action that flows necessarily from it will be equally good in the same way. It is from this angle that we consider the people's worldview as the basic moral heritage of that people, in so far as it provides the basic conceptual platform from which other concrete values derive.

(b) Extended Family System

Under the above lists, we first identify, perhaps, the most basic, or, the African extended family practice, which has remained the bedrock of communal caring and sharing in the society. In other words,"apart from giving the African a distinctive mark of identity as against the West, extended family practice (communalism), has remained with him over the years, being a veritable 'insurance' in justice for his life, and properties."[25] Due to its central concern on 'man', not as a discrete entity but as a being-in-relation-to- others; it is often characterized as 'African humanism' or 'African brotherhood'as Julius Nyerere would like to call it. Basic to this brotherhood is 'feeling-involved- with- others' analogous to, and yet, distinct from Heideggerian concept of man as a 'being-with.'[26]

It is this unique vision of man as a being- in-African- world that makes extended family practice an invaluable African moral heritage. From extended family system, one can talk of wider practice of individual\ communal relationship in terms of communalism. Because of the many implications of this way of life amidst some criticisms,[27] it is worthwhile to give it a more detailed attention.

(c.) Communalism and Human limitations

The significance of communalism is better felt in the context of human limitations and scarcity. The Igbo, as the Africans, in general share the common conviction that the earthly existence is fraught with great imperfection, powerlessness, and contingencies, which beg for urgent meaning and solution. The principle of human limitation *uwa ezu oke, and uwa- bunjo- na- mma,* implies scarcity of human resources, powerlessness and ambivalence in the face of earthly disasters and evil fortunes. These forces seem to pose so great a challenge that only with concerted effort of communalism can they be effectively wrestled with. This organized action is better facilitated by an expectation in justice based on the principle of I am because We are and since we are, therefore I am. The moral implication arising from this basic relationship is here articulated under four existential moments:

Justice- as- co-existence

Justice- as- acceptance

Justice- as- care

Justice- as concern

The import of justice- as- co-existence in tackling the problem of limitation and ambivalence is better brought out in the remark of C. B. Okolo where he states that the African is not just a human being but is also essentially a "being- with", the very basis of his claim to the title, "African."[28] It means a sense of belongingness of life and destiny among members of a given community. If there is any unique characterization that Placide Tempels observed in the people of Bantu it is the fact that they had strong affinity to one another and to their basic customs. Hence, he remarks that:

> Just as Bantu (black Africa) ontology is opposed to the European concept of individuated things existing in themselves, isolated from others, so   Bantu psychology cannot conceive of man as an individual, as a force existing by itself and apart from its ontological relationship with other living   beings.[29]

In communalism, there are also individual and collective dispositions to feel concerned for the less privileged, or justice as- concern. This has often given rise to the derivative name given to least advantaged members of the Community. In African-Igbo of Nigeria, such deprived members are called (Ogbenye or analytically, *Ogbe- enye*), meaning 'community- gives,'[30] or 'community supported member\s.' Here, what the community provides is mostly material sustenance. All these ethical provisions are readily promoted in the context of communalism. Other values coming as offshoots of this system of life include; kinship groupings and brotherly affinity, common religious identity, consensus and representative democracy, philosophy of participations, appreciation of 'age' and integrity as a veritable condition of leadership. However, there is no doubt that the contemporary understanding of these values and how they are appreciated and practiced today will certainly create a dramatic twist as will be given some considerations in the subsequent sections.

(D) Leadership by Example

From what has been studied earlier, G.J. Warnock is not alone in justifying the reasonableness of morality as a way of countervailing the ugly effects of human predicament. But while he finds the possible solutions in the enlargements of human sympathies beyond other four notable factors he identified, the Africans will naturally locate the solution in the expression of justice- in communalism, the dimensions of which have been briefly enumerated above. Human condition is, to a large extent, as dynamic as man himself, presenting as it were, not just one but divergent face. Consequently, it appears to be better confronted from, not just one, but from many equally effective angles. The import of communal coexistence is a rational provision aimed at a better understanding and appreciation of man, not as a discrete individual but as a being-with. This understanding has provided an enduring manner of attending to man as a being with an inalienable interconnectivity with the rest of men. And so, the idea of coexistence as bedrock of caring and concern (sympathy) is highly significant in Africa as a whole. Hence, the Igbo people normally talk of power as belong to the multitude ('Igwe- *bu- ike'*). In fact, the very concept of the multitude is in itself understood as a source of power and authority. In a society, like Africa that operates a basic kinship system of government, the power resides in the kindred itself. In other words, kindred is power. That is "umunna- bu- ike." This underscores the pre-eminence of the community over the individual especially in terms of *locus* of power and not necessarily with regard to the assertion of rights. That is to say that, 'no man however great can win judgment against the clan,'[31] as power resides on the multitude. Kwasi Agyeman recognizes the similarity between the concept "*we, the people* ..." as used in the framing of the modern democratic Constitution of Ghana and the phrase used in the installation of a king or chief by the Yorubas of Nigeria, Bawules of Ivory Coast, Dagares of Burkina Faso, Kikiyus of Kenya, Fulanis of Mali and Guinea, Ewes of Togo, Akan of Ghana, Bantus of South Africa.[32] During the occasion, the people are said to tell the King/Queen or chief what they should do and what they should not attempt doing before they bind the authority. By this singular gesture, the King or the chief becomes only a custodian of the interest or well being of the people. The use of the phrase, "the people,"according to Agyeman insures that, "the Africans leave none aside, so the strength and sense of the people lie in the provision it makes for the protection and service of all, mostly the disadvantaged among them ...."[33]

It is equally in the context of this need to provide the enduring structure for attending to human welfare in the society, that path of good leadership becomes highly significant in African socio- ethical scheme of things. Apart from dearth of human resources in the society, man is a problem unto himself (*'mmadu- bu- ala- adiro- mma'*). He is ethically ambivalent, as rightly noted above. It means then that without communal ideals, concerted efforts and encouragements, even the most articulated noble ideals could collapse. But a crucial question often asked in connection with this is: who watches the watchmen themselves? And how many watchers would be sufficiently employed to watch the people and more especially, the *watchmen*, human beings, being what they are? For G.J. Warnock, if this effort is to succeed, the monitoring machinery ought to be indeed, ubiquitous, if only to be effective. But, "if nothing but coercion (or coercive watching) kept people in order, then the machinery of coercion would have to be very vast... or at any rate somehow ubiquitous and powerful enough...."[34] But this difficulty refers to the problem of the organization of people in the society. But what seems to constitute more difficulty to Warnock is in fact, on how to control the excesses of the watchmen themselves, and in our own case, *the leaders*.

The concept of "leadership" in traditional Africa is an act of "standing for" somebody or else, it is a means by which leaders "mediate" between the living members of the community and the ancestors. According to C.K. Meek "the real rulers of the community are the ancestors or spirits and the living persons who act as rulers are merely the agents of the ancestors."[35] This explains why all those that are involved in traditional leadership as lineage heads (Okpala), the titled men, leaders of various age-grades and groups, often chosen by virtue of their ripe age, are always "on the watch less they offend"[36] the ancestors whom they actually represent. In other words, there is an understanding of leadership as divine trusts meant for communal service and caring. In his study of Igbo people of Africa, C.U. Ogu reports that: "The desire to preserve community harmony and therefore the integrity of traditional morality is institutionalized in such titles as *"ozo."* This is because "genuine "ozo" initiates claim that the continuity of every lineage is linked with the existence of good living men, who uphold both publicly and privately the laws of the land, its taboos and religious rituals of the community."[37] Hence, like communalism, leadership becomes a valued moral instrument, providing solutions to human predicaments.

(f) Custom And Tradition ('Ome-na- ani')

Before we eventually settle to talk about the present challenges facing the African moral heritage as highlighted above, it is still important to examine the impact of African custom and tradition (*'omenani'*) to moral disseminations and cultivations. The Igbo concept of custom and tradition *'omenani'* literally means, "as it is done, or supposed to to be done in the land."[38] This is equivalent to Igbo 'ethical-ought' as opposed to its ethical 'ought not' or, 'nso- ala,'(taboo). In fact, the concept of taboo (*'nso'*), abomination (*'aru'*) and purification (*'ikpu- aru'*) has been part and parcel of the history of the Igbo as indeed, of the Africans in general. "The spirit of omenani,"according to E. Edeh, "is always linked with the sense of mystery and supernatural. The idea of making sure that all is in tune with the sensory and the supersensory realities is always in the background of the thought and actions of the people...."[39]In fact, what is generally considered as either the custom (*'ome'*) or the taboo (*'nso'*) is thus, culturally determined and derived from the nature of man, his general vision of the universe and the situation, in which he finds himself. In other words, the ethical-ought is supposed to promote the welfare of man and the communal well-being and harmony. This corresponds to the general object of moral evaluation which for Warnock is to contribute in some respects, by way of the actions of rational beings, to the amelioration (welfare) of the human predicament- that is, of the conditions in which these rational beings, humans, actually find themselves (the communities). The ethical ought-not (the taboo) is meant to check the human excesses, the evil inclinations in man. In other words, it is recognition that man is ethically ambivalent; a being that harbors paradoxically, good and evil inclinations. Hence, without collective ideals and encouragements, evils are likely to triumph over the good. These collective ideals and encouragements are, as it were, provided by custom and tradition as well as by the inhibiting forces of taboos (*'ome-na- ala'* and *'nso- ala'*).

4. Challenges of African moral Heritage

Discussing the general situation of things in the modern world of today, the second Vatican II draws our attention to the fact that: "Ours is a new age of history with critical and swift upheavals spreading gradually to all corners of the earth. They are the product of man's intelligence and creative activity... We are thus, entitled to speak of a real social and cultural transformation whose repercussions are felt too on the religious level."[40] Here, the council Fathers give us the general overview of the underlying cause of the worldwide instability and the consequent crises resulting there from. It means a critical and swift upheaval, sweeping across the entire nations of the world in man's rational attempt to make a better bargain in his chequered existence. It means a strong influence of world cultural and social changes. It brings a transformation that is not simply peculiar to Africa alone, neither is it directed to its moral values in particular. It is rather a force that touches every domain of human life in every continent, in so far as it falls within the ambient of its cultural compositions. Our introductory section explains how this cultural transformation takes place in terms of four basic processes, undergone by every cultural activity in its effort to incorporate certain new elements considered amenable to its existing values.

Although, these observed challenges do not affect the African continent alone, their negative impacts are felt more in Africa, as a black continent and especially, as they affect its moral domains. In the case of Africa, the modern upheavals so illustrated have tended to obliterate or at best distort her ontological, historical, cultural and moral values. Here, there is hardly any cherished African traditional way of life that is not affected in one way or the other.

There is first of all a perceived distortion in the way and manner of conceiving the world. Hitherto, the African sees the moral world as dualistic and unitary at the same time. In its worldview, there is a basic relationship between the material world of man and the spiritual world of the ancestors. To live means an aspiration to satisfy the demands of the two worlds or to bear the consequence. Again to act is to be responsible not only to the living, the community and the yet- unborn but also to the spiritual world of the ancestors.

Perhaps, the much talked about modern upheaval deals its greatest blow on this African moral perception to the extent that today the modern African acts without any motivational vision, except perhaps, to maximize personal profit and gain. The ready challenges posed by this state of affairs are no doubt tremendous, especially, when we remember the present day corruption and embezzlement of public and private funds in Nigeria and in African countries as a whole. Today, the African lives and acts as if his moral world begins and ends in the world of man without any reference to the spiritual world of his ancestors. But that is not the only challenge facing African moral heritage.

The extended family practice that has hitherto earned the African a great respect in the committee of nations is today steadily tested and challenged by western individualistic life styles and its undue affinity to capitalistic and legalistic systems. Before this time however, " communalism", according to Okere, "has been so much appreciated politically that it provides the ideological base for all the known theories of African nationalism." Like African extended family system, "it (communalism) has been much maligned mainly on account of the economic constraints it may place on the well-to-do individual."[41] The recurrent crises and challenges facing this unique life style is such that, Nyerere has to put up a timely admonition, as mentioned earlier, in his suggestion that: "Our (Africans) first step, must be to re-educate ourselves to regain our former attitude of mind. In our traditional African society we were individuals within a community. We took care of the community and the community took care of us,"

And for Marcien Towa, "Africa will not really attain its cultural (historical, political, moral and economic) maturity as long as it does not elevate itself resolutely to a profound thinking of its essential problems, that is to say, to philosophic reflection."[42] In a sober moment, under a serious rational engagement, a person is drawn to discover that the colonial denigration of African moral values brought with it, an undue preferences of foreign values; a situation that still remains unabated. It means a basic attitude of preferring and choosing values other than ones own. It implies a choice of imported materials and a preference for that, in place of what one has as a possession. Not that everything so imported is necessarily bad but the basic alienation of oneself from ones inherited values is in itself a great challenge facing African moral values.

Notable among these factors, as earlier mentioned are the forces of colonialism, urban migration, and modern cravings for foreign fashions and ideology. Others include: secularism, militarism and materialism in the midst of abject poverty. There are also evils of bribery and corruption, armed robbery, drug addictions, institutionalized prostitution. All these socio-ethical maladies witnessed on daily basis are the consequences of sudden estrangement of the African from his co-existent traditional life style. Individualism takes the place of this cherished collectivity in living, planning and execution. At the root of these crises are some notable factors.

(a) Colonialism

Basic to the effects of culture- contacts in Africa is *colonialism* as we tried to discuss from the onset. Although, objectively speaking, colonialism, as a lop-sided socio-political and cultural relationship of the colonizing powers and the colonized nations abroad is no longer in force in Africa, its effects still linger for many years to come in form of neo-colonialism and imperialism. In fact, the aftermath of colonialism seems more devastating and enduring than colonialism itself. Here, nobody forgets in a hurry the various degrees of denigration brought on the Africans individually as persons and collectively as a continent of a black race. It was then fashionable to deny that the Africans are human beings or at best, the 'real' human beings as the rest of mankind. Emil Ludwig had exclaimed in the following terms when talking about African religious experience: "How can the untutored Africans conceive God? How can this be? Deity is a philosophical concept which savages are incapable of framing."[43]

Neither this encounter nor that of Euro-American sense of *'evangelizing mission'* could have left the African without what C.B, Okolo of blessed memory, calls the African *'Uprootedness of self.'*[44]

There is therefore, in these derogatory statements no small

negative impacts in the psyche of the average Africans. The African becomes then a man afflicted with many complexes, inferiority complex, not in the least. Consequently, he (the African) soon begins to romance, and crave for other foreign moral ideologies, preferences, and values, other than his own. This is as it were a basic challenge confronting African moral heritage. It means resolving how to be an African in the midst of seeming attractive influences brought about by colonialism.

Again, as earlier highlighted, the African is born in an environment that cherishes communal living as a moral value, rooted in the basic extended family system. Here, he lives and acts as part and parcel of the community. Just as he lives for the community, the community, as it were, also exists for him. In this way, an ontological symbiosis is maintained all for the mutual well being of each party. Here, the individual is free but his freedom is seen as a freedom within the community. He is free within the context of the community. The resultant effect of this state of living is that the community insures the individual's existence and vice-versa. The insuring benefit derived from this mutual connection is anchored on the principle that, 'I am because we are and since we are therefore I am.' This has served as an African contribution to the world and its philosophy, being as Richard H. Bell observes "an inversion of the well known Cartesian 'cogito ergo sum' which places emphasis on the self, the 'I in isolation with the 'we- are.'"[45] But today, this significant traditional facility for cushioning the ugly effect of human predicament appears to be giving way to survival of the fittest as a system of life both in socio- political and moral dealings.

This aside, there are also the effects of modern upheavals on African custom and tradition, as a next in our consideration. Today, there is hardly any agreement on what the society should regard as ethical right or wrong. The lack of consensus which is the bane of modern moral crisis seems to be the result of different ways of conceiving man, his vocation on earth, his relationship to his fellow man, and the place of the Supreme being in the universe in which he lives. While some Africans hold to the moral expectation of traditional customs, which is called *'ome-na-ala'* in Igbo, others allow the modern fashionable trends to dictate for them while others follow what their religion tells them as good or bad. And today, there are thousands of such religious affiliations.

(b) Leadership crisis in Africa

Governance in African is not spared of this dislocation. In fact today, African moral heritage is facing an enormous leadership crisis. In every time and place, what people generally believe in, and how they act are to a large extent due to how they are governed. In other words, there is a sense in which a chaotic society promotes chaotic behaviors, just as organized community influences mature behaviors. The long practiced military governments in Africa are to a greater extent, contributive to the present day moral disorientations in Africa, especially Nigeria, considered recently, by *Transparency International*, as the second most corrupt country in the world.

Compared to African traditional leadership style, the contemporary leadership in Africa is at best an aberration and at worse, a betrayal of enduring objective of leadership. The modern crisis of governance in Africa lacks something that compels the human convictions and consciences unlike the traditional African *para types*. This has given rise to fraud, manipulations and to insincerity connected with the morality of apparent observance of the letters of the law without personal convictions. Instead of fostering genuine leadership, this ends up promoting pretences, eye-service, and different degrees of sycophancy. This is not different from what Chinua Achebe remarked concerning lack of moral content in African leadership, as illustrated with Nigeria. In fact, he summarized Nigerian (African) problem as "the unwillingness or inability of its leaders to rise to the responsibility, to the challenges of personal example, which are the hallmarks of true leadership."[46]

5. Conclusion

So enormous were the mistakes made in the past by earliest African critics, that today, it is no longer fashionable to speak of Africans, as not possessing a moral heritage like the rest of men. These mistakes, as we studied, appear to be borne of a glaring lack of appreciation that every morality (or moral heritage), to be relevant and meaningful to its people, ought to be understood in the context of the culture that produces it, and not outside it.[47] So that African moral heritage ought to be sought and known within the overall gestalt and 'sitz im lebem' of the African culture. But what is painful is that these identified valued heritages that were once pragmatically significant to the lives and existence of the Africans, are today becoming increasing mitigated and distorted by alien influences. They have been so adulterated in many cases that they now serve neither as African moral heritage nor western paratypes. These phenomena seem to constitute no little challenges to contemporary moral practice in Africa. Our study considers the challenges, simply as crises brought about by the negative colonial influences in Africa as well as a problem occasioned by a sudden drift of the bulk populations of the Africans to urban cities in search of better means of livelihood. In other words, the challenges facing African moral heritage today are part of what Chinua Achebe called "things fall apart" in Africa.

Hence, the "things" that actually fell apart are the basic mitigation of African worldviews, the dismantling of communal life style in preference to individualistic urban system of life, disparate institutions and interpretation of law as against a common legal vision in terms of custom and tradition. All these and more have become a cog on the wheels of continued existence and preservation of African moral heritage.

Notes

[1]. For Gadamer "a pedagogical question implies the direction of its answer but leaves some distance the student must cross in order to reach the answer." C.f, Joel C.Weinsheimer, *Gadamer's Hemeneutics: A Reading of Truth and Method* , New York: Vail-Ballou,1985, p.207.
[2]. Bertrand Russell's, *The Problem of Philosophy,* London: Oxford University 1976, p.6
[3]. Our interest here is not primarily in answering all these philosophical questions posed but in generating the puzzles surrounding the very topic itself. Hence, in philosophy questions appear more important than the answers.
[4]. Albert.K.Obiefuna, "Some Aspects of Traditional Moral Heritage With Particular Reference To The Igbo People of Nigeria", *Lucerna,* No.1 Vol 1 (1978), p.18. The same denial also trailed the domain of religion: Emil Ludwig had exclaimed in this manner about African religious experience: "How can the untutored African conceive God? How can this be?" "Deity is a philosophical

concept which savages are incapable of framing." Bolaji Idowu, *African Traditional Religion*, London: SMC, 1973, p.88.

⁵. Lord Lugard, *The Dual Mandate In British Tropical Africa*, Edinburgh: Blackwood and sons, 1921, p.1921, quoted from Albert .K. Obiefuna, *Loc. Cit.*

⁶. G.T, Basden, *Among The Ibos of Nigeria*, Lagos: Academy, 1983, p.34, Bracket mine.

⁷. Theophilus Okere, " The Assumption of African Values As Christian Values,"*Lucerna*, No.1, Vol.1 (1978), p.6.

⁸. Loc. cit.

⁹. K.C, Anyanwu, *The African Experience In The American Marketplace*, New York: Exposition, 1983, p.21, Emphasis mine.

¹⁰. K.C, Anyanwu, *loc.cit.*

¹¹. Ashley Montagu, *Man in Process*, New York: The New American Library, 1961, p.20.

¹². T.U, Nwala, *Igbo Philosophy*, Lagos: Lantern Books, 1985, p.26.

¹³. K.C, Anyanwu, *loc.cit.*

¹⁴. Ibid, p. 22.

¹⁵. Richard A. Wright (ed.), *African Philosophy An Introduction*, Washington D.C: University Press of America, 1984, pp.43-45. Adaptation is mine.

¹⁶. Kwasi Wiredu, *Philosophy And African Culture*, London: Cambridge University, 1980, pp.6-7.

¹⁷. G. J, Warnock, *The Object of Morality*, London: Methuens, 1971, p.16.

¹⁸. Ibid, p.21

¹⁹. Austin Fagothey, *Right And Reason*, New York: The C.V.Mosby, 1953, p.112

²⁰. Loc.cit.

²¹. Loc.cit.

²². Kwasi Wiredu, *op. cit*, p.6.

²³. T.U. Nwala, *loc cit.*

²⁴. Ibid, p.54

²⁶. John C.Ekei, *Justice In Communalism: A foundation Of Ethics In African Philosophy*, Lagos: Realm Communications, 2001, p.1.

²⁶. Loc.cit.

²⁷ Extended family system is often criticized "on account of the economic constraints it may place on the well- to- do individual," (Theophilus Okere, *op.cit*, p.12) and of course, "its anti-competitive and anti explorative visions"(John C. Ekei, *op. cit*, pp.242-243).

²⁹. C.B.Okolo, *What Is To Be African?* Enugu, Cecta, 1993, p.5.

²⁹. Placide Tempels, *Bantu Philosophy*, Paris, Presence Africaine, 1953, 103, quoted   from C.B. Okolo, *Ibid*, p.6.

³⁰. John C. Ekei,"Is There An African Moral Philosophy? A Hermeneutical Investigation Into African-Igbo Ethics,"*Understanding Philosophy*, Enugu:

Snaap, 2003, p.65.

[31].T. U. Nwala, *op. cit*, p.152.

[32] Kwasi Agyeman, "The Quest For Moral Democracy," A paper presented at Bigard Memorial Seminary, Enugu, Nigeria on 18th-20 Nov.2002 during the International Conference *On Philosophy And The Quest For* Responsible *Governance In Africa*, pp.2-3.

[33]. Loc.cit.

[34]. G.J, Warnock, The *Object of Morality,* op cit., pp.74-75.

[35]. C. K. Meek, "The Religions of Nigeria," *Africa*, Vol. xiv, No. I, (1943), p.113.

[36]. G.T, Basden, *Niger Ibos,* London: Frank Cass, 1966, p.xiv.

[37]. C.U. Ogu, "Offence In Traditional African Societies: The Igbo Case," *Lucerna*, No.2, Vol.1, (1981), p.45.

[38]. C.O, Obiego, "Igbo Idea of God," *Lucerna*, No.1, Vol.1 (1978), pp.27-28.

[39]. Emmanuel M. Edeh, *Igbo Metaphysics,* Chicago: Loyola University, 1985, p.61.

[40].Vatican 11, Gaudium et Spes, no. 4.

[41].Theophilus Okere,"The Assumption Of African Values As Christian Values,"*op.cit.* Pp.12-13.

[42]. Marcien Towa, "Conditions for the Affirmation of a Modern African philosophical Thought," *African Philosophy: The Essential Readings*, ed. Tsenay Serequeberhan, New York: Paragon House, 1991, p.187.

[43]. Bolaji Idowu, *African Traditional Religion,* London: SCM, 1973, p.88

[44].D, Lugard, *The Dual Mandate In Tropical Africa, op. cit,* p.437.

[45]. '*Uprootedness of self*'- used by C. B, Okolo to describe the colonial destruction of African ontological integrity.

[46].Richard Bell, *Understanding African Philosophy,* New York, Routledge, 2002, p.60.

[47].Chinua Achebe, *The Trouble with Nigeria,* Enugu: Fourth Dimension Publishers, 1983, p.1.

[48]. K. C Anyanwu, *op. cit*, pp.35-37.

19

From Okere to the Rest of Us
A Philosophy of Life

Michael Sunday Sasa

1. Introduction

I welcome you to these few pages on Msgr. Theophilus Okere, a Catholic priest, a philosopher, a pioneer researcher and projector of African philosophy, a teacher, a manager and a motivator. We are celebrating a land mark in his life. We want to dig out of his life some hidden but perceived philosophy of life we can learn from, and even propose to fellow Nigerians and all men of good will for emulation or adoption.

Having anchored our subject-matter, let us settle the case of what qualifies me to want to dig this out of him. Msgr. Okere did not teach me directly in the classroom. He however taught me at meetings, seminars, conferences and workshops. I was the first ever General Secretary of the Catholic Theological Association of Nigeria (CATHAN), while he, Theophilus Okere, was the first President and the then Rev. Fr. Anthony Obinna, now Archbishop Obinna, was and still remains a foundation member. Since then, himself, Archbishop Obinna of Owerri and I have been close friends. It was this Association that brought us close and we worked together at a close range. Simply put, I admire both of them. However, our focus today is on Msgr. Theo. Okere.

While working on this paper, I caught sight of Professor Chinua Achebe's work, entitled *The Trouble With Nigeria* first published in the year 1983[1]. I found it a good tool in hand. Going through my library, I stumbled on Arthur A. Nwankwo's *Can Nigeria Survive?*[2] Nwankwo becomes relevant to this topic in his very last chapter (Towards a Self-Reliant Economy). In the case of Msgr. Okere, his concern was towards a self-reliant Catholic Church in Nigeria, personnel-wise. God gave him the opportunity in Seat of Wisdom Major Seminary, Owerri, where he had been the founding Rector. He proved equal to the task. Let us use a recent speech development: "to God be the Glory". In deed, the glory goes to God while we praise Msgr. Okere for responding positively to that divine grace. To God be the glory still.

2. Motivational Philosophy

The priest has a unique relationship with men. The Epistle to the Hebrews, says the priest is "appointed on behalf of men." His whole being is dedicated to the service of others. He does not exist for himself. He has a function which orientates him with his whole life: his talk, his action, his example, his sacrifice and suffering, his relationship with other human beings. He is an apostle, just an apostle sent to serve. That is Msgr. Theophilus Okere for you. Meet him. Taste what it means to be a priest, a Catholic priest. He has been a leader.

We have many leaders in Nigeria today who do not have the gift of personnel motivation. That accounts for why they fail to carry people along. A good leader should be able to motivate those under him or those working with him. It is a necessary quality for effective leadership.

Okere had once quoted one J. A. Coleman in his synthesis of the general debate in the workshops of the 1971 Synod of Bishops on justice in the World. Here, Coleman had written to ask inter alia:

How is it that after 80 years of modern social teaching and 200 years of the gospel of love the Church has to admit her inability to make more impact upon the conscience of her people…It was stressed again and again that the faithful, particularly, the more wealthy and comfortable among them, simply do not see structural social injustice as sin. They simply feel no personal responsibility for it and feel no obligation to do anything about it. Sunday observance, the Church's rules on sex and marriage tend to enter the Catholic consciousness profoundly as sin; but to live like Dives with Lazarus at the edge is not even perceived as sinful.[4]

I am bringing this in to show the working of Msgr. Okere's mind. He sites this to corroborate a point of great importance in his mind. His human touch and consequent sympathy for the plight of the poor and the needy can easily be noticed here. Can we place this in contrast with a situation Prof. Chinua Achebe describes in his book, *The Trouble With Nigeria*:

> Recently, the Shagari administration found it difficult to pay the new national minimum wage which was raised from One Hundred Naira (N100.00) per month to One Hundred and Twenty Naira (N120.00). One had thought that the chance would be seized to peg salaries at the top for the next five years or so. But not on your life! You might as well expect landlords to form a national committee for the sole purpose of lowering house rent![5]

Still further, comparing Msgr. Okere with some notable figures in this country, let us revisit Prof. Chinua Achebe's book quoted above. He has two of our great leaders brought side by side in their intention to make themselves rich and comfortable. Let us take a look at the statements credited to both leaders and compare with the person of Msgr. Okere.

According to Prof. Achebe, in a solemn vow made by (Nnamdi) Azikiwe in 1937, he pledged, saying: "That henceforth I shall utilize my earned income to secure my enjoyment of a high standard of living and also to give a helping hand to the needy."[6] In like manner, he quoted Obafemi Awolowo as being even more forthright about his ambitions "I was going to make myself formidable intellectually, morally invulnerable, to make all the money that ..."[7]

Motives relate to the "why" of human behaviour. Ideas come before action. Ideas make a man. If our basic, fundamental ideas lack depth, our subsequent action is not likely going to be of any useful value. Hence, Chinua Achebe concludes saying:

> Thoughts such as these are more likely to produce aggressive millionaires than selfless leaders of their people. An absence of objectivity and intellectual rigour at the critical moment of a nation's formation is more than an academic matter. It inclines the fledgling state to disorderly growth and mental deficiency.

What people do, how they do it, when or where it is done are all important. Still further is the question of why people do what they do. This, in fact, is the motivational question. Jack R. Frymier asks series of questions to illustrate motivational questions thus:

Why do workers go on strike?
Why do teachers teach?
Why do some students try to learn in school?
Why do some students not try to learn in school?
Why do some people back-bite?
Why do some people gossip? Etc.[8]

Frymier observes that motivation gives both direction and intensity to behaviour. A statement like this merely begs the question, he concludes. To be more precise, he defines motivation as that which gives direction and intensity to behaviour.

Thomas F. Gilbert, a former professor of psychology, published a book entitled *Human Competence: Engineering Worthy Performance*[9] in which he said that if managing and motivating people is about anything, it is about finding ways for people to be competent and perform at their full potential. Anyone who is close enough knows that Msgr. Okere's approach to teaching and contact with people, both at meetings, conferences, workshops, and even at casual street conversations, bear motivational mark. This forms a part of his credit.

3. His Cheerful Look

How many of us agree to be cheerful today? Many people would rather write all their problems on their faces, appealing to all who care to read their faces to sympathise with them or simply pass by without a smile. What an appeal!! Msgr. Okere's cheerful and inviting face could easily be taken for granted. But such is not common to all men. This alone can even account for why it should not be taken for granted. One's facial look can either promote or kill motivation. That one is serious-minded does not in any way mean that one should look gloomy. One's facial appearance is a gate-way for people to either commence conversation with one or to quickly change one's address or location. How many people send away others by their looks? Msgr. Okere has always invited others by his look. Students are invited and encouraged to listen to him and to learn from him; all by his look and approach. Are teachers reading or hearing this?

4. Motivation and Intelligence

We have been told that in many ways, the problem of motivation is similar to the one we face in dealing with intelligence in an educational setting. We always infer the nature and degree of intelligence from observation of a student's behaviour. No one seems to know what intelligence is, so we watch what a student does or watch or study his performance on standardized tests. Based on these, we make inferences about the student's intellectual ability. Who says he can adequately measure intelligence? Not even those who virtually make a dogma of IQ. They seem to forget that measured ability (i.e., IQ) is the most influential variable involved. Frymier says : "IQ scores appear to be exact, while other variables such as motivation or personality or cognitive style seem slippery and difficult to pin down with precision."

Motivation and ability are often taken as relatively discrete phenomena. However, while ability summarizes observations about what an organism can do, motivation summarizes observations about what an organism will do or wants to do.

5. Okere and African Philosophy

Albert Einstein once asked the question: What is the meaning of human life, or, for that matter, of the life of any creature? To know an answer to this question means to be religious... [10]

Okere believes that religion has always understood itself to be a way of life, and whenever it is left free fully to express itself, it seeks to encompass the whole of man's life, both private and public, individual and communal. According to Okere, to exclude religion from any major area of life would amount to a major, disabling amputation which would reduce drastically its effectiveness and indeed distort its meaning.

Of great interest is Okere's connection between culture and philosophy. In one of his write-ups, Okere holds that the philosopher, by the fact of the nature of his research, is already contaminated, and perhaps, consummated by the culture which he has inherited and to the extent that that culture has been, and continues to be, itself contaminated and influenced by other cultures. All of the philosopher's past and present, merge in the single experience which has been his from his first dawn of consciousness. It is too late therefore to treat the past as some object that is distinct, distant and apart. It is noted that the past involves the present consciousness. One may, as it were, create the past, but real philosophical creativity is perforce in the present, from the totality of the "as is". Okere maintains, it is a pure case of hermeneutics. He says:

> We must now discuss hermeneutics. Since …to define philosophy and relate it to culture will revolve around the subject of Hermeneutics…it is only within the context of hermeneutics that African culture can give birth to African philosophy. If we have rejected the various attempts so far to write an African philosophy, it is in fact due to the failure of these authors to realize that philosophy and culture (a) are heterogeneous and (b) must be mediated by preliminary hermeneutical work which comprises of various levels.[11]

While Heidegger, in his wisdom, considers hermeneutics as man's way of being.[12] Paul Ricoeur looks at hermeneutics rather as a method. His own way is not that of a philosophy of hermeneutics but that of a philosophical hermeneutics, a graduated, methodological approach; an effort to enlist the methods and concepts of interpretation already elaborated by hermeneutical sciences into the services of the problem of the truth of existence.[13]

Simply put, Okere's thesis is that there is a dialectical relationship between philosophy and culture. Then, the logic of it. The above, having been established, we can proceed in thought. There is no doubt that Black Africans have their own cultures. They can and do have their own proper philosophies by deriving and elaborating them from their own cultures. He keeps insisting that it is not enough to have a culture in order to have also a philosophy; a mediation, a passage from culture to philosophy is necessary. This passage is hermeneutical in nature.[14]

What thrills me most, and perhaps interests me best, is the relationship Okere draws between language and thought. Surely, there is a relationship between the form of a language and the modes of thought of its speakers. I perfectly agree that this fact should not be taken to mean that a language is the photocopy of a philosophical system, or that the structure of a language represents the structure of a philosophy. Caution is called for. Okere goes further to say:

The Bantu languages have a class system for all the nouns, whereas French, German, Latin, and Greek, but not English, have a gender system. Has this any philosophical significance? No, except in a philosophical discourse. The idea of a philosophy literally taken out of a dictionary or deducible from the grammar of a language cannot be illustrated from the history of philosophy; in fact, it is rather contradicted.[15] To further explain the above, Okere says:

> If to each language there was a corresponding philosophical system, it would be impossible to conceive two distinct and much less two opposed philosophies in one language and there would be no difference between Thales and Plato, Aristotle and Parmenides.[16]

6. Okere's Leadership Style

Leadership is the process of directing the behaviour of another person or persons towards the accomplishment of some objectives. Thus, leadership is exercised whenever a person influences the behaviour of another person or a group of people towards achieving an objective.[17]

Leadership is basically for service rather than being served. Those who have ever worked with Monsignor Okere would readily agree that this is true of him. But, that is not all that there is to him. Leadership should be flexible so that appropriate styles of leadership can be used in various situations. Example can be given of differences in styles in situational leadership. The style of leadership that is required in an urgent and dangerous situation should be different from that which should be used in a different, non-urgent and non-dangerous situation. For a personality like Monsignor Okere, who has handled successfully, at various times, both parish and school communities, principles like this only say what Okere already proclaims in practice.

Leaders must constantly call to mind the essence of leadership, outside of which leadership looses its essence. Leadership is for SERVICE. Leaders are to SERVE others. Leaders are SERVANTS. Okere remains a leader-servant till date.

Leaders seek to empower others. Leaders train others to avoid "break in transmission". This means that the leader trains others so that when the time comes for him or her to step down as the leader, those whom he or she has trained may carry on. Okere proves this in his apostolates.

The leader is to see God as the ultimate leader to whom he or she looks up to for inspiration and leadership. The leader is a steward or stewardess who knows he or she must ultimately render account to God. He or she therefore carries out his or her duties in love and fear of God. Who needs help in order to see this in Monsignor Okere.

7. Conclusion

Albert Einstein has said:

> Numerous are the academic chairs, but rare are wise and noble teachers. Numerous and large are the lecture halls, but far from numerous the young people who genuinely thirst for truth and justice. Numerous are the wares that nature produces by the dozen, but her choice products are few...[18]

We are no longer complaining. All cannot be Okere. Okere has his charisms. Others have theirs. All put together, compliment one another. The world goes on and better for it. I only hope that the youths are hearing. I also hope our elders are seeing. I want to believe we are moving and hope that our destination is clear to us.

Okere calls us to a sober reflection. What way our country? How are we going about it? What method are we using? Who leads? Who are the followers? How convinced? How committed? What state of mind? It is in deed good to pause from time to time to take stock. It is good to know how far. It is good to know how near. It is good to know how well. It is good to know what error. It is good to know what remedy. It is good to know where we are strong. It is good to know how to continue. It is good to remember where we are coming from. It is good to realise where we are. It is equally good to remind ourselves of where we are going to. All these will help us to remain focused.

Let us embark on an exercise. Let us compare the spirit which animated the youths in our seminaries and universities some five or six decades ago with that prevailing today. Do we notice a difference? We might readily agree that the youths of decades ago had deeper faith in the amelioration of human society, more respect for every honest opinion, tolerance and respect for human life.

But, it is not all negative today. We must admit the fact that there is an urge toward social progress, toward tolerance and freedom of thought. The most devastating news is that the students in our Nigerian Universities have ceased as completely as their lecturers to embody the hopes and ideals of the people. Are you saying that our Universities are reflections of our larger society? I open this to discussions. But, wait a little. Is our reasoning level so low in this country? Has journalism gone that low in Nigeria? It was reported on page four of the Sunday Sun Newspaper of March 7th 2004, that:

> As the family of the slain, former Managing Director of Nigeria Airways, Andrew Agom agonize over his killing, its spokes person, Mr. Anthony Agom has revealed that Andrew, a true Catholic was fasting in the spirit of lent when he was killed on Wednesday (3rd of March, 2004).

The Sunday Sun had for its front-page caption:

'AGOM DIED FASTING'

What an irresponsible caption! It is heavily misleading.

But, what is your opinion? This, I believe, is a commercial strategy to attract the attention of prospective newspaper buyers. Is that not too much for its motive?

The above is not all. There is a new dimension to political trend in this country. It is a political passion that has translated into political madness. We are talking of political assassinations. This new development also shows the type of perforated security net-work we operate in this country. Nobody is safe! Not even the president. What is happening? Is there a government? I also leave that to discussion. Where the wise rule, wisdom is seen. Sanity prevails. What is next? Discussions continue. Thanks to Msgr. Okere.

Notes

[1] Published by Fourth Dimension Publishers Co. Ltd, Enugu, Nigeria.
[2] The same Publishers as above, first published in the year 1981.
[3] See Hebrews 5 : 1.
[4] J. A. Coleman, ed., *One Hundred Years of Catholic Social Thought: Celebration and Change,* New York: Orbis Books, 1991, P. 306, quoted in Theophilus Okere, *The Poverty of Christian Individualist Morality and An African Alternative,* (Book in photocopy, title and Publisher, unknown). This has to do with the observed divorce between Religion and Public Life.
[5] Chinua Achebe, *The Trouble with Nigeria,* op. cit., p. 23.
[6] Ibid., p. 11.
[7] Ibid., p.. 11.
[8] Jack R. Frymier, *"Motivation: The Mainspring and Gyroscope of Learning"* in *Teaching Today: Tasks and Challenges,* Edited by J. Michael palardy , New York: Macmillan Publishing Co., Inc., 1975, p. 258. I added a few of my own questions.
[9] See J. Boyett & J. Boyett, *The Guru Guide: The Best Ideas of the Top Management Thinkers,* John Wiley & sons, inc., 1998, p. 233.
[10] Einstein, Albert, *Ideas and Opinions,* New York: Wings Books, (no date of publication indicated), p. 11.
[11] Okere, Theophilus, *African Philosophy A historico-hermeneutical investigation of the conditions of its possibility,* Lanham: University Press of America, 1983, p. 15.
[12] Okere brings forth a good defence of Heidegger on page 29 of his (Okere's) book quoted above in footnote number 10. Heidegger's statement here does not mean that he understood hermeneutics altogether differently. He (Heidegger) distinguishes several levels of hermeneutics and makes it quite clear that he is concentrating on one level, the ontological level, see *Sein Und Zeit,* Pg. 33. (Sein und Zeit in German means Being and Time in English). Hermeneutics in *Sein U. Zeit* , Heidegger later says," means neither a doctrine of the art of interpretation nor interpretation itself, but rather the attempt to determine the essence of interpretation from the hermeneutical being itself" (see Unterwegs zur Sprache, PP. 97-98).
[13] See Ricoeur, Paul, *Le Conflit des Interpretations,* Paris: Edition de Seuil, 1969, Pg. 10.
[14] See Okere, T., *African Philosophy,* Op. Cit., Pg.xiv.
[15] Ibid., Pg. 9.
[16] Ibid., Pg. 9.

[17] Kapena, Sumbye, *How to be a Wise Leader Principles that Work*, Paulines Publications Africa, 2001, Pg. 13.
[18] Einstein, Albert, op. cit. Pp. 28 29.

20

Theophilus Okere
My Philosophical Odyssey

Interview by J. Obi Oguejiofor

1. Question: You are one of the first Nigerian priests to specialize in philosophy. What in your upbringing, education and life made this route possible?

Okere: As priests we had our first contact with philosophy in the major Seminary, since philosophy always formed the first half of our academic preparation for the priesthood. In Bigard Memorial Seminary, Enugu I took a special liking for it, mainly because it involved deep thinking and was always confronting riddles. The fact that texts were in Latin and teachers often inadequately prepared, rather than bore me, became such a challenge. There were other limitations to scholastic philosophy. A copy of Descartes' *Discourses on Method* which I bought in the Enugu CMS Bookshop was the first original copy of a philosophy classic I ever saw. But within a week it was confiscated by the Rector of the seminary on the grounds that it was on the Index of forbidden Books.

So I left Bigard with whetted but unsatisied appetite. The opportunity to further my special interest in philosophy came as I finished my degree in English Language and Literature in Dublin and I was offered admission to study philosophy in Louvain.

Finally it was much later on in life when from my interactions with my father, I found out that the old man had such a thirst for knowledge and information as well as a knack for argument and generalizations. And that at least seemed to explain to me where I got some of the natural ingredients that made philosophy so congenial and so natural to me.

2. Question: What factors or combination of factors influenced your choice of the Catholic University of Louvain as the appropriate university for advanced philosophical studies

Okere: Louvain was my natural choice for philosophy. It had a great name - the oldest Catholic University in the world, the home base of Cardinal Mercier and his popular thomistic revival, the alma mater of Archbishop Fulton sheen, the star intellectual of Catholic America, and the one university producing the greatest number of *Periti* to the just concluded Second Vatican council. It was so exciting that as the council was concluding, I was being admitted into Louvain.

3. Question: Philosophy was studied in the senior seminary before you entered the staff of Bigard Enugu in the early 70s. In what ways did your study in Louvain bring a change in focus in philosophical studies in the seminary?

Okere: I already pointed out the limitations of the teaching of scholastic philosophy in the seminary at Enugu. On my return from Louvain I found myself teaching philosophy in my Bigard alma mater. In that post conciliar and post Biafran-war intellectual climate l was encouraged to update the curriculum and programme of philosophy studies, I made sure that, just as in Louvain, our philosophy students should be introduced to the original writings (in translation of course) of the philosophers. Reading philosophy is after all nothing much more than reading philosophers. So in came Plato, Aristotle, Kant, the banned Descartes, Heidegger, etc, and titles like the *Thaetetus* and *Protagoras*, the *Metaphysics* and the *Nichomachean Ethics*, the *Critique of Pure Reason* and *Sein und Zeit* became commonplace in the Seminary. The real texts of these works and even of the *Summa Theologiae* of Aquinas were being read verbatim for the first time. Hitherto students had only seen these authors used as convenient straw men to be parodied and their works briefly mentioned, often out of context, in the objections section of the relevant scholastic thesis.

We also tried to give a new direction and a more truly philosophical face to what was then called African philosophy but was perhaps little more than the uncritical collection of myths and proverbs.

4. Question: It appears you became famous in African philosophical discussions on account of your doctoral thesis which pointed a new direction in the then philosophical discussions in Africa. What was your inspiration in writing this thesis? Which authors influenced you most?

Okere: My doctoral thesis in Louvain was an early and bold attempt to examine what would be the criteria and conditions of possibility for philosophy and more specifically, for a philosophy that could be called African. My inspiration for writing the thesis was perhaps the admiration I felt for what had been achieved elsewhere and how it was achieved. I mean the magnificent tradition and harvest of reflection and thought, the great human conversation and symposium, at which I felt we had been absent when we should have been present. In that great edifice of the *Histoire de la pensee* [history of thinking], there was not a modest niche, scarcely even a mention of Africa. Yet those who made these contributions, as we now see it, on behalf of themselves and their peoples and cultures still made them as if they spoke for all mankind. My reaction to my philosophical education was to think; If they, why not we? We too should be able to speak from our cultures and do so as if we spoke for all mankind.

I Wanted also to take a closer look at what was being called African philosophy and saw that raw narratives of folk tales and myths or even grammars of certain languages were being passed off as African philosophy. Since other cultures had, beside their own folktales, myths and grammars also their philosophies which were in a distinct and different category, then it was clear we could not go on taking our own myths, folktales and proverbs to be our philosophy. That looked too much like a lazy short cut.

All my acquaintance with philosophy wherever it was practiced and acknowledged as such, showed that these elements of culture provided only raw material for the manufacture of philosophy, making philosophy more or less a philosopher's personal interpretation of his culture. Philosophy was interpretation, a work of art, a personal reading of life and experience.

The authors whose works helped me best articulate this view were of course the modern philosophers of Hermeneutics namely Heidegger and Gadamer and Paul Ricoeur. But, as a chapter of the thesis shows [chapter 5 of the published version], the work of virtually every philosopher could be summoned as witness to prove my point, which is, that philosophy, regardless of its content, its emphasis or its bent, works from and on its ambient culture and that there is no philosophy otherwise.

5. Question: How does one explain the fact that your works appear to be much better known in the United States and some French speaking African countries than in Nigerian philosophy departments?

Okere: I suppose my work has been better advertised in the French speaking world mainly because of the Belgian Louvain connection and the fact that African philosophy had been much longer discussed in the French speaking African world - (Placid Tempels, Alexis Kagame, Fabien Eboussi Boulaga and Paulin Houtondji). The thesis was also first published as a book in the United States, where, l later also taught philosophy.

6. Question: Most of your academic career took place in the seminaries: Bigard Memorial Seminary, St. Joseph's Seminary, and Seat of Wisdom Seminary. In what ways did this create advantages and/or disadvantages to your philosophical engagement?

Okere: Most of my career has meant teaching in our Seminaries and, since half of seminary training meant studying philosophy, teaching philosophy to a captive audience of highly motivated serious young men was very exciting and challenging. Still it was the extra curricular lecture circuit that created for me multiple occasions to reflect creatively, that is, philosophically on *n'importe quoi* as the French would say. On the other hand, ten of the twenty years I spent in Seminary work were also essentially ten years of institutional administrative work, the formation of candidates for the priesthood and supervising some extensive building construction. Some of this time could be reckoned as a loss to philosophy but certainly not the wisdom and experience gained in the process.

7. Question: For some years you were on the staff of St. Joseph's University in Phaladelphia. How do you compare this stint with your long years in the seminaries in Nigeria?

Okere: I taught philosophy for four years at the Jesuit St. Joseph's University in Philadelphia. It was a welcome opportunity to return to teaching philosophy and teaching it in a secular, academic environment. I enjoyed the freshness of a younger, wilder audience, different from our disciplined, mature seminarians. Very few of the students would ever go on to become professional or academic philosophers but, in the Jesuit system, philosophy was necessarily part of the liberal studies curriculum offering a stable core of the intellectual culture that every educated person, from whatever discipline, must have.

8. Question: In your book *African Philosophy: Historico-Hermeneutical Investigations into the Conditions of Its Possibility*, you were of the view that it is possible that some form of real philosophy existed unnoticed in some parts of Africa, but that "we cannot be dogmatic about the existence of philosophies yet unknown, undiscovered, or unpublished." (p.ix) What do you say about this position now, given the discovery, the edition and the publication of the 5 volumes of Ethiopian philosophy by Claude Sumner, some of which manuscripts date back to the 16ᵗʰ century?

Okere: "We cannot be dogmatic about the existence of philosophies yet unknown, undiscovered or unpublished." Until something is known or discovered or made public how could any one say for sure that it exists? I think that was a prudent statement on my part at the time and it remains true even now. This was without prejudice and indeed with certain openness to future discoveries such as those of Prof. Sumner. Now he has found us something to be dogmatic about and hopefully there may be future discoveries of even earlier, heretofore unknown philosophies existing beyond our present radar screen. Of course once such discoveries are made, the question: Can there be an African philosophy is already answered by force of an *Ab actu ad posse.*

9. Question: In general, what has been the major direction of your academic output since your days in Louvain?

Okere: I must confess that I have not been publishing as much as I have been writing or lecturing. But I have had time to write, lecture and generally to exercise my mind philosophically on a variety of topics other than African philosophy, and, usually on topics suggested by my interest and profession as a priest. These have included the ethical problems of peace and war, of politics, democracy and good governance, again, as the urgency of our peoples' desperate situation has dictated. I have given some time to questions of culture, of the identity and the survival of minority cultures such as ours in a fast changing world. I have done some reflection on epistemological issues. The range of my interest may be vaguely reflected in the following recent titles.
Is there one Science, Western Science?
Philosophy and Intercultural dialogue.
The Kite may Perch, the Eagle may Perch,
Egbe bere ugo Ebere: An African concept of peace and justice.

Christianity mediating between North and South.

10: Question: Since you came back to Nigeria a few years ago from the United States, you have founded and directed the Whelan Research Academy. What is the inspiration and aims of this academy? What has it achieved so far, and how do you see its future?

Okere: The Whelan Research Academy has been founded by the Archdiocese of Owerri to consolidate the work of its first Irish missionary Bishop Joseph Brendan Whelan. Its mandate is to undertake scholarly research, publish and disseminate information on the culture of the Igbo people of Nigeria, and the impact of Christianity and western civilization on this culture and thus contribute to the relevance of both culture and religion to the developing society.

It is well known that the Igbo have been, of all Africa's major groups, one of the most receptive both to the Christian religion and to western modernity. Yet the study of their culture and history and religion has been either by design or default, one of the most underdeveloped. The problem of the scanty recording of their illiterate past is compounded by the fast, silent disappearance of the aged, culture-bearing generation, while the impact of Christianity and the external pressure of the modern, secular culture poses even a greater threat to survival. We intend to fully record the story of this clash of cultures as they struggle to achieve some creative interaction or at any rate to work to salvage what we can lest this rich culture be totally lost to humanity.

A lot of the work will focus on in-depth research and studies on the one hand of Igbo culture, its complex, tonal language, its wisdom and law and social institutions, in particular, its traditional religion which was ignored and condemned largely unexamined by the missionaries. On the other hand, there will be an intense study of the entire Christian tradition, with emphasis on scripture and the early Fathers, but also the itinerary of the gospel among the various cultures of the world. The aim is to enable for the first time a direct encounter between the mature thought of Igbo religion and that of the Christian religion, as a way to encourage both to enter into a fruitful dialogue. A practical result of the research program is to have the Academy act as a think-tank that offers critique and debate on society and its development and on public policy from the perspective of Christian and indigenous principles. As Nigerian society muddles on almost without focus and almost with no vision for its millions, it has become absolutely necessary to have some powerful voice guided by reason and faith, based on the Christian gospel and on the perennial principle of the indigenous spirituality to promote a sense of the public good.

To undertake these tasks, the Academy will employ the services of a first class team of scholars and fellows dedicated to fulltime research, writing and lectures. A fully equipped modern library with archives from colonial and missionary history, a computerized data base, and a museum of art and culture will form the core of a research and learning village where lectures and workshops and seminars will be scheduled through the academic year. A journal will serve as the organ for the publication of the results of research. A lot of plans and good intentions, but we are somewhat far from actual achievements. We are yet training some personnel, building up some staff strength and hoping for some financial support to help us with infrastructure. In the meantime we have been able to host two international symposia, something we are determined to hold annually if we can. We are also talking with Louvain University Theology department with a view to future affiliation.

11. **Question**: Do you plan to give more time to philosophy and theology in future?

Okere: I mean to continue to give more time to philosophy and theology in the future. I have been thinking, among other things, of the Nigerian situation, a real challenge to any Nigerian who has been exposed to philosophy. I somehow think that we philosophers should endeavour to make some contribution to the national debate, by articulating a rational vision of a just society. While many talk about the inadequacies of the counterfeit constitution we are operating, it is time to have some thinkers start tinkering with some draft of a well-thought out, just and balanced new constitution. This would be some serious service to the fatherland. And it looks like the way to go.

LIST OF CONTRIBUTORS

Joseph Achike Agbakoba,
Dept of Philosophy, University of Nigeria, Nsukka, Nigeria.

Martin Ferdinand Asiegbu
Faculty of Philosophy, Bigard Memorial Seminary, Enugu, Nigeria.

Pauline Aweto
Formerly, Consultant of International Organisation for Migration, Rome.

John Chukwuemeka Ekei
Pope John Paul II Seminary, Awka, Nigeria.

Evaristus Ekweke
Faculty of Philosophy, Seat of Wisdom Seminary, Owerri, Nigeria.

Innocent Enwe
Institut Supérieur de philosophie, Université Catholique de Louvain, Louvain-la-Neuve, Belgium.

Emmanuel Chukwudi Eze
Department of Philosophy, DePaul University, Chicago, USA.

George F. Maclean
Emeritus Professor
School of Philosophy, Catholic University of America, Washington, D.C., USA.

Marco Massoni
Department of Philosophy, Terza Università degli Studi, Rome

Francis O. C. Njoku
Claretian Institute of Philosophy, Nekede, Owerri.

Sylvanus Ifeanyi Nnoruka
Faculty of Philosophy
St. Joseph's Major Seminary, Ikot Ekpene, Nigeria.

Boniface E. Nwigwe
Department of Philosophy, University of Port Harcourt, Port Harcourt, Nigeria.

Augustine Okechukwu Oburota
Pope John Paul II Seminary, Awka, Nigeria.

Josephat Obi Oguejiofor
Faculty of Philosophy
Bigard Memorial Seminary, Enugu, Nigeria.

Godfrey Igwebuike Onah
Institute for the Study of Non-Belief, Religion and Cultures, Faculty of Philosophy, Pontifical Urban University, Rome.

Maduakolam Innocent Osuagwu
Provincial Department of Church and Society, Owerrri, Nigeria.

Mogobe Ben Ramose
Department of Philosophy, University of South Africa, Tshwane, South Africa.

Michael Sunday Sasa
Faculty of Philosophy, All Saints' Seminary, Ekpoma, Nigeria.

Cletus Umezinwa
Faculty of Philosophy, Bigard Memorial Seminary, Enugu, Nigeria.